THE WELFARE STATE IN CANADA

THE WELFARE STATE IN CANADA

PAST, PRESENT AND FUTURE

Edited by

RAYMOND B. BLAKE

PENNY E. BRYDEN

J. FRANK STRAIN

Mount Allison University

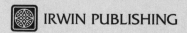 IRWIN PUBLISHING

Published by
Irwin Publishing
1800 Steeles Avenue West
Concord, Ontario
L4K 2P3

Canadian Cataloguing in Publication Data

Main entry under title:

The welfare state in Canada : past, present and future
ISBN 0-7725-2397-5

1. Public welfare - Canada. 2. Canada - Social policy. 3. Welfare state.
I. Blake, Raymond b. (Raymond Benjamin). II. Bryden, Penny. III. Strain, J. Frank

HV108.W45 1997   361.6'1'0971   C97-930570-5

Cover image: © Will Crocker/The Image Bank

Printed and Bound in Canada

1 2 3 4 5 01 00 99 98 97

Contents

Preface

WELFARE STATES ALL OVER THE WORLD ARE IN THE PROCESS OF BEING reconsidered. Canada, with its assortment of federal and provincial legislation designed to ameliorate the economic and social problems of underemployment, ill health, poverty, and old age, is no exception. Staggering deficits and increasing globalization have prompted successive governments to re-evaluate the efficacy of social welfare legislation in Canada and the result seems to have been, thus far at least, a declining commitment to maintaining the high-cost programs that had been put in place by the end of the 1960s. Some programs seem to be relatively immune to massive overhaul, largely because of the public support for continued benefits as an inherent right of citizenship. The Canadian system of state-sponsored health insurance is the most obvious example: having equated medicare with the Canadian identity, voters are loathe to let their elected official tamper with its basic design. Other programs, however, have been less fortunate in maintaining high levels of acceptance. Those policies that sought to provide benefits to the unemployed or underemployed are most frequently targeted as undermining the work ethic and creating a general lethargy in the Canadian work force that impedes the growth of the national economy.

Thus, the political and economic environment of the mid-1990s has produced a certain schizophrenia of opinion of the welfare state. For some, governments in the years since the Second World War and especially since the 1960s, have been regarded as profligate with Canadian taxpayers' money. The spending on social programs, either directly to recipients or through grants to the provinces, has skyrocketed in the last generation and now represents the largest expenditure in the national budget. For many, this is identified as the root cause of our massive deficit and relatively high levels of unemployment. For those who regard the welfare state as the major cause of the current economic woes, the only solution seems to be the elimination of benefits the public has come to enjoy. Others point to our social welfare programs as the heart of the nation, performing the dual function of establishing Canada's distinctiveness from our neighbours to the south and asserting a political commitment to public betterment. Superficially at least, the Canadian social welfare state is regarded as either good or bad; as either defining or debilitating.

The contributors to this collection avoid the trap of selecting between these extremes in their assessment of the current welfare state. Instead, they offer sophisticated interpretations of the complexities of the issues involved and thoughtful prognostications for the future. They have not been misled by the emotionalism of the issues surrounding the future of the welfare state, and they have refused to engage in the production of panaceas. Working within the constraints imposed by the economic realities facing Canada today, they offer a variety of solutions to some of the problems equated with specific welfare legislation, as well as some prescriptions for the welfare state as a whole.

The articles in this collection were all first delivered as papers at a conference at Mount Allison University in New Brunswick on the past, present, and future of the welfare state in Canada. The participants came from different sectors of society and brought to the proceedings a wide variety of political perspectives. As their work here suggests, however, they shared a number of similarities. All are experts in the field of social welfare, and all have played an active role, either within the academic community or as commentators in the public debate, in defining the terms of the policy approach to the future of the welfare state in Canada. All have turned the tools of their particular disciplinary approach to the questions plaguing the very existence of a continued role for the state in the provision of social welfare benefits. All admit the necessity of redesigning at least some elements of the current system or re-evaluating the conceptual underpinnings of our current philosophy of social welfare. Their research into the changes that the system has undergone since it was first somewhat haphazardly put in place, and the implications of those changes, should therefore be of enormous interest to those legislators and policymakers charged with the responsibility of determining where Canada takes its welfare state at the dawn of the millennium.

ɔ̃ ɔ̃ ɔ̃

The preparation of this volume, and the organization of the conference that originally brought these people together, would not have been possible without the generous support of a number of institutions and individuals. The editors would especially like to thank: the Department of Human Resource Development, the government of New Brunswick, and Mount Allison University for financial assistance; Allan Zeesman of Human Resources for helping to pull everything together; Kim Mitton for technical assistance at all stages of the project; and the Canadian Studies Student Association for assistance at the conference.

PART ONE

Understanding Change

A RE WE CURRENTLY WITNESSING 'WHAT APPEARS TO BE A FUNDAMENTAL reinvention of the welfare state as we know it?'[1] Why now? What does the future hold in store for the welfare state? Can we choose alternative paths of development? Or are we caught in a vortex of change that seriously constrains our options? Questions like these play an important role in social policy debate, and each contributor to this volume attempts to address them, either directly or indirectly. The papers in this section were chosen to provide a broad cross-section of opinion on social change and its implications for the Canadian welfare state.

Recent history has forced students of the welfare state to reconsider the importance of social change. Between 1867 and the late 1970s, governments in Canada gradually expanded the scope of their activities. In the process, a complex system of health care, education, employment, and social transfer policies was created in an attempt to ensure that all Canadians enjoyed an adequate income and security against dramatic income fluctuations. Initially, the system grew slowly and governments introduced policies reluctantly. But by the end of the Second World War, the public expected government to solve 'social problems' and generally believed that it had the capacity to do so. During the fifties and sixties, governments responded by introducing policy after policy. By the late sixties, the core of the Canadian welfare state was in place. The pattern was clearly one of expansion (with steady but gradual improvements in income adequacy and security) with some tinkering at the margins.

Two features of development of the Canadian welfare state stand out. The first is the role played by the national government. The British North America Act of 1867, which provided a constitutional framework for Canadian federalism, did not anticipate the expansion of the welfare state. It assigned most important revenue sources to the national government while leaving provincial governments responsible for health care, education, and income security. In principle, the de jure distribution of legislative powers should have constrained the development of the welfare state since provincial governments lacked the resources to expand and the national government lacked the authority to do so. Canadian federalism, however, proved remarkably flexible with the federal government assuming a key role through constitutional amendment, fiscal transfers to provinces, and use of the spending power clause. By 1982, when the BNA Act was patriated and incorporated in the Constitution Act, a strong federal role was widely accepted (especially outside Quebec).

2.   The second feature is the gradual move from a residual to a universalist welfare state. This distinction, originally drawn by Wilensky and Lebeaux, separates the residual welfare state from the universal welfare state according to coverage.[2] A residual welfare state focuses on the poor, with public provision of services to those who pass an income test and private provision to all considered nonpoor. A universal welfare state, on the other hand, involves public provision to all socioeconomic groups. In the post-Second World War period, Canada introduced a variety of universal programs including the family allowance, old age security, and public health insurance. By 1982, many of the services provided through the federal welfare state were considered entitlements or social rights and the Constitution Act explicitly committed the government of Canada and the provincial governments to: (1) promote equal opportunities for the well-being of *all* Canadians; (2) further economic development to reduce disparity in opportunity; and (3) provide essential public services of reasonable quality to *all* Canadians [italics added].

    The path of welfare state development in Canada through the late seventies loosely followed the industrialism theory proposed by Wilensky and other students of the welfare state.[3] Industrialism theory suggests that industrialization simultaneously generates: (1) the demand for welfare state policy by undermining traditional, nonmarket sources of security; and (2) the capacity of society to supply welfare state policy by generating the income needed to meet the new needs. The industrialism theory was relatively successful in explaining the development of the welfare state over time and across countries. Events in recent years, however, have challenged the industrialism thesis.

    By the late 1980s, it was becoming clear that the trajectory of welfare state development in Canada had changed. Rather than being characterized by expansion, the welfare state in Canada entered a holding pattern. Fiscal restraint became the preoccupation of both federal and provincial governments as they now faced unsustainable deficits and strong resistance to tax increases. At the same time, the assumption that government could solve social problems came under increasing attack and many began to believe that government was the source of problems rather than the solution. By the mid-1990s, restraint and relatively ad hoc tinkering at the margins had generated significant changes in the structure of the Canadian welfare state. Indeed, many observers of the welfare state argue that we are on a new path of welfare state development and that without a conscious change in policy direction the national government will lose its role and services will be increasingly delivered on a highly selective, residual basis.

In the first paper of this section, Tom Courchene argues that a set of powerful forces largely outside our control 'are informing and, to some extent predetermining the evolution of Canada and Canadian policy as we approach the millennium.' These forces—glocalization, internationalization, and the national debt—constrain the set of possible policies available to Canadians at this point in time. Indeed, Courchene suggests that the policy framework of the postwar Canadian welfare state may well lie outside the feasible set.

Tom Courchene is one of Canada's most influential economists and social policy analysts and his contribution to this volume confirms this. Despite being known as a tireless supporter of a social policy framework that emphasizes income testing and provincial dominance, Courchene does not attempt to marshal the normative case for his preferred policy alternative (this can be found elsewhere in Courchene's work). Instead, he argues that his preferred alternative is inevitable. Thus, even if one believes that a residual, decentralized social policy framework is undesirable, one must face Courchene's argument that it is a dynamic equilibrium or steady state outcome being generated by a complex set of forces largely beyond our control.

Courchene's position is a direct challenge to those on both the 'left' and 'right' of the political spectrum who argue that it is possible to choose the 'best' policy framework. On the political left there are many who argue that the current situation is simply a product of misguided national government policy (implemented under the strong influence of the business lobby). According to this view, the crisis in the welfare state can be traced to the debt crisis, which in turn is largely a product of past tax cuts and the high interest rate policy of the Bank of Canada—this not only increases the cost of debt service but also raises the unemployment rate, thus increasing social spending and reducing tax revenues). They argue that a better macroeconomic policy mix (lower interest rates and greater public sector infrastructure expenditures) and the right trade policy can put the debt on a sustainable base to allow the postwar welfare state and postwar rates of economic growth to be restored.

On the right side of the political spectrum there are many who believe that Canadians face few constraints when choosing a framework for social policy. But rather than argue that the crisis of the welfare state is caused by policy mistakes, they suggest that welfare state policies are themselves misguided. Specifically, they argue that welfare state policies have resulted in lower incomes for the average Canadian without improving the position of the poor.

Why? Government programs introduce adverse incentives (discouraging work, risk taking, and other productive activity) and are vulnerable to 'rent-seeking behaviour' (which results in a redistribution of income from Canadians generally to special interest groups). Consequently, they argue that we simply need to choose the right policy mix, albeit one that involves a significantly reduced role for the public sector.

Courchene's argument that a set of powerful forces is informing—and to some extent predetermining—the evolution of social policy in Canada should not be dismissed as a right wing rationalization. Boyer, Aglietta, and Lipietz in France, Bowles, Gintis, Edwards, and Gordon in the United States, and Offe in Germany (all social scientists on the left) hold views on social change that are remarkably similar to those of Courchene.[4] Their work focuses on the interaction of a broad set of interlocking social institutions (ideology, government policies, corporate organization, international political and economic alliances, etc.) and the process of capital accumulation and profit making. Their analysis, which is heavily influenced by Marx and his theory of social change in a capitalist society, suggests that the institutional framework of a capitalist society is occasionally vulnerable to crisis and transformation because of conflicts between the social institutions and the need to make profits.

David Gordon is representative when he argues that 'interdependencies among individual institutions create a combined social structure with a unified internal structure of its own—a composite whole, in effect, whose intrinsic structure amounts to more than the sum of the individual institutional relationships' and 'changes in any one constituent institution are likely to reverberate throughout the entire structure.'[5] This vision, especially the emphasis on nonlinear interaction, is also found in recent work with complex dynamical systems in evolutionary biology, cognitive science, physics, and chemistry. It suggests that free trade, the death of Keynesian demand management policy, changes in labour/management relations and the declining power of unions, corporate restructuring, pressures on the nation state, the crisis in Canadian federalism, and new directions in the welfare state are all inextricably linked. Moreover, there is no turning back the clock to return to the post–World War II institutions. By emphasizing the linkages between social policy and changes in the broader social structure, Courchene and the new left theorists force anyone interested in Canadian social policy to consider the relationship between social change generally and the evolution of the welfare state.

In the second paper in this section, Andrew Parkin identifies how a number of social justice movements have already developed a sophisticated analysis of changing social policy and its relationship to broader social change. He reviews how these movements have moved beyond traditional approaches to identify alternate avenues for political mobilization and new policy alternatives. Parkin's analysis is based on survey work undertaken at the 1995 People's Summit, a meeting of social justice groups that coincided with the meeting of G-7 leaders in Halifax.

The Parkin paper not only identifies alternatives to a reduced, income-tested welfare system, but also illustrates that the social justice groups are changing in lockstep with other social institutions. One of the most important catalysts is 'increasing disillusionment with the conventional political process and escalating scepticism about the benefits of participation within the formal institutions of representative democracy.' Like Courchene, the social justice groups see the debt and globalization as factors that have severely weakened the ability of national governments to respond to demands for a more demo-cratic and egalitarian society. As a consequence, these groups are seeking a 'new terrain for political struggle which is not exclusively national in its para-meters.'

The third paper by Patricia Armstrong also focuses on a profound social change that is affecting the evolution of the Canadian welfare state. Armstrong notes that the Canadian welfare state has been 'about values as well as about practices.' The emergence of a federal universalist welfare state in Canada coincided with the emergence of a widespread consensus on values; that is, a 'consensus on collective responsibility and shared risk as well as a recognition that many forces were beyond individual control and other forces needed to be kept in check through regulation.' During the eighties and nineties, however, this consensus disappeared to be replaced by 'a new emphasis on individual rights and responsibilities' and what can be crudely characterized as 'a move from caring and sharing to greedy and mean.'

As Armstrong notes, the change in values assures 'that alternative ways of fighting the debt have become unthinkable and the idea that we have over-spent on the luxury of shared rights and responsibilities has become part of our common sense.' Nonetheless, Armstrong is not convinced that Canadians completely abandoned the values that underpin the universalist welfare state. In fact, she suggests that the value shift is being led by elite groups in the private sector, government, and the media. Her article implicitly asks Canadians to analyze the 'new values' critically and to decide if they really support the redefinition of what it means to be a Canadian lurking within the new approaches to social policy.

Guy Chiasson's contribution to this section also focuses on an ongoing change in values. Chiasson, using recent documents produced by the Atlantic Canada Opportunities Agency (ACOA) as an empirical base, argues that the mode of discourse used by government officials severely limits the scope of debate over government policy and thus the very nature of Canadian democ-racy. For Chiasson the most important innovation in social policy discourse over the past two decades is what he calls the economic necessity argument. The economic necessity argument—or TINA (There Is No Alternative) as it has been called by others—states that the global economy and its imperatives, the government debt, and the failure of past interventionist policy leave governments no option but to increase reliance on market forces. In other words, the 'real world' constrains the possible.

The impact of TINA is evident in Canadian regional policy. Whereas past regional policy reflected a commitment to override the market in order to engineer social and economic equality, the new regional policy seeks to 'promote possible comparative advantage of the regional economy within the logic of the market economy.' This involves encouraging entrepreneurship (including supporting the introduction of an entrepreneurship curriculum in the public school system), innovation and technological transfer, human resource development, and marketing and trade development while discouraging industrial policy initiatives and social transfer payments that could slow the structural adjustment of the region.

However, Chiasson asks us to question the assumption that we are caught in a vortex of social change that seriously constrains our options. Following Charles Taylor, James Farr, and others, Chiasson argues that reality is not independent of discourse. Indeed, reality 'is shaped and given meaning by discourse.' Nothing is inherently inevitable. Chiasson argues that a mode of discourse that assumes there is no alternative embodies an ethical outlook: the liberal conception of citizenship. Moreover, given the ethical outlook is hidden from view, debate between ethical positions is closed. Consequently, democratic choice between alternative value systems becomes more difficult.

The Armstrong and Chiasson contributions both point to positive feedback mechanisms in social change. High rates of unemployment, the increased uncertainty that accompanies dramatic social change, and serious deficits have two consequences. First, they put direct pressure on social policies by undermining the financial basis for these policies. Second, people lucky enough to keep their jobs (still the vast majority of Canadians) turn inward and place priority on their personal well-being, on the future of their families, and on their immediate community. This turn inward manifests itself in a change in values and the change in values 'feedback' to further undermine commitment to centralized universal social policies. The existence of this type of positive feedback is a challenge to those who oppose the move to a decentralized and residual welfare state. The future of the welfare state may not be predetermined, but it will be difficult to change.

The following selection in this section is written by Leslie Pal, a political scientist at Carleton University. Pal argues that civil society is changing and with it the role of nongovernmental organizations (NGOs). Pal refers to this process as civic re-alignment, and his paper explores the complex and sometimes contradictory elements of this process.

One aspect of the process of re-alignment is disengagement, a phenomena that involves the deliberate withdrawal of state support and legitimacy from the NGOs. Disengagement assumes a variety of forms including, but not limited to, cuts to government financial grants to the NGOs. Disengagement, however, does not imply a withering away of the NGOs. Indeed, Pal argues that the process of re-alignment also involves re-engagement. Reduced government leaves a void that can be potentially filled by the NGOs, especially those that provide social services on a volunteer basis. As well, Pal expects some NGOs to benefit as governments seek policy expertise and the involvement of the public through consultation. Pal's framework allows him to generate some reasonable predictions about which NGOs will survive and which are at risk. Finally, Pal argues that re-alignment will involve displacement or changes in the site of NGO activity. Parliament has been the traditional site of activity, but with decentralization, increased emphasis on charter rights, and the emergence of international NGO networks, more attention will be directed to the provinces, the courts, and international forums. Some NGOs are better situated than others to adapt to this phenomena.

Like other contributors to this section, Pal believes that there is a powerful social dynamic that is shaping the development of the NGO sector. Moreover, Pal believes the welfare state at the millennium will be smaller, that individuals will have to become more self-reliant, and that market mechanisms will be more prominent. But he also believes the NGO sector will remain central to the well-being of Canadians.

The final contribution is by Allan Moscovitch from the Faculty of Social Work at Carleton. Moscovitch's piece is a fitting bookend to the section since it involves a detailed examination of the Canada Health and Social Transfer (CHST), perhaps the key piece of legislative change in the current period of restructuring. According to Moscovitch, the CHST has three important implications. First, it eliminates many important national standards in Canadian social policy and in the process seriously constrains the role of the federal government in social policy development. Second, the CHST leaves the provinces with almost complete responsibility for the poor while giving the national government almost complete control over macroeconomic policy tools. Moscovitch argues that this removes 'any incentive to the federal government to undertake economic policies that would improve welfare recipients chances of employment.' Finally, the CHST does not take provincial differences in fiscal need (differences in the proportion of the population needing social assistance and social services) and fiscal capacity (the ability to raise revenue into account). Moscovitch fears that this will result in dramatic differences in the treatment of persons in need according to province of residence.

The contrast between Courchene and Moscovitch is especially striking. Both argue that CHST represents a dramatic change in the Canadian welfare state. Unlike Moscovitch, however, Courchene believes the provincial governments will be able to arrive at a system that maintains the most significant standards while encouraging productive competition and innovation. At this point it is impossible to determine who is right. Indeed, it will be several years before we will be in a position to assess the consequences of the CHST experiment.

There is a general recognition by other contributors to this volume that changes in the welfare state are closely tied to broader social changes. But there is no consensus on the constraints imposed on social policy by changes outside the welfare state. Nor is there a consensus on the future of the welfare state. Readers must carefully weigh the arguments and arrive at their own conclusions.

NOTES

1. Leslie Pal, 'Civic Re-alignment: NGOs and the Contemporary Welfare State,' p. 88 of this book.
2. Harold L. Wilensky and Charles N. Lebeaux, *Industrial Society and Social Welfare* (New York, 1965).
3. Harold L. Wilensky, *The Welfare State and Equality* (Berkeley, 1985).
4. See, for example: Aglietta, *A Theory of Capitalist Regulation: The U.S. Experience* (London, 1979); Boyer, 'Technical Change and the Theory of Regulation,' *CEPREMAP*, no. 8707 (March 1987); Lipietz, 'Behind the Crisis: The Exhaustion of a Regime of Accumulation. A "Regulation School" Perspective on Some French Empirical Works,' *Review of Radical Political Economics* 18 (1/2)(1986), 13–23; Gordon, 'Stages of Accumulation and Long Cycles' in T. Hopkins and E. Wallerstein, eds., *Processes of the World System* (Beverly Hills, 1980), 9–45; Gordon, Edwards, and Reich, *Segmented Work, Divided Workers* (Cambridge, 1982); Bowles and Gintis, *Democracy and Capitalism* (New York, 1984); and Offe, in John Keane, ed., *Contradictions of the Welfare State* (Boston, 1984).
5. Gordon, Edwards, and Reich, *Segmented Work, Divided Workers,* 17.

CHASTE and Chastened

Canada's New Social Contract   •

THOMAS J. COURCHENE

Director, John Deutsch Institute for the Study of Economic Policy
Queen's University

The published program of this conference indicates that my topic is 'Towards a New Social Contract.' This is the sort of title that normally appeals to me since it places few, if any, constraints on the subsequent analysis. However, in 'A Blueprint for Social Canada' (the final chapter of *Social Canada in the Millennium*) I have attempted precisely this—an unconstrained restructuring of Canada's social contract for the twenty-first century.[1] Thus, something else is called for in the present context.

Accordingly, I have opted for a quite different approach to the emerging social contract, namely what are the likely longer-term implications of the powerful domestic and international forces—economic, fiscal, and even social—for the evolution of social Canada? Phrased this way, the implication is that large parts of the ensuing analysis are predetermined. To a certain extent this is true, but readers are best advised to view what follows as largely subjective, although informed by these larger forces. Since the Canada Health and Social Transfer (CHST), itself largely shaped by exogenous global, fiscal, and social factors, is the principal integrating vehicle in what follows, the paper can be recast as follows: What are the steady state features of CHASTE?—the Canada Health And Social Transfer Equilibrium.

The first section focuses on the set of (largely exogenous) forces impinging on Canada's society and economy. Included here are the implications of glocalization, of internationalization, of national indebtedness (although self-inflicted, the indebtedness is largely exogenous to the future evolution of social Canada), and of other factors such as the national unity issue. The following section then focuses on Ottawa's initial social policy response—the Canada Health and Social Transfer (CHST). With this as backdrop, the analysis then focuses on the likely evolution of the federal–provincial jurisdictional interface. This seeming detour is necessary because it spells out the likely federal–provincial environment within which CHASTE will evolve. Several principles relating to federal–provincial arrangements are developed—the principle of subsidiarity, the spending power principle, the new notion of regional equity, the principle of duality, and the principle of competitive federalism. In the next section, the focus is on CHASTE. The analysis deals in turn with the implications for the Canadian social union, for the likely evolution of the CHST, for the future of UI. The section concludes with some analysis of the intergenerational equity issue, particularly as it relates to the CPP/QPP. The role of the following section is to assess the manner in which Ottawa has opted to rein in its fiscal excess. What the analysis suggests is that the federal government has protected its own turf while exacting a substantial fiscal toll on both provincial finances and on social insurance programs (UI and CPP/QPP). Implicit, if not explicit, in this section is the observation that the federal government is taking an enormous social policy gamble. My interpretation of this gamble is that the federal government has effectively transferred substantial control over the evolution of social Canada to the provinces; the implications of this are not as yet clear. In the process, however, the nature of social Canada has changed dramatically and permanently.

FORCES INFORMING THE EVOLUTION OF CANADIAN POLICY

Underlying the analysis is the assumption that there is a set of powerful forces that are informing and, to some extent, predetermining the evolution of Canada and Canadian policy as we approach the millennium. While some of these forces are domestic rather than international, they are all external or exogenous to the social envelope.

GLOCALIZATION

Globalization is tending to transfer powers both upward (WTO, NAFTA, Maastricht) and downward from central governments of nation states. While the evidence for the downward transfer is more tenuous, one aspect of this is reflected in the implications deriving from the existence of democracy deficits: as important aspects of decision-making relating to citizens are passed upward and, therefore, beyond their direct control, citizens appear to be focusing more and more on the concept of community, where they can still exert some degree of control. One key aspect of this is the resurgence of interest in what Canadians would refer to as *distinct societies*. Given that international super-structures like the North American Free Trade Agreement (NAFTA) and the European Union (EU) are replacing 'national' superstructures, it is increasingly possible for 'nations' like Scotland, Wales, Catalonia, and Quebec, among others, to contemplate latching on to this new superstructure and pursuing a fully or more autonomous future within this new macro environment. Presumably this is part of what Peter Drucker meant when he proclaimed that we are witnessing at the same time an integrating global economy and a splintering global polity. This simultaneous emphasis on the global and local is captured by the term glocalization.

THE INTERNATIONALIZATION OF THE CANADIAN ECONOMY

Relatedly, but probably much more important, is the fact that global forces are 'internationalizing' Canada's regions. In his insightful overview paper to this conference, Tom Kent alluded to the fact that only Prince Edward Island now exports more to the rest of Canada than to the rest of the world. Table 1 presents the relevant data. Focusing on exports (the first three columns of the table), in 1981 exports by all provinces to the rest of the world (ROW) were 87 percent of their exports to other provinces (ROC). Only four provinces (Newfoundland, New Brunswick, Saskatchewan, and British Columbia) recorded ROW exports in excess of ROC exports. By 1994, however, only Prince Edward Island, as noted, exports more to ROC than to ROW. And at the aggregate level, exports to ROW are 168 percent of exports to the rest of Canada. Two provinces in 1994, Ontario and British Columbia, export more than twice as much to ROW than to ROC.

On the import side, the aggregate data for 1981 and 1994 are similar to those for exports—in 1981 imports from ROW were 90 percent of imports from ROC, but by 1994 ROW imports were 171 percent of imports of ROC. This is driven by the Ontario data where imports from ROW for Ontario are 3.6 times imports from ROC. Quebec (1.71) and British Columbia (1.20) are the only other provinces where the ratio of external imports to domestic imports is greater than unity.

The implications of these data, and particularly the trends in the data, are far reaching. They confirm the growing importance of north–south trade

TABLE 1   Internal and International Trade (goods and services, 1986 dollars)

	Exports			Imports			Trade Balance			E/GDP
	ROC (1)	ROW (2)	ROW/ROC (3)	ROC (4)	ROW (5)	ROW/ROC (6)	ROC (7)	ROW (8)	Total (9)	(Col 1 + Col 2) /GDP (10)
CANADA										
1981	116.58	101.85	.87	116.58	105.3	.90	0.0	3.45	3.45	.49
1994	133.98	225.82	1.68	133.98	229.10	1.71	0.0	-3.28	-3.28	.60
NEWFOUNDLAND										
1981	.85	1.98	2.33	3.32	.97	.29	-2.47	1.01	-2.46	.47
1994	1.13	2.01	1.78	3.55	1.92	.54	-2.42	.09	-2.33	.43
PRINCE EDWARD ISLAND										
1981	.50	.19	.38	.87	.15	.17	-.37	.04	-.33	.56
1994	.69	.32	.46	1.07	.31	.29	-.38	.01	-.37	.52
NOVA SCOTIA										
1981	2.97	1.81	.61	5.00	3.02	.60	-2.03	-1.21	-3.24	.44
1994	3.15	3.45	1.10	5.56	4.56	.82	-2.41	-1.11	-3.52	.44
NEW BRUNSWICK										
1981	2.31	2.47	1.07	4.05	2.48	.61	-1.74	-.01	-1.75	.59
1994	3.70	3.73	1.01	5.02	4.06	.81	-1.32	-.33	-1.65	.62
QUEBEC										
1981	27.60	21.94	.79	24.13	23.51	.97	3.47	-1.57	1.90	.47
1994	29.49	41.62	1.41	28.13	47.93	1.71	1.36	-6.31	-4.95	.53
ONTARIO										
1981	47.04	45.07	.96	30.00	47.76	1.57	17.04	-2.69	14.35	.54
1994	54.05	113.59	2.10	34.50	124.31	3.60	19.55	-10.72	8.83	.70
MANITOBA										
1981	5.11	2.65	.52	6.37	2.75	.43	-1.26	-.10	-1.36	.49
1994	5.30	6.00	1.13	7.14	5.60	.78	-1.84	.40	-1.44	.58
SASKATCHEWAN										
1981	3.55	4.21	1.19	7.84	2.96	.38	-4.29	1.25	-3.04	.52
1994	5.53	7.00	1.27	8.58	3.61	.42	-3.05	3.39	.34	.66
ALBERTA										
1981	18.20	9.01	.50	19.31	11.28	.58	-1.11	-2.27	-3.38	.51
1994	19.54	25.42	1.30	20.75	14.65	.71	-1.21	10.67	9.46	.63
BRITISH COLUMBIA										
1981	8.21	12.51	1.52	13.45	9.27	.74	-5.24	3.24	-2.00	.38
1994	10.64	22.06	2.07	17.69	21.22	1.20	-7.05	.84	-6.21	.44

SOURCE: *Provincial Economic Accounts, Annual Estimates: 1981–94*, table 3.

(international) relative to east–west trade and, in the process, offer evidence that Canada should not be viewed as a single, east–west economy. Moreover, since goods and services are mobile across international borders, whereas labour typically is not, it is increasingly appropriate to view Canada as a social policy railway rather than an economic policy railway.

Undoubtedly, the key message is that further decentralization is probably inevitable. Given that the provinces are becoming integrated more internationally than domestically (in terms of exports), it will almost surely follow that they will want to design their social and economic policies in accordance with their new economic realities and prospects. And what might be appropriate for British Columbia as a Pacific Rim region may not work for Ontario as a Great Lakes economy. Drawing from the European regional science literature, we are probably witnessing the development of a *regional–international interface* in place of the former conception of a *national–national* interface. This is inherently decentralizing.

THE EMERGENCE OF REGION AS AN ECONOMIC FORCE

Decentralization is one thing. Viewing provinces as 'economic nations' is quite another. Yet Michael Storper provides a rationale for the latter when he notes that the principal dilemma of contemporary economic geography is 'the resurgence of regional economies and of territorial specialization in an age of increasing ease in transportation and communication of inputs and outputs and of increasingly scientific organizational rationalities of managing complex systems of inputs and outputs.'[2] Storper proposes that the success of Silicon Valley, Route 128, and other 'hot spots' resides in the concept of 'untraded interdependencies' or what economists might call 'locational positive externalities.' Arguably, this is, at an analytical level, what the provinces are increasingly about—positioning themselves across a broad range of fronts to become competitive within their new economic (cross-border/international) environments. To do this, the provinces require greater operational and policy flexibility. Intriguingly, this desire for greater flexibility is not about beggar-thy-neighbour federalism, nor is it about decentralization for its own sake. Rather, it is about positioning the provinces and their citizens more effectively vis-à-vis their competitors (which are less and less their sister provinces). In this sense, what Ontario is currently all about is probably not all that different than what Italy within the EU framework is all about. It is important to note that the attempt of provinces to position themselves competitively within North America is not limited to the have provinces—New Brunswick is also an excellent example.[3]

THE DEBT/DEFICIT OVERHANG

Thus far the enumerated forces are largely exogenous to Canada. A key domestic force that is driving the system is the enormous debt/deficit overhang. While other countries (Italy, Belgium) have higher debt/GDP ratios than Canada, we are unique in that we also have very high international indebtedness (unlike Italy and Belgium) and are also running a large current account deficit (again unlike Italy and Belgium). The result is that we have effectively transferred aspects of sovereignty to the 'kids in red suspenders' (the international money markets). The result of all of this was the 1995 federal budget—a devolution of power to markets (privatization, deregulation, contracting out, etc.) and a decentralization to lower levels of government (a 45,000-person reduction in the federal civil service, which speaks in part at least to the disentanglement and elimination-of-duplication imperatives, and a decentralization in terms of powers relating to the social envelope, i.e., the shift to the CHST block fund). Moreover, we are far from out of the woods here since the real rate of interest still exceeds the real GNP growth rate. This implies that, left to itself, the debt/GDP ratio will spiral off explosively.[4]

NATIONAL UNITY

A second domestic force that informs most aspects of Canadian policy is our constitutional 'neverendum.' At the time of writing (April 1996), Canadians in countless groups and networks are once again fully engaged in attempting to generate yet another set of proposals aimed at maintaining Quebec in the Canadian family. A common feature of these proposals is a devolution of further powers to Quebec which, given our new-found principle of symmetry, means a generalized devolution to all provinces. Spearheading this latest round is the Throne Speech commitment to transfer manpower training, among other powers, to the provinces.

MISCELLANEOUS

Others may wish to extend this list. A natural inclusion would be the Free Trade Agreement (FTA) and North American Free Trade Agreement (NAFTA). While these agreements reflect the first three of the above forces, they go further in that they begin to embrace a common institutional framework as it relates to the trading environment. And while the FTA and NAFTA need not affect policy goals, they do place constraints on the range of instruments that can be used to implement these goals.

Many Canadians would also include the Bank of Canada's pursuit of price stability. Even those who celebrate our achievements on the inflation side would probably concede that the costs of success were high, one aspect of which is that the debt/deficit overhang was exacerbated in the process.

Any one of these forces would present a daunting policy challenge. Together, however, they have reinforced each other and have become over-powering in the sense that they will influence Canadian policy well into the next century.

The Social Policy Response: The CHST

On the social policy front, the federal government's response to these forces was the CHST—the rolling of Canada Assistance Plan (CAP) and Established Programs Financing (EPF) into a single superblock fund embodying a cut in cash transfers to the provinces from roughly $18 billion currently to just over $11 billion in 2001. While one can probably argue that Ottawa need not have responded this way, the thrust of this paper is the obverse, namely that the CHST makes eminent sense in the overall context of the forces outlined, and, later, what the characteristics of a CHST equilibrium (CHASTE) are likely to be.

To this end, the CHST (although not necessarily the attendant cuts in cash transfer) can be viewed as a positive step in the social policy challenge. First, the shift in emphasis on the health front from 'correction' (medicare) to 'prevention' (well-being) is facilitated by an approach that integrates the health and welfare spending envelopes. Second, given the changing nature of the labour market, the traditional Canadian approaches were increasingly offside. The notion that welfare was largely to support the disabled (or unable to work) while UI was to tide able-to-work persons over the business cycle has long since been displaced by the fact that reliance on both UI and welfare is structurally driven and that the rolls increasingly comprise the able-to-work. Hence, new approaches are needed and the relaxation of some of the former CAP restrictions may provide some needed flexibility in this regard. But the CHST is only one step in this direction: indeed, the later focus on CHASTE will look at long-term implications in this area.

There is another reason why the greater flexibility of the CHST approach can be viewed as appropriate. In the Pearson era when the social infrastructure was being set in place, Ottawa played a critical role via cost sharing, the exercise of the spending power, and the establishment of a set of binding principles. In effect, this served to convert the various provincial programs into national ones. Now, however, these programs have to be reworked. But since Ottawa does not deliver these programs (except, perhaps, to the First Nations), this challenge falls largely by default to the provinces. Flexibility is essential so that the provinces have the ability to experiment with alternative design and delivery systems, and the CHST is one approach to provide this much needed flexibility.

The CHST also resonates well with the set of forces outlined earlier. In particular, the CHST became an appealing vehicle for federal deficit shifting. One of the remarkable features of the past two federal budgets is that annual cash transfers under the CHST will, by the turn of the century, be roughly $7 billion less on an annual basis than they were prior to the CHST. While these cuts are only now coming into force, few predicted that the federal government would have been able to pare cash transfers by this amount. By arguing (1) that the CHST was transferring greater powers to the provinces and (2) that the unconditional nature of the CHST meant that Ottawa was not prejudging how this cut would be absorbed by the provinces, the federal government has, thus far at least, been able to fend off criticism. Indeed, with the announcement of the $11 billion floor to cash transfers in the 1996 federal budget, Ottawa has even managed to convince Canadians that it is now committed to preserving our social infrastructure. Setting aside the consequences of all of this, it is clear that the CHST was a masterful political strike, especially from the Finance Department's perspective.

The consequences of the CHST are quite another matter. Most obviously, the resulting fiscal squeeze at the provincial level will result, as it has already, in its own set of provincial policies relating to downsizing, contracting out, privatization, and the like.

JURISDICTIONAL REALIGNMENT AND THE PRINCIPLE OF SUBSIDIARITY

The forces already noted speak with one voice in the direction of a decentralization of powers, a greater reliance on markets, and a generalized downsizing of governments. The recent Throne Speech complemented this by proposing federal disengagement from manpower training, by recommending outright federal withdrawal from areas such as forestry, mining, and recreation, and by placing limits on the exercise of the federal spending power. The Throne Speech's *quid pro quo* for all of this is some 'rebalancing' or shifting upward of powers (e.g., in the area of securities regulation) and a joint federal–provincial implementation of a more thoroughgoing social and economic union.

Although these initiatives accord well with the emerging global and domestic realities on the economic/fiscal fronts, of and by themselves they do not constitute a set of organizing principles upon which to rebalance and revitalize the jurisdictional and institutional workings of Canadian federalism. The purpose of this section is to propose such a set of principles. Admittedly, this is a very subjective exercise, but one that is nonetheless informed by the factors enumerated earlier in the paper. As an important aside, nothing that follows involves formal constitutional amendment. The cornerstone of this rebalancing is the principle of subsidiarity.

THE PRINCIPLE OF SUBSIDIARITY

By way of introduction, subsidiarity has a long philosophical and political history, particularly in Europe but also in Quebec. At the request of the German federation, among others, subsidiarity underpins the Maastricht Treaty in the European Union. On this side of the Atlantic, the principle of subsidiarity featured prominently in Quebec's *Royal Commission of Inquiry on Constitutional Problems* (the Tremblay Report, which led to the creation of Quebec's personal income tax system). There are two components to subsidiarity. The first, and the one that is most frequently associated with subsidiarity in the public's mind, is that powers should be delegated to the lowest level of government at which they can be exercised effectively—clearly a decentralist thrust. The second aspect of subsidiarity is that where externalities or spillovers exist at the lowest government level or where there are national dimensions associated with these powers, then a rationale exists for moving the jurisdiction upward.

If one takes both components of subsidiarity into account, the result is a principled and nonconstitutional approach to *rebalancing* the allocation of powers. Powers should be shifted upward to the federal government only if externalities or spillovers cannot be handled in any other way.

As alluded to earlier, the proposals contained in the Throne Speech implied an application of the subsidiarity principle. Another good example is the recent *Environmental Management Framework Agreement.*[5] The federal government's authority in the environment area would be recognized in national and transboundary measures, in conducting Canada's international environmental relations, in environmental matters relating to federal lands, in the relationship with aboriginal peoples, and in working with the provinces in protecting nationally significant ecosystems. The provinces would assume primary jurisdiction in most other areas. This is subsidiarity in action!

Thus, the proposition advanced here is that the subsidiarity ought to be the key operational principle in the renewed federal–provincial jurisdictional accord. As well, it would serve to inform any exercise relating to duplication.

To be sure, the concept of subsidiarity is open to differing interpretations. This is not necessarily a problem in an era where everything appears to be in flux. At the core, however, is the presumption that powers should be devolved unless arguments to the contrary can be sustained. At the same time, however, the federal–provincial interface must also maintain 'process' flexibility. For example, some provinces might have neither the desire nor the resources to draw down authority over, say, forestry. They should be able to request that Ottawa continue to act on their behalf. To be sure, this may complicate the overlap issue, but such flexibility is central to revitalizing the overall management of the federation. There is another aspect of flexibility that needs to be addressed—the role of the federal spending power.

THE SPENDING POWER PRINCIPLE

As noted earlier, the exercise of the federal spending power in postwar Canada gave us our decentralized yet 'national' set of social programs. Reworking the federal–provincial interface on the basis of the principle of subsidiarity may well strait-jacket the exercise of the spending power. This would be contrary to the notion of revitalizing the federation: the federal government ought to be able to act in what it perceives to be the national interest. This is especially the case given that globalization and the information revolution are serving to catapult traditional provincial areas (such as education) into key competitive determinants in the next century. To disempower the federal government from taking a leadership or a legislative role in areas critical to national competitiveness does not make economic or political sense.

Therefore, I would endorse a version of the Meech Lake recommendation with respect to the spending power. Specifically, Ottawa should have a free hand in designing and funding programs in areas of exclusive provincial jurisdiction provided that the provinces can opt out with adequate compensation if they mount equivalent programs or already have them in place. In effect, this maximizes the freedom to manoeuvre on the part of both levels of government without violating the underlying principle of subsidiarity. Intriguingly, while endorsing this version of the spending power, the recent Throne Speech may actually go *too far* in attaching self-imposed constraints on the ability of the federal government to innovate and legislate in areas of national interest.

EQUITY AS A PRINCIPLE IN FEDERAL PROGRAMS

Equalization is the overarching redistributive program ensuring that all provinces have access to reasonably comparable tax revenues at reasonably comparable tax rates. Established in 1957, the equalization program became so integral a component of Canada's political economy that it was enshrined in the Constitution Act, 1982. Beyond this program, however, federal spending in other areas should strive for equality of treatment for both provinces and individuals. Programs such as Old Age Security/Guaranteed Income Supplement (OAS/GIS) for the elderly are universally acclaimed by Canadians, in large part because they do not discriminate among Canadians based on where they reside. This is not true for unemployment insurance (where unemployed Canadians are twice as likely to be UI recipients in New Brunswick than in Ontario) or for the Canada Assistance Plan, now part of the CHST, where per capita payments vary arbitrarily across provinces.[6] While federal programs must conform to section 36(1) of the Constitution Act, 1982 (which commits governments to promote equal opportunities for the well-being of all Canadians), my position here is that differential federal treatment should be restricted to the formal equalization program. If this is deemed to require some equalization on the 'cost' side, so be it. But national programs such as UI and the CHST should treat similarly situated recipient units (province or individual) equally. To fail to do so will eventually undermine support for the formal equalization program.

This principle will have very significant implications for the evolution of CHASTE, as elaborated later.

THE PRINCIPLE OF DUALITY

Central to the rebalancing and revitalization of the Canadian federation must be the recognition of Quebec's cultural, legal, and linguistic distinctiveness. The full articulation that this fundamental duality of Canadian federalism is a source of Canadian strength and richness may eventually have to involve formal constitutional amendment. The purpose of this section is more circumscribed: to present the case that the principle of duality must inform any reworking and revitalization of the operation of Canadian federalism.

It is instructive to come at this issue from a quite different perspective than is normally proffered. What follows are a few of the principles of the 'preamble' of the much-celebrated recent Yukon Indians' Self-Government Agreement. This is an agreement among the Government of Canada, the Government of the Yukon, and the Yukon First Nations. (In the specific case cited, the agreement involves the Champagne and Aishihik First Nations.) This agreement provides wide-ranging powers to the Yukon First Nations, much like the powers of the provinces. The preamble reads, in part:

Whereas

- the Champagne and Aishihik First Nations have traditional decision making structures based on a moiety system and are desirous of maintaining these structures;
- the Parties wish to support and promote the contemporary and evolving political institutions and processes of the Champagne and Aishihik First Nations...;
- the Parties recognize and wish to protect a way of life that is based on an economic and spiritual relationship between Champagne and Aishihik people and the land;
- the Parties wish to protect the cultural, political and economic distinctiveness and social well being of the Champagne and Aishihik people;...

Now therefore, in accordance with...the Parties agree to the following.

Surely it would be difficult to construe this as anything but a complete and generous recognition of the cultural, political, and economic distinctiveness of the Yukon Indians within the Canadian society and polity. And the agreement, replete with these principles, is in the process of being enshrined in the Constitution under the provision of section 35 of Part II of the Constitution Act, 1982. How can we conceive of a less generous approach to one of the founding nations of the Canadian federation?

Another example may be in order. Many Canadians make the point that goods and capital can often flow more freely across the nation-state boundaries of the European Union than across provincial boundaries in Canada. A major objective of this paper is to ensure that, henceforth, this statement will not be true. For present purposes, however, a different point is in order: the single European market is a triumph in achieving harmony within diversity. For example, unitary state, English-speaking, individualist and common-law Great Britain has agreed to mutually recognize and respect in matters of trade, regulation, etc., the federal, German-speaking, collective rights and civil-law Federal Republic of Germany.

The force of these two examples surely argues that the linguistic, cultural, and legal (civil law) reality of Quebec must also be revitalized as part of any rebalancing. This may, and likely will, imply asymmetrical arrangements. But there are already some significant asymmetries in the system. Quebec has its own personal income tax, its unique set of financial institutions, its own Quebec Pension Plan, its own deposit insurance corporation, etc. Other provinces could replicate all of these, but they choose not to. As noted, more asymmetries may arise. This is especially the case given the pervasiveness of the information revolution. Areas such as human capital formation (including training), research and development, labour market strategies, telecommunications, etc., have to be integrated into the cultural and linguistic specificity of Quebec in order that Quebeçois have the full opportunity to earn a North American living standard operating in French. We can leave this to Ottawa, in which case the provisions will take on a pan-Canadian reach or we can devolve these powers to Quebec. My view is that only the latter approach fully recognizes and respects the aspirations of Quebec within Canada. Hence, the principle of duality must inform any rebalancing and revitalization of the federal–provincial accord on the jurisdictional interface.

The Principle of Competitive Federalism

The motivation for ensuring that Ottawa maintains flexibility in terms of the exercise of the federal spending power has its counterpart in ensuring that the provinces retain the freedom to experiment in the area of design and delivery of social programs. In the economics literature, this is typically referred to as *competitive federalism.* Currently we are witnessing an explosion of creative provincial responses across the full social policy spectrum—new approaches to drug plans for the elderly, new ways to make the welfare-to-work and the school-to-work transition, innovative approaches to the welfare–health (well-being) integration, and creative ways to design and deliver health care. But competitive federalism must also be constrained. It must operate within the overall parameters set down by the Canada Health Act (CHA) principles, the parameters of the Agreement on Internal Trade (an agreement among governments in Canada to reduce barriers to trade within Canada), etc. More on this later.

Summary

Readers will recognize that the above articulation of principles relating to the rebalancing and revitalization of the federal–provincial economic and jurisdictional interface is at the same time highly speculative and highly subjective. However, these five principles correspond rather accurately to the pervasive global and domestic economic and political forces impinging on the evolution of federal and provincial policy choices. In turn, this evolving nature of the federal–provincial jurisdictional interface circumscribes the options for the evolution of social Canada. Phrased differently, the backdrop is now in place to address the likely future of the Canadian social contract.

CHASTE AND SOCIAL CANADA

STRENGTHENING THE CANADIAN SOCIAL UNION

The market-driven and decentralist thrust of the imperatives of globalization as they apply to Canada and the evolving federal–provincial jurisdictional interface pose significant challenges for the preservation, let alone promotion, of the Canadian social and economic union. This is the Achilles heel of the entire exercise: if social Canada begins to fragment, Canadians will surely put a stop to decentralization. Hence, fragmentation cannot be allowed to occur. The fallback position is the maintenance of the five existing CHA principles and the prohibition of residency requirements for access to welfare.

But these existing principles are increasingly inadequate. In my view, this is why the finance minister in the last two budgets, as well as the Throne Speech, have called for the development of some 'mutual consent' federal–provincial principles to underpin the CHST. To see why the existing set of principles may fall short of the challenge, it is appropriate to come at the social union from a somewhat different perspective.

Although Canadians have much to celebrate in terms of the postwar development of our social policy infrastructure and of our social union, nonetheless, we have some distance to go before we can match the social unions of other federations, such as the Swiss or German or Australian. Our traditional approach to promoting the social union has been to leave this to Ottawa with the exercise of the federal spending power and the regulatory oversight of sets of principles (e.g., the Canada Health Act principles). This has served Canadians well, but it is not enough. In the language of the Charlottetown Accord, this is top-down or 'negative' integration, namely a series of 'thou shalt nots' (e.g., thou shalt not extra-bill). With the erosion of federal cash transfers and the accompanying diminishment of Ottawa's moral authority in the social sphere on the one hand and with the enhanced powers of the provinces on the other, something more is needed. Specifically, we must combine this negative integration with 'positive' or horizontal integration, namely a proactive integration or meshing of provincial policies designed to ensure that there are pan-Canadian rights on the social policy front. In other words, preserving and promoting the Canadian Social Union (CSU) must be the joint responsibility of both levels of government. This principle will inform the remainder of the analysis of the CSU.

At this juncture, it is instructive to focus on where and why the existing CHA principles may be falling short in terms of the ongoing health challenges faced by Canadians. One problem is that the CHA principles focus rather narrowly on sickness and not on the emerging shift towards well-being. Another is that the CHA does not apply to long-term care. Finally, but hardly exhaustively, the CHA principles are becoming undermined by fiscal constraint and the march of technology. For example, limiting patients to two days in hospital instead of, say, six days does not violate any CHA principle, but it does 'privatize' the recuperation period. It is becoming increasingly evident that Canada needs a Canada Well-Being Act, replete with its own set of binding principles, to replace the Canada Health Act if we are to address the emerging well-being needs of Canadians. The provinces must be involved in developing these principles since they will be delivering the services.

At this juncture, it is instructive to note that the provinces are actually co-operating in developing pan-Canadian social policy principles. Although much-criticized by the press, the December 1995, *Report to Premiers* by the Ministerial Council on Social Policy Reform and Renewal is quite a remarkable document. If one strips away some of the rhetoric directed against the federal deficit shifting in connection with the introduction of the CHST, then the document takes on very encouraging dimensions. The four central themes are:

- social programs must be accessible and serve the basic needs of all Canadians;
- social programs must reflect our individual and collective responsibility;
- social programs must be affordable, effective, and accountable;
- social programs must be flexible, responsive, and reasonably comparable across Canada.[7]

Table 2 elaborates on the principles relating to each of these themes. The conclusion I draw from this table is that there is a lot of common ground from which to reconstitute the principles underpinning social Canada.

Sceptics can and will focus on the ongoing disputes between Ottawa and British Columbia (over residency requirements for welfare) and between Ottawa and Alberta (over health care) as evidence that the system is about to fragment. Although one cannot deny this possibility, I read these disputes quite differently. Basically, these provinces are in a pitched battle against Ottawa's deficit shifting, including the perceived inequities associated with the cap on CAP that applies to them and has been incorporated into the CHST allocations across provinces. The proposals in the 1996 budget to narrow these provincial allocations by 2001 and to place a $11 billion floor on cash transfers will go some way to redressing this inequity. But not far enough as I will argue below. Nonetheless, although this may complicate the negotiations pursuant to the establishment of a set of mutual consent principles, the bottom line is that citizens in all provinces will ensure that the Canadian social union will continue to exist and, in many areas, be strengthened.

TABLE 2 Principles to Guide Social Policy Reform and Renewal

Social Programs Must Be Accessible and Serve the Basic Needs of All Canadians

1. Social policy must assure reasonable access to health, education, and training, income support and social services that meet Canadians' basic needs.
2. Social policy must support and protect Canadians most in need.
3. Social policy must promote social and economic conditions which enhance self-sufficiency and well-being, to assist all Canadians to actively participate in economic and social life.
4. Social policy must promote active development of an individual's skills and capabilities as the foundation for social and economic development.
5. Social policy must promote the well-being of children and families, as children are our future. It must ensure the protection and development of children and youth in a healthy, safe, and nurturing environment.

Social Programs Must Reflect Our Individual and Collective Responsibility

6. Social policy must reflect our individual and collective responsibility for health, education, and social security, and reinforce the commitment of Canadians to the dignity and independence of the individual.
7. Partnerships among governments, communities, social organizations, business, labour, families, and individuals are essential to the continued strength of our social system.
8. There is a continuing and important role, to be defined, for both orders of government in the establishment, maintenance, and interpretation of national principles for social programs.

Social Programs Must be Affordable, Effective, and Accountable

9. The ability to fund social programs must be protected. Social programs must be affordable, sustainable, and designed to achieve intended and measurable results.
10. The long-term benefits of prevention and early intervention must be reflected in the design of social programs.
11. Federal constitutional, fiduciary, treaty, and other historic responsibilities for assurance of aboriginal health, income support, social services, housing, training and educational opportunities must be fulfilled. The federal government must recognize its financial responsibilities for aboriginal Canadians, both on and off reserves.
12. Governments must co-ordinate and integrate social programming and funding in order to ensure efficient and effective program delivery, and to reduce waste and duplication.

Social Programs Must be Flexible, Responsive, and Reasonably Comparable Across Canada

13. Social policy must be flexible and responsive to changing social and economic conditions, regional/local priorities, and individual circumstances.
14. Governments must ensure that all Canadians have access to reasonably comparable basic social programming throughout Canada, and ensure that Canadians are treated with fairness and equity.
15. Social policy must recognize and take into account the differential impact social programming can have on men and women.

SOURCE: Ministerial Council on Social Policy Reform and Renewal, *Report to Premiers*, Mimeo (December 1995).

Toward Skills Mobility

As noted earlier, the Canadian social union falls short of the social unions of the Swiss, the Germans, and the Australians. Our most glaring shortcoming is that we do not guarantee full portability of Canadians' skills and certification. Short of Ottawa usurping provincial powers, this challenge has to be addressed by the provinces. The preferable approach is for the provinces to follow the Australians in adopting 'mutual recognition' of other provinces' standards for occupational training and certification. Actually, chapter 7 of the 1994 Agreement on Internal Trade makes very substantial progress in this direction. The task remaining is to carry these provisions forward to ensure that presumption of equivalency of standards must rest with Canadians wishing to ply their trades in other provinces. Phrased differently, the burden of proof that standards are not equivalent must rest with the provinces, not with individuals. Were the provinces, acting with or without Ottawa, to provide for this enhanced degree of occupational and skills mobility, this would probably be the most significant improvement in the Canadian social union of the last few decades. In my view, the provinces have no choice here: Canadian citizens in this increasing human capital era must have full access to the pan-Canadian market for themselves and their skills, training, and certification. Indeed, some version of mutual recognition is a precondition for reworking the federal–provincial bargain and for promoting the Canadian social union.

To recapitulate a bit, Canadians will insist that some binding principles remain in place in terms of guaranteeing our social union. If for some reason new principles cannot be agreed upon or cannot be made binding on governments, then the fallback position will be the existing CHA principles and the prohibition of residency requirements. My best guess is that compromises will be found. I would also venture a guess that the Canada Health Act (or preferably the Canada Well-Being Act) will be extended to cover new areas with the *quid pro quo* that provinces will be allowed to fall back on some private financing for covered services provided that this financing is progressive. Ontario might lead the way here. If the Harris government follows through with its intended tax cut replete with a health care surcharge on persons with higher incomes, the stage would be set for utilizing the income tax system as a vehicle for private contributions to financing health care. In this context, it is important to note that several provinces have now followed Saskatchewan's lead in replacing free drugs for the elderly with a system based on ability to pay. Such initiatives have, in general, been well received, even by the elderly. The proposition advanced above is that this ability-to-pay approach to drugs will begin to spread into the traditional health care area.

In a sense, this is the easy aspect in terms of the implications of CHASTE. Much more difficult are the likely implications for the have/have-not subsystem in terms both of unemployment insurance and the evolution of the CHST. I will deal with these in turn.

EQUALIZATION AND THE CHST

In reworking the federal–provincial transfer system in the 1995 federal budget, the federal government:

- maintained equalization intact;
- sharply reduced cash transfers under the new CHST—from $18 billion last year to just over $11 billion early next century (this latter figure includes the further cut in the 1996 budget);
- allocated the CHST entitlement for 1996–7 (the first year of the CHST) on the basis of combined CAP and EPF allocations in 1995–6. This had the effect of carrying over the cap on CAP (applied to the have provinces) into the CHST allocations for the initial year.

These provisions, and particularly the cap on CAP carryover to the CHST, are viewed as patently unfair by the have provinces and they constitute the principal reason why, for example, British Columbia and Alberta are challenging Ottawa. In the 1996 budget, Ottawa moved to reduce this latter inequity. Henceforth, provincial shares will reflect population movements and the uneven entitlement allocations will be reduced by half by 2001–2.[8]

This is probably not going to carry the day. At a minimum, Ottawa will have to move to per capita equality in CHST *entitlements*. But pressures will build for equal-per-capita *cash* transfers. Once the $11 billion cash transfer floor becomes binding, then it will be increasingly appropriate to view the CHST solely as a cash transfer (i.e., ignoring the implicit tax-transfer component). And, in turn, it will become progressively more difficult to sell anything but an equal-per-capita allocation of this CHST cash. The have-provinces' rationale will be straightforward—if some differential treatment is needed, then put this in the formal equalization program, not in a national program like the CHST.[9] With the 1996 federal budget, Ottawa has recognized, in principle, the validity of this line of argument. The only question is how far this move toward equality will go. This is especially the case since the issue of fairness will surely play front and centre in any negotiation of mutual consent principles to underpin the CHST.

EQUALIZATION AND UI

The Unemployment Insurance program (or Employment Insurance as the new proposal refers to it) is an even greater challenge. There are two quite distinct ways in which UI, as currently constituted, is way offside with the emerging reality elaborated earlier in this paper. One relates to the set of forces outlined earlier and the other to the likely evolution of the federal–provincial interface. These are lumped together in the following analysis.

There has long existed a substantial body of evidence, some of it undertaken by governments, to the effect that the regional entry and benefit provisions of UI have played havoc with allocative efficiency—among other aspects, the twelve-week job syndrome and the emergence of transfer dependency. On the equity side, the problems are equally severe—as already noted, recent evidence suggests that an unemployed New Brunswicker is more than twice as likely to collect UI benefits as an unemployed Ontarian. It is not just that the structure of the current UI program fares woefully on equity and efficiency grounds, but that this negative perception of the program is beginning to unwind Canadians' acceptance of the entire east–west social contract.

The proposed solutions in the EI (Employment Insurance) bill actually exacerbate the existing problems. To be sure, there are some reform provisions, like the shift to an 'hours' basis, which are most welcome. By and large, however, the effect of the proposals is not to tackle the long-recognized structural deficiencies, but rather to grind down the program a bit. This leaves the poorer regions with a larger percentage cut in benefits than the richer regions. To ensure that this is not the final result, Ottawa will offer five types of employment benefits (wage subsidies, earnings supplements, self-employment assistance, etc.) that will be allocated regionally so that the overall percentage cut in total benefits is equal across all provinces. This leads to two wholly inappropriate results.

The first is that similarly situated unemployed persons in different provinces will now be treated differently in terms of accessing these employment benefits, because these benefits are allocated regionally. This is way offside of an insurance program where all employees contribute on an equal basis. Second, Ottawa has created a new set of services for a select group of Canadians, namely UI beneficiaries. Persons on welfare will not be able to access these new federal benefits since they can only go to UI recipients. The result will be massive jurisdictional entanglement. Active labour market policies on the part of the provinces will now run into enormous complications since a special group of provincial citizens will be eligible for select treatment from EI funds. Among other things, this wreaks havoc with the Throne Speech that devolves labour market policies to the provinces.

We ought to do better. Two polar approaches merit serious consideration. First, convert UI to an insurance scheme with equal entry and benefit rules across the country and with a reward for long-term labour force attachment, i.e., UI should not be an income-support program for tenuous labour force attachment. These new rules can be introduced gradually in order to minimize transitional problems. Nonetheless, it may be necessary to mount some transitional funds for hard-hit provinces or regions that could, for the transition, be financed by premiums. But premiums would eventually be determined by benefit levels, not by social policy aspirations of the department of Human Resources Development (HRD). If HRD wants to mount employment-related programs, they should be financed from consolidated revenues and not by a tax on employment. If the result of such a program is longer-term hardship for some regions, then the way to handle this is through the equalization program. This would leave the UI program to be applied equally to all similarly situated Canadians regardless of where they reside. Ottawa is undoing the national glue by introducing a regional component in every 'national' program. This is especially the case for premium-financed programs.

The other alternative, which I prefer and which would be more consistent with the CHST, is to 'provincialize' UI, namely turn UI over to the provinces and 'equalize' premiums, i.e., bring UI premiums formally into the equalization program to ensure that all provinces have access to the national-average premium income on a per capita basis. Then leave it to each province to design its own system replete with a set of binding principles (minimum premiums, portability, publicly administered with an appeal process, etc.). One can be sure that provinces would not long tolerate the inefficiencies and inequities that currently exist. Not only would this approach complement the thrust of the Throne Speech but the longstanding jurisdictional impediment to the development of integrated labour force strategies at the provincial level would be eliminated. Thus, we could anticipate the integration of education, training, welfare, and UI into a unified and rationalized whole. It matters less which level of government does this than that some level be able to forge the needed integration.

THE INTERGENERATIONAL TRANSFER

One of the more intriguing policy anomalies of the 1980s is that, in both Canada and the United States, administrations elected on a conservative fiscal platform felt little compunction about borrowing heavily from future generations during what was the longest postwar economic boom. The result is that these future generations will come into the world with a very substantial negative dowry. Recent fiscal initiatives, driven more by the 'gnomes of Zurich' and international competition than by concern for intergenerational effects, are welcome in this context, but it will take a while before the aggregate (all-government) debt/GDP ratio in Canada falls below one hundred percent. However, the intergenerational equity and intergenerational transfer issues transcend the debt-servicing burden. In terms of the former, the current generation of young people is the first that is less well off than the elderly. In an era where the prospects of the young require greater investment in skills than was true for earlier generations, Ottawa is in the process of maintaining, even enriching, its programs for the elderly (the new proposal for OAS/GIS in the 1996 federal budget) while reducing the cash transfers to the provinces by $7 billion annually—transfers that in part at least support welfare and PSE.[10] Moreover, with the new emphasis on markets and self-reliance among other things, younger Canadians are being required to bear more of the costs of their education via much higher tuition fees and, soon perhaps, income-contingent-repayment schemes. Although it is, in principle, difficult to argue with this, it is likely to exacerbate the intergenerational equity issue. In terms of the latter, namely the intergenerational transfer, the societal challenge is how to cope with the doubling of the elderly cohort over the next quarter century or so.

Both the equity and transfer issues have come to the fore in terms of the reform proposals for the CPP/QPP. The unfunded liability here is estimated by the CPP chief actuary to be in the range of $550 billion. The root cause of this underfunding is that no one, young or old, has contributed or is currently contributing anywhere near the amount of premiums needed to make the CPP a market-equivalent plan. Premiums would have to be somewhere in the 8 to 10 percent range (depending on the nature of the plan). Yet for the first twenty years of the CPP they were only 3.6 percent and are now only between 5 and 6 percent.

It is not difficult to return the CPP to fiscal integrity. All one has to do is manipulate the various parameters of the 'mathematics of annuities.' Hence, the various reform proposals generally:

- increase contribution rates;
- argue for pre-funding invested at market rates;
- increase the age of retirement (which lengthens the contribution period and reduces the benefit period); and
- decrease CPP benefits either by stealth (de-indexation) or discretionary measures.

The problem with all of these reform proposals is that not only do they saddle future generations with fully paying for their own pensions (which is obviously acceptable), but also with contributing substantially to pay off the existing unfunded liability (which is not acceptable). Specifically, the way in which this unacceptability will reveal itself is that future generations will simply renege on the CPP if they are required to participate in a pension scheme yielding way less than market returns.

It is not evident how all of this relates directly to CHASTE, except that Canadians are now wrestling with how to cope with the CPP unfunded liability in the context of the overall debt/deficit overhang. My preferences (reflected in *Generation X vs. Generation XS*) are in the direction of preserving the CPP, but saddling most of the burden of the underfunding on the present generation.[11] For example, each dollar of CPP benefits yields roughly 30 cents in tax revenues. These revenues ought to be put back into the CPP fund: if the CPP unfunded liability were cast in after-tax terms, the unfunded liability would be less than $400 billion rather than the CPP's chief actuary's figure of $550 billion. Moreover, given that this unfunded liability is a 'sunk' cost, it should be financed along ability-to-pay lines by those generations or cohorts who are the principal beneficiaries. This does not include future generations!—except that they ought to contribute to their public pensions on an actuarially fair basis.

Two final observations are in order. The first is that there is an influential movement afoot to convert the CPP into an individually based RRSP-type system, along the lines of the World Bank recommendations.[12] It is not difficult to rationalize this on market/fiscal/individualist grounds. And it *will* come to pass if we attempt to unload the unfunded CPP liability on future generations. But my preference is to maintain the CPP as an intergenerational public pension. (Note, however, that in the context of 1996 and beyond, this would imply that it is the turn of the existing generations to play their role, on an ability-to-pay basis, to ensure that the CPP is viable for future generations.) My reasoning is straightforward: if we shift to an individualist market (RRSP-type) approach to compulsory contributory pensions, we will begin the process of severing the intergenerational transfer link. If intergenerational sharing is no longer an implicit contract, how long will it be before within-cohort sharing will no longer be a feature of Canadian social policy. As already noted, I think that CHASTE can still go either way on this issue, but thus far those who favour an RRSP-type approach and/or saddling future generations with much of the underfunding appear to be carrying the day.

The second observation is really a lead into the final section of this paper. Ottawa is receiving high marks for its performance on the deficit-cutting front. Even the Fraser Institute has recently showered accolades on Finance Minister Paul Martin's performance. Yet, as indicated above, Ottawa (and the provinces) stand to pocket roughly $200 billion (30 percent of the $550 billion unfunded liability) in taxes on CPP/QPP benefits if future generations could be cajoled into remaining in a system where they would contribute not only to their own pensions but also to unwinding the unfunded liability. But are these Ottawa's revenues? To this and related revenue issues I now turn.

CHASTE AND FEDERAL–PROVINCIAL FINANCES

While no one doubts that the federal government has undertaken substantial *internal* initiatives (the significant downsizing of the federal civil service, albeit with incredibly generous buy-out privileges), it is also the case that Ottawa has engaged in very substantial deficit shifting. The most obvious exemplar here is the scaling down of cash transfers to the provinces—from $18 billion now to $11 billion early in the millennium. This is an absolutely enormous cut whose effects for social Canada are only beginning to be felt at the provincial level. As already noted, this has been, thus far at least, orchestrated masterfully by the feds, so much so that the public may well end up holding the provinces, rather than Ottawa, to task when their favourite programs are scaled back.

However, it is not just the provinces that have felt the impact of federal deficit shifting—so have the contributory programs CPP/QPP and UI. Earlier in this paper, I alluded to the fact that over the last decade Ottawa has shifted much of the administration of HRD as well as several employment-related programs from consolidated revenue funding (CRF) to premium funding. It has also introduced a claw-back of UI benefits for high-income UI recipients. This is inappropriate for a social *insurance* program: it is similar to clawing back fire insurance payments for rich persons whose houses burn down. This is another way of stating that there is precious little of the insurance principle that remains in UI. Most importantly, for federal deficit purposes, Ottawa is pocketing about $5 billion of premiums income in the current year to establish a UI 'fund' so that premiums will not have to rise in the next recession. Up to a point, this can be justified, but there is nothing in the 1996 budget that suggests that premiums will be rolled back once the appropriate fund is in place.

CPP contributors do not come off much better, but here the culprits are both levels of government since the CPP is a joint federal–provincial program. The tax reform in the mid-1980s skimmed somewhere in the neighbourhood of $1 billion a year by converting CPP contributions from a deduction to a *credit* at the lowest tax rate. Yet RRSPs and RPPs remain a deduction. Moreover, a large part of the reason for the rapid growth of the unfunded CPP liability results from arbitrary increases in benefits (largely but not exclusively in the area of disability benefits). And as noted in the previous section, the proposed

CPP reforms suggested by the joint federal, provincial, and territorial governments' CPP information paper include raising premiums, reducing benefits, raising the retirement age, etc., but nowhere do they even hint that the taxes raised on CPP benefits might be rolled back into the CPP fund to assist future generations in terms of offsetting the unfunded liability.[13] What is the equity or efficiency rationale for raising CPP premiums on future generations to the proposed 14 percent so that Canadian governments can pocket $200 billion? If we were to view the CPP a pure intergeneration savings and transfer scheme, then the public pension scheme is viable at premium rates that are roughly in line with those in market alternatives. Why are our legislators not considering this option?

Beyond these measures, Ottawa has been particularly adept in recent years at *indirectly* increasing its own revenues (or reducing its expenditures) at the expense of the provinces. For example, the 1996 budget proposes that, beginning in 2001, the OAS/GIS will be converted into a nontaxable benefit with the benefits decreasing with increasing income. In other words, the OAS component will also be converted into a GIS. Hitherto, the OAS was taxable, with the taxes shared by both levels of government. Henceforth, the provinces will be out of luck since the new program for the elderly will be net of tax: the costs of this measure to the provinces will be in the billions of dollars, particularly as the number of elderly persons increases. One can argue that it was inappropriate in the first place for the provinces to share in tax revenues from a *federal* OAS payment. But this was the status quo and it will soon be history.

Finally, it is obvious that Ottawa is ensuring that its *own* programs remain intact. The increase in the basic level of the new OAS/GIS proposal as well as the fact that it is fully indexed for inflation stands in stark relief to the roughly 40 percent cut in cash transfers to the provinces over the same time frame. Moreover, intergenerational equity considerations are hardly well served by this special treatment of the elderly. Evidence suggests that the Consumer Price Index (CPI) likely overestimates the degree of inflation by a percent or two: hence, all that was needed to maintain elderly benefits at a constant *real* level was something like an indexation equal to the CPI *less* 1 or 2 percent. Thus, full indexation is inappropriate in terms of what the program intends to do, let alone with respect to how the federal government is treating programs outside of its own jurisdiction.

The provinces have been remarkably silent in the face of all of this. I suspect that this is because they are totally shell-shocked in terms of how they are going to accommodate the major paring in their cash transfers. More to the point, Ottawa has cleverly finessed all of this, even to the point of placing an $11 billion (temporary?) floor on the level of cash transfers and, in the process, masquerading itself as the saviour of 'national standards.' The reality,

I submit, is quite different: in the face of cuts and caps and freezes on federal transfers over the last decade, the provinces have done, and are doing, a magnificent job in attempting to preserve the essence of social Canada, for which they are getting no credit from Canadians. In effect, this is brinksmanship on Ottawa's part—sharply reducing cash transfers in the hope that certain social programs are well enough established that the provinces will be forced to undertake massive redesign and redelivery approaches that will maintain existing levels of service.

This gamble may well pay off. But I doubt it. More likely, the richer provinces (who have been particularly hard done by in terms of the federal initiatives or at least perceived themselves to be) will begin to flex their muscles. Part of this flexing was anticipated in the earlier sections on the likely evolution of UI and of the CHST. My guess is that as a result of all of this, Canada will finally become an effectively decentralized country: the notion that Canada is now decentralized is surely spurious if, as clearly is the case, unilateral federal action can fiscally clobber the provinces. Under the provisions of the 1996 federal budget relating to cash transfers to the provinces, a modest provincial sales tax in Alberta (e.g., 3 to 4 percent) would more than offset this province's total cash transfers from Ottawa and, hence, remove it from any and all federally imposed national standards. Indeed, Alberta's budget surplus for the current year is well above the level of cash transfers it receives from Ottawa. At this point, effective power shifts to the provinces: this may well be the lasting legacy of the 'successful' initiatives on Ottawa's part of setting its own fiscal house in order! Certainly, the evolution of global forces is largely consistent with powers being transferred downward.

In this sense, the longer-term implications of CHASTE are that Canadians will be forced to look to the provinces rather than to Ottawa as the ultimate guarantors of social Canada. The reality is that the federal government has mismanaged its fiscal responsibilities within the federation and that the nature of its chosen solutions are effectively serving to decentralize powers and responsibilities within the federation. I have no doubt that I am among a very small minority of Canadians who believe that the provinces are up to the task of maintaining and even strengthening social Canada, but within a framework that is consistent with the set of global and economic forces outlined earlier. But let there be no doubt—CHASTE has chastened social Canada. We may look longingly on the Canada of the sixties and seventies in terms of social policy, but the relevant message for the romanticists is that 'these are the good old days.'

CONCLUSION

The thrust of the foregoing analysis is that Ottawa's response to the constellation of pervasive forces (internationalization, fiscal burdens, national unity, etc.) has been to launch social Canada into unchartered territory. The federal government's chosen instrument on the social policy front, the CHST, cannot be the final word: it will trigger its own internal dynamic which, in turn, will affect other social programs. This new equilibrium, referred to as CHASTE, will likely have profound implications for the evolution of UI and for the CHST itself. In effect, whereas in 'old Canada,' the have-not provinces essentially drove aspects of social Canada, especially on the regional front, under CHASTE the have provinces will attempt to occupy the driver's seat. In part, this is a result of the way in which the federal government off-loaded its deficit to the provinces. In part also, however, this reflects the new reality where trade flows are increasingly north–south (or international) rather than east–west. In pursuing this new *regional/international interface*, Ontarians, on the economic front, for example, are likely to look more to Queen's Park than to Parliament Hill—Ottawa's financial clout within the federation has diminished substantially, particularly for the have provinces, and its moral authority has literally plummeted.

As a result, Canadians (or at least non-Quebec Canadians) are going to have to resort to something quite un-Canadian, namely looking to the provinces for preserving and promoting the Canadian social union. In *Celebrating Flexibility*, I noted that Quebecers have long associated Quebec with 'nation' and Canada with 'state,' whereas non-Quebec Canadians associated both with Ottawa.[14] Ottawa's policies are forcing Canadians to turn more and more to the provinces to define important aspects of their social and cultural nationhood. Disturbing as this may be to many of us, this is the reality of CHASTE.

NOTES

1. The final chapter in Thomas J. Courchene, *Social Canada in the Millennium: Reform Imperatives and Restructuring Principles* (Toronto, 1994).

2. Michael Storper, 'The Resurgence of Regional Economics Ten Years Later: The Region as a Nexus of Untraded Interdependence,' Paper presented at the conference Cities, Enterprises, and Society on the Eve of the XXI Century (Lille, France, March 1994), 22.

3. Thomas J. Courchene, 'Glocalization: The Regional/International Interface,' *The Canadian Journal of Regional Science* 18/1 (Spring 1995), 1–20.

4. Events change rapidly. Between the time of writing (April 1996) and editing (December 1996), not only is the current account deficit disappearing, but also real interest rates have fallen dramatically. This alters the details contained in the paragraph, but the underlying concerns themselves are still relevant.

5. Canadian Council of Ministers of the Environment, *Environment Management Framework Agreement,* Mimeo (Winnipeg, 1995).

6. Timothy C. Sargent, 'An Index of Unemployment Insurance Disincentives,' Working paper no. 95-10 (Ottawa, 1995), fig. 17; Thomas J. Courchene, *Redistributing Money and Power: A Guide to the Canada Health and Social Transfer* (Toronto, 1995), table 9.

7. Ministerial Council on Social Policy Reform, *Report to Premiers*, Mimeo (Dec. 1995).

8. By way of backdrop for these comments, the 1996–7 allocation of entitlements under the CHST gives Quebec 111 percent of the national average per capita level while Ontario, Alberta, and British Columbia will receive 95 percent, 92 percent, and 96 percent, respectively. These data are from T.J. Courchene, *Redistributing Money and Power* (Toronto, 1995), table 5. The 1996 federal budget promises to reduce these differentials by one-half by the millennium. However, all of this relates to entitlements—cash transfers plus the value of the equalized tax points associated with the CHST. The per capita differentials in cash transfers could well increase over this period. For more detail, consult Courchene, *Redistributing Money.*

9. I may be more biased here than in other parts of this paper, since in *Redistributing Money and Power*, I argued for equal-per-capita cash transfers under the CHST. And, as long as the UI program remains in place (with its own set of equalizing provisions), the evidence that I surveyed suggested that cost differentials in any and all of welfare, health, and postsecondary education argue for *more* money for the have provinces, not less.

10. There is some new and important evidence from the Canadian Institute for Advanced Research relating to the determinants of well-being and population health. As Mustard reports, the ability to cope in later life is often a function of the adequacy of social support networks in early childhood. They need not imply the necessity for preschool daycare since the evidence shows 'that children in poor socio-economic environments who were able to interact with "substitute parents or grandparents" during their early life did much better in later life than those that could not get this adult support.' However, it probably does imply that decreasing support for children may be creating even larger (and more expensive) social challenges later. Mustard's recommendation is to 'make children the highest socio-economic priority and put in place measures of what is happening to children'; J. Fraser Mustard, 'Technology, Information and the Evolution of Social Policy: The Chips for Neurons Revolution and Socio-Economic Change' in Thomas J. Courchene, ed., *Policy Frameworks for a Knowledge Era* (Kingston, ON, forthcoming).

11. Thomas J. Courchene, 'Generation X vs. Generation XS: Reflections on the Way Ahead,' in Keith Banting and Robin Boadway, eds., *Reform of the Retirement Income System* (Kingston, ON, 1996).

12. See Estelle James, 'The Agenda for Reform: An International Perspective' in Banting and Boadway, *Reform of the Retirement Income System*; William B.P. Robson, *Putting Some Gold in the Golden Years: Fixing the Canada Pension Plan*, Commentary no. 76 (Toronto, 1996); the Reform Party proposals; and the *Globe and Mail* editorials.

13. Federal, Provincial, and Territorial Governments of Canada, *An Information Paper for Consultations on the Canada Pension Plan* (Ottawa, 1996).

14. Thomas J. Courchene, *Celebrating Flexibility: An Interpretive Essay on the Evolution of Canadian Federalism* (Toronto, 1995).

SOCIAL JUSTICE MOVEMENTS AND THE CRISIS OF THE WELFARE STATE

Observations from the Halifax People's Summit

ANDREW C. PARKIN

Department of Sociology and Social Anthropology
Dalhousie University

> In this society, they're cutting back medical care, they're cutting back social services, there's a rise in militarism, they're talking about privatizing the jails, and on and on and on. Somebody has got to fight that.[1]

> Invention is always born of dissension.[2]

This paper provides some reflections on the response by some social justice movements to the current crisis of the Canadian welfare state: the actual and expected cut-backs in the funding by federal and provincial governments of a variety of social programs, particularly in health care, social assistance and income support, unemployment insurance and employment training, but also in higher education, cultural and artistic programs, international development aid, and the protection of the environment. Historically, social justice movements have played a key role in mobilizing popular support for such programs, and in pressuring governments to undertake to establish and extend them. It is hardly surprising, then, to find that these same movements now oppose the reduction or abolition of funding for these programs. The precise way in which social justice movements are formulating their response to the current crisis, however, is a matter that warrants further scrutiny and discussion. I argue that rather than simply protesting cut-backs in a manner that fails to take the current fiscal crisis of the state seriously, or conversely resigning themselves to the inevitability of cut-backs given the inescapability of this crisis, a number of movements have been remarkably innovative in developing a sophisticated analysis of the issues, in articulating viable policy alternatives, and in identifying new avenues for political mobilization.

The social justice movements that I focus on in this paper are those that participated in the 1995 Halifax People's Summit. The People's Summit, also known as the P-7, was a week-long series of events organized by local social justice movements, public interest groups, and interested citizens at the time of the meeting of the Halifax G-7 Summit.[3] The main purpose of the People's Summit was to present, evaluate, and publicize alternatives to the policies of the G-7 governments and the international financial institutions (such as the World Bank and the International Monetary Fund [IMF]) which these governments *de facto* direct.[4] The types of events held during the People's Summit ranged from workshops to speeches, to rallies and 'speak-outs,' to art shows and street theatre. These events were organized by, among others, labour unions, feminist groups, development workers, environmentalists, peace groups, civil rights and antiracism activists, youth groups, and artists. The People's Summit was unique: never before in Halifax had such a wide array of social movement activists, organizers, and sympathizers assembled together for the same purpose.

My study of the People's Summit began in March 1995. As well as participating in the People's Summit and assisting with aspects of its organization, I conducted interviews with eleven members of the People's Summit Co-ordinating Committee, the body that oversaw the genesis of and preparation for the People's Summit, and that effectively ran the final event. I also conducted interviews with three other individuals who played key supporting roles in the People's Summit. A complete round of fourteen interviews was conducted prior to the event, and nine of the members of the co-ordinating committee were interviewed for a second time after it. The conclusions that I have drawn based on this informative but limited study clearly cannot be said to apply to Canadian social justice movements as a whole. Instead, this paper considers this case as a revealing snapshot of a recent instance of social movement activity in one part of the country.

CONCEPTUALIZING THE CRISIS

With regard to the current crisis of the welfare state, there are two features of the discussions that took place among the participants at the People's Summit that warrant particular attention. First, the crisis of the Canadian welfare state was consistently conceptualized by participants in a global context: the Canadian state was not viewed as an isolated and autonomous unit, but rather as but one player within a global economic system. The main actors in this economic system were seen to be, not only other nation states, but also multinational corporations, currency speculators, bond traders and stock brokers, and international credit raters. Moreover, these corporations and traders were seen as having the ability to move large amounts of capital around the world instantaneously, dramatically affecting currency values, domestic interest rates, and levels of employment, and thereby constituting a serious constraint on the scope of action of the Canadian government with regard to domestic public policy.[5] In other words, the participants at the People's Summit allowed that the degree to which the Canadian government has a free hand to shape domestic policy is limited, given the exigencies of the global economy. As one group of participants concluded: 'transnational corporations have colossal powers and have outdistanced the capacity of nation states to regulate and act on behalf of citizens.'[6]

This means that the participants at the People's Summit embraced an analysis that on the surface appears similar to that of their political opponents, among them the federal government—that 'Canada has become excessively vulnerable to the volatile sentiments of global financial markets,' and that the country therefore has 'suffered a tangible loss of economic sovereignty,' meaning that it does not have freedom of choice in terms of public policy.[7] As will be shown, however, the similarities between the analysis of the P-7 and that of its political opponents are limited.

The nature of the participants' analysis of the situation facing Canada can be illustrated in an impressionistic and anecdotal sense through a consideration of the movements' choice of symbolic representation or personification of its political adversary. The social justice movements gathered in Halifax often caricatured their typical 'opponent' as a youthful and reckless bond trader or currency speculator working on Wall Street or in Singapore, who with a touch of a computer button causes dramatic fluctuations in currency values, stock prices, and interest rates, thereby derailing national governments' economic plans. This differs in interesting ways from the opponent which similar movements would have identified at the previous countersummit held in Canada in 1988 at the time of the free trade debate. This was most often Ronald Reagan (or perhaps the more generalized 'Uncle Sam'), or Brian Mulroney, particularly in his capacity as Reagan's sycophant. Importantly, at the 1995 countersummit, Jean Chrétien was not seen to be coddling international stock brokers in the way Mulroney was seen in 1988 as coddling Ronald Reagan. Instead, Chrétien was seen to have been made irrelevant by the stock brokers, and hence, to a certain extent, less as an political adversary than a fellow victim.

The second significant feature of the consensus that emerged among the participants of the People's Summit concerning the current crisis of the welfare state is their increasing disillusionment with the conventional political process and their escalating scepticism about the benefits of participation within the formal institutions of representative democracy. This, in a sense, is a corollary of the view that the Canadian government's 'room to maneuver' is presently restricted in the face of the pressures exerted by the international economic system: if public policies are no longer determined, in the last instance, by political decision-makers, then a popular campaign to influence these decision-makers now appears misdirected. It makes little sense, in other words, to expend the energies of a movement to gain access to politicians if the latter have effectively become powerless.[8]

This is a conclusion which several of the participants at the People's Summit said they had drawn on the basis of their recent experience of the process of social program reform. For example, health care workers attending a People's Summit workshop on the future of Canada's social programs described how their lobbying efforts and their participation in government consultations and public hearings at the provincial level bore little fruit in the end, despite indications along the way in party policy documents and government committee reports that their arguments had held sway. The final policy decisions were seen to be taken in the interest of international economic actors, an interest which apparently overruled the consensus that previously had been developed between the provincial government and the health care workers. The conclusion reached by the workers, then, was that the conventional means for influencing government policy formation (such as preparing briefs and submissions for government committee hearings and task forces, working to gain the support of politicians and political parties, and engaging in elite-level negotiations between politicians or bureaucrats and leaders of unions or public interest groups) could no longer be relied upon. In order to make oppositional voices heard, therefore, the health care workers, among others, felt that a shift to more unconventional methods of political action was needed.

This stands as an illustration of what the political sociologist Claus Offe has claimed has been a general trend within liberal democratic countries for over fifteen years. Offe argues that once public policy ceases to be formulated through democratic processes as formally provided for by democratic institutions, but instead is formulated through an informal and secretive process of negotiations between public officials and representatives of the private sector, then the public itself can be expected to turn increasingly to nonconventional methods of expressing their political will and fighting for their interests: 'if democratic institutions such as the party system, elections and parliamentary government are reduced in their ability to provide for the articulation of political conflict, *alternative channels of conflict are likely to develop and to absorb the political energies of the people.*'[9] The nature of those alternative channels identified at the P-7 will be explored later.

The analysis of the crisis of the welfare state that emerged at the People's Summit, as described above, has a number of significant implications. First, the position adopted by the participants at the People's Summit was one that enabled them to avoid two simplistic poles of argument. On the one hand, they were able to avoid the argument that the country simply can no longer afford the social safety net: that given the debt and deficit crisis, the necessity and so the legitimacy of sizeable cuts in social spending are self-evident and unquestionable. This argument could be avoided because of the People's Summit globalist approach, an approach that did not take the international context for national public policy formation as an unchangeable given. The P-7's approach, in other words, did not take it for granted that the priorities of international finance capital must take precedence over all others in the formation of Canadian public policy; it did not prevent them from exploring alternate means of solving the debt and deficit crisis, such as the lowering of interest rates; and, as will be seen, it did not exclude from consideration the possibility of regulating and constraining the global economy in order to allow the national state more leeway with respect to domestic spending. This is what differentiates the P-7 approach from that of the federal government, despite the superficial similarities mentioned above.

On the other hand, the participants were able to avoid the equally simple argument that there is no need to seriously re-evaluate public policy, since the debt and deficit crisis is exaggerated, if not fictitious. This second line of argument appears as overly simple in the face of the situation in which roughly as much money is being spent on servicing the debt as on social programs. The position of the participants at the People's Summit therefore was politically sophisticated in that it allowed that a certain fiscal crisis genuinely existed while denying that the government had 'no choice' but to cut social programs. This ability to navigate the conceptual waters between the Scylla of the inevitability of cutting back social programs and the Charybdis of accepting the status quo is a significant feature of the People's Summit approach, for it necessarily prompts a much needed search for innovative policy alternatives.

Another significant implication of the People's Summit's approach to the welfare state is that it enabled activists and movement intellectuals to draw attention to the connections that exist between Canadian political and economic concerns and those of other countries, both in the North and in the South. Canadians, peoples of other G-7 countries, and peoples of countries of the South were all portrayed as victims of the new global economic order, under which spending on health, education, and job creation are sacrificed in favour of the repayment of debt, the liberalization of trade, and the de-regulation and privatization of economic activity. In a communiqué issued following a workshop on economic issues held in preparation for the People's Summit, one group of participants declared that 'as a group, we recognize that Canada is beginning to face the effects of the same structural adjustment policies that are so adversely affecting the developing countries of the world.'[10] This is not to say that it was argued that the severity of poverty in the North and the South is the same, but rather that similar processes and interests are at work in both parts of the globe. As one organizer stated, 'structural adjustment programs are hitting Canada, and the same financial interests are at work. We don't borrow from the World Bank...but the same overseas financial interests are saying "here's the hoop and jump through it: cut your social programs or else."'

This emerging sense that poor, unemployed, and marginalized peoples in the North and the South are essentially related victims of the same global economic practices is noteworthy for at least two reasons. First, it provides some additional conceptual grounding upon which a coalition between different social justice movements, concerned with or active in different areas of the globe, can be built. In other words, it highlights the common ground shared by, for instance, antipoverty groups active in Canada, and Canadian organizations concerned with economic and social development in the South, thereby contributing to the goal of strengthening the unity and solidarity among oppositional movements in the country. Second, by globalizing the outlook of movements concerned with social justice in Canada, the sense that the economic situations facing people from different parts of the world are linked can be seen as contributing to the development of an expanded sense of political identity and community that prefigures the making of a global citizenship or global civil society.[11] The tendency of activists to view local social justice issues as particular manifestations of global phenomena, the consequent strengthening of a sense of connectedness to and solidarity with peoples from other parts of the world, and the formation of linkages and alliances among different social justice movements from across the globe, produces a phenomenon that Richard Falk has called 'globalization from below'[12]—and which David Held has equated with a cosmopolitan conception of democracy[13]—which mirrors or shadows processes of the globalization of capital.

A third implication of the approach to the welfare state articulated by social movements at the People's Summit has already been discussed above: it leads to a critique of institutional politics, which by extension implies a growing interest in noninstitutional politics as a means for pressing the movements' claims concerning the future of the welfare state. This, as I have argued, is congruent with a larger trend toward 'the increased use of noninstitutional or nonconventional forms of political participation, such as protest, demonstrations, and unofficial strikes,' which political sociologists such as Claus Offe have argued is a characteristic of Western politics since the 1970s.[14] Of course, the interest in noninstitutional politics professed by many at the People's Summit may have been superficial: radical tactics may well have been advocated in words during P-7 meetings, but there is no guarantee that this verbal endorsement will be matched by concrete actions. Recent developments in many areas of the country, including protest marches and direct actions in Ontario, New Brunswick, and Nova Scotia, indicate, however, that the disillusionment of social movements with institutional politics may not lead only to resignation and quiescence.[15] In addition to these instances of protest against Canadian governments, social movements are increasingly engaging in an altogether different form of noninstitutional politics, one that bypasses the institutions of the nation state and targets multinational corporations directly. This latter strategy will be discussed later.

The increasing disillusionment with the institutional avenues of policy formation and the growing interest in noninstitutional politics also has implications in terms of the audience whom the social justice movements are trying to reach. At the People's Summit, the majority of participants showed little interest in reaching the leaders of the G-7 Summit, despite the fact that the latter group's meeting in Halifax was the very *raison d'être* for the P-7. As one organizer put it, 'I'm not sure I really intend the G-7 leaders to listen to what I have to say. I think I intend the people to listen to what I have to say.' Another organizer explained the thinking on the matter as follows: 'Politicians, surprisingly enough, have not been a major audience for us; we're not trying to really influence a G-7 agenda. ...They already have their communiqus written ...We feel that if we can create more of a milieu out there, more of a general public demand for or interest in alternatives, then the politicians will inevitably have to follow.'

Despite the stated intention 'to present our analysis to the G-7 decision makers' then, the People's Summit did not view itself primarily as a lobbying organization bent on gaining the ear of politicians and bureaucrats.[16] In practice, the People's Summit placed much greater emphasis on the need to communicate with the general public, either directly or through the media.

At the same time, as mentioned above, a distinct effort was placed on exploring the possibility of influencing the behaviour of corporations directly, rather than indirectly through means of prompting the state to act against corporations on the movement's behalf. For if it is the case that the authority of the nation state is currently being bypassed by corporations that operate on a global level, then it follows that the efforts of opposition movements need to be redirected accordingly. As one organizer remarked: 'Maybe in some ways lobbying governments is a waste of time, because it's really the corporations and big business that we have to talk to, and that's going to involve a very different strategy than what we're used to doing.' The participants were encouraged to think in these terms by a number of the featured speakers at the People's Summit, including Maude Barlow, who argued for the need for Canadians to build a social movement directly in opposition to 'corporate rule,' and Vandana Shiva, who provided her audience with salient examples of successful direct actions in India against multinational corporations, including the physical tearing apart of unwelcome chemical factories by local citizens.[17]

ARTICULATING THE ALTERNATIVES

It is important to note that the participants at the People's Summit did not only attempt to develop an understanding of the current crisis of the welfare state. Nor did they focus exclusively on mobilizing protest against those government policies concerning the welfare state with which they disagreed. For as well as denouncing the failures of the G-7 governments, the participants placed great stress on the need to develop viable policy alternatives. As one organizer explained, 'I think the number one objective [of the P-7] is to talk about, come up with, and present alternatives...to the media and to the people.' Or, in the words of another: 'It's not just enough to say this is what we're against, but it's also very important for us to say what we're for. And if there's any balance on that scale, I would say the P-7 is definitely more about what we're for, as opposed to what we're against.'[18]

A number of different policy alternatives were put forward by the organizations taking part in the People's Summit. Many of the most interesting of these did not concern the social welfare programs directly, but rather concerned the international economic and political forces currently shaping governments' domestic policies in the ways discussed above. In general, the People's Summit demanded 'a changed relationship among government, business, and the people' and insisted that 'people, through an authentic process of democracy, must regain control over business and commerce.'[19] More specifically, in order to accomplish this, various groups proposed such measures as:

- the implementation of a tax of 0.5 percent on international currency transfers (the Tobin tax), with the proceeds being used to further human security throughout the world;

- the introduction of international taxes on multinational corporations, and charges (rents) for the use of the global commons;
- the insertion of a Social Clause in the constitution of the World Trading Organization, committing its members to observe core labour rights, including: freedom of association and the right to organize and bargain collectively; freedom from forced or compulsory labour; freedom from child labour; equal renumeration for men and women; and freedom from discrimination with respect to employment and occupation;
- the definition and enforcement of common labour practices and environmental standards among member countries of the NAFTA;
- the holding of multinational corporations accountable to international agreements on human rights including those concerning the rights of children;
- the requirement that lending by the World Bank or the IMF be subject to stricter criteria in order to ensure that projects that receive funds are neither environmentally destructive nor involve the violation of human rights and norms of democracy;
- the making of decision-making at international bodies such as the United Nations, the IMF and the World Bank more transparent, open, and accountable to public scrutiny;
- the creation at the United Nations of an economic security council, allowing the broader world community a greater say in the governance of the global economy;
- the facilitation of participation by nongovernmental organizations (NGOs) in intergovernmental forums and decision-making processes.

The intended benefits of these policies are at least threefold. First, they are designed to regulate the international economy in such a way as to decrease the extent to which international economic actors can exert a de facto veto over national policy initiatives (such as those designed to preserve, rather than dismantle, the welfare state). As one of the organizations participating in the People's Summit argued, the Tobin tax and related mechanisms are required in order to control global currency transfers that currently 'undermine the stability of global and national economic systems' and generate a climate of fear and uncertainty that 'destabilizes economies and undermines national sovereignty, ecological security, and efforts at reducing poverty.'[20] Or, as another report put it, measures such as the Tobin tax 'would replace the monetary chaos of the present situation with order. Designed to reduce speculation, while allowing legitimate financial trading...currency market volatility would be reduced...*and the degree of autonomy for government policy making would be expanded*.'[21]

paradox:
of internalization → of ineffectiveness
of full action →

Second, proposals to encourage if not enforce adherence by both national governments and multinational corporations to <u>minimum standards in the realm of labour practices, the environment, democracy, and human rights</u> are <u>also designed to increase the control of political agents over economic activity</u>. More specifically, they are designed to ensure that national governments ultimately are not forced to abandon domestic programs designed to benefit society and the environment in order to stay competitive with those areas of the world in which no such standards prevail.

Third, the reform of international institutions in order to allow for greater public scrutiny and wider representation of the world's citizens is similarly intended to <u>allow citizens to gain</u> control over the economic activities and <u>decision-making</u> that affect their lives. The involvement of NGOs in the decision-making of international bodies that regulate international commerce, for instance, would facilitate efforts to revise the priorities of these bodies so that they ultimately act to promote economic and social justice, rather than to simply 'liberalize' economic activity. In sum, then, the policy alternatives noted above are designed to contribute to the goal of 'the creation of new democratic processes and institutions for the control and regulation of monetary speculation and corporate power.'[22]

As mentioned, this collection of policy alternatives is designed to help preserve the welfare state indirectly by tackling the operations of the international political and economic system. As argued above, this tendency to conceptualize domestic policy problems and solutions within an internationalist framework, and indeed to mobilize internationally to confront not only nation states but international decision-making bodies and multinational corporations, is one of the striking features of contemporary social movement activity. As Zsuzsa Hegedus argues, politics since the 1980s has been characterized 'by the eruption of social practices, public opinion campaigns, and civil initiatives in the international arena.'[23] Although social movements of the 1970s may have had global relevance and resonance, they nevertheless tended to focus on the nation state as the terrain and object of struggle. By contrast, movements today 'are basically global, planetary and transnational not only with regard to the issues they address but, above all, in their interventions.' In other words, contemporary movements 'are not limited to national boundaries, nor to actions which merely pressure governments or oppose states. They now intervene in a newly autonomous manner in the international arena by directly addressing different issues formerly managed by states in the framework of inter-state relations.' These interventions, argues Hegedus, 'challenge the conceptual exclusion of social movements from the international arena.' Indeed, as it was put in one P-7 communiqué, 'the fact that the P-7 is meeting at all demonstrates the vitality of <u>global civil society</u>.'[24]

THE CREATIVITY OF MOVEMENT POLITICS

At this point, several cautionary notes are in order. First of all, participants at the People's Summit were by no means unanimous with respect to the points discussed above. There were many who felt uncomfortable with any approach to the crisis of the welfare state that was premised upon the notion of the limited sovereignty of the nation state. Such a notion, some felt, merely served to let national political leaders 'off the hook,' as responsibility for cut-backs in social spending was passed on to international bond rating agencies and currency speculators. It was also felt that this notion served to deflect energy away from confrontation with the national state and toward campaigns for reforms in international agencies such as the IMF, campaigns that might be laudable but that do not address the immediate and pressing crisis posed by the actual ongoing cuts in unemployment insurance, closures of hospitals, introduction of exploitative and disciplinary programs such as workfare, and so on. Thus while some participants explored the potential for building new democratic institutions and processes at the international level, others chose to concentrate more straightforwardly on lobbying the national government to abandon planned cuts in social programs.

For example, following the workshop on the future of Canada's social programs, a number of activists faxed a letter to the Senate Committee on National Finance stating: 'We demand that the Senate suspend passage of Bill C-76 until there have been ample opportunities for public discussion and input across Canada, and an impact assessment of the effects of this Bill has been completed.'[25] Other organizations demanded the increase of taxation on corporations and wealthy individuals within Canada in order to increase funds available for social programs, as well as the reduction in length of the work-week in order to alleviate unemployment, thereby reducing demand for social programs such as unemployment insurance. The globalist approach articulated by many at the People's Summit was thus not the only approach in evidence, and it certainly did not replace more state-centred political strategies. In my opinion, the adoption of contrasting strategies by the different social justice movements involved with the People's Summit should be viewed as evidence of a functional division of labour, wherein different movements continue to work at different levels, be they the international level, the national, provincial, or municipal level of government, or even the level of the neighbourhood or individual person.

As a second cautionary note, it should be stated that the social justice movements participating in the People's Summit were more successful in articulating policy alternatives with respect to certain issues than others. For instance, little consensus existed as to the appropriate response to the growing devolution—whether from the federal to the provincial level of government, or from provincial bureaucracies to local boards and councils—of the delivery and administration of social programs. Several participants who addressed this issue seemed unsure as to the extent that such devolution should be supported at least in part as a step towards democratization and the return of power from the bureaucracy to the community, or opposed wholesale as a pretence on the part of governments for the cutting back of total expenditure on social programs and the abandonment of national standards.[26] At times, then, there was some uncertainty among participating groups as to what their response should be to many of the transformations that are currently taking place within the Canadian welfare state.

Finally, it is apparent that not all of the policy alternatives proposed by the participants at the People's Summit are ones that could be implemented instantaneously and unproblematically. Writing in support of the Tobin tax, for instance, one participating group added that 'the practical difficulties in imposing a Tobin tax should not be underestimated, however, as the decentralized, unregulated, electronically mediated nature of the foreign exchange markets pose particular challenges.'[27] Social justice movements at the People's Summit, therefore, may have had alternative solutions to offer to pressing issues, but they did not have in their possession the equivalent of a magic wand. This should not come as a surprise: given the limited financial and infrastructural resources which these movements have at their disposal, it is particularly unrealistic to expect them to have proven, straightforward answers to complex problems at the ready. As one organizer remarked, 'I get annoyed when the government, having gone for years and years and years with billions of dollars with all their expertise that they're paying for all the time, then turns around and expects citizens' groups to have all the answers for how we can get out of this mess or how we can pay the debt off.'

This point should not be belaboured, least the impression be created that the alternatives put forward at the People's Summit were not serious, well-researched, and ultimately viable. Nevertheless, to the extent that the particulars or even in some cases the substance of many alternatives remain to be defined, two further points can be made. First, the G-7 leaders gathered in Halifax, supported by their ministers and policy advisors, and with full access to the policy-making apparatuses of their respective governments and political parties, failed to identify a single policy innovation to address persistently high levels of unemployment, poverty, and social alienation within their own countries. They did, however, reaffirm the need 'to further reduce public deficits.'[28] In effect, this means that the leaders were able to offer no new thoughts on how to manage a situation of declining expenditures on social programs combined with the likely persistent if not the increasing demand for social assistance on the part of citizens. As the economist Michel Chossudovsky points out, 'the G-7 Summit draft *Communiqué* denies the existence of a global economic crisis...despite the wave of plant closures, mounting unemployment and the instability of global financial markets.'[29] In comparison with the G-7, therefore, the P-7 fares quite well as a forum for policy innovation.

The second point here is that the role and responsibility of social justice movements ultimately is not to provide political leaders with the ready-to-implement solutions which the latter have previously overlooked. Their goal is more generally to bring into question prevailing political and economic orthodoxies, and to prompt public debate on the current priorities of governments and other decision-making agencies. As Jean Cohen and Andrew Arato have argued, movements such as those involved with the People's Summit aim to 'create new associations and new publics, try to render existing institutions more egalitarian, enrich and expand public discussion in civil society, and influence the existing public spaces of political society, potentially expanding these and supplementing them with additional forms of citizen participation.'[30] Similarly, Craig Calhoun argues that 'movements are crucial to re-orienting the agenda of public discourse, bringing new issues to the fore,'[31] while Ron Eyerman and Andrew Jamison maintain that social movements act 'as moments of collective creation that provide society with ideas, identities, and even ideals.'[32] Forums of public communication such as the People's Summit thus are designed, in the final analysis, not to provide definitive answers, but rather to confront institutions such as the G-7 with the persistent demand that government actions and policies be oriented so as to meet the needs and demands of the citizens whose lives they affect, and to alert the public to the existence of other choices in the area of economic and social policy. As one P-7 organizer explained, the goal of the People's Summit was 'to constantly reinforce the option of choice,' and to emphasize that 'their [the G-7's] vision isn't the only vision and their way is not the only way.' To this, the organizer added: 'to continue to routinely introduce the concept of choice...is one of the fundamental underpinnings of a good democracy.'

I will conclude by reiterating some of the basic points of the argument developed above. The current crisis in the welfare state, which has been prompted by the overarching concern on the part of governments with the goal of reducing overall public expenditure in order to eliminate budget deficits, has not been met with either paralysis or resignation on the part of social justice movements. Instead, these movements have tended to respond in three ways. First, they have developed a sophisticated analysis of the current situation that, by conceptually positioning the Canadian state in a global economic context, has allowed them to question the idea that the government has no choice but to cut back on social welfare spending, without at the same time requiring them to deny that a fiscal crisis actually exists at present. Second, they have articulated a number of policy alternatives, many of which concern ways in which the effective sovereignty of national governments can be increased vis-à-vis multinational corporations and other extranational financial interests. Third, they have begun to map out a terrain for political struggle that is not exclusively national in its parameters, but that incorporates, on the one side, networks and alliances of social movements from around the world, and on the other, multinational corporations, international political and economic decision-making bodies, as well as national governments. In the context of frequent political set-backs and a decline in the availability of the resources needed to mobilize, what is most remarkable about the response to the crisis of the welfare state by the social justice movements involved with the People's Summit is their innovativeness, creativity, and resilience.[33] The conclusions that I have drawn from my study of both the 1995 Halifax G-7 Summit and the 1995 Halifax People's Summit thus lend support to Warren Magnusson's assertion that the world of critical social movements 'is the world in which entrepreneurial initiative, popular mobilization, global networking, and political innovation are most apparent.'[34] According to Magnusson, it is to social movements, rather than politicians, that we must look to find viable alternatives to current political crises.

NOTES

My research on the Halifax People's Summit and the preparation of this paper was made possible through the support of the Killam Trust.

1. Response by an organizer of the People's Summit to the question: Is there a need for an oppositional social movement in Canada at this time?
2. Jean-François Lyotard, *The Postmodern Condition: A Report on Knowledge*, trans. by Geoff Bennington and Brian Massumi (Manchester, 1984 [1979]), xxv.
3. This was not the first time that such a summit had been convened at the time of the meeting of the G-7 in Canada: the 1995 Halifax People's Summit was preceded in 1988 by the Citizens Summit in Toronto, and in 1981 by the Popular Summit in Ottawa. In fact, in almost every year since 1984, similar countersummits have been held in each of the seven member nations concurrent with the official G-7 Summit.
4. More specifically, the objectives of the People's Summit were listed as follows: '(1) To raise public and media awareness of the impact of the G-7 Summit policies on people, communities and the environment, and to present our analysis to the G-7 decision makers; (2) To offer public education and media outreach on economic, social and political alternatives to the G-7 agenda—locally and globally; (3) To demonstrate these alternatives in action and directly support those who provide fair, equitable and environmentally sustainable products and services; (4) To be a catalyst for sharing and starting alternatives here in the Atlantic region' (statement of the People's Summit objectives, as written in the People's Summit publicity and registration pamphlet).
5. The economist Michel Chossudovsky, a panelist at the People's Summit workshop entitled 'The Failed Development Model,' argues as follows: 'The debts of parastatal enterprises, public utilities, state, provincial and municipal governments are carefully categorised and "rated" by financial markets. Moreover, ministers of finance are increasingly expected to report to the large investment houses and commercial banks. Moody's downgrading of Sweden's sovereign debt rating in January was instrumental in the decision of the minority Social Democratic government to curtail core welfare programs including child allowances and unemployment insurance benefits. Similarly, Moody's credit rating of Canada's public debt was a major factor in the adoption of massive cuts in social programs and lay-offs by the Canadian Minister of Finance in February.' See Michel Chossudovsky, 'The G7 Policy Agenda Creates Global Poverty,' Paper prepared for the People's Summit, 3.
6. *Communiqué from the People's Summit Conference on Human Security and Development for All: Building a Better World*, (Halifax, 1995).
7. Federal Finance Minister Paul Martin's economic policy paper *Agenda: Jobs and Growth*, released October 1994, quoted in the *Globe and Mail*, 18 Oct. 1994, A19.
8. As one participant stated: 'There are so many institutions that even nominally are supposed to be operated by government that are unresponsive to the electors' will. They are responsive either to the wills of the business council on national issues, or the Bank of Canada, or the bond market, or the currency exchange markets. And that's the fundamental problem.'
9. Claus Offe, 'The Separation of Form and Content in Liberal Democracy,' in John Keane, ed., *Contradictions of the Welfare State* (Cambridge, MA, 1984), 166.
10. *Communiqué* issued by the participants of the People's Summit workshop on 'Deficit Cutting: What Is the Agenda of the G-7?', Halifax, May 13, 1995. The communiqué continues: 'These policies, largely developed by investment interests and implemented through the influence of the International Monetary Fund and World Bank, include: cutbacks in social spending; deregulation; privatization; downsizing; devaluation of currency; high interest rates; reduced environmental protection standards; reduced labour standards.'
11. See Richard Falk, 'The Making of Global Citizenship,' in Bart van Steenbergen, ed., *The Condition of Citizenship* (London, 1994).
12. Falk, 'The Making of Global Citizenship,' 139.

13. David Held, 'Cosmopolitan Democracy and the Global Order: Reflections on the 200th Anniversary of Kant's "Perpetual Peace",' *Alternatives* 20/4 (Oct.–Dec. 1995), 415–29.

14. Claus Offe, 'Challenging the Boundaries of Institutional Politics: Social Movements Since the 1960s,' in Charles S. Mair, ed., *Changing the Boundaries of the Political: Essays on the Evolving Balance Between State and Society, Public and Private Life in Europe* (Cambridge, 1987), 63. See also Jürgen Habermas, *The Theory of Communicative Action, Volume Two: Lifeworld and System: A Critique of Functionalist Reason*, trans. Thomas McCarthy (Cambridge, 1987 [1981]), 391–6.

15. I am thinking of such recent actions as the occupation of the Canada Employment Centre on Gottingen Street in Halifax by community activists protesting its closure, the disruption of speeches by local members of parliament in New Brunswick by those protesting cut-backs in unemployment insurance, and the storming of the Ontario Provincial Parliament by student activists.

16. Statement of the People's Summit objectives, as written in the People's Summit publicity and registration pamphlet.

17. Maude Barlow, National Volunteer Chairperson of the Council of Canadians, spoke in Halifax as part of the People's Summit Marquee Series on June 11, 1995; Vandana Shiva, a physicist and philosopher of science, spoke as part of the same series on June 16.

18. Commenting on the need to go beyond political protest and articulate concrete alternatives, organizers offered statements such as the following: 'I think it will help us be taken seriously by some people, like people get tired of the protesters'; and 'anger has its role, but at the same time if we'd just done that it would backfire terribly. The public would just go:"what are your alternatives"?'

19. *Communiqué from the People's Summit*, 16 June 1995, item #3.

20. Letter from the Sierra Club of Canada to Prime Minister Jean Chrétien, 22 March 1995.

21. Trade Union Advisory Committee to the Organization for Economic Cooperation and Development, *Trade Union Statement to the OECD Ministerial Council and Halifax Summit* (May–June 1995), 4. This document was not prepared for the People's Summit, but was circulated at the People's Summit by the Canadian Labour Congress, a key participant in the event [emphasis added].

22. *Communiqué from the People's Summit*, 14 June 1995.

23. Zsuzsa Hegedus, 'Social Movements and Social Change in Self-Creative Society: New Civil Initiatives in the International Arena,' in Martin Albrow and Elizabeth King, eds., *Globalization, Knowledge, and Society* (London, 1990), 266, 277. See also Warren Magnusson, 'Decentring the State, or Looking for Politics,' in William K. Caroll, ed., *Organizing Dissent: Contemporary Social Movements in Theory and Practice* (Toronto, 1992).

24. *Communiqué from the People's Summit*, 14 June 1995.

25. Message to the Senate Committee on National Finance from members of the P-7, 13 June 1995.

26. Participants were nevertheless able to agree that 'social security reforms [should] not be imposed on peoples in the developed or developing countries. All constituencies...must join as equal partners with federal and provincial governments in debates about fiscal restraints, allocation of resources and social reform.' *Communiqué from the People's Summit*, 16 June 1995, item #5.

27. Letter from the Sierra Club of Canada to Prime Minister Jean Chrétien, 22 March 1995.

28. *Communiqué from the People's Summit*, 17 June 1995, paragraph #5.

29. Michel Chossudovsky, 'The G7 Policy Agenda Creates Global Poverty,' Paper prepared for the People's Summit, 5. Chossudovsky adds: 'It is worth recalling that a similar aura of complacency prevailed during the frenzy of late 1920s in the United States.'

30. Jean L. Cohen and Andrew Arato, *Civil Society and Political Theory* (Cambridge, MA, 1992), 548.

31. Craig Calhoun, 'Introduction: Habermas and the Public Sphere,' in Craig Calhoun, ed., *Habermas and the Public Sphere* (Cambridge, MA, 1992), 37.

32. Ron Eyerman and Andrew Jamison, *Social Movements: A Cognitive Approach* (University Park, PA, 1991), 4.

33. One organizer remarked: 'It is very hard to organize period, right now...because all groups are feeling, not lethargy, but downheartedness...with the economy...all we hear is cut, cut, cut, and...we're losing a lot of people.'

34. Warren Magnusson, 'Critical Social Movements: De-centring the State,' in Alain-G. Gagnon and James P. Bickerton, eds., *Canadian Politics: An Introduction to the Discipline* (Peterborough, ON, 1990), 527.

THE WELFARE STATE AS HISTORY

PAT ARMSTRONG

School of Canadian Studies
Carleton University

The term *welfare state* is meant to imply intervention carried out in the name of promoting general prosperity and providing personal protection or support. The private sector had not only failed to provide efficient and effective services, it had also created enormous hardship and fundamental unrest. The welfare state developed as a response to demonstrated needs and articulated demands, particularly from unions, from professional organizations, and from community groups but also from the business community. And it was about values as well as about practices. Especially in the period following the Second World War, government reports, academic research, and social commentaries emphasized the Canadian commitment to social responsibility and to sharing the risks of ill health, disability, poverty, age, and unemployment. These values were clearly evident in the introduction of federal programs and regulations designed to share risks and responsibilities among both people and provinces. Such programs simultaneously reflected and reinforced the notions of caring and sharing, in the process becoming central to our Canadian identity.

Because it reflected and reinforced power relations and ideological commitments, the welfare state has always been the subject of criticism and debate, never fulfilling the promise of equity for some and intervening far too much for others. There have always been opposing voices and variations among classes, races, cultural groups, regions, and sexes. But there was, for a while at least, a widespread consensus on collective responsibility and shared risk, as well as a recognition that many forces were beyond individual control and other forces needed to be kept in check through regulation.

Today, the critiques developed by those seeking equity are increasingly used by those seeking a new kind of state to argue that the ideas and programs of the welfare state are out of date, inefficient, and ineffective. The contention is both that the welfare state did not work to eliminate inequality and that the global economy gives us little choice but to compete through an unbridled market. There is emerging a new emphasis on individual rights and responsibilities. Social programs reflecting the old values are being downsized and transformed. A wide variety of programs, based on a range of criteria, are being collapsed and 'rationalized' into an integrated project that determines access on the basis of individually demonstrated need. Increasingly, social security and social services are being 'targeted' or privatized. Privatization in this sense refers not only to the transfer of responsibility from the public to the private sector, but also from the collectivity to the individual and from the state to the home. At the same time, regulations that protected individuals and equity-seeking groups are being eliminated.

This assault on the welfare state represents and structures new power relations and a new ideology. General prosperity is increasingly defined in terms of what encourages private investment, while the proper role for the state is defined as supporting this investment and assisting the deserving poor in extreme conditions.

It could be characterized as a move from caring and sharing to greedy and mean. However, this would not only fail to capture the complex, contradictory, and tension-filled value transformations that are underway in Canada today but also the contradictions that have always been present in the welfare state. While that state helped increase equality and encouraged collective responsibility, it also perpetuated many divisions and failed to resolve many conflicts, providing some of the conditions for the current backlash. These tensions have helped make it possible to attack the welfare state and the ideology on which it is based, but they have also made it necessary to frame the debate in terms of saving our most cherished social programs and ensuring, in the words of former Human Resource Minister Douglas Young, that we are 'getting every penny we can into the hands of the people we think should be receiving it.'[1] Conscious of how critical these programs are to Canadian identity and Canadian values, policymakers vociferously claim a commitment to ensuring equity and accessibility, while stressing the need to lower the deficit by reducing social spending. This seemingly contradictory purpose is to be achieved by shifting from access based on rights to programs targeted at those who are most deserving and most in need. In the process, the values embedded in the institutions are being profoundly altered. Yet the new developments are still often justified in terms of the old ones of collective responsibility and equity.

This paper explores these developments. It begins by examining the range of federal government programs, services, and regulations introduced in the postwar period and the rationale on which they were based. It then moves on to outline the kinds of changes that are underway. The purpose is to demonstrate that it is not only programs, services, and regulations that are being transformed but also our view of ourselves as Canadians.

COLLECTIVE RESPONSIBILITY AND SHARED RISK

In the 1943 *Report on Social Security for Canada*, Leonard Marsh made it clear that the social safety net was about 'the collective pooling of risks.' As he put it,

> In modern economic life there are certain hazards and contingencies, which have to be met, some of them completely unpredictable, some of them uncertain as to time but in other ways reasonably to be anticipated. They may be met in hit-or-miss fashion by individual families or they may never strike any individuals or families; but we know from experience that, collectively speaking, these problems or needs are always present at some place in the community or among the population.[2]

Marsh, and the rest of the generation that survived the Depression and fought a war, knew that everyone was at risk, even though not everyone would suffer. They also knew that very few had the kinds of incomes that could offer the financial protection necessary if ill health or unemployment hit. The market could not provide and individual effort was not enough. As Marsh explained, 'it is impossible to establish a wage that will allow every worker and his family to meet the heavy disabilities of serious illness, prolonged unemployment, accident and premature death. These are budget-shattering contingencies that strike most unevenly.'[3] Therefore, Marsh went on to argue, it is necessary to establish a social safety net that recognizes our shared vulnerability to forces beyond our individual control.

Marsh was certainly not alone in holding these values. The federal government's position was made clear at the 1945 Dominion–Provincial Conference: 'In familiar terms, our objectives are high and stable employment and income, and a greater sense of public responsibility for individual economic security and welfare. Realization of these objectives for all Canadians, as Canadians, is a cause in which we would hope for national enthusiasm and unity.'[4]

The objectives would be attained by federal programs to protect Canadians from 'large and uncertain individual risks, for such hazards, and disabilities as unemployment, sickness and old age.'[5] They would also be achieved through regulation of the market and intervention to support employment. As Armine Yalnizyan so eloquently puts it in 'Securing Society: Creating Canadian Social Policy,' the 'shiver of universal risk had swept over everyone, and people started demanding protections by pooling that risk across society.'[6]

With these kinds of values as a public guide, a variety of programs, services, and regulations were established or expanded in the years following the Second World War. Some were based on rights as citizens, some on rights as workers and some were specifically designed to support and protect the most vulnerable. Certainly the programs had flaws and many failed to fulfil the stated objectives. Some perpetuated inequality while others ignored such objectives entirely. Almost all were the result of struggle and compromise, conflict and debate. But all of the initiatives discussed here were based on the notion that Canadians had shared rights and shared responsibilities and that they deserved some protection from the excesses of the market.

CITIZENS' RIGHTS

The programs, services, and regulations that best exemplified this notion of shared responsibility and risk were those that applied either to all citizens or to all citizens who fell into particular demographic groups. These were ours by right of citizenship and required only a demonstration that we were Canadians who belonged to that group.

The most obvious of what we think of as a universal program is health care. Gallup polls in both 1944 and 1949 indicated that 80 percent of Canadians supported the notion of a federal National Health Plan.[7] A sickness survey demonstrated 'an inverse relationship between income and sickness and a direct relation between income and volume of care received.'[8] And research revealed significant variations in health care services from province to province. Clearly, there was inequality in access to care and Canadians shared the view that the collective risk should be recognized and dealt with by the government.

The federal programs designed to use federal financial resources to create a national health care system required that all necessary care be provided under uniform terms and conditions to all Canadian citizens. All citizens were eligible and means testing was unacceptable: 'Also eliminated were the commercial insurance concepts of deductibles, non-insurable conditions, limitations with respect to age, employment, or membership in groups, and experience rating—all the devices that protect insurance funds but frequently at the expense of individual hardship.'[9]

The national consensus on shared risk was translated into a universal program with eligibility based on health needs and publicly provided services rather than on individual economic resources or characteristics. The distribution of health care services among provinces and among individuals became more equal while the system ensured that no Canadian risked economic hardship or personal bankruptcy in order to receive care.[10] No means test was required. Health care also became much cheaper than it is in the individually based, private system in the United States.[11] Although inequalities in access to health care and to health remained, research demonstrated significant improvements in the care provided to the poorest groups.[12] Moreover, business got a cheaper and healthier work force, because the costs were shared and access increased. Not surprisingly, health care remains Canada's most popular social program, and its existence has helped reinforce the notion of Canada as a caring and sharing nation. Indeed, many Canadians see our health care system as what primarily distinguishes us from the United States.

Although we may seldom think of them in these terms, services such as parks, airports, and roads are also universally available to citizens without regard to ability to pay. Similarly, some cultural events and recreational services are open to the entire population. Regulations such as those requiring seat belts for riding in cars, safety inspection for trucks, for meat, and no smoking in airlines reflect our notion of shared responsibility. Other regulations, like those forbidding discrimination or pollution and protecting human rights, are also both universally applicable and reflective of the value placed on collective responsibility. Here, too, the programs were seldom completely successful in achieving their stated goals but they did indicate at least a willingness to recognize collective rights and responsibilities.

In addition to those services or regulations that apply to all citizens, there are ones that give collective rights to all those who fall into particular demographic groups. Old Age Security (OAS) is an obvious example. The evidence of widespread poverty among Canada's seniors clearly demonstrated that the elderly collectively shared risks that could not be attributed primarily to individual inadequacy, especially given compulsory retirement. Moreover, it was equally clear that the elderly have made important contributions to our society, contributions that should not be repaid by poverty in old age. The old age security, paid to every Canadian over a specific age who had lived in Canada for a specified period, was a recognition of both the shared risk and the shared responsibility.[13] As the National Council of Welfare put it, 'It was a universal program, free of stigma for recipients and subject only to minimal residence requirements. The administration of the program was a model of simplicity and low cost.'[14] Moreover, it unquestionably contributed to the decline in poverty rates among the elderly and especially among the female elderly.[15] Additional funds were made available under the needs-tested Guaranteed Income Supplement (GIS) and Spouses' Allowance. More expensive to administer than a universal plan, it still went to the majority of elderly. In 1972, nearly two-thirds of women over sixty-five and half the men qualified for the supplement.[16] Those in higher–income brackets were not excluded from supplemental, targeted programs, given that tax benefits such as deductions for investment in RRSPs helped them. Like other programs, these did not eliminate inequality or even poverty but they certainly reinforced the idea of collective rights and reduced the enormous gaps in income that had existed among the elderly.

Family Allowance was also a universal program paid to all mothers of children under a certain age. Although it was partly designed to put money in the hands of women who had become accustomed to having their own earnings during the war, it was also a clear expression of a collective responsibility for children.[17] The family allowance meant that motherhood brought rights as well as responsibilities. As was the case with old age security, the government offered supplements to this support based on means-tested need. It also offered some benefits to higher-income groups through tax deductions related to children.[18]

Like motherhood, postsecondary education too was defined as something that brought benefits for all Canadians and that therefore deserved support from all Canadians. Through a program similar to that developed for medicare, the federal government heavily subsidized postsecondary education across the country. The contribution was based on the assumption that the national government 'possesses a specially recognized jurisdiction over such matters as research and manpower training,'[19] that the costs of education restricted access[20] and that countries needed educated work forces. The assumptions were evident in the *Fifth Annual Review* of the Economic Council of Canada, published in 1968, which took as given 'the large economic, social and cultural values of education.'[21] The transfer of federal funds to the provinces contributed to the enormous expansion in colleges and universities across Canada, making them more accessible: 'Only 6 percent of the 18–24 age group participated in postsecondary education in 1951. By the early 1970s almost 20 percent of this age group were enabled to participate in one or another form of the postsecondary education process.'[22] Individual employers got an educated work force and individual students graduated, but the country as a whole also benefited. Students were charged user fees, but the overwhelming majority of costs were covered by the government for any student admitted to a postsecondary educational institution. In addition to paying for a significant part of operating costs in order to provide public education services, the federal government also offered needs-based support for living expenses through the Canada Student Loans Act. And governments introduced regulations that not only forbid institutions to restrict access for women, the disabled, aboriginals, and visible minorities, but that also required them to take positive steps to encourage participation from members of these groups. Funds were provided as well for independent research that helped expose unequal access and distribution, demonstrating the systemic discrimination. Inequalities were certainly not eliminated by these developments in education, and the victories did not come without struggle. But these provisions nonetheless were based on and perpetuated the idea that anyone in such groups had a right to protection and support.

The programs, regulations, and services provided to Canadians by right of citizenship simultaneously reflected and reinforced the notion of shared responsibility. Together they helped distinguish Canada from the United States in terms of both values and lifestyles and helped make Canada a more egalitarian society. So did the programs and regulations based on the rights of workers.

WORKERS' RIGHTS

In addition to the rights available on the basis of citizenship, the postwar period established rights based on employment. The Great Depression had clearly demonstrated that unemployment was not primarily the result of personal failure. The war effort had left Canadians convinced that they deserved better conditions of work. The combination of Keynesian economic theories, a fear of mass unemployment and protest in the aftermath of war, an emphasis on working together for a better life and collective action by unions and various popular organizations, led to a series of government actions designed to ensure workers' rights.

Perhaps the most obvious of these is Unemployment Insurance (UI). Bryce Mackasey, then Minister of Manpower and Immigration, made the purpose of the plan clear when, in 1970, he introduced revisions intended to expand the scheme to cover most workers, not only those employed in what had been thought of as precarious industries. It was designed to ensure that 'workers who became unemployed could claim benefits with dignity and self-respect, because they had contributed a substantial share to the unemployment insurance while working.'[23] Mackasey made it clear that 'everyone, to a greater extent than ever before, is vulnerable to a temporary disruption of earnings' and that we must rely 'upon the good will and responsibility of more fortunate, better-placed Canadians toward those who through lack of education and opportunity are in less secure occupations.'[24] Unemployment insurance, then, acknowledged both that all workers were at risk of becoming unemployed through no fault of their own and that the federal government had a responsibility to intervene to remove the fear of unemployment. It did so by pooling the costs and sharing the risks among both employers and employees. Workers had a right to income when their job disappeared. Not everyone benefited equally from the plan, and this was especially the case for women, but it did significantly improve the position of a working majority.

Like unemployment insurance, the Canada/Quebec Pension Plan requires contributions from employers and employees and covers most employees. It gave workers the right to retirement pensions and supplementary benefits, including 'surviving spouses pensions, disability pensions and supplementary benefits for orphans and children of the disabled contributor.'[25] And like UI, it was a response to the demonstrated need for income in old age. In *Better Pensions for Canadians*, the federal government claimed that their pension schemes were designed to provide Canadians with 'security, dignity, and fulfilment in retirement.'[26] The amount of pension given by right was based on a formula related to earnings and work history, not to need. While such formulas help perpetuate existing inequalities in pay, they do nevertheless support the notion that we need collective protection and that employers have responsibilities beyond the workplace.

In addition to the schemes that provided cash income to workers, the federal government introduced a series of regulations that also reflected the recognition that workers had certain rights that would not be protected by the market and that were beyond individual workers' control. Labour standards legislation was designed to ensure minimum conditions of work, just as minimum wage legislation was designed to ensure minimum levels of pay. Health and safety regulations were also introduced and enforced by government agencies. Such regulations not only provided some protection for individual workers; they also protected the employers' collective interests. Workers' rights to strike and to bargain collectively were recognized by legislation, and employers were required to bargain in good faith with workers. Similarly, the right to maternity leave was guaranteed to women, as were some other protections, such as pay equity, that recognized women's shared and particular needs as workers. A significant number of employees, such as female domestics, were excluded from this kind of legislation, but the need for some collective protection was recognized for the majority of employed.[27] And programs such as employment equity acknowledged the systemic nature of discrimination, even if they failed fundamentally to change the composition of the labour force.

Although workers' rights depended on being an employee or former employee, they also reflected and reinforced a notion of shared risk and responsibility. Payments under UI and the pension plan were not based primarily on how much workers contributed. They were based on the idea that everyone should contribute in order that those who needed assistance would get it by right. These plans and the regulations of work assumed that employers too had a responsibility to their employees, a responsibility that the market did not enforce.

INDIVIDUAL RIGHTS

In addition to the universal rights and workers' rights, there were programs, services, and regulations that were based on the assumption that Canada had the responsibility to ensure that no individual went without a minimal level of food, shelter, and clothing and that their other basic human rights were protected. For the most part, what we often call welfare programs are distributed on the basis of means or needs tests. As we have already seen, means-tested plans supplemented the universal pensions, family allowance, and postsecondary education support.

Most of the federal support for needs-tested programs, however, has been funded under the Canada Assistance Plan (CAP). This federal cost-sharing program covers social assistance payments and some services such as childcare and homecare. A major goal of the program was 'the prevention and removal of the causes of poverty and dependence on public assistance' and 'the provision of adequate assistance to persons in need.'[28] As is the case with medicare, the program requires that the provinces meet certain conditions in order to get funding. The conditions for funding under CAP 'ban residency requirements, require that assistance be paid to persons in need without any conditions attached (for example, workfare or liens), and mandate an appeals procedure.'[29] The federal government also establishes limits on earnings exemptions. Even though the program requires that assistance be determined on a case-by-case basis through a needs test, the federal guidelines reflect the assumption that those in need have a right to support from the collective funds, without punishment or loss of dignity.[30] Certainly the programs were not always administered in this fashion, but there was at least an official acknowledgment of rights to basic support.

The government intervened in other ways as well. For example, in response to both public pressure and established need, the federal government introduced legislation intended to limit abuse, rape, and harassment. It provided some funding for daycare centres and shelters. It changed immigration requirements to address concerns about racism and introduced a Charter of Rights and Freedoms.

In the quarter century following the Second World War, then, Canada developed a series of programs, services, and regulations that established rights based on a notion of collective responsibility. They grew out of demonstrated needs and of demands for change. They acknowledged that many Canadians faced risks over which they had little control and for which they could not individually provide. They placed limits on employers at the same time as they often supported their collective interests. None of the programs, services, and regulations were free of flaws. And all were limited in the extent to which they fulfilled their promise, especially in terms of what are often called the equity-seeking groups. But these developments did provide a variety of supports and a range of services to Canadians by right. Moreover, some of them at least served to encourage values based on sharing and caring for others, even if they were introduced after considerable resistance and were never fully accepted by some. And they not only reflected but also contributed to shifts in power relations, strengthening many individuals and communities. But by the 1970s, there were signs that opposition to these values, and to the welfare state, was growing. In the 1990s, there has been a consolidation of efforts to change both the programs and the values on which they are based.

PRIVATE RESPONSIBILITY AND INDIVIDUAL RISK

Long-time Tory Dalton Camp characterized the changes underway as an argument over 'affordable Canadians':

> Canada's social security system has long represented confirmation of a
> social contract between Canadians and their federal government. Most of
> the contract has been proposed, endorsed and enacted in my lifetime and
> it has created a society until now determined to meet its responsibilities to
> its children, the aged and those who are ill.
>
> I believe these measures have defined the country. And not only
> because of what they provided, but the kind of society that flourished as a
> result....But we have enjoyed an activist political agenda, a progressive
> political tradition, and a social culture of tolerance and compassion.[31]

Camp goes on to say that 'What Canada's critics seek is a new commercial contract to replace the social contract that has shaped us as a people.' But it is not only the critics outside Canada identified by Camp who are pushing us in this direction. The arguments within Canada for changing the social contract, however, have been framed as a way of reducing the debt while saving our social programs. In the name of necessary debt fighting, federal governments have been transforming Canada's social safety net along with the values of Canadians. As John Ralston Saul put it, 'Received wisdom blamed the growing deficit on spending and set about slashing programs.'[32] The approach, as Saul points out, is not based on evidence that either spending on social programs caused the debt or that slashing spending can solve the debt problem. Indeed, there is considerable evidence to the contrary.[33] Rather, he says, the attack has taken the form of a religious crusade and calls for a debate without the 'standard religious fear sermons about inflation and debt or the hysterical denunciation by columnists and lobby groups (often posing as think tanks) to which we have grown accustomed.'[34]

It is precisely because Canadians are committed to the values of the social contract that cut-backs have been justified as necessary in order to save them; that politicians have declared social programs a 'sacred trust' and vowed to defend them while practising 'social policy by stealth.'[35] Nowhere is this more evident than in the federal discussion paper on *Improving Social Security in Canada*. The paper begins with the following description of Canadian values:

> Canada's social security is the hallmark of our nation. Through it, we have defined ourselves as a country that aspires to give our children the best possible start in life, to enable all Canadians to meet their basic needs, and their families to live with dignity. It is a system dedicated to supporting the most vulnerable in our society, while creating opportunity for all Canadians to improve their lives. Social security embodies the values of justice, tolerance and compassion that mark our country.[36]

It is important to note that this description, while recognizing a collective responsibility, does not recognize a shared risk. Although there is talk of allowing all Canadians to meet their needs, the stress is on 'the most vulnerable' rather than on the 'public responsibility for individual economic security' which had been the concern of the Dominion–Provincial Conference. It speaks of compassion, rather than of rights or a 'pooling of risks.' Similarly, the 1996 federal budget speech sets out as its fifth principle (after deficit cutting, economic growth, frugality, shutting down some programs and focusing on others), a commitment to be 'fair and compassionate,' because 'It is the most vulnerable whose voices are often the least strong.'[37] These documents represent a significant shift away from the values embodied in the programs, services, and regulations that formed the basis of the Canadian social contract. This fundamental change is not only evident in the rhetoric; it is also evident in what has happened to the components of the welfare state described above.

*✴ this is not shared value.
This is rational choice Theory*

CITIZENS' RESPONSIBILITIES

The value transformation is particularly evident in the move away from the universal programs given to people as a matter of citizenship rights. Journalist Linda McQuaig has captured the essences of this value shift in the titles of her books. *The Wealthy Banker's Wife* refers to then Prime Minister Brian Mulroney's justification for abandoning the universal programs such as family allowance.[38] He asked: 'Are we making proper use of taxpayer's money by giving a bank president who makes five hundred thousand to six hundred thousand dollars a year a baby bonus?'[39] The abandonment of universal rights in the case of family allowance was based on the idea that, in debt-ridden times, money should not go to the un-needy rich but rather should be targeted at the deserving poor. Combining both the notion of a debt crisis and a social contract, the family allowance was discarded in favour of a means-tested program. Not incidently, this strategy did little to re-distribute income to the poorest children but did have an impact on our ways of seeing social security.[40] No mention was made of additional taxes for the wealthy banker and his wife as a way of pooling the risks and solving the debt crisis, however.

In her book *Shooting the Hippo*, McQuaig describes how the argument has now been taken a step further.[41] Here the reference is to the killing of a baby hippo because there are no more resources to provide for its needs. According to the new values, we not only have to abandon universality in favour of selectivity based on need but also sacrifice some programs altogether and make others more efficient by either privatizing them, applying private sector techniques to their delivery, or charging user fees. This move away from universality has profound implications for our shared values. As the Ecumenical Coalition for Economic Justice makes clear: 'While universality reinforces social solidarity, selectivity undermines majority public support for a program. It becomes difficult to maintain political will among the majority of the population for programs that benefit a small sector of society.'[42] Erosion in other areas is already well underway and the ideological stage has been set for further cut-backs.

While *Improving Social Security in Canada* avoided a discussion of Canada's very popular universal pension and health care schemes, this does not mean that these programs have been excluded from the ideological shift. Indeed, reforms are well underway in these areas and government documents, supported by think tank reports, have become increasingly hysterical in claiming that spending here is out of control and threatens all our futures. The government does not yet seem prepared to go as far as the wealthy banker who

+ 72% relation to what/when?

has recently called for a 'massive decentralization and further dismantling of Canada's welfare and health-care systems,' but the erosion is clearly evident in a number of areas.[43]

In the case of health care, the federal government has for a number of years been slowly reducing the cash transfer to the provinces and with it the opportunity to use its spending power to enforce national standards of access. When the federal government made the cash transfers conditional on meeting the five principles of health care, they were ensuring a universally accessible publicly controlled program based on uniform standards and conditions. Without this cash transfer, the federal government has few means of enforcing these standards, as is already evident in the emergence of for-profit eye clinics in Alberta. Moreover, it seems to be the case that the principles will now be enforced only through cabinet review, making the process of enforcement inaccessible to Canadians. With evaluation hidden away, the opportunity to reinforce values related to shared responsibilities is reduced.

In addition, the reduction in cash transfers and the massive cuts euphemistically called the new Health and Social Transfer have led to cut-backs in provincial health care provision. This in turn has contributed to a privatization of services. In fact, the proportion of health care spending paid for by all governments has been steadily declining in recent years. In 1993, only 72 percent of total health care spending in Canada was accounted for by government expenditures.[44] This privatization took a number of forms. More services, such as rehabilitation, were provided on a for-profit basis. More care was transferred to institutions such as homes for the aged where user fees are permitted. More services and drugs were delisted and thus became available only to those who could pay. And more of the caring work was transferred to the private home where much of it was done without pay by female relatives.[45] This privatization means that access is increasingly dependent on ability to pay rather than on rights. Indeed, those who are in need of care are increasingly called consumers in the government literature. And when those who can pay face deteriorating services in the public system, they demand access to privately provided ones.

Meanwhile, cut-backs continue and there is every indication that the federal government intends to further transform the values on which health care is based. Prime Minister Chrétien has claimed that our spending is out of line with other countries and that health care was never meant to cover anything but major surgery.[46] Both assumptions can be challenged but the point is that the ground is being prepared for a major value shift in terms of the right to care and an increasing actual shift to the private sector.

Both the value shift and the pressure on values is evident in a poll conducted by Environics Research Group and published by the *Toronto Star*. It maintains that, while nearly a third of Canadians polled thought the promotion of economic growth was the number one government priority, only 17 percent felt that maintaining social and health programs should be the number one priority of the government.[47] The poll pressures people to choose one priority, suggesting with the questions that these are mutually exclusive alternatives and suggesting with the publication of the answers that Canadians do not strongly support social programs. Moreover, the poll lumps together all social programs, including health, thus eliminating the possibility that people strongly support public health care. Yet another poll conducted during the same period reported that 81 percent of Canadians outside Quebec support health care run by governments and this was the case for more than three-quarters of the entire population.[48] This poll received less attention in the media. The combining of all social programs in the more publicized study camouflages the wide support for public health at the same time as it helps undermine that support.

In the case of pensions, the federal government tried once to attack the pension plan directly and faced strong opposition. Instead, it introduced the claw-back scheme to take benefits back from seniors whose income was above a fixed limit and has slowly eroded the value of the pensions that remain through de-indexation.[49] The government now claims that the pension plan cannot stand the pressure of an aging population, even though, as Monica Townson points out, it has long been known that the population was aging and the government had plenty of time to build this into the program.[50] Indeed, it still has time.[51] But the 1996 budget announced a new Seniors' Benefit that 'will make the system more affordable and sustainable' because it 'will target help to those who need it most.'[52] With justifications reminiscent of both the wealthy banker's wife and shooting the hippo, OAS and GIS pensions will be combined and paid on the basis of demonstrated family need, not on the basis of right. Recognizing the value attached to these plans and fearing strong opposition, the government has promised that 'pensions for everyone 60 and over will be protected.' The real story comes, though, in the line that says the 'Seniors Benefit will provide adequate time to prepare.'[53] In this phrase is hidden the privatization and individualization of pensions; the shift from collective provision that recognized 'seniors had made a contribution to society and that society as a whole would acknowledge that by paying them benefits in their older years.'[54] It will be each person for themselves in old age, unless they are defined as vulnerable people requiring compassion.

Improving Social Security for Canada did address the question of education. And here the combination of espousing old notions related to universally accessible services while fundamentally challenging the values on which they are based is particularly evident. The report acknowledges that 'it is true that replacing federal cash transfers would put upward pressure on tuition fees.' However, it goes on to say that 'This may be a necessary price to pay to put in place a permanent system for ensuring accessibility to postsecondary education.' The shift to both the private sector and to individual responsibility is clearly evident in the solutions offered.

> Federal funds would be used to lever private money which would sustain and expand access to higher learning. The new forms of assistance to individual learners would be used both by young people going to college or university; and by mid-career boot-strappers keen to upgrade their skills. This approach would also reinforce the idea of encouraging mutual responsibility among Canadians for managing a greater share of their own social security.[55]

There is no explanation or evidence provided for how private money will expand and sustain access, even though the reliance on private money could mean that only money talks. Meanwhile, the promotion of income contingent repayment loans makes it clear that individuals rather than services will be targeted for support that must be repaid directly in financial terms, not indirectly through other contributions to Canadian society. This is stated even more explicitly in *A New Framework for Economic Policy*. According to this government document, 'while society gains collectively from the skills of its citizens, the greatest beneficiaries of investment in human capital are individuals themselves, in terms of both a lifetime financial return and potential for human development.'[56] According to this perspective, individuals rather than the society in general must take the responsibility for education, given that individuals are defined as the major beneficiaries. This contrasts sharply with the notion that the country gains socially, economically, and culturally from investment in higher education. The 1996 budget offers only income tax deductions for individuals as a means of compensating for the reduction in collective support for education.

Universal rights of citizens are also being undermined in other areas through fees and deregulation. There is increasing talk of building roads and airports with private resources and introducing tolls or special fees. Here, too, the debt is used as the explanation and the justification is better access. Fees for parks are being raised on the grounds that users should pay and regulations on the environment are being loosened in the name of promoting the shared economy. Cut-backs in regional offices enforcing human rights legislation leave citizens with less protection, and the money for the support of public cultural events has been severely reduced or eliminated. Access to such services is increasingly dependent on money rather than on citizenship and choices are increasingly based on ownership rather than citizenship. In the process, what it means to be Canadian is being fundamentally altered.

Universal programs gave everyone a stake and shared the risk. They promoted a notion of collective citizenship and of Canadian distinctiveness at the same time as they reflected this notion. The dismantling of universal programs places both the risk and blame on the individual and transforms universal programs claimed by right and with dignity into privileges granted on the basis of 'compassion' and needs tests. We are to become responsible for ourselves, not for each other. More and more universal rights have become programs targeted to those defined as deserving poor, and fewer citizens are defined as deserving. Universal rights are increasingly becoming welfare claims and in the process the very meaning of Canadian citizenship is being redefined.

WORKERS' RESPONSIBILITIES

It is not only citizenship rights that are disappearing but also those of workers. The restructuring and downsizing in the economy is making employment more precarious and more risky.[57] At the same time, the federal government is contributing to that risk by significantly altering or eliminating workers' rights and by challenging the values on which they were based.

While work is becoming more precarious, so is the insurance scheme that was designed to protect workers from the fear of unemployment. The federal government's Advisory Group on Working Time and the Distribution of Work made it clear that the 'configuration of working hours and the availability of work in general is largely determined by employers and their assessment of the demand for their products or services.'[58] In other words, the risk of unemployment is not mainly in the hands of the worker. Yet, in spite of the recognition that unemployment is not primarily the fault of individuals, governments have been increasingly reducing the right to unemployment insurance and shifting the burden to individuals, maintaining that the old scheme was, like the welfare state as a whole, designed for another time and is out of step with the times.

A New Framework for Economic Policy claims that UI was 'originally intended to cushion the income loss for short jobless spells and thus give people reasonable time for search for a new job that would be a good fit.'[59] This claim is made in spite of the fact that, according to Mackenzie King, unemployment insurance was intended to 'prevent much of the...industrial dislocation which might otherwise be the aftermath of war.'[60] The framework document goes on to say that because unemployment is now the product of restructuring and creates long-term unemployment, UI must be transformed. But it also says that the program must be transformed because the rules have 'encouraged chronic, repeat use,' mainly by those unemployed for short terms.[61] The solution, according to the report, is to remove the incentives that lead to chronic, repeat use by individuals and business.[62] Similarly, *Improving Social Security for Canada* recommends that UI support be 'conditional on their willingness to participate in programs that make them more employable,' suggesting that unemployment is the fault of the individual's failure to develop their skills.[63] This report also supports an income test that would virtually eliminate any notion of rights based on contributions through work.[64] Not all of this was translated into the new 'employment insurance' scheme but the 'massive changes mean people will have to work longer to qualify for smaller benefits and they will get them over a shorter period.'[65] Repeat users will get progressively smaller benefits over time. Earlier changes in the 1990s had already reduced the proportion of unemployed collecting insurance from 'almost 90 percent to less than 50 percent' and now even fewer will qualify.[66]

So, in spite of the recognition that unemployment is structural, indeed because it is structural, more of the responsibility has been shifted to the individual and rights have become even more circumscribed. Again, the effect is to reduce collective responsibility for unemployment and to make UI payments more contingent, based on need rather than on rights. And, in spite of the budget commitment to fairness, those in regions with high seasonal unemployment and the mainly women who work part-time will be particularly hard hit while being blamed for their own unemployment.

Employment-related pensions, like the universal scheme, are also under threat. While there are not yet specific recommendations, the 1996 budget says changes are required and there has been considerable talk about employer taxes such as pensions discouraging employment. Moreover, there is no indication that provisions will be made for the increasing numbers of people with nonstandard employment who are not eligible for employment-related pension schemes or unemployment insurance. Women, the disabled, immigrants, visible minorities, and aboriginal people are more likely than white men to have such employment. With fewer people eligible for pensions, there is less sharing of risk and less sharing of responsibility. There are also fewer people with a stake in the plan.

At the same time, regulations protecting workers' rights are being undermined. Many of the labour standard regulations do not apply to the increasing number of people with precarious employment and the same is true of such rights as maternity leave. Other measures designed to recognize the need for special protections, such as pay equity legislation, are also under attack. The government has appealed an order to the Human Rights Tribunal to make pay equity adjustments, on the grounds that such adjustments would discriminate against men. Perhaps this is what is meant by the concern for fairness. Minimum wages have not kept up with prices. And there is an increasing polarization of work hours, with some people employed for very short workweeks while others work very long workweeks. Although they recognized this problem, the Advisory Group on Working Time and the Distribution of Work recommended only voluntary strategies to address the problem.[67] The number of people employed to ensure the enforcement of health and safety standards has not kept up with need and there are increasing attacks on benefits assigned under Worker's Compensation, another support workers' claimed by right. Meanwhile, workers' right to bargain collectively and in good faith has been eroded by government wage freezes. The International Labour Organization has ruled that this government action 'in no sense corresponds to the fair and reasonable compromise required' in collective bargaining.[68] But no action has been taken by the government to restore these rights.

A New Framework for Economic Policy makes it clear that there is to be less collective, national provision and less sharing of risks among workers. More will be done by the provinces, the individual, and the private sector: 'All other government activities are being assessed to determine if they still serve a public interest and, if so, if there continues to be a necessary and appropriate role for the federal government. If not, the activities must be devolved to the provinces or transferred, all or in part, to the private/voluntary sector.'[69]

The shift in ideas is obvious, as is the 'commercialization' that accompanied and promoted it. Private provision and interest are the new norms.

INDIVIDUAL RISK

Although the entire report is supposed to be about social security, it is in a chapter titled 'Security: Building Opportunity for People in Need' that *Improving Social Security in Canada* discusses those programs aimed at individual support. All of the hard-won rights designed to recognize shared risk, collective responsibility, and rights are collapsed into a chapter that is focused on the few in need. 'Social security is society's commitment to take care of its most vulnerable citizens' sums up the new approach to all collective provision.[70] And vulnerability is to be more and more narrowly defined.

The transfers under the Canada Assistance Plan have been significantly reduced and, as is the case with health care, there is no guarantee that national conditions will be maintained. The 1996 budget only promises to oppose the residency requirement for social assistance recipients and remains silent on workfare.[71] This process opens the way for workfare programs that require people to take any job at any price and leaves few rights for those who are defined as employable. The shift is to be toward 'better-targeted programs' and the idea of a guaranteed annual income that was supported by many of those who appeared before the Human Resources Committee reviewing social security is rejected as unaffordable in these times.[72]

*ceud is not 'cautious' a market metaphor?!

CONCLUSION

There can be no question that there is room for reform of the Canadian welfare state. Many initiatives have been poorly conceived, inappropriately introduced, or meanly administered. Some have failed in their purpose or had effects opposite to those promised while others need considerable expansion. Some do not serve the current population or address the current economic conditions. Some have perpetuated inequality and inhibited prosperity. But the issue here is not whether or not there should be reform or whether we should be nostalgic about a past that was problematic at best. Rather, the issue is the ideas on which the reform is based and the role the welfare state plays in creating or perpetuating values at the heart of being Canadian.

In the name of efficiency, effectiveness, and ending the debt, the variety of programs and regulations that reflected notions of shared risks, shared rights, and shared responsibility are being transformed or eliminated. The welfare state is under attack for being out of step with the times or as having failed to create equality. But the reform is reducing both the variety and the access, collapsing all programs on the basis of a single notion that restricts support to the few who can demonstrate they are truly in need and access to those with money. Increasingly, the values, and the language, are those of a commercial rather than of a social contract. Patients become customers and parents become stakeholders. And everybody but the corporations and those running the bond markets are defined as interest groups that do not represent the new Canada. Education and health are evaluated in value-added terms, and productivity rather than people is the focus of concern.

The justification for reforms in recent government documents begins with a recognition of 'those public endeavours—including health care, education, cultural development and assistance for the needy, among others—that have made Canada one of the world's most civil societies.'[73] Such justifications clearly acknowledge the values on which Canada is based and their relationship to social programs. But the next step in current reform is to maintain both that Canada can no longer afford such programs and that the programs can only be saved through transformation, privatization, and targeting. Indeed, it is suggested that the new versions will be more flexible, democratic, and closer to home, even though fewer people will have access and access will increasingly depend on financial resources or compassion. Of course, both processes serve to alter fundamentally the programs and services along with the ideas on which they are based.

The only line is the bottom line. Alternative ways of fighting the debt have become unthinkable and the idea that we have overspent on the luxury of shared rights and responsibilities has become part of our common sense. More and more Canadians, especially women, visible minorities, the disabled, immigrants, and aboriginal people are targeted as abusers rather than as people at particular risk who have a right to support or protection. The welfare state becomes history. In the words of the 1996 budget, 'The full response lies in recognizing where we are in the evolution of the country, in the evolution of the world beyond our borders. It is time to turn the page.'[74] What it means to be Canadian is being redefined and, increasingly, the only debt we worry about leaving our children is a financial one.

NOTES

This is a revised version of a paper initially presented to the International Council of Canadian Studies conference, 'Languages, Cultures and Values in Canada at the Dawn of the 21st Century,' Ottawa, June, 1995.

1. Quoted in Margaret Philip, 'Ottawa Insists on National Social Standards,' *Globe and Mail*, 8 Feb. 1996, A7.
2. Leonard Marsh, *Report on Social Security for Canada 1943* (Toronto, 1975), 9–10.
3. Marsh, *Report on Social Security*, 10.
4. Quoted in Malcolm Taylor, *Health Insurance and Canadian Public Policy* (Montreal, 1987), 50.
5. Ibid.
6. Armine Yalnizyan, 'Securing Society: Creating Canadian Social Policy,' in Armine Yalnizyan, T. Ran Ide, and Arthur J.Cordell, eds., *Shifting Time* (Toronto, 1994), 31.
7. David Naylor, *Private Practice, Public Payment* (Montreal, 1986), 158.
8. Taylor, *Health Insurance*, 176–7.
9. Taylor, *Health Insurance*, 328.
10. Philip E. Enterline, Vera Salter, Alison D. McDonald, and J. Corbett McDonald, 'The Distribution of Medical Services Before and After "Free" Medical Care: The Quebec Experience,' *New England Journal of Medicine* 289 (1973), 1174–8.
11. This is the case whatever measures are used. Just about the same proportion of government spending goes to health care in both the United States and Canada, but the United States covers only the military, the very old, and the very young, while we cover everyone. *OECD Health Systems Facts and Figures, 1960–1991*, Vol. 1 (Paris, OECD, 1993), table 7.1.5.
12. See B. Singh Bolaria and Rosemary Bolaria, eds., *Racial Minorities Medicine and Health* (Halifax, 1994).
13. Kevin Collins, *Women and Pensions* (Ottawa, 1978) and Louise Delude, *Women and Aging* (Ottawa, 1978).
14. National Council of Welfare, *Pension Reform* (Ottawa, 1990), 16.
15. National Council of Welfare, *Poverty Profiles, 1993* (Ottawa, 1995), 10.
16. Collins, *Women and Pensions*, 102.
17. Canada, Advisory Committee on Reconstruction, *Post-War Problems of Women, Final Report of the Subcommittee* (Ottawa, 1944).
18. The Ecumenical Coalition for Economic Justice, *Reweaving Canada's Social Programs* (Toronto, 1993), 24–7.
19. R. Taylor Cole, 'The Universities and Governments under Canadian Federalism,' *The Journal of Politics* 34/2 (May 1972), 527.
20. Marion R. Porter, John Porter, and Bernard Blishen, *Does Money Matter?* (Toronto, 1973).
21. Economic Council of Canada, *Fifth Annual Review, The Challenge of Growth and Change* (Ottawa, 1968), 59.
22. Wilfred Martin and Allan Macdonnell, *Canadian Education*, 2nd ed. (Scarborough, ON, 1982), 23.
23. See Pat Armstrong, 'UIC: Reform or Revolution?' *Perception* 3/4 (March/April 1980), 31–3.
24. See Armstrong, 'UIC,' 32.
25. Collins, *Women and Pensions*, 112.
26. See Michael MacLean and Eric Shragge, 'Groping for Pension Reform,' *Perception* 6/5 (Summer 1983), 26.
27. See Patricia Daenzer, *Regulating Class Privilege: Immigrant Servants in Canada 1940s–1990s* (Toronto, 1993).
28. Ontario, Social Assistance Review Committee, *Transitions* (Toronto, 1988), 9.
29. Ontario, Social Assistance Review Committee, *Transitions*, 498.
30. Ontario, Social Assistance Review Committee, *Transitions*, 495.
31. Dalton Camp, 'Canada's Social Critics Want to Drop Social Contract for a Commercial One,' *Toronto Star*, 1 Feb. 1995, A19.

32. John Ralston Saul, 'McQuaig Throws Doubt on Economic Policies,' *Globe and Mail*, 22 April 1995, C25.
33. Hideo Mimoto and Philip Cross, *The Canadian Economic Observer* (June 1991).
34. Saul, 'McQuaig Throws Doubt on Economic Policies,' C25.
35. Gratton Gray, 'Social Policy by Stealth,' *Policy Options* (March 1990), 17–29.
36. Human Resources Development Canada, *Agenda: Jobs and Growth—Improving Social Security in Canada* (Ottawa, 1994), 7.
37. Paul Martin, Minister of Finance, *Budget Speech* (Ottawa, 1996), 7.
38. Linda McQuaig, *The Wealthy Banker's Wife* (Toronto, 1993).
39. Quoted in Ecumenical Council for Economic Justice, *Reweaving Canada's Social Programs*, 11.
40. Francis Woolley, Judith Marshall, and Arnt Vermaeten, 'Ending Universality: The Case of Child Benefits,' in Meg Luxton, ed., *Gerstein Family Research* (Toronto, forthcoming).
41. Linda McQuaig, *Shooting the Hippo* (Toronto, 1995).
42. Ecumenical Council for Economic Justice, *Reweaving Canada's Social Programs*, 13.
43. Canadian Centre for Policy Alternatives, *CCPA Monitor* 2/2 (June 1995), 11.
44. Health Canada, *National Health Expenditures in Canada, 1975–1993* (Ottawa, 1994), 3.
45. Pat Armstrong, 'Closer to Home: More Work For Women' in Pat Armstrong et al., *Take Care: Warning Signals for Canadian Health Systems* (Toronto, 1994).
46. *Toronto Star*, 'Devote Less of Economy to Medicare, PM Urges,' 6 March 1995, A3.
47. William Walker, 'Deficit Still Big Concern Survey Finds' *Toronto Star*, 20 April 1995, A15.
48. Vector Opinion, Results, 10–29 March 1995, field work.
49. National Council of Welfare, *Pension Reform* (Ottawa, 1990).
50. Monica Townson, *Our Aging Society: Preserving Retirement Incomes into the 21st Century* (Ottawa, 1996).
51. See Townson, *Our Aging Society*.
52. Department of Finance, 'The Seniors' Benefit: Securing the Future' (Ottawa pamphlet, unpaginated).
53. Ibid.
54. Townson, *Our Aging Society*, 3.
55. Human Resources Development Canada, *Agenda: Jobs and Growth—Improving Social Security*, 63.
56. Human Resources Development Canada, *Agenda: Jobs and Growth—A New Framework for Economic Policy* (Ottawa, 1994), 41.
57. See Advisory Group on Working Time and the Distribution of Work, *Working Time and the Distribution of Work* (Ottawa, 1994).
58. Advisory Group on Working Time and the Distribution of Work, *Working Time*, 24.
59. Human Resources Development Canada, *Agenda: Jobs and Growth—A New Framework*, 51.
60. See Armstrong, 'UIC.'
61. Human Resources Development Canada, *Agenda: Jobs and Growth—A New Framework*, 52.
62. ibid., 53.
63. Human Resources Development Canada, *Agenda: Jobs and Growth—Improving Social Security*, 44.
64. ibid., 46–7.
65. Susan Bourette, Greg Keenan, and Casey Mahood, 'UI Overhall Meets With Mixed Reviews,' *Globe and Mail*, 2 Dec. 1995, B1.
66. Nancy Riche, 'In Defence of Unemployment Insurance,' *Globe and Mail*, 18 Dec. 1995, A13.
67. Advisory Group on Working Time and the Distribution of Work, *Working Time*, 25.
68. In Leo Panitch and Donald Swartz, 'What Happened to Freedom of Association?' *Globe and Mail*, 7 April 1995, A19.
69. Human Resources Development Canada, *Agenda: Jobs and Growth—A New Framework*, 57.
70. Human Resources Development Canada, *Agenda: Jobs and Growth—Improving Social Security*, 69.
71. Martin, *Budget Speech*, 11.
72. ibid., 75.
73. Human Resources Development Canada, *Agenda: Jobs and Growth—A New Framework*, v.
74. Martin, *Budget Speech*, 25.

THE 'CRISIS IN THE WELFARE STATE' AND DEMOCRACY

A Discourse Analysis of ACOA

GUY CHIASSON

Department of Political Science
University of Ottawa

The main discourse at the present time on the welfare state is one that emphasizes its crisis. The crisis comes from an incapacity to continue to be the leading mode of social regulation in Western societies. Such incapacity is seen by that discourse as being caused by economic imperatives. As Pierre Rosanvallon points out, the leading explanation of the crisis is one that argues that the slowing down of economic growth does not enable Western states to keep on facing the rising social expectations of their populations. In other words, the state's action and evolution are determined by the economic imperatives.[1]

The economic necessity argument is, however, quite puzzling and it surely doesn't yield a consensus on its validity. One can ask why should economic logic automatically prevail over the entire society? It seems important to have a closer look at that economic necessity argument in order to show that it is not as compelling as it asserts. We will show that the economic necessity argument is very much linked to a moral position and social choices. By promoting economics to the rank of necessity, the usual position on the crisis of the welfare state blurs and confuses the issues by excluding itself from the level of political debates. This paper will try to clarify the discourse on the welfare state by showing how it is grounded in politics.

Tracing the main discourse on the crisis in the welfare state as political (in the sense of implying a political and ethical debate) permits us to raise the question of democracy. The importance of democracy for understanding public discourse is asserted by Ian Robinson, among others. For him, democracy should be seen as a form that should have precedence in the making of public policy. The importance of democracy is justified by the fact that it is 'an inherent political good.' On the other hand, economic growth and market logic don't have that inherent character. Their value only stems from their capacity to promote human well-being.[2] What we can retain from Robinson's work is the notion that thinking about democracy is not irrelevant to the study of public policy. In fact, considering the importance of democracy as a central element of politics, it becomes important to understand what conception of democracy is promoted by the public discourses. In other words, it is important to establish a framework that will permit us to understand welfare state politics from the point of view of its contribution to a particular understanding of democracy.

This framework will be applied to one particular case of public policy. That case is the discourse of the Atlantic Canada Opportunities Agency (ACOA). ACOA is a regional development agency created by the federal government in 1987. Regional development is a very interesting case for the study of the discourse behind state intervention. It is not usually seen as part of welfare state politics. In fact, when we think of the welfare state we think of the more clearly social areas of intervention such as health care and education. Regional development remains very relevant to welfare state politics in the sense that it is at the crossroads of economic and social policy. It therefore asks, in a very acute way, the question of the relation between the social and the economic. It is that same question that is asked by the privatization movement in the more social areas of policy.

We can clearly see that a new way of looking at the relation between economic and social considerations has been a driving force in the evolution of regional policy in Canada since the 1980s. Many authors have identified two phases in such a policy.[3] The first phase, which extends from the mid 1950s to the end of the 1970s, comprises a relatively social approach. The initiatives in that phase were seen as part of a wider regional approach that includes social transfer payments.[4] The efforts in regional development were seen as going hand in hand with social redistribution. There was a sort of commitment from the federal government to the idea that intervention could bring social and economic equality across the regions. As Donald Savoie puts it: 'The mid- and late- 1960s saw strong but uneven growth in the national economy and, relatively speaking, a burgeoning federal treasury. The government moved toward explicit redistributive priorities, as seen in the Canada Pension Plan, the Medical Care Act (medicare) and programs for economic development, some of which I have just described. Keynesian thinking in Ottawa was clearly dominant, and so was its notion of balance in the national economy.'[5]

The second phase of regional development is driven by a conception that is less concerned about the social dimension of the regional problem. It adopts a more clearly economic approach where the private sector is the motor to development in slow-growth regions. The responsibilities of the federal government in these regions is economic development in a more narrowly defined way.

By seeing economic logic as separated from social considerations, the new discourse on regional development presents market logic as a compelling necessity that has to be the priority over other considerations. The separation from the social, presents economic logic as a self-sustaining logic that is not dependent on social (and ethical) logic (and then becomes what we called economic necessity). In other words, the separation of the economic from the social sets the stage for economic necessity as a guiding principle of public policy. The shift to a second phase of regional development then becomes a good example of the changing discourse in and on the welfare state. Therefore, when studying ACOA's discourse as a main proponent of that second phase, one can get some important indications leading to a better understanding of the mutations in welfare state discourse. More particularly, we will be examining ACOA's discourse through an analysis of its public documents that were published between 1987 and 1995.

Our analysis will have two sections. The first section will examine how ACOA legitimizes its approach to regional development.[6] Although at first glance the agency appears to find its only legitimacy in economic necessity, our argument will be that the legitimacy is actually to be found in a particular conception of citizenship, the liberal conception. In other words, the reason given by ACOA for passing to a more economically defined regional development occludes the fact that the new approach is grounded in a particular moral outlook.

In the second section, our attention will be focused on the consequences of that economic necessity argument on democracy. Even though ACOA's documents never mention democracy, it can still be argued that by denying the links of its conception to a particular moral outlook, ACOA's discourse does not allow the issues to be debated in the public sphere. We propose to explore this tendency through an examination of how the government agency defines the needs of the population it serves. These two sections will prepare the ground for the conclusion where we hope to affirm the relevance of democracy as a perspective for evaluating the changes happening in the welfare state.

THE ATLANTIC CANADA OPPORTUNITIES AGENCY

ACOA has two major programs, the Action program (by which ACOA directly promotes the creation of small business in Atlantic Canada) and the

Co-operation program (focusing on the facilitation and signing of federal provincial accords in economic development). These two programs are where the majority (85 percent) of ACOA's yearly budget of about $371 million is spent. ACOA also has another important mandate, which is to defend the interests of the Atlantic provinces inside the federal government. In other words, it is supposed to get involved with the different concerned ministries in order to develop favourable and co-ordinated policies for the Atlantic. That last function is obviously the responsibility of the Ottawa office whereas the Action and Co-operation programs are mostly under the national office (in Moncton) and the regional ones (in Fredericton, Halifax, Charlottetown, and St. John's).

The documents analysed are a sample of the public literature published by ACOA. They include not only literature published directly by the agency but also a certain number of evaluations commissioned by ACOA.

THE ECONOMIC NECESSITY ARGUMENT AND CITIZENSHIP

This first section will examine more closely the central argument used by ACOA to legitimize its action in order to see what importance it gives to the idea of economic necessity. We do this as part of an effort to deconstruct that argument in order to show how it neglects to point out its moral roots.

ACOA's CENTRAL ARGUMENT

ACOA's public literature seems to be guided by one central argument that is present more or less explicitly in all of the texts. At the least, we can say that key parts of that central argument are present in all of these texts. We will examine this argument from two different but very interrelated perspectives, the first being the identification of the problem, the second being the solution identified.

The Problem

According to ACOA, the globalized economy and its pressures mean that state intervention in general and intervention in regional development has to change.[7] Government cannot keep on managing regional development as it did in the past, that is, by interfering with market forces in order to favour the regional slow-growth economies. That Keynesian type of economic appreciation led to many forms of economic approaches (growth pole, industrial subsidization, and market stimulation, etc.), but it is not an option any more (considering these approaches have failed in the past and probably considering the globalization of the economy).[8] Contrary to the assumption of previous experience, government should not try to go against the grain of the market forces when they undertake regional development. In other words, governments should not try to implement measures like industrial expansion and social transfer payments that could slow down the structural adjustments of the region.[9] They should rather try to promote the comparative advantage of the regional economy within the logic of the market. The role of government is to help regional economies to adjust to structural necessities and therefore become more competitive by the use of their own forces.[10]

That competitivity argument is central to the interpretation put forward by ACOA. For instance, in one key document of seventy-eight pages the words *competitivity* and *competition* were used twenty-eight times.[11] The frequent use of these terms shows that competitivity is an important concern for ACOA. Looking at the number of occasions in which the word *competitivity* is used, two interpretations are possible: Is competitivity being considered as desirable in itself or rather as something implicitly linked to the conditions imposed by the global economy? In either case, economic necessity is the determining factor that should guide ACOA's actions.

The Solution: Building Entrepreneurship

ACOA's insistence on competitivity inevitably leads it to see the solution to the regional problem as being one that is in accordance with the imperatives of competition. That solution is what we could call the building of entrepreneurship.[12] If in the past the strategy for regional development has very often centred on industrial expansion supplemented by federal social transfer payments, the latest vision has set aside that path in order to favour the creation of small-scale business emanating from the Atlantic provinces.[13] The term *building entrepreneurship* is used in the sense that the role of regional development is to make easier the creation and the stability of small business. ACOA's role is not only to help finance some projects that refer to creating and expanding businesses but also to put in place (directly through the Action program and with the participation of the provinces in the Co-operation program) other conditions favourable to a business climate.

Basically, these are elements that are meant to help the most promising businesses in their adaptation to structural adjustments.[14] The major elements that will help the business sector to face structural pressures are identified as the following by one text: training of the workforce, education, human resource management. According to that same text, assuring these new conditions for economic growth constitutes the new role for governments: 'Le rôle du gouvernement est de comprendre ce processus et de fournir de l'aide et des conseils afin d'accroître la promotion de l'entreprenariat dans la région.'[15] The role of government is one of advisor and supporter to the private sector. It is there to ensure that things like research and development, training, technological advances, and education (defined in terms of what is necessary for productivity) are promoted in order to give the cutting edge in economic competition to the Atlantic provinces' business sector.

THE CENTRALITY OF ECONOMIC NECESSITY

ACOA's central argument that we have just presented is based on an evaluation that seems to consider economic logic as inherently compelling. The omnipresence of competitivity as a concept guiding ACOA's action suggests that market logic has to prevail and determine regional development. The promotion of regional development cannot choose to go against the imperatives imposed by the competitive structure of the economy.

The solutions proposed by ACOA also follow market logic. The insistence on entrepreneurship is based on an enhancement of the capacity of the local business class to appropriate their share of markets. As we mentioned earlier, the role of government is seen as promoter of private sector competitivity. ACOA's mandate is therefore thought of in terms of helping the private sector. Elements such as education and training are of interest to the agency simply because they are useful for business and not because of other social advantages they might promote. Education is not considered valuable because it promotes a balanced and healthy citizenship, but only because it enhances its productive capacities.[16]

Donald Savoie confirms the fact that ACOA has espoused that market-conscious approach when he states: 'la majorité des gouvernements (de l'OCDE) affirment maintenant clairement, et de plus en plus, l'importance de la composante régionale dans les rajustements structurels et les politiques qui les favorisent. Il y a donc tendance à faire perdre aux politiques leur caractère social et à les canaliser vers les rajustements structurels....Les conclusions de l'OCDE sur le développement régional s'appliquent au Canada de bien des façons. Notamment, elles indiquent que l'APÉCA est sur la bonne voie.'[17] ACOA's regional development strategy is an important part of a larger governance strategy oriented toward the marketization of the role of government.

ACOA'S CONCEPTION OF CITIZENSHIP: A CRITIQUE OF THE ECONOMIC NECESSITY ARGUMENT

The notion of economic necessity presumes that reality is self-evident. The realities of this world (especially the economic ones) are independent of what people think of it or say about it. Ironically enough, Marx's base superstructure distinction creeps up in ACOA's discourse. However, this position is highly contested; one can also argue that reality is not detached from discourse. Authors like Charles Taylor and James Farr would point out that reality cannot be seen as independent from discourse. Reality is shaped and given its meaning by discourse. As Farr asserts, political change has to be seen in a constant relation with what he calls 'conceptual change': 'when we acknowledge that practices are *constituted* by concepts, we remind ourselves how very much of language is "in" the political world and how decisive this is for our understanding of it. This, too, is an important political reality, for where there are different concepts, there are different beliefs, and so different actions and practices.'[18]

If we recognize the political salience of concepts, we have to address the issue of the inevitability of economics in a different way. Economics cannot in itself be naturally and inherently compelling. Its necessity is created at the level of concepts or in other words at the level of discourse. ACOA's case doesn't differ from that framework proposed by Farr. Although the agency's discourse legitimizes its action on the inevitability of economics, we would suggest, following Farr's argument, that it cannot be separated from a particular moral outlook: 'The belief that the developmental validity of the market is historically inevitable forms part of the substance of classic neo-conservatism. These arguments are not, I would suggest, completely sustainable. There is a recursive pattern in either individualistic or communal explanations of social policy that cannot be side-stepped by an appeal to the power of an historic linear ascendancy of ideas.'[19]

For our purpose, we will talk about ACOA's moral outlook in terms of its conception of citizenship. In doing this we are following authors, such as John Scott, who see the development of the welfare state as very much linked to changes in the conception of citizenship.[20] Scott proposes a threefold conception of citizenship: the liberal conception, the social democratic, and the radical conception. The liberal conception is based on work. Full participation in society (in other words, citizenship) is defined by participation in the work force: 'The rights of citizenship are grounded in the obligation to work.'[21] Citizens are to find their well-being through the fruits of their labour, which means that they realize themselves through the competition of the market.

The second conception, the social democratic conception, is also based on work. The difference between this and the liberal one is that there is a commitment on the part of the society to provide work for its citizens. There is what Ian Culpit calls a 'social obligation,' or a collective responsibility to ensure that members of the citizenry have access to a minimum amount of welfare through their participation in the work force. Market logic can be twisted somewhat in order to meet that principle of collective responsibility.[22] The radical conception defines membership in the public sphere as automatic and therefore not linked to any condition. Society should provide for its members independently of their contribution to that society.

ACOA seems to embrace at least partially the liberal conception of citizenship.[23] As we have shown before, ACOA's main argument is based on the idea that regional development has to be geared toward an enhancement of the region's capacity to face market competition. The insistence on the market is presented as an absolute. ACOA doesn't present any other form of justification for the predominance of market logic over social relations. In light of John Scott's contribution, it seems reasonable to question that assertion. The economic argument does not make sense when it is not put in relation to an ethical conception. Individuals will best benefit from their citizenship when they do it by conforming to the competition. That vision implicitly refers to an outlook that sees competition as a healthy medium for the management of society.

To add to that argument, we can also refer to Culpit's analysis. He presents the neo-conservative critique of the welfare state (the same critique can also be found on the left) as a critique of the paternalism of state bureaucracies.[24] The critique of the right sees bureaucracy as an impediment to human autonomy. State intervention is dangerous not only because it costs a lot of money (in the sense of being inefficient), but also because it creates a dependency on government that doesn't allow the full expression of human autonomy.[25] Culpit comes back to the central ideas of the liberal conception of citizenship in the sense that collective responsibility as embodied by the state is seen as paternalistic.

It seems that the idea of the state as a paternalistic reality is necessary to give some meaning to the economic argument. It is because one is arguing that individuals are at their best when free of state intervention that the economic price to pay for solidarity becomes relevant. By putting up front the economic necessity argument, ACOA neglects the fact that welfare state politics are guided by societal choices that are more deeply rooted than the economic argument.

THE DEMOCRATIC CONTRIBUTION OF ACOA

Until now, we have criticized ACOA's argument, showing that contrary to its assertion, the economic necessity argument is not self-evident. In this section, we would like to understand what ACOA's argument means for democratic discourse. In other words, what version of democracy is implied when a public agency bases the legitimacy of its action on economic logic. Denying the grounding of its discourse in a particular definition of citizenship blurs the prospect of a public debate or open discussion of that conception. We will illustrate this argument by borrowing from Nancy Fraser's framework on needs assessment.

For Fraser, it is important to understand how needs are defined by public agencies because these represent 'an idiom in which political conflict is played out and through which inequalities are symbolically elaborated and challenged.'[26] Needs are not naturally defined. The definition of needs is therefore a totally political matter. For Fraser, by defining needs, public agencies have the power to determine what issues are political (and debatable in the public sphere) and what issues are private. That politicization process is, in her view, very much linked to democracy. Someone concerned with democracy has to understand such questions as: Which needs are included in the public debate? How is that happening (what and who determines the inclusion and the rejection of certain issues in the public debate)?[27] It is these questions that have to be asked in the case of ACOA in order to understand what importance it gives to democracy.

ACOA's DEFINITION OF NEEDS

The objective here is not to give a complete picture of what ACOA perceives to be the needs that it wants to address, but rather to see in general how it addresses the question of needs. To do that, our strategy will be to look at two different areas—the statistics presented in the agency's documents and the strategic themes that are emphasized.

The Statistics

Statistics are very important in the case of ACOA's publications, not only because there are a lot of them but also because they tend to be central arguments in the presentation of the problem.[28] Table 1 presents the distribution of different sets of statistics according to different themes.[29] The table demonstrates in a very striking manner that the sets of statistics presented by ACOA construct reality largely in terms of economic criteria. For instance, if we combine the themes employment, small business creation, and budget, they make up more than 60 percent of the sets of statistics used. Equally significant is the fact that social statistics were only found five times in all of the documents.[30] This creation of an economic reality then influences all the interpretation. For example, elements like the number of small businesses created or the number of jobs created are not desirable because of their contribution to social well-being. The definition of these elements is very much market-

TABLE 1   Themes of ACOA's Statistics

Themes	Number	Percentage
Budget (1)	51	15.7
Employment (2)	79	24.2
Population (3)	8	2.5
Regional development spending (4)	12	3.3
Small business creation (5)	70	21.6
Business profile (6)	5	1.5
Formation and education (7)	8	2.5
Government deficit and revenues	4	1.2
Investment (8)	16	4.9
Production (9)	28	8.6
Service to entrepreneurship (10)	22	6.9
Revenue (11)	16	4.9
Social statistics (12)	5	1.5
Total	324	100.0

1. *Budget:* by sectors, by program, budget for each theme
2. *Employment:* % of active population, unemployment rate, by sectors, growth of unemployment insurance payment, cost of employment creation, jobs lost in the last recession
3. *Population:* total population of the Atlantic (compared to Canada), emigration, age pyramid
4. *Regional development spending:* in proportion of total federal spending in the Atlantic
5. *Small business creation:* number of businesses created by ACOA, successful projects, success by sectors, jobs created, small business financing, autonomous workers
6. *Business profile:* corporation profits, technological concentration, industrial diversity
7. *Formation and education:* public funds for research, business spending on research and development, years of education of the population
8. *Investments:* ratio of public–private investments, investment needs
9. *Production:* GDP growth, ACOA's GDP contribution, growth of export, growth of sales
10. *Service to entrepreneurship:* information, business counselling, client satisfaction
11. *Revenue:* revenue per capita, transfer payments
12. *Social statistics:* proportions of houses with sanitary installation and refrigerators, provincial spending on health and education

centred. The statistics presented quite clearly assume the legitimacy of the economic logic since they are at the centre of the problem to be tackled.

The Strategic Themes

The second element that can give us an idea of ACOA's definition of needs is its strategic themes. These themes are the priorities that should guide ACOA's action and the criteria according to which the success of ACOA is to be evaluated. These themes are the following: (1) *entrepreneurship,* (2) *innovation and technology transfer,* (3) *human resource development,* (4) *marketing and trade development,* and (5) *the environment.* Once again, all these themes are valid because of their contribution to economic development. They are means by which governments can create a healthy climate for the creation of small businesses.

Rather than examining them all in detail, we will look at one example, that of the environment. Even that theme, which at first looks like it might not be linked to market logic, is presented as a priority because of its contribution to economic development. In Donald Savoie's interpretation, the environment is to be protected because it is essential to economic development (mostly as a resource base) and at the same time environmental protection can also be a potential area of activity for small business. The same argument is used for all the other themes, including human resource development.[31]

The construction of reality through the use of statistics and of strategic themes is totally coherent with the liberal discourse on citizenship. The construction of the problem doesn't leave any room for the social aspect of the issues. Citizens are responsible for their well-being through work. Social well-being is not a public matter. It is a private matter that is derived from work, which is public (but the definition of work is limited by the parameters of the market).

AN ECONOMIC APPROACH TO NEEDS INTERPRETATION

The other question that is very relevant to our discussion is what approach is used to define the needs. Nancy Fraser asserts: 'Such theories assume that the politics of needs concerns only whether various predefined needs will or will not be provided for. As a result they deflect attention from a number of political questions. First, they take the interpretation of people's needs as simply given and unproblematic; they occlude the interpretative dimension of needs politics—the fact that not just satisfactions but need interpretations are politically contested.'[32] ACOA seems to be using that kind of approach denounced by Fraser. By using the argument of economic necessity, it denies the possibility or at least the relevancy of a debate that could discuss what is political and what is not. In fact, because it denies its linkages to a particular conception of citizenship, ACOA closes the door to a debate between the various ethical outlooks. In a more practical way, the closing of the debate takes place through the refusal to admit that the definition of what is political varies across ethical outlooks and is therefore not inherent. In other words, ACOA, by its use of the economic necessity argument, tries to establish that the needs it defines as political are 'naturally' the ones to be met.

A definition of needs that does not allow the public sphere to discuss on the definition of the political, leaves a very limited role for democracy. In ACOA's example, democracy as embodied by the public sphere is not capable of determining which ethical outlook is preferable. It is market logic that is the determining factor in deciding to privilege the liberal conception. The refusal of the agency to talk about social needs is not necessarily antidemocratic, but the fact that the public sphere is not in a position to discuss which conception it prefers poses some serious questions from the standpoint of democracy. The democracy that ACOA's discourse allows cannot be of a substantial kind because it does not debate ethical questions.

Such a refusal to associate democracy with substantial choices amounts to what Ron Perrin calls a neo-realist version of democracy. Perrin sees neo-realist democracy as the main definition in the social sciences. It is the opposite of democracy defined in normative terms. Democracy in neo-realist terms is limited to the presence of elected institutions.[33] It is opposed to any capacity of democracy to reflect on more substantial questions like the contribution of the public sphere to the fulfilment and empowerment of individuals.[34] By promoting a neo-realist definition of democracy, ACOA does not allow that concept any power to orient public policy.

Conclusion

One of this paper's main objectives was to assert the relevancy of democracy as a criteria for judging the changes happening to the welfare state. By examining the discourse of ACOA, we see that the argument of economic necessity used to explain the evolution of the welfare state loses its power unless its links to an ethical outlook, in this case the liberal conception of citizenship, are suppressed.

By putting forward the economic necessity argument, ACOA promotes a neo-realist version of democracy. Needs are defined in narrow economic terms leaving all social concerns outside of public scrutiny. This type of approach is in accordance with a liberal version of citizenship. On the other hand, by putting forward market logic as the determining factor that defines the political, the agency does imply that democracy has no capacity to define what is political and has no capacity to choose between ethical conceptions present in society.

The neo-realist version of democracy is based on the idea that the conceptions of the political are not relevant to politics. If we admit that these conceptions cannot be separated from politics, then a democratic choice between ethical outlooks becomes possible. Social scientists, once they have relativized the legitimacy of economic logic to guide public policy, could then criticize ACOA for putting democracy on the sidelines of public policy evaluations.

ACOA's case seems conclusive enough to give some clear indications about the importance of democracy for an understanding of public policy and notably of the current welfare state politics. The changes in state social intervention because of their use of the economic necessity argument can probably, as the case of ACOA suggests, be seen as promoting a neo-realist vision of democracy. To see this is the first step toward the promotion of a more substantial vision of democracy, a vision that could use democracy as a criteria for determining the evolution of state intervention. Democracy would then mean that public policy would reflect social choices between conceptions of the political.

Notes

1. See Pierre Rosanvallon, 'Introduction' in *La crise de l'État-providence* (Paris, 1981).
2. Ian Robinson, *North American Trade as if Democracy Mattered* (Ottawa, 1992), 3.
3. See for instance Pierre-Marcel Desjardins, 'VENI, VICI, VIDI: Le cas des efforts de développement régional au Canada Atlantique' in Donald Savoie, ed., *Les provinces Maritimes: un regard vers l'avenir* (Moncton, 1993), 108–9.
4. The main initiatives in that phase and the most documented ones are taken by the Department of Regional Economic Expansion (DREE).
5. Donald Savoie, *Regional Economic Development: Canada's Search for Solutions* (Toronto, 1986), 27.
6. That approach is the one of the second phase of regional development, which is characterized by a particular vision of the relations between economic and social considerations. The economic considerations are seen as compelling and therefore having precedence over social considerations.
7. 'Dans la mesure où les forces économiques modifient le tracé du développement régional au Canada, la politique gouvernementale devra changer. En créant l'APÉCA le gouvernement fédéral a formulé des politiques de développement régional suffisament flexibles et efficaces pour récolter les bénéfices de la mondialisation de l'économie.' Guy Baumier, *L'agence de promotion économique du Canada atlantique: les programmes Action et Coopération* (Ottawa, n.d.), 18; Donald Savoie, *L'APÉCA face à l'avenir* (Moncton, 1991), 3–4; and APÉCA, *Rapport quinquennal présenté au Parlement 1988–1993* (Ottawa, 1993), 2.
8. Donald Savoie, *Constitution de l'agence de promotion économique du Canada Atlantique* (Ottawa, 1987), 1–2.
9. James Feehan, *Évaluation du programme Coopération: Rapport sommaire et conclusions* (1994), 56; and Donald Savoie, *Constitution de l'agence*, 44.
10. Savoie, *Constitution de l'agence*, 16–18.
11. APÉCA, *Rapport quinquennal présenté au Parlement*.
12. 'Dans une économie mondiale de plus en plus concurentielle, le succès allait désormais venir du développement de la petite entreprise et de l'entrepreunariat, ainsi que de l'amélioration du marketing et de la compétitivité, par l'emploi de la technologie et du perfectionnement des compétences des gestionnaires de la main-d'oeuvre.' APÉCA, *Rapport quinquennal présenté au Parlement*, 4.
13. Savoie, *Constitution de l'agence*, 40.
14. Savoie, *L'APÉCA face à l'avenir*, 7.
15. APÉCA, *État de la petite entreprise et de l'entrepreunariat dans la région de l'Atlantique* (Moncton, 1994), 10.
16. For a good example illustrating ACOA's conception of education see Savoie, *Constitution de l'agence*, 44–8.
17. Savoie, *L'APÉCA face à l'avenir*, 6–7.

18. James Farr, 'Understanding Conceptual Change Politically,' in T. Ball et al., eds., *Political Innovation and Conceptual Change* (Cambridge, 1989), 29. See also Charles Taylor, *Human Agency and Language* (Cambridge, 1985) on language and its constitutive capacity.

19. Ian Culpit, *Welfare and Citizenship: Beyond the Crisis of the Welfare State?* (London, 1992), 13.

20. That type of argument can also be found in the works of many other authors. See A. Cordell et al., *Shifting Time* (Toronto, 1994) and Theodore Lowi, 'The Welfare State: Ethical Foundations and Constitutional Remedies,' *Political Science Quarterly* 101/2.

21. John Scott, *Poverty and Wealth: Citizenship, Deprivation and Privilege* (London, 1994), 149.

22. Ibid.

23. We say partially because these conceptions are always impure in reality and especially in the case of a discourse on regional development. Regional development is in itself a form of market distortion in favour of regions plagued by slow growth and therefore as something that does not follow the liberal conception. However, it is still useful to talk of a liberal conception in the case of ACOA because of the emphasis on market forces, particularly with the recent shift toward a more liberal discourse.

24. Ian Culpit, *Welfare and Citizenship*, 27–9.

25. 'The general tenor of that argument is that public sector bureaucracies are too cumbersome and expensive; that they create an administrative structure which inhibits personal responsibility.' Ian Culpit, *Welfare and Citizenship*, 8.

26. Nancy Fraser, 'Talking About Needs: Interpretative Contests as Political Conflicts in Welfare State Societies,' *Ethics* 99 (Jan. 1989), 291.

27. See Fraser, 'Talking About Needs,' 294–5 and 313.

28. Statistics are particularly relevant to our process here because they are the result of a particular set of assumptions that are validated through the apparent factual character of quantification. These assumptions help to draw the line in the definition of the problem. By classifying statistics we can have a general picture of what are the main areas that are to be seen as part of the problem and what is assumed as outside of the problem (that being the elements that are not quantified) See Jean-Pierre Gaudin, *L'aménagement de la société, la production de l'espace aux XIXème et XXème siècles* (Paris, 1979), 314.

29. We say 'sets of statistics' to refer to the statistics that are used in the same argument by the author for describing the same reality.

30. All those social statistics were used to present a period before the creation of ACOA and seemed to imply at least in two cases that the social problem was mainly resolved. ACOA's mandate was therefore to take care of the economic problems. See Savoie, *Constitution de l'agence*, 7–8.

31. Savoie, *L'APÉCA face à l'avenir*, 93–104; and also APÉCA, *Rapport quinquennal présenté au Parlement*, 8; Savoie, *Constitution de l'agence*, 44–8.

32. Nancy Fraser, 'Talking About Needs,' 293–4.

33. For an author like Ron Perrin, the neo-realist version of democracy is dominant in social sciences. Although that version is very often associated with authors like Joseph Schumpeter, it is also present in much of political science. See Ron Perrin, 'Rehabilitating Democratic Theory: The Prospect and the Need' in John P. Burke et al., eds., *Critical Perspectives on Democracy* (Lanham, 1994), 2. On Schumpeter, see Carole Pateman, *Participation and Democratic Theory* (Cambridge, 1970).

34. For Perrin, normative democracy finds its legitimacy both in tradition (what has been standard understanding in the community) and in the critique of that tradition. For that author, human understanding doesn't have a meaning in itself. It always finds its roots in the horizon of a particular community. The critique of tradition also finds its roots in tradition and cannot be understood other than as a reflection on tradition: 'In this regard the significance of "liberty" as a primary value in democratic theory is less a feature of the philosophical merits or demerits of natural law doctrine than it is of the historical and emancipatory interest in supplanting the rule of dogma and arbitrary force by reflective standards of reason and the principles of constitutional law.' Perrin, 'Rehabilitating Democratic Theory,' 8.

CIVIC RE-ALIGNMENT
NGOs and the Contemporary Welfare State

LESLIE A. PAL

School of Public Administration
Carleton University

The *welfare state* is a misleading term. It is not merely a state, but a system of governance, policies, and of civil society. The development of the Western welfare state has also been the story of the development of a welfare society, and we cannot understand one without the other. Liberals and other supporters of the welfare state have long argued that the classical version of the welfare state was necessary because of weaknesses in civil society—churches, families, and voluntary groups simply could not cope with the exigencies of a modern, industrialized economy. Only the state, with its capacity to redistribute wealth and manage economic cycles, was equal to the challenge. Conservative critics of the welfare state have told another story about the relation of governance to civil society, a narrative wherein the state has gradually colonized whole portions of our social life and sapped their vitality. The state in this version is not the answer but the problem.

It is impossible to tell whether every welfare state gets the society it needs or deserves, but it is probably that over the decades the two parts of the system settle into some sort of equilibrium peculiar to historical circumstances. The mix in the United States is different from that of Canada or Germany, even while all three systems share some generic welfare state features. Of course, the welfare state was constantly evolving over the twentieth century, and so we can expect that civil society was constantly adapting as well. Nonetheless, for roughly twenty-five years (1960–85), we can say that the welfare state/society equilibrium was relatively stable. In retrospect, this stability masked major changes and challenges under the surface, ones which eventually erupted through the 1980s and culminated in what appears to be a fundamental reinvention of the welfare state as we know it.

If the welfare state is changing, then civil society will change with it. As programs are cut or altered, the people, communities, and associations linked to them will change as well. Central questions in the future of the welfare state, therefore, are what type of civil society will it engender and what type of civil society will it need? A crucial component in this change will be nongovernmental organizations (NGOs)—including advocacy, research, and service organizations. What changes are in store for them, and how should they adapt for a twenty-first–century version of the welfare state?

If one adopts the view that the current policy shifts underway at the federal and provincial levels are a root-and-branch attack on social policy, then there may not be much to discuss. This essay takes the view that the changes, while in some cases drastic, will nonetheless still leave a relatively large state sector. Moreover, despite the negative impact of these cuts on many NGOs and sectors such as health and education, there are important countertrends that suggest, if anything, an enhanced role for NGOs. Something more complex than mere cuts is going on. This paper will explore some of these current patterns, arguing that they demonstrate a process of civic re-alignment between state and society that involves several distinct and contradictory dynamics. It will then pose the question of what role NGOs can be expected to play in the new welfare state configuration, and how they should prepare themselves for that challenge.

CIVIC RE-ALIGNMENT

Canada, along with other Western states, has witnessed a major change in the way in which NGOs participate in and affect the policy process. This change is actually the result of a variety of incremental initiatives undertaken over the last decade. Budgetary pressures, for example, have gradually eroded the financial support that NGOs have come to expect from federal and provincial governments. As well, the familiar debates over 'reinventing' and 're-engineering' government have led all jurisdictions to alter their service delivery patterns.[1] For some NGOs and community-based service providers, this has meant 'partnerships' wherein they co-operate with government agencies in the provision of social and other services.[2] As part of this process, governments have also been bitten with the consultation bug, and now routinely bring NGOs into the policy formulation phase as well as implementation.[3] There is broad consensus that the Charter has enhanced the role of the courts and made them a new target for interest group pressures through litigation.[4] At the same time, internalization of domestic public policy is changing the range of NGO actors on the domestic scene,[5] as well as inducing Canadian-based NGOs to project their domestic policy concerns internationally.[6] Finally, as something of a countertrend to increased consultation, governments have been increasingly pressured to regulate the lobbying industry.[7]

The potential universe of NGOs is too great to be embraced within this paper, and so I will focus my attention on the federal level and, for the most part, on NGOs drawn from the advocacy, service, social movement, and public interest sectors.[8] NGOs and social movements are key elements in the modern *civitas* or civil society; indeed, the idea of civil society is itself considered central to a conceptualization that goes beyond simple dichotomies of state and economy.[9] Civil society, however, is not insulated from the state. In modern polities, the state structures civil society and its associations, and in turn, those civil associations focus much of their energies on trying to shape state policy and behaviour. The civic re-alignment that has occurred in Canada over the past decade has features peculiar to this country, but also shares in some dynamic forces that have been evident throughout the OECD countries. Grouping some of the developments described above, this re-alignment entails strategies of (1) disengagement, (2) re-engagement, and (3) displacement.

DISENGAGEMENT

The visible dynamic in the process of civic re-alignment is disengagement, or the deliberate withdrawal of state support and legitimacy from the voluntary sector. This itself has had three distinct features. The first is the reduction in program expenditures. As governments have cut health, education, and social security, they have inevitably destabilized groups and organizations active in those fields. The key factor here is that these moves have been couched as a means of shrinking government, reducing excess expenditures, and privatizing to some extent services that were previously delivered through the public sector. As I note below, this reduction in state activity can and often does imply an increase in nonstate or NGO/community activity, but it has also been accompanied (certainly in more conservative regimes like Alberta and Ontario) with an emphasis on the introduction of market mechanisms such as contracting out, and private, fee-charging delivery mechanisms. The effect, therefore, is less directly fiscal than it is in the broad legitimacy given to the public sector and voluntary, nonprofit community action.

The second form that disengagement takes is the attack on public sector unions. Labour strife has been characteristic of every jurisdiction that has tried to balance its budget, though governments like Ontario's have been more adamantly anti-union than Liberal or NDP governments. The same dynamic is at play in all regimes, whatever their 'good cop–bad cop' routines. Public sector wages at the federal level are not a major contributor to the deficit, but they do account for a larger portion at the provincial level. For both provincial and federal governments, however, the point is less about money in the short term (as important as that is) than about labour market flexibility in the long term.

The third mechanism is more directly fiscal: the reduction or elimination of funds to groups themselves, either for advocacy, for research, or even service delivery. At the federal level, one of the clear trends since the late 1980s has been to question the legitimacy of advocacy organizations, and in particular to query the degree to which they are truly representative of the population at large. Like the United States and Britain, Canada has enjoyed a strong tradition of voluntarism and philanthropic action to deal with social ills and the needs of the community.[10] While the potential legitimacy of voluntary action and service provision by civic associations is, if anything, greater today than in recent years,[11] the legitimacy of advocacy organizations is increasingly challenged.[12] These groups, many allied to major left-of-centre, 'counterconsensus' social movements in Canada,[13] grew rapidly in the 1960s and 1970s around social justice concerns.[14]

This frayed legitimacy has been reflected in attacks on the government funding of these groups. Once again, it is important to distinguish advocacy or public interest groups[15] from service-oriented organizations. The former typically face major collective action problems, since they purport to represent broad interests—from a public choice perspective, this should make 'free riding' by potential members quite attractive, and therefore make it difficult to raise funds. As Walker has shown in the American context, the way around this problem is sponsorship.[16] In the United States, foundations have played a key role in supporting advocacy organizations; in the Canadian case, it has been government. Thus cuts to government funding of organizations presents substantial logistical as well as financial challenges. Federal support for public interest groups—especially women's organizations—has been whittled away over the last decade, and the February 1995 federal budget promised to cut further. John Bryden, a Liberal MP, issued a report in 1994 severely critical of government funding of advocacy-oriented NGOs.[17]

Another example of this type of disengagement, though indirect, is the recent cuts to arm's length agencies that in turn support important segments of the NGO community. The amalgamation of the Canadian Advisory Council on the Status of Women with other government agencies devoted to women's issues will probably have little effect on feminist-oriented research per se, but it removes an important node in feminist policy networks. Budget cuts to the Canadian Human Rights Commission and to the Canadian International Development Agency also will result in cuts to NGO support as well as a weakening of the fabric of related policy networks.

If disengagement is indeed going on, what does it imply about the type of welfare state–welfare society system that we once had and now appear to be forging anew? The leitmotif in this dynamic of disengagement is one of separation and delegitimation. Despite the often adversarial relationships between the NGO sector and government in the building of the Canadian welfare state, in fact that old system was characterized by a substantial degree of clientelist politics. This style of regime had several key features. First, it relied on fairly segmented policy fields—certainly a division between economic and social policy, but even within each of these broad spheres, further subdivisions into industrial, trade, technology, labour, health, welfare, and more recently multiculturalism, women, language groups, and so on. As government expanded into each of these fields over the postwar period, at both the provincial and federal levels the response was to establish distinct agencies and departments, which then in turn developed relationships with client groups within that sector. A second feature—alluded to earlier in contrasting the Canadian pattern to the American one—was the fact that many Canadian NGOs involved in advocacy, research, and service delivery relied on government for core funding in one way or another. The Canadian Council on Social Development (CCSD), for example, used to be primarily an umbrella organization for a host of social policy groups. Both the CCSD and these groups relied heavily on government for support. A third characteristic of this regime was that in any given policy field, the number of groups was relatively small and there was some clear dominance by one or a cluster of groups. The self-regulatory health sectors are perhaps the prime example of this, but the same could be said of the Canadian women's movement and the National Action Committee on the Status of Women in its classic period in the 1970s and early 1980s.[18]

This clientelist regime began to erode through the 1980s for several reasons, only one of which was clearly related to governments' new determination to deal with the deficit. That was certainly a factor, but funding for groups of this type was never a big ticket item—the real reasons were deeper. Certainly a key one was the increased numbers in NGOs themselves, and the growing complexities of the social sector. Whereas in the early years, clientelist politics could make sense because one could plausibly claim a coherent client base of activists and organizations, that assumption gradually sunk under the weight of the growth first of splinter organizations within the same sectors that shared broad ideology but had slightly more focused agendas (e.g., in the women's movement, among the disabled), and later with the rise of more conservative organizations that challenged the consensus in the first place. The imbroglio over funding for REAL women in the mid-1980s was significant for this reason.[19] Another reason was the broadening and deepening of social policy itself. While the connection between economic and social policy was seen from the beginning, it was only a decade ago that the intimate connection between human capital and economic performance was made and taken seriously outside of academic circles. That overlap was complemented by new directions in contemporary social policy that emphasized rights gained through the Charter and the courts rather than through expenditure programs per se. The 'equity' agenda expanded to include recognition of various minorities as something going considerably beyond the alleviation of poverty per se.

In short, the dynamic of disengagement is only partly driven by ideological forces. The nature of the policy field and of the NGOs in that field have changed radically in the last two decades as well, and it is unlikely that the cozy (if still domineering) relationship between government departments and NGOs could be sustained in this new environment.[20] As social policy expands, virtually everyone can be viewed as a social policy advocate. The range of groups and their strategic foci have broadened to the extent that it is unclear who or what the constituencies are. As Boase demonstrates in her study on regulation of the health professions, as the NGO universe gets more complex, it is more and more difficult for government to maintain the old patterns.[21] Disengagement, particularly from groups who claim to speak for this or that constituency, is the likely result.

RE-ENGAGEMENT

The politics of deficit-cutting is so dominated by harsh rhetoric on the government's side and howls of injured outrage on the nongovernment side, that at first blush it appears that disengagement is the complete story. Governments want to be smaller, they cut programs and connections, and we end up with both an impoverished state and a devastated civil society.

Civic re-alignment, however, is more complex than a simple disengagement of government and the state from NGOs and civil society. At the same time that advocacy and public interest activity is criticized by government and challenged by what might be inelegantly called 'counter-counterconsensus' groups, other segments of the NGO community are being treated more favourably through a process of re-engagement. The rhetoric of 'smaller, leaner, meaner' has dominated government discourse at federal and provincial levels for the last decade, with the corollary that government should make room for the market. Another corollary of this discourse, however, has been the celebration of voluntarism and the 'community.' The antithesis to 'big government,' in short, is not always the 'market' but the community or the voluntary sector. This way of framing the issue appeals to both left and right, and its popularity should not be surprising. What it means, however, is that even as governments cut funds to some groups and rupture their policy networks, they seek to reconnect with other organizations that can plausibly be portrayed to represent the community. Since the real intent of most of these maneuvers is to download programming to the provincial, municipal, and local levels, in practice this entails a focus on service-oriented community groups. For the moment, to take Ontario as an example of what this can mean *in extremis*, the previous government had launched major community-based initiatives in long-term care and citizens' advocacy.[22] In the case of long-term care, Queen's Park sought to establish Multi-Service Agencies that would weave together thousands of community-based service providers into a province-wide plan. A federal example comes from the tobacco reduction strategy announced by Ottawa in conjunction with its cuts to cigarette taxes. Public information campaigns and other smoking reduction programs are being funnelled through community-based organizations on the assumption that a lifestyle issue like smoking can best be tackled by groups and individuals close to the ground. These initiatives are consistent with a focus on 'partnerships' discerned in federal policy several years ago.

Paralleling this strategy of partnership and government service delivery through NGOs is the recent emphasis on consultation. The roots of this no doubt can be traced to the de-legitimization of Canada's parliamentary institutions during the constitutional fiascoes of Meech Lake and the Charlottetown Accord, and the commensurate pressure to connect with the people more directly in routine policy making.[23] The PS2000 blueprint (largely of historical interest now after federal government program review) stressed the importance of consultation, and some academic observers have even gone so far as to highlight the 'stewardship of policy communities' as a key management function.[24] The forms of consultation vary by policy sector,[25] but include imaginative attempts to incorporate business and NGOs into roundtables,[26] as well as wider consultation through parliamentary committees in the review of government policy statements or legislation. Two recent examples of this latter exercise were the social policy review, and the joint parliamentary committee on foreign policy. In both cases, hundreds of witnesses appeared before the committees, and in both those, appearances were dominated by nonbusiness, nonlabour NGOs.[27] This may in part reflect the Chrétien government's penchant for cheaper forms of public consultation (the Mulroney governments were prone to Royal Commissions, e.g., reproductive technologies, aboriginal peoples), but it is consultation nonetheless, and implies a re-engagement of state and society that runs counter to the first dynamic of civic re-alignment to separate the two spheres.

The reasons behind this re-engagement for both service delivery and consultation are as complex as the ones behind disengagement. Certainly, the drive behind greater consultation is in part shaped by the declining role of political parties, the sheer growth in the NGO community, and the need to 'sell' policy by getting opponents on board. Governments are also consulting, however, because they have limited policy-making capacity. Defined broadly, this would include the lack of legitimacy of parties and incumbent govern-ments. Governments need to consult in order to build a consensus that is no longer achievable through pure parliamentary mechanisms. As well, however, policy capacity refers to the ability to manage information and develop new ideas. One of the consequences of smaller government—which has already dawned on governments themselves—is that they reduce their own abilities to make new policy. This is especially important in the new information economy. Issues change constantly, have an international dimension, and are routinely coupled in very complex ways to other policy fields (witness the overlap in economic and social policy considerations). Governments are consulting more because in part they need better intelligence about their still-crammed agen-das. Information management and the organizational capacity to generate ideas are important contributions that the research-based NGO community can make.

What of service delivery? It would be tempting to ascribe almost all of this to a desire to off-load former government programs onto the voluntary sector. It saves on the wage bill, and can even cut on administrative overhead. The Canadian welfare state has traditionally relied a great deal on voluntary orga-nizations and semiprofessional nonprofit groups to deliver a wide variety of services, particularly in the health field. As hospital budgets are cut, and as the population ages, it would be natural to expect these types of associations and organizations to become even more important. But this is an old-fashioned rationale, which while still important, does not fully capture the forces under-pinning this deliberate state re-engagement with sectors of the NGO commu-nity. One important implication has to be the recent concern with 'social capital' and the role of key social institutions in fostering values of citizenship and participation.

Social policy in the welfare state for many years was defined in terms of an equity agenda, focused first on obvious income inequalities, and later on recognition of fundamental group rights and characteristics. Social policy is still about this agenda, but there has been a move across the political spectrum to reorient social policy (and hence the welfare state) towards the protection of fundamental democratic values. The reason this counts as social policy, and not simple civics, is the accumulating work on social capital that argues that these fundamental values are nurtured in the civic associations that dot the social landscape, from bowling leagues to the family itself. As Aaron, Mann, and Taylor state in their introduction to *Values and Public Policy*:

> In the jargon of the social sciences, analysts have begun to recognize that values and norms are not 'exogenous,' or independent of public policy. And the idea that values can change, combined with the recognition that responses to policies depend on people's preferences—that is, their values —leads to thinking about how public policy might change values directly or indirectly and thereby change the responses to public policies themselves.[28]

The success of Robert Putnam's book, *Making Democracy Work*, has encouraged policymakers to think about how values can be supported and nurtured.[29] Although it betrays a certain conservative temperament to look askance at the role government might have in this process, it accords with the general view that social capital—especially trust, its key ingredient—cannot be created by the state. As James Q. Wilson puts it, 'A government program to foster personal redemption will come equipped with standardized budgets, buy-America rules, minority set-asides, quarterly reporting requirements, and environmental impact statements and, in all likelihood, a thinly disguised bias against any kind of involvement with churches.'[30]

This is not to suggest that Canadian politicians closely study academic treatments of Italian civic traditions for clues about social policy (though Professor Putnam has been invited to brief the U.S. president several times). What it does mean is that the disengagement described in the previous section will be balanced by pressures to re-engage in a variety of ways, to carve out spaces for NGO associational action, complemented by the state. But NGOs that purport to represent constituencies rather than serve them, and those that have more of a professional than a volunteer character, are less likely to garner official support. In an era of values, social capital, and trust, the favoured NGOs will be small, service-oriented, and volunteer-based.

DISPLACEMENT

The dynamics of engagement and disengagement pertain to broad outlines of state/society relations in the specific form of NGOs and their place in the policy process. In these dynamics, NGOs are either drawn in or pushed out, but there is another dynamic that demands attention as well: instances where the intensity of NGO-government interaction is less affected than the site of that interaction—it is displaced. This is more than a mere institutional relocation of practices: once the site of NGO-government interaction changes, so too does the nature of that interaction. Unlike the first two dynamics, however, it is not a matter of 'more' or 'less' but 'different.'

Perhaps the most vivid example of this phenomenon is the rising prominence of courts and the Charter over the last decade.[31] The introduction of the Charter in 1982 and particularly the implementation of section 15 in 1985 gave new resources and opportunities to 'equality-seeking' groups to challenge federal and provincial legislation on constitutional grounds. According to Russell, the actual impact of the Charter in overturning government legislation has been modest,[32] but others have argued that with the Charter has come a significant judicialization or legalization of the Canadian political process.[33] Women's groups in particular have used the Charter to argue high-profile cases such as abortion, childcare, and rape shield.[34] The Charter is not the sole basis for NGO-inspired legal action, of course, as the challenges to the federal government's environmental assessment procedures around the Rafferty–Alameda dam project demonstrate. The key point—one that is intrinsically difficult to prove but that seems intuitively plausible—is that some NGOs are pursuing their political agendas through the relatively new technique of litigation. Cost remains a problem, but at least at the federal level, the Court Challenges program has been re-established under a new corporate body that includes stakeholder representation. There has been some discussion in academic circles on the utility of pursuing social policy through the courts or in league with a social charter.[35]

Reliance on courts and litigation is more than simply another technique for achieving traditional aims. With the displacement of political action to the courts come certain consequences for policy processes. Typically, if policy issues are argued in constitutional terms, especially in connection with the Charter, the 'rights talk' that characterizes this form of discourse is usually less amenable to compromise and routine forms of political horse-trading.[36] Indeed, it is possible that the displacement of some policy issues to the courts has an 'echo effect' in more traditional policy venues such as parliamentary committees insofar as NGOs will frame issues differently depending on whether the courts have pronounced upon them or not.[37]

Another important form of displacement is the increasing participation by at least some NGO sectors in international fora. Domestic policy is increasingly becoming 'internationalized,' and with this displacement of sovereignty comes a commensurable displacement of NGO activity. The logic behind interntionalization is complex, and embraces several distinct dynamics. In some cases, integration comes about primarily as a result of technological forces such as computerization and telecommunications. In other cases, such as the environment, the simple logic of common property resources and externalities drives the agenda. Economic integration, particularly of capital markets, often makes decisions taken in Tokyo, London, or Washington more salient than ones taken in Ottawa or Toronto. Finally, governments have acted (albeit slowly and reluctantly) to establish universal standards of civilized practice through the UN's and regional human rights' machinery. The 1993 Vienna World Conference on Human Rights and the 1995 Copenhagen World Social Summit attest to these developments. Canadian NGOs recognize that with internationalization and the development of global standards come opportunities to pursue 'domestic' policy issues through international means. Aboriginal organizations, for example, have fought hydro projects such as the Great Whale scheme by lobbying in New York.[38] Housing advocates have used the occasion of Canada's reports to the UN Committee on Economic, Social, and Cultural Rights as an opportunity to press for policy changes. The 1995 federal budget was protested by several Canadian NGOs—but to the Committee on Economic, Social, and Cultural Rights in Geneva.

The evolution of the machinery of domestic reporting on domestic compliance with international covenants shows how the institutional intertwining of domestic social policy departments and the foreign affairs function has become more complex. While the federal government has the exclusive power to sign international treaties, it cannot force provincial legislation to be consistent with these treaties. In the social policy and human rights field, up to the mid-1970s, no formal mechanism had been developed to deal with this structural problem. Indeed, it was exogenous pressure that provided the impetus for Canada to move away from this ad hoc approach. In anticipation of the ratification of the International Covenants on Civil and Political Rights and on Economic, Social, and Cultural Rights the following year, the Federal–Provincial–Territorial Continuing Committee of Officials on Human Rights was established in 1975. Moreover, a Federal–Provincial Conference of Ministers in charge was held in December 1975 that reached agreement on the ratification of the two covenants and the design of a new reporting machinery about their implementation.

Consistent with its long-standing attitude about its own constitutional rights and division of responsibilities, Quebec had serious concerns that Ottawa might try to unilaterally draft reports to the UN on provincial legislation, and/or to speak 'for all of Canada' in explaining the provincial sections of the reports. To get unanimous consent on the 'Modalities and Mechanisms' document that formed the basis of the Continuing Committee, therefore, the federal government had to address Quebec's concerns. In doing so, it was agreed that before the federal government acceded to future international human rights covenants or amended existing ones it would consult with the provinces and territories. Provinces have the opportunity to serve as representatives on the Canadian delegation, and hence the ability to respond to any criticisms emanating from an international body concerning provincial laws or institutions. Finally, there is acknowledgment of the right of provinces to prepare their sections of Canada's reports in concert with the federal government.

Canadian federalism adds other, ongoing, twists as well to the modification and reporting requirements for human rights and social policy instruments. As the scope of the international social agenda has expanded, so has the range of possible disputes. An interesting example of this phenomenon stemmed from the Convention on the Rights of the Child. Alberta failed to endorse the Convention, influenced by some provincial opinion that it thought would undermine parental authority, but Ottawa went ahead and ratified it anyway in 1992. Concerns raised by aboriginal peoples also forced Canada to enter reservations on the issue of adoption. Although the normal procedure is that the review of legislation undertaken before ratification will reveal statutes that are inconsistent with an international convention, leading to amendments at the provincial or territorial level, these concessions attract high-level political attention. Provincial agreement to ratification of a human rights convention is usually conveyed through a letter from the premier or the responsible minister, or alternatively through an order-in-council of the provincial cabinet. Quebec goes so far as to pass a decree to the effect that it has acceded to the international convention.

Federalism is not the only complicating institutional feature to the reporting and ratification process. The internal structures even at the federal level alone have become considerably more complex over time. The Human Rights Directorate of the Ministry of Canadian Heritage co-ordinates the overall preparation of all human rights reports, drawing together federal, provincial, and territorial input. In addition to this co-ordinating role, the Human Rights Directorate may also take the lead in drafting the federal portion of some reports (e.g., Convention on the Elimination of Racial Discrimination, or the Covenant on Economic, Social, and Cultural Rights). In other cases, however, other federal departments will draft the federal section; the Department of Justice, for example, is the federal lead for the Covenant on Civil and Political Rights. The Directorate is the federal liaison for the Continuing Committee of Officials, and draws together reports from other federal departments as necessary in the ratification and reporting process.

The mandate of the Human Rights Directorate is to serve as the central point of reference for the federal government's domestic interest in human rights. It has overall policy responsibility at the federal level for the understanding of, development, and respect for human rights. It accomplishes this through human rights education and promotion (principally through a grants and contributions budget of $858,000 in 1994–5), the Court Challenges Program,[39] and preparation of reports to the UN. While the Directorate is responsible for preparing these reports, it relies on federal, provincial, and territorial departments for relevant information. In Canada's first report under the Convention on the Rights of the Child, for example, Justice and Health played the lead roles in the initial drafting of the federal portion of the report. The Department of Justice is routinely involved in most reports through reviews of federal statutes. The current report prepared for the Covenant on Economic, Social, and Cultural Rights will similarly have input from several departments, including Human Resource Development, Environment, and the Canada Mortgage and Housing Corporation.

The institutional machinery has become more complex, and at the same time has provided new points of entry to NGOs. It is not clear that the international agenda is actually being set by either social policy ministers or the international NGO community, but the international level is clearly more relevant as a site of NGO activity.[40] Paradoxically, so is the local and provincial level, as provincial authorities play a greater role in generating the information required by international institutions. As policy-making has become more globalized, so have NGOs. One could argue that social policy–focused NGOs— beginning with the labour movement—have always had a strong international orientation, but the development of new information and communications technologies makes possible a new level of interconnection. For example, the Association for Progressive Communications (APC) is one of the most important and best known networks. It claims to have member networks in 19 countries, partner networks and local hosts in 133 countries, linking together over 28,000 individuals and organizations. Information is available through the APC, of course, but the purpose of APC itself is to provide communications and information-sharing capacity to organizations and individuals. The Canadian partner is Web Canada, and itself consists of partner networks: the Environment Intern-Network, Women's Web, Access to Justice Network, International Development, Human Rights and Peace, Education and Youth, Social Policy and Social Services (still under construction), and Faith & Justice.

A final example of displacement is speculative at this point, but would appear to be underway with Ottawa's restructuring of social transfers to the provinces. The new Canada Health and Social Transfer will actually reduce cash transfers, and in exchange Ottawa has offered to give the provinces greater (almost exclusive) discretion in spending those monies. This displacement of policy capacity will probably lead to a shift in NGO focus to the provinces, where the key programmatic decisions will be made.

LIVING WITH RE-ALIGNMENT

Taken together, the process of civic re-alignment shows a complex restructuring of the relations between welfare state and civil society as represented in NGOs. It is clear that some sectors and groups will be severed from the close relation that they have traditionally had with government. This seems principally to affect advocacy groups that have depended on government funding. At the same time, processes of re-engagement appear underway where service NGOs are being relied upon more as partners in the delivery of social programs, and other groups are being brought into the policy process. Finally, the locus of NGO-state interaction seems to be shifting across domestic institutions and even from domestic institutions to international ones. Table 1 summarizes these patterns of civic re-alignment.

TABLE 1 Patterns of Civic Realignment		
	Traditional Welfare State	**Emerging State–Society Relations**
POLICY FIELDS	Segmented	Integrated
DEPARTMENTS	Many, fragmented	Few, co-ordinated
NGO (types)	Mix of distinct types: advocacy, service, research; professional and volunteer	Pure advocacy in decline; overlapping characteristics
NGO (numbers)	Growth in 1960s and 1970s, but as policy fields kept distinct, numbers in any one field are stable	As fields overlap, number of potential players increases exponentially
NGO (preferred mode of interaction with government)	Key client organization	Broad consultations with many actors
NGO (favoured type)	Advocacy as representing constituency; professionalism favoured	Service and policy capacity
NGO FOCUS	Balanced between federal and provincial	Increasingly bifurcated between local and global; possible shift to courts

The discussion in this paper has been deliberately broad—trying to discern patterns from a welter of details. For every trend identified, there will clearly be counterexamples. As well, there are significant developments that have been overlooked—for example, the possible emphasis on business associations as social policy partners (this flows from an emphasis on human capital, but also the 'it's your turn now' syndrome once the pain has been spread through social policy programs). However, one virtue of generalization is that it provides a sense of perspective about big changes that might be obscured through a focus on details. Moreover, deliberately trying to capture the contradictory dynamics in this process helps avoid too pat a portrait of what, after all, are indeed inconsistent and confusing developments.

A final issue concerns the type of NGOs that will thrive in this new, re-aligned world of the Canadian welfare state. Advocacy organizations of the type we have seen in the past—supported largely by government grants, and geared to representation rather than research—are in for a hard time. Core funding is gone, and if governments do support groups it is through project-based funding. This is easier for governments to control, but it also shifts NGO activity towards more specific service and research functions. Advocacy groups will not disappear—think of the National Action Committee on the Status of Women, or any of the major environmental groups—but they will have to change the way that they operate. Without reliance on government funds, they will have to seek support elsewhere, either from business or through some contractual exchange of services. It is likely therefore that the pure type of organization will evolve into something more of a hybrid form, with cross-subsidization of activities. The CCSD has evolved in this way, earning its money through targeted research and using revenues to support some of its more traditional advocacy.

Government will continue to need advice and information, and so the research sector is likely to continue to exist and even grow as the demands of integrating complex policy fields become more pressing. We should expect the development of both broader international networks and movements as the international level becomes increasingly relevant to social policy, coupled with a greater focus on local service delivery. Organizations in the later category that can show that they have the potential to contribute to social capital formation and the support of fundamental community values are well positioned, especially if they do this through a judicious mix of voluntarism and professionalism.

It is clear that the welfare state in the new millennium will be smaller and spend less. It is also clear that individuals will have to become more self-reliant and that market mechanisms will be a more prominent form of service delivery. What is not clear, however, is that all of this will be necessarily accompanied by a wholesale withering of the NGO sector. It will change, it will re-align to a newly configured state, but it will continue to be central to the well-being of Canadians.

NOTES

1. Evert Lindquist, 'Recent Administrative Reform in Canada as Decentralization: Who Is Spreading What Around to Whom and Why?' *Canadian Public Administration* 37 (Fall 1994), 416–30.

2. Susan Phillips, 'How Ottawa Blends: Shifting Government Relationships with Interest Groups,' in Frances Abele, ed., *How Ottawa Spends 1991–1992* (Ottawa, 1991), 183–210; Ken Kernaghan, 'Partnership and Public Administration: Conceptual and Practical Considerations,' *Canadian Public Administration* 36 (Spring 1993), 57–76.

3. On PS2000 and consultation, see Canada, Privy Council Office, *Task Force Report: Service to the Public* (Ottawa, 1993), chap. 4; and Leslie A. Pal, 'The Federal Bureaucracy: Reinventing the Links Between State and Society,' in Michael Whittington and Glen Williams, eds., *Canadian Politics in the 1990s*, 4th ed. (Toronto, 1994).

4. Rainer Knopff and F.L. Morton, *Charter Politics* (Toronto, 1991); W.A. Bogart, *Courts and Country: The Limits of Litigation and the Social and Political Life of Canada* (Toronto, 1994).

5. Andrew F. Cooper, 'Questions of Sovereignty: Canada and the Widening International Agenda,' *Behind the Headlines* 50 (Spring 1993), 1–16; and Andrew Fenton Cooper and J.-Stefan Fritz, 'Bringing the NGOs In: UNCD and Canada's International Environmental Policy,' *International Journal* 47 (Autumn, 1992), 796–817.

6. Robert M. Campbell and Leslie A. Pal, *The Real Worlds of Canadian Politics* (Peterborough, 1994), chap. 4.

7. A. Paul Pross and Iain S. Stewart, 'Lobbying, the Voluntary Sector and the Public Purse,' in Susan D. Phillips, ed., *How Ottawa Spends: 1993–94: A More Democratic Canada?* (Ottawa, 1993), 109–42.

8. To some degree these categories overlap, and there is no consistent usage. In combination, however, they point to nonbusiness, nonlabour organizations.

9. John Keane, *Democracy and Civil Society* (London, 1988).

10. A. Paul Pross, *Group Politics and Public Policy*, 2nd ed. (Toronto, 1992).

11. For theory, see Paul Hirst, *Associative Democracy: New Forms of Economic and Social Governance* (Amherst, 1994).

12. W.T. Stanbury, 'A Sceptic's Guide to the Claims of So-Called Public Interest Groups,' *Canadian Public Administration* 36 (Winter 1993), 580–605; and Susan Phillips, 'Of Public Interest Groups and Sceptics: A Realist's Reply to Professor Stanbury,' *Canadian Public Administration* 36 (Winter 1993), 606–16.

13. On idea of counterconsensus applied in foreign policy and ODA sector, see Cranford Pratt, 'Dominant Class Theory and Canadian Foreign Policy: The Case of the Counter-Consensus,' *International Journal* 39 (1983–84), 99–105.

14. Leslie A. Pal, *Interests of State: The Politics of Language, Multiculturalism and Feminism in Canada* (Montreal, 1993).

15. For a definition, see Jeffrey Berry, *Lobbying for the People: The Political Behavior of Public Interest Groups* (Princeton, NJ, 1977).

16. Jack Walker, *Mobilizing Interest Groups in America: Patrons, Professions and Social Movements* (Ann Arbor, 1991).

17. John Bryden, MP, *Special Interest Group Funding*, 2 vols. (Ottawa, November 1994).

18. Jill Vickers, Pauline Rankin, and Christine Appelle, *Politics As If Women Mattered: A Political Analysis of the National Action Committee on the Status of Women* (Toronto, 1993).

19. Pal, *Interests of State*.

20. Rodney Haddow, *Poverty Reform in Canada: 1958–1978: State and Class Influences in Policy Making* (Montreal, 1993).

21. Joan Boase, *Shifting Sands: Government-Group Relationships in the Health Care Sector* (Montreal, 1994).

22. Terry Milne, (PhD diss. research proposal, Carleton University, (1996).

23. Leslie A. Pal and F. Leslie Seidle, 'Constitutional Politics 1990–92: The Paradox of Participation,'

in Susan D. Phillips, ed., *How Ottawa Spends: 1993–94: A More Democratic Canada?* (Ottawa, 1993), 143–202; Robert M. Campbell and Leslie A. Pal, *The Real Worlds of Canadian Politics* (Peterborough, 1994), chap. 3; Peter H. Russell, *Constitutional Odyssey: Can Canadians Become a Sovereign People?* 2nd ed. (Toronto, 1992); Alan C. Cairns, in Douglas E. Williams, ed., *Disruptions: Constitutional Struggles, from the Charter to Meech Lake* (Montreal, 1991).

24. Evert Lindquist, 'Public Managers and Policy Communities: Learning to Meet New Challenges,' *Canadian Public Administration* 35 (Summer 1992), 127–59.

25. For an example from the foreign policy sector, see Leslie A. Pal, 'Competing Paradigms in Policy Discourse: The Case of International Human Rights,' *Policy Sciences* 28 (May 1995), 185–207.

26. Glen Toner, 'The Canadian Environmental Movement: A Conceptual Map,' Unpub. ms, 1991; Glen Toner, 'Whence and Whither: ENGOs, Business and the Environment,' Unpub. ms, 1990.

27. For the foreign policy review, over half the appearances before the committee were by nonbusiness, nonlabour NGOs (a total of 277). See Canada, Parliament, Special Joint Committee of the Senate and the House of Commons, *Canada's Foreign Policy: Principles and Priorities for the Future* (Ottawa, 1995); Leslie A. Pal, 'Advocacy Organizations and Legislative Politics: The Effect of the Charter on Interest Group Lobbying over Federal Legislation, 1989–91,' in F. Leslie Seidle, ed., *Equity and Community: The Charter, Interest Advocacy and Representation* (Montreal, 1994), 119–57.

28. Henry J. Aaron, Thomas E. Mann, Timothy Taylor (eds.), *Values and Public Policy* (Washington, DC, 1994), 3.

29. Robert Putnam, *Making Democracy Work: Civic Traditions in Modern Italy* (Princeton, NJ, 1993).

30. James Q. Wilson, 'Culture, Incentives, and the Underclass,' in Henry J. Aaron, Thomas E. Mann, Timothy Taylor, eds., *Values and Public Policy* (Washington, DC, 1994), 75.

31. There is a mountain of literature on this, but see Alan Cairns, *The Charter versus Federalism* (Montreal, 1992).

32. Peter H. Russell, 'Canadian Constraints on Judicialization from Without,' *International Political Science Review* 15 (April 1994), 165–75.

33. Michael Mandel, *The Charter of Rights & the Legalization of Politics in Canada*, rev. ed. (Toronto, 1994); also F.L. Morton, 'The Charter Revolution and the Court Party,' *Osgoode Hall Law Journal* 30 (Fall 1992), 627–52.

34. Generally, see Sherene Razak, *Canadian Feminism and the Law* (Toronto, 1991).

35. Martha Jackman, 'Constitutional Contact with the Disparities in the World: Poverty as a Prohibited Ground of Discrimination Under the Canadian *Charter* and Human Rights Law,' *Review of Constitutional Studies* 2 (1994), 76–122; and Robert House, 'Another Rights Revolution? The Charter and the Reform of Social Regulation in Canada,' in Partick Grady, Robert House, Judith Maxwell, *Redefining Social Security* (Kingston, ON, 1995), 99–161.

36. Mary Ann Glendon, *Rights Talk: The Impoverishment of Political Discourse* (New York, 1991).

37. Pal, 'Advocacy Organizations and Legislative Politics.'

38. Radha Jhappan, 'A Global Community?: Supernational Strategies of Canada's Aboriginal Peoples,' Paper presented to the Annual Meeting of the Canadian Political Science Association, Charlottetown, PEI, 2 June 1992.

39. The Court Challenges Program was cancelled in 1993 by the former Conservative government but was reinstated by the Liberals after the federal election that year. The program is now delivered by an arm's length corporation called the Court Challenges Program of Canada, run by equality-seeking groups. The Directorate manages the contribution agreement with the corporation.

40. Keith Banting, 'A House Divided Against Itself,' in G. Bruce Doern, Leslie A. Pal, Brian Tomlin, eds., *Border Crossings: The Internationalization of Canadian Public Policy* (Toronto, 1996).

THE CANADA HEALTH
AND SOCIAL TRANSFER

ALLAN MOSCOVITCH

School of Social Work
Carleton University

On 1 April 1996, the Canada Assistance Plan (CAP) and the Established Programs Financing (EPF) passed into history.[1] They were replaced by a new federal funding mechanism called the Canada Health and Social Transfer (CHST).[2] Under the CHST, the federal government will provide a block grant to the provinces and territories for the funding of welfare, social services and child welfare, hospital and personal medical care, and postsecondary education.

CAP was the legislation through which the federal government has provided 50/50 open-ended conditional cost-sharing of agreed provincial social assistance and social services expenditures.[3] Notice of termination of the Canada Assistance Plan was given by the federal government in the February 1995 budget.[4] Through the EPF, the federal government has contributed funds to the provinces for postsecondary education, and for hospital and personal health care. EPF was converted from per capita to block funding in 1977 and renewed every five years since.

Although the financing and administration of health care and postsecondary education are important topics, here the focus will be on the social assistance and services portion of the new Canada Health and Social Transfer. The chapter opens with an explanation of the reason for the termination of the Canada Assistance Plan and the introduction of the Canada Health and Social Transfer. Three reasons are examined here. First, the purpose of the CHST is to terminate the standards of CAP funding that have limited the way the provinces can spend social service and assistance funding. The second reason is to divest control over social assistance and services to the provincial governments. A third reason is to limit federal funding of provincial social programs by terminating the open-ended cost-sharing features of the Canada Assistance Plan. Until agreement with the provinces is reached on an alternate funding formula, the federal government will allocate funds under the CHST. The next section explores how this will occur and what the implications are.

In establishing the CHST, the federal government has offered to negotiate social transfer standards with the provinces. What the federal government has so far stated and what the provinces appear to be offering as a basis for negotiation is covered in the next section of the chapter. A clear difference in the federal government's approach to standards for health care and for social services is also explored. Finally, the chapter reviews the possibilities for enforcement of whatever standards are agreed upon between the provinces and the federal government.

WHY IS THE FEDERAL GOVERNMENT TERMINATING CAP AND CREATING THE CHST?

The federal Finance Minister outlined his reasons for the termination of CAP and the creation of the CHST in the 1995 budget:

> At present transfers under the Canada Assistance Plan come with a lot of unnecessary strings attached. They limit the flexibility of the provinces to innovate. They increase the administrative costs. In short the cost-sharing approach of the past no longer helps the provinces, who have clear responsibility to design and deliver social assistance programs, to do so in a way that is as effective as possible and in tune with local needs.
>
> So we are prepared to address those issues by funding CAP in a similar way as we fund the existing EPF transfers for health and post-secondary education.[5]

STANDARDS FOR SOCIAL ASSISTANCE AND SERVICE

This statement requires some translation into plain language. First, when the Budget Speech says that the Canada Assistance Plan funds came with strings it is referring to the CAP standards for social assistance and social services. Several of these standards were in the CAP legislation while the rest were located in the regulations and in the manual which the Ministry of Health and

Welfare developed and used over the past thirty years to administer CAP.

Under Part 1 of the Canada Assistance Plan each province and territory receiving funds agreed to:

- provide social assistance to any person in the province who is in need;
- *not* require a period of residence in the province as a condition of eligibility;
- establish a social assistance appeals procedure within one year of the signing of the agreement;
- account for all spending on social assistance and welfare services in the province;
- supply copies of all relevant provincial Acts and Regulations to the Federal government.

CAP introduced the principle that social assistance be available to applicants in need regardless of their personal characteristics. To assess need, provinces had to account for an applicant's budgetary requirements and the income and resources available to him to meet them.[6] This test of needs also became an administrative standard.

CAP prohibited the provinces from requiring social assistance applicants to accept employment *as a condition of receiving assistance*. While based on federal interpretation and enforcement, this too has become a 'standard' of social assistance administration. The CAP guidelines limited the earned income that recipients could keep without penalty and the assets that they could hold and still be eligible for assistance. These guidelines were also considered 'standards.'

Lastly, CAP introduced cost sharing for welfare services, which would lessen, remove, or prevent the cause of poverty, child neglect, or dependence on public assistance.[7] The list in the Act included rehabilitation, casework, counselling, assessment and referral, adoption, homemaker, daycare, and community development services.[8] This was the first federal funding for welfare services and was a key reason for the expansion of the social services since the 1960s.

The new Canada Health and Social Transfer will have three components—postsecondary education, health care, and social assistance and services. The social assistance and services portion of the CHST which was replaced has only one standard—all provinces and territories receiving funds under the CHST must ensure that they not impose a residence requirement on social assistance applicants or recipients.[9] To qualify for the social portion of the CHST, the provinces will have only to ensure that residence is not a condition of eligibility for financial support. This is the only national standard for social assistance and social services set out in Bill C-76, the budget implementation legislation that became law on 6 June 1995.[10]

This standard is more limited than it appears since it will only apply to social assistance and not to social services. On the latter, the provinces will be free to set their own standards. For example, otherwise eligible applicants could be denied a childcare subsidy on the grounds that they have not lived in the province previously. It is less clear if social service programs that are tied to social assistance administration could be restricted by province of residence. Will a disabled person not on welfare who changes provinces be able to access supplementary medical services that may be available through social assistance administration? Will a low-income senior who is not receiving welfare be able to move and access dental services? Since the CAP manual has been thrown away, and the federal government has disbanded the Cost Shared Programs Branch that administered CAP, who will decide and how will they do so?[11]

The health care component will have standards—the five standards of the Canada Health Act. It is worth quoting what the Minister of Finance had to say about standards for health care: 'There are national goals and principles we believe must still apply, and which the vast majority of Canadians support. Our goal must be to combine greater flexibility with continued fidelity to those principles....The conditions of the Canada Health Act will be maintained. Universality, comprehensiveness, accessibility, portability, and public administration....For this government, those are fundamental.'[12]

The postsecondary education component has never had standards associated with it. Since the switch to block funding in 1977, provinces have not been required to spend the funds on postsecondary education. The grant has simply been another way of transferring funds to the provinces. No change was suggested in the 1995 budget to add standards for the postsecondary education portion of the CHST.

What is not explained is why the federal government will continue to impose national standards for health care, no less a provincial responsibility than social assistance, while the full range of CAP standards for social assistance and social services will not be imposed. Neither will it introduce standards for the provision of postsecondary education by the provinces. Instead, the federal government will drop all but one of the national standards for social assistance and services, while leaving open the possibility that through discussions with the provinces it will arrive at a set of 'shared principles and objectives' for the CHST.[13]

DIVESTING CONTROL OF SOCIAL ASSISTANCE AND SERVICES TO THE PROVINCES

The phrase in the 1995 Budget Speech that designates the province as the body with 'clear responsibility to design and deliver social assistance' is also an important one. Here the federal government is indicating that it is willing to fully divest responsibility for social assistance, an area which the provinces have historically claimed. Social assistance has always been administered by the provinces and municipalities. What changed was the introduction of several federal conditional grant programs to share the cost of the provinces providing income assistance to specific categories of deserving persons. The first of these was the Old Age Pension, established in 1927. It was later converted to a universal pension in legislation in 1951.

Between 1951 and 1956, the federal government implemented a series of measures to cost share provincial social assistance for persons with disabilities and for the unemployed. In 1966, the Canada Assistance Plan combined these measures into one piece of legislation, but it also added cost sharing for single mothers previously assisted by provincial mother's allowances and for anyone else in need. CAP also provided cost sharing for social services.

Why now the sudden interest in divestiture? Two reasons are apparent, the two main concerns of the 1995 budget: Quebec and the deficit.[14] Divestiture gives back to all the provinces, including Quebec, the full authority for social assistance. They will not be restricted by Canada Assistance Plan standards nor will they be accountable to the federal government for how they spend the federal share of social assistance and social service funding.

Divestiture also makes easier the reduction of a major slice of federal social expenditures. It is expenditure control that is the primary issue for the federal government. The open-ended cost sharing of the Canada Assistance Plan made it impossible for the federal government to control a substantial portion of its expenditures since social assistance payments have depended on the willingness of each province to support its unemployed and poor people. In future, regardless of the need, the federal government is off the hook once it transfers $25.1 billion; it will be the provinces that will be solely responsible for the poor.

TERMINATING COST SHARING OF SOCIAL ASSISTANCE AND SERVICES

The Minister of Finance noted that the primary purpose of the 1995 budget was to deal with the debt and deficit. He also made clear that raising taxes was not his preferred way of proceeding: 'Our budget must focus on cutting spending—not raising taxes.'[15]

If we accept the logic that the deficit is to be reduced and taxes are not raised to do it, then the conclusion is that spending must be cut. As the Minister notes, the introduction of the CHST is also and equally about expenditure reduction: 'Our major transfers to the provinces currently amount to $37 billion in cash and tax point. The cash portion alone represents about 21 per cent of our total programs spending....Addressing our fiscal challenge simply does not allow us to leave that spending untouched.'[16]

block funding is a sum, $. all may initially be set on basis of per capita transfers, but not later ⟵

The combined CAP and EPF payments were estimated in the budget to be $29.4 billion for 1994–5. These payments will be reduced by $2.5 billion in 1996–7 to $26.9 billion and by roughly another $2.0 billion in 1997–8 to $25.1 billion.[17] The withdrawal of $7 billion in funding represents a 23.6 percent decline in social transfers to the provinces over a two-year period. Under the plan outlined in the 1996 budget, the CHST will be maintained at the 1997–8 levels for the years 1998–9 and 1999–00. Subsequently, CHST funding levels are projected to be increased to $27.4 billion in 2002–3.[18]

Since 1989–90 the Canadian economy has been in a recession with relatively high rates of unemployment prevailing. At the same time, changes to unemployment insurance to reduce the value of benefits as well as a growth in the number of claimants who have exhausted their benefits has led to substantial increases in the numbers of welfare recipients. Consequently, on the social assistance side, 1994–5 social assistance expenditures were at a relatively high level. They form a large base from which the federal government is withdrawing funds. However, the ceiling placed on Canada Assistance Plan funding in British Columbia, Alberta, and Ontario in 1990 has already effected a significant reduction in the level of total federal payments to the provinces.

Social assistance, it should be remembered, is a demand-driven program. The numbers of social assistance recipients are closely related to unemployment and the general health of the economy. The federal reduction of expenditures on the former EPF and CAP programs will make for difficult choices even for provincial governments that have the political will to maintain the living conditions of people who are obligated to resort to social assistance. For provinces eager to reduce welfare budgets they will have an added incentive to do so: reductions in the federal funding for social programs. Either way, the choices facing the province are to pay an increased share of the costs of maintaining the unemployed, single parents, and disabled persons or to reduce the level of benefits and/or eligibility for social assistance or some combination of the two.

The shift to block funding will also remove any incentive to the federal government to undertake economic policies that would improve welfare recipients' chances for employment. Block funding means never having to take financial responsibility for the poor. In this respect, in the name of deficit, debt, and provincial rights, the welfare state has been returned to the pre-1956 period when the level of government with primary responsibility for economic policy had no corresponding responsibility for Canada's poor. The negotiation of some additional standards will not alter what is a fundamental change in the nature of Canadian federalism undertaken in the name of expenditure reduction.

How Will the CHST Allocate Funds to the Provinces?

For 1996–7, payments under the CHST will be allocated to the provinces according to the proportion of provincial entitlement to EPF and CAP payments in 1995–6. As Mendelson points out, this will result in anomalies; Quebec's per capita payments will be $1001, while those of a have-not province like New Brunswick will be $901. Other have-not provinces such as Prince Edward Island will be at $906 per capita and Newfoundland will be at $942 per capita. As a result of the freezing of the ceiling on CAP funds introduced in 1990, the so-called have provinces will be grouped between $840 for Alberta to $877 for British Columbia.

The allocation for 1997–8 and subsequent years is still to be negotiated.[19] It is clear that a move to average per capita funding will provide a substantial increase to the have provinces without regard to the costs of social assistance in the province nor to the impact of federal government monetary and fiscal policy.

In the 1994 Budget Speech the federal government committed itself to a reform of the social security system in Canada. One of the objectives of the reform was 'to restore greater fairness in federal support for the whole system throughout Canada.' No indication was given of what a fairer system would look like. It is possible that when the allocation for 1997–8, is actually negotiated with the provinces, a 'fairer system' of financing social programs will emerge.

But how does a 23.6 percent reduction in federal transfers represent the route to a fairer system? This reduction will provide at least some provinces with an imperative to make substantial cuts in the funding for the most disadvantaged, social assistance recipients. Whether another approach to the distribution of the CHST will be taken has so far not been indicated. Should funds be distributed on an equal per capita basis? Should funds be weighted to the poor provinces? Should account be taken of the changing demands on the provinces, using regional unemployment or changes in unemployment as an index of weighting?

The shift to a block grant insulates the federal government from the effects of a policy of favouring the reduction of inflation over the reduction of unemployment. Should the federal government with authority for and responsibility for employment and economic growth pay more if its policies lead to an increasing cost of social assistance to the provinces? These are the types of questions that should be raised in any subsequent negotiations on the methods of payment.

PRINCIPLES AND OBJECTIVES FOR
SOCIAL ASSISTANCE

The government did commit to inviting representatives of the provinces to participating in a process of 'developing through mutual consent, a set of shared principles and objectives that could underlie the new Canada (Health and) Social Transfer.'[20] Little progress toward this end has as yet been made. In December 1995 a joint provincial and territorial Ministerial Council on Social Policy Reform and Renewal released a report that they intend will be a part of a larger process of reform of federal–provincial relations in social policy. The document has two key elements: a Statement of Principles and a Framework and Agenda for Change and Renewal. Neither element is specifically meant to address the issue of principles and objectives for the social transfer component of the CHST. Instead, the purpose of the document is to provide a basis of review of the federal–provincial division of authority and funding for social welfare policy.

The Statement of Principles to Guide Social Policy Reform and Renewal contained in the document has four central themes:

- social programs must be accessible and serve the basic needs of all Canadians;
- social programs must reflect our individual and collective responsibility;
- social programs must be affordable, effective, and accountable; and
- social programs must be flexible, responsive, and reasonably comparable across Canada.[21]

Would these general principles be valuable 'principles and objectives' for the CHST? Certainly it is important for social assistance to be accessible and serve the basic needs of Canadians although it is not clear if this is the same thing as the CAP principle that income assistance be available to everyone who is demonstrably in need. Does serving basic needs require a test of needs or would it permit a reversion to the older means test? That is, would applicants be asked about their income only (a test of means) or would they also be asked about their expenditures (a test of needs)?

While only a few would dispute that social programs should reflect both individual and collective responsibilities, the principle is too abstract for administration. For example, under this principle could recipients be asked to treat welfare as a loan—part of their responsibility being to repay their welfare cheques? It appears that almost any form of administration could be justified since neither the responsibilities of the collectivity nor the individual are stated.

Social programs should be publicly accountable and transparent. Is this what is meant? Accountability was an important part of the CAP regime. Social assistance should certainly be effective but as a standard this one would be impossible since there is so much ideological debate about what effectiveness means. For example, in one of the most prominent disputes in the welfare field in the United States, the Democrat-sponsored Employment Training (ET) program in the state of Massachusetts was a very effective program; however, the state Republicans were convinced that it was not. They disputed its success and cost and believed that they could be more effective with a more punitive approach that did not provide as much state assistance. As soon as they came to power in 1991 they cancelled the program, installed senior administrators hostile to the program, and introduced much more punitive measures. If they were both effective, then the principle is trivial.

Certainly social programs should be affordable, but it is hard to understand this as a standard for administration unless the point is that there should be an income security fund provided through a tax. This may be an idea whose time has come in Canada. But affordability is only meaningful in relation to adequacy and eligibility. Who is eligible and how much they get determines how much the social assistance administration spends. Social assistance should also be affordable in a different sense—it should afford those who are dependent on it a decent standard of living and a decent opportunity to get training, social services, and other support to move on in their lives. This is not a principle that is evident in the provincial list, but it is the most important one from the point of view of the individual or family dependent on social assistance.

Social programs should also be flexible; an inflexible regime is difficult to administer with sensitivity. But is flexibility simply a code word for permitting the introduction of more punitive measures that have been prohibited by CAP, such as work for welfare? These programs should also be responsive but to whom? One would hope that they would be responsive to the client.

Social assistance should also be reasonably comparable across the country. This is an important concession from provincial politicians who for many years have consistently opposed making data publicly available for provincial comparisons despite the CAP reporting requirements. But what is reasonable? Within a standard percentage of the poverty line? But will all the provinces accept the Statistics Canada low-income cut-offs as the standard?

The provincial statement would need some work were the themes to be the basis for standards in the CHST legislation. Admittedly, the themes were developed for what the provinces anticipated would be a wider review of federal provincial responsibilities. In relation to the CAP standards what is missing is a commitment to need as the main criterion for benefit and for administration, and to due process and appeal. What was missing in CAP and here as well is a fundamental commitment to adequacy.

If the provinces *and* the federal government could come up with agreed upon principles, the federal government would have to amend Bill C-76, the budget implementation legislation, if the principles are to have the force of law. Clause 13.1.d of the legislation makes clear the federal government has already determined it will promote whatever principles and objectives are agreed on. However, promote is not the same as maintain or enforce. The federal government's intention does not appear to be adding additional enforceable standards.[22]

DIFFERENT STANDARDS FOR HEALTH AND FOR SOCIAL ASSISTANCE

Why the difference in approach between health and social assistance and services? Health and social assistance and services are each no less provincial responsibilities, but only in the case of social assistance does the government consider the reduction of standards appropriate; social services do not appear even to have been considered. The answer to the question lies in the politics of public policy. Universal health care is popular. Any government that abandoned national standards while provincial governments have been attempting to dismantle health care benefits would lose popularity. Health care recipients could be anyone. An illness is not regarded as the fault of the person.

Social assistance is not popular. Social assistance recipients are regarded by many as someone else, someone who is responsible for their own unemployment. Events like the Great Depression made many people aware of their own dependence on the vagaries of the economy and the labour market. Those in need ceased for many to be regarded as personally at fault. The present generation of politicians and business leaders grew up in a time of plenty. They have not had the experience of mass unemployment nor of strikes and marches that forced their predecessors to take action. In this sense, it is the very effectiveness of the welfare state that has created the conditions for the belief that it is politically beneficial to reduce expenditures on social assistance and other income-support programs.

In the 1960s and 1970s, social equality was regarded as a virtue and greed a vice. In the public sector this was translated into left-leaning governments and the construction of the contemporary welfare state. Social programs were the solution to the problem of maintaining employment and sharing the growing wealth. Social programs could be generous since unemployment was low and expected to remain so.

Without doing a history of the last twenty years, by the mid-1980s business organizations had made inflation the number one problem, followed closely by the size of the budgetary deficit and public debt. The imposition of the

Bank of Canada's zero inflation monetary policy led to a rise in levels of unemployment. The latter has led to increasing demand for income support from the social programs—particularly unemployment insurance and social assistance—which are intended to provide for people who are unemployed. Without the tax revenues to pay for the increased cost of unemployment, reductions in social program conditions and in social expenditures have been viewed as a key part of the solution to the problem of deficits.

Attitudes to social assistance do appear to be fluctuating. The bill for social assistance has been rising rapidly. Recipients, in the eyes of some, are overrepresented by the workshy and the fraudulent. Social assistance is cited repeatedly by business organizations as a form of spending that should be reduced. Social assistance is in the midst of a cycle of unpopularity. Some provincial governments have been pressing the federal government for many years to loosen the rules to permit workfare; others have been elected to get tough on welfare. In these circumstances, and boxed in by the policy of the Bank of Canada and the expectation of the business institutions that offered them electoral and financial support, the federal government is in the process of sacrificing the poor on the altar of debt and deficit.

THE CANADA ASSISTANCE PLAN, THE CHST, AND WORKFARE

CAP's standards included the requirement that the provinces and territories *not* require recipients to take a job as a *condition* of receiving social assistance. It is this standard that is the key. Several of the provinces have been pressing the federal government for more than ten years to permit cost sharing of workfare—compulsory work for welfare.[23] They believe, without sufficient evidence, that there are substantial numbers of lazy and fraudulent recipients on welfare. Workfare will teach the workshy a lesson, that if they go on welfare then they can expect life to be more painful. Workfare is also supposed to teach work skills and lead to a job. But the conclusion from previous efforts at workfare in the United States and Canada is that it is not effective at increasing employability without putting more resources to work. And the point of workfare for some provincial governments is to cut expenditures, not to increase them.[24]

ENFORCEMENT OF STANDARDS

Several commentators have already noted that enforcement of even the one social assistance standard of the CHST could be rendered impossible if the cash portion of the transfer disappears at some point in the future.[25] In the recent 1996 budget, the federal government has indicated that it will in future maintain a minimum cash grant to the provinces. It is promising that for the period from 1998–9 to 2002–3, it will provide 'a legislated guarantee that the cash component of the transfer will never be lower than $11 billion at any time during this period.'[26]

How they will accomplish this is not clear. The federal government estimates that the value of the 1997–8 cash transfer will be $12.3 billion falling to $11.1 billion in 1999–00 and in 2000–1. At the same time, the Department of Finance expects to stabilize the value of the CHST at $25.1 billion during this period.[27]

The CHST (the combined CAP/EPF entitlement) is equal to the total of the provincial tax point transfer and the cash transfer. Without increases in the total entitlement, the rising value of the tax points would likely lead to a reduction in the cash transfer. The Caledon Institute estimates that the cash portion of the combined EPF/CAP transfer to the provinces would be $10.3 billion by 1997–8 and without changes in the funding formula it would decline further after that.[28] It appears that in order to set a floor on the cash portion and a ceiling on the level of CHST entitlement, the federal government would have little choice but to unilaterally alter that method of distributing tax points. If it is prepared to do that, why did it not consider a reduction in the value of the tax point for noncompliance?

Is this guarantee of a cash floor an important concession? Not really. While the federal government is guaranteeing a floor on the cash transfers, it will not be increasing CHST funding until the year 2000. In the meantime, a drastic funding reduction will have been translated, in most instances, by provincial governments into significant reductions in the level of support available to the poor. Further, the existence of a cash transfer will have little meaning for the administration of provincial social assistance without significant legislative standards. The 1996 budget gave no indication of any change in this respect. As we have seen with the changes to CAP in 1990 and its termination in 1995, promises incorporated in legislation mean little to future governments determined to effect a further reduction in social program funding. What is important is only what governments do in 1999, not what they promise to do now.

CONCLUSION

Why then is the federal government replacing the Canada Assistance Plan with the social portion of the Canada Health and Social Transfer? Of the three reasons cited, the principal reason appears to be the federal government's determination to limit its social expenditures.[29] Why social expenditures have become a target has been the subject of several recent books. Without reviewing the literature here, it is worth noting several of the key issues. There is no doubt that in the 1980s the number of persons supported by social assistance has grown dramatically. In 1980 at the beginning of the decade the number of persons receiving social assistance was 1.418 million people. This number rose to 1.894 million in 1983 and as a result of the recession of the early 1980s. It did not significantly decline after the recession was over. In 1987 at the peak of the mini boom of the 1980s the numbers were still at 1.853 million people. At the end of the 1980s a deeper more profound recession manifested, with an impact on employment exacerbated by the underlying changes in the labour market and by the federal government's monetary policy and abandonment of full employment as an economic and social policy.[30] These are the major explanations for why by 1992 nationwide there were 2.723 million people receiving social assistance.

It is important to understand that these numbers are not an indication of a profound problem with the Canada Assistance Plan or social assistance administration across the country. There were problems to be addressed, but in general the social assistance system and the Canada Assistance Plan, which provided the framework for it, were doing what they are supposed to: providing minimum income to people in need, a floor of support below which no one should fall during a period of economic recession and high unemployment.

Why then the demand for reform? Why the claims that the welfare system is not working and the perennial claims of widespread fraud? The demands and concerns have little to do with the workings of the welfare system. They have to do with deeply conflicting views about human nature held by many in society. On the one hand, there are those who believe that the poor should be taken care of; on the other, there are those who believe that the poor are themselves responsible for their condition. In good times many people believe that the poor are deserving because they are subject to forces greater than themselves, but when social expenditures rise dramatically, sympathy for the poor alters and many come to believe that if only the poor were more responsible and worked harder to help themselves then government could cut down on costs.

The view that the poor are lazy, undisciplined, and therefore responsible for their own fate has been with us for a long time. It is a part of the Poor Law tradition that predated the Canada Assistance Plan. The Canada Assistance Plan was planned and developed in the 1960s to put the Poor Law behind us in favour of a citizenship approach in which people in need have the right to access income assistance. The accomplishments of the Canada Assistance Plan should not be ignored or forgotten in the rush to reform governmental finances.

The Canada Health and Social Transfer, which has replaced the Canada Assistance Plan, will take away much more than funding. It will take away the national framework for the administration of social assistance. It will also take away any financial cost to the federal government for economic policies that emphasize the reduction of inflation over the reduction of unemployment. With the CAP framework gone, and with no discernable reason why the provinces and the federal government should come to an agreement under the CHST, the strongest likelihood is that they will not. Instead, the range of difference between provinces will likely widen as governments undertake a range of social experiments with welfare recipients. At least some provincial governments seem determined to see whether more punitive conditions for social assistance will drive more people from the province. Undoubtedly, if this does occur, then there will be increased tension between provinces over welfare and residence.

Far from accomplishing the renewal of social programs as they promised, the federal government will have created the conditions for the dismemberment of what was once a national minimum income program. Until the 1990s and while social welfare remained popular with business and the public, the Liberal Party has repeatedly presented itself as the party that created the welfare state. Will they be so proud to present themselves as the party that did more to dismantle it than any other since the 1960s?

NOTES

I wish to thank John Stapleton, Graham Richies, Richard Splane, and an anonymous reviewer for their comments on earlier drafts of this paper. I alone am responsible for the opinions expressed and any errors that remain.

1. According to Bill C-76, the 1995 budget implementation legislation passed by the House of Commons on 6 June 1995, the Canada Assistance Plan will actually be formally repealed on 31 March 2000. See section 32. This is simply to allow five years to wrap up the outstanding federal obligations under the Canada Assistance Plan. Under Section 31 no payments can be made for fiscal years beyond 1 April 1996.
2. The 1995 budget referred to the creation of a Canada Social Transfer but the implementation legislation refers to a Canada Health and Social Transfer. See Paul Martin, Minister of Finance, *Budget Speech* (Ottawa, 27 Feb. 1995) 18 and Part V of Bill C-76, the budget implementation legislation.
3. For an explanation of the operation of the Canada Assistance Plan, see A. Moscovitch, 'The Canada Assistance Plan: A Twenty Year Assessment,' in K. Graham, ed., *How Ottawa Spends, 1988–89* (Ottawa, 1988).
4. Martin, *Budget Speech*, 1995, 17–19. The Canada Assistance Plan required one year's notice on either side for termination or change. In 1990, the federal government unilaterally changed the Canada Assistance Plan to limit the funding to the provinces of Ontario, Alberta, and BC. BC took the federal government to court over unilateral change without notice. The court rules that Parliament is supreme; the federal government may make changes at will and cannot be tied by such legislative clauses.
5. Martin, *Budget Speech*, 1995, 17.
6. Canada Assistance Plan, 713.
7. Canada Assistance Plan, 711.
8. Canada Assistance Plan, Section 2; 'welfare services,' and 'welfare services provided in the province.'
9. The standards are outlined in section 13 and 19 of Bill C-76, 6 June 1995, the Act to Implement Certain Provisions of the Budget Tabled in Parliament, 27 Feb. 1995. The explanation contained

in the background papers to the recent federal budget was written by someone who does not understand the one social assistance standard that will prevail. The text suggests that the prohibition against a residence requirement applies only to 'social assistance recipients who move from one province to another.' (See Paul Martin, Minister of Finance, *The Budget in Brief*, 6 March 1996, 12.) It does not. A reading of the government's own legislation suggests that the restriction will apply to *recipients* and *applicants*. It is an important distinction. Perhaps the Finance Department Staff should consider talking to someone over in Human Resources Development who understands the difference. There are still a few left.

10. Bill C-76, the budget implementation legislation, makes this point clear in section 13.1.c, 24.

11. The government has already decided to test the application of the residence principle by declaring that it will continue to require welfare applications to have lived in the province for three months before applying.

12. Martin, *Budget Speech*, 1995, 18.

13. Ibid.

14. Martin, *Budget Speech*, 1995, 2.

15. Martin, *Budget Speech*, 1995, 7.

16. Martin, *Budget Speech*, 1995, 18.

17. Martin, *Budget Speech*, 1996, 31. See also Michael Mendelson, 'Looking for Mr. Good-Transfer; A Guide to the CHST Negotiations' (Caledon Institute for Social Policy, 1995), 3.

18. Martin, *Budget Speech*, 1996, 10–11, 31.

19. Mendelson, 'Looking for Mr. Good-Transfer,' 6–7.

20. Martin, *Budget Speech*, 1995, 18. The author has added the words in brackets. The name of the block grant was changed to the Canada Health and Social Transfer when it appeared in legislation later in 1995.

21. Ministerial Council on Social Policy Reform and Renewal, *Report to Premiers,* December 1995, 1.

22. See Michael Mendelson, 'Establishing a Social Investment Framework,' in Canadian Council on Social Development, *Roundtables on the Canada Health and Social Transfer, Report,* January 1996, 131–2.

23. The 1985 Federal Provincial Agreement on Enhancement of Employment Opportunities for Social Assistance Recipients was a method of diverting CAP dollars to provinces that instituted programs to take welfare recipients off welfare and put them into employment training programs. The argument for the agreements went like this. If a provincial training program keeps someone off welfare then the province loses the federal government's 50 percent of the funding for the person were they on welfare. Therefore, the provinces wanted the federal government to ante up on the foregone cost sharing. This is what the federal government agreed to do rather than activate or amend the work activity section of CAP. Agreements under the work activity section of CAP must include a clause stating that 'no person shall be denied assistance because he refuses or has refused to take part in a work activity project.' (Canada Assistance Plan, C-1, 1966–7, 724.)

24. The C.D. Howe Institute recently released its contribution to the workfare debate entitled *Helping the Poor: A Qualified Case for Workfare* (Toronto, 1995). It was joined by the Institute for Research on Public Policy (IRPP), which produced *Workfare: Does it Work? Is it Fair?* (Montreal, 1995). An earlier IRPP volume, *Income Security in Canada: Changing Needs, Changing Means* (Montreal, 1993), contained several articles on workfare including one by Judith Gueron, a leading U.S. scholar, on workfare in the United States. She cautions against the search for simple solutions to complex problems and notes that where welfare to work as been successful it has too often left the former welfare recipient working full-time but still poor.

25. See for example, Caledon Institute, 'Lest We Forget: Why "Canada Needs Strong Social programs,"' November 1995, 4; Mendelson, 'Looking for Mr. Good-Transfer,' 4; Caledon Institute, Constitutional Reform by Stealth,' May 1995.

26. Martin, *Budget Speech*, 1996, 11.

27. Martin, *The Budget in Brief*, 1996, 12, chart 3.

28. M. Mendelson, 'Looking for Mr. Good-Transfer,' 4.

29. The material in this section is based on my Brief to the House of Commons Committee on Human Resources Development, Ottawa, 1994 and on a background paper prepared by Allan Moscovitch and Leon Muszynski, 'Mr. Axworthy's Green Paper on Social Security,' prepared for the Communications Energy and Paperworkers Union, November, 1994.

30. See, for example, Linda McQuaig, *Shooting the Hippo* (Toronto, 1995).

PART TWO

Change in Historical Perspective

T HE WELFARE STATE IN CANADA IS A RELATIVELY MODERN CREATION.
Although colonial governments in New France and in British North
America offered limited assistance to the most destitute of their citizens, Canada's welfare state emerged, albeit piecemeal, only in the period
following the Second World War. Despite the short history, those involved in
the current debates about the nature of the welfare state in Canada must realize that an understanding of the past is crucial as the country wrestles with the
thorny question of reforming Canada's current social security system.
Canadians have come to see the social safety net that has been put in place by
both the federal and provincial governments as one of the most important
elements in their society. Not surprisingly then, the debate over the past few
years on Canada's social security programs has been acrimonious. Yet, most of
those involved in the debate have often ignored the origins of the various
programs and have failed to consider the circumstances and reasons behind
the introduction of programs as varied as medicare, the Canada/Quebec
Pension Plans, unemployment insurance, and a diverse group of others. As
contemporary Canada wrestles with a fundamental re-invention of the welfare
state in the face of fiscal restraint and the restructuring of governments, the
historical development of Canada's social security system offers considerable
insight if not guidance to the public and policymakers alike. The essays in this
section suggest that we might consider change in a historical perspective as
many of the problems and crises that we see in contemporary Canada have
been addressed in the past.

This is particularly true of the apparent impending crisis with a rapidly
aging population about which we hear so much these days. Edgar-Andre
Montigny reminds us that this is not a new concern in Canada. He claims that
a study of Ontario's nineteenth-century policies concerning the relationship of
the family to the state for the care of the dependent aged 'can reveal much
about the potential impact of social reforms upon the aged and their families
today.' In a thoughtful essay that examines the fiscal crisis that faced the

government of Ontario in the early 1890s, Montigny reminds us that more than a century ago governments were also concerned about the impact of an aging population on the ability of the welfare state to provide for its citizens. In that earlier period of fiscal restraint, the government of Ontario redefined 'the boundary between state responsibilities and family obligations.' The government socially constructed a crisis of the aged, he claims, who were often the most visible beneficiaries of public support. The government of Ontario decided that it had to 'abdicate much of its responsibilities for caring for aged people,' and, in the interests of restraint and austerity, it forced families to assume primary responsibility for the care of the dependent elderly. Such policies, Montigny concludes, often did little to meet the genuine needs of the aged, their families, or the state, but in the name of financial exigencies this has not prevented governments from frequently trying to redefine the boundary between state responsibilities and family and individual obligations to reduce expenditures on social welfare. In the current fiscal crisis, when governments are again asking Canadians to reconsider the role of the family in providing care and support in areas that we have come to expect the state to provide, Montigny's essay is instructive.

Shirley Tillotson from the Department of History at Dalhousie University is interested in a similar question. As she points out, many fiscal conservatives suggest that the governments must reduce taxation, play a more limited role in the delivery of social services, and encourage greater community involvement in caring and giving. Too much government involvement, they further maintain, has fostered selfishness and individualism. In her essay on the relationship between charitable fundraising and the origins of the welfare state, Tillotson argues that fundraising for the Community Chests—the federated appeals along the lines of the contemporary United Way campaigns—served to educate 'the mass of Canadians and not just the social elite in the ways of a modern, rationalized system of funding social services.' The Community Chest movement from the 1920s onward helped create a new conception of the taxpayer willing to fund an expanded state. Her evidence clearly shows that even as Canadians paid an increasingly larger proportion of their earnings in income tax to support an expanded welfare state, the federated charities also proposed and expanded. Rather than a defining competitive relation between public and private provision for welfare needs, Tillotson sees a mutually reinforcing one.

Geoffrey E. Hale continues with the dichotomy between the public and private realms in his discussion of Marc Lalonde's pension reforms of 1982–4. While reminding us that pension reform and concerns about the Canadian and Quebec Pension Plans are not new to Canadians, Hale asks if there are 'lessons that can be learned from [pension reform in the early 1980s] that can usefully be applied to the current debate over pension reform'? After examining the various factors and issues that influenced the earlier debate about pension reform, he demonstrates that there are lessons to be learned from earlier attempts at social policy reform. Although he does not offer a prescription for the actors in the current round of pension reform, Hale warns social policy activists that it will be virtually impossible to implement reforms that ignore the current fiscal and economic realities and the fact of diminishing public expenditures. Social security policies, he claims, must be integrated with those that promote medium-term economic growth and job creation. And it is likely that the federal Department of Finance will take control of the pension debate. Above all, Hale concludes, current policymakers can learn from earlier attempts at pension reform that Ottawa and the provinces must pursue 'a strategy of purposeful, incremental change [that] is more likely to be more productive than grand strategies for the recasting of large elements of social policy.'

James Struthers, perhaps the leading historian of the welfare state in Canada, returns to the subject of the elderly introduced in Montigny's article and elaborates on the relationship between the state and the voluntary sectors that Tillotson introduces. In his essay on state regulation of private nursing homes in Ontario after the Second World War, Struthers shows how the aged increased substantially in number after 1940 and the difficulties the state faced in providing institutional care to those who required it. What emerged in Ontario was a series of private nursing homes that the state slowly and reluctantly incorporated into its regulatory regime. Struthers' study of nursing homes shows the relationship that has emerged in Canada between the public and private within welfare policy. As he reminds the reader, long-term care remains a rapidly growing island of private profit 'within a health care sector otherwise dominated by the much-celebrated expansion of public responsibility for hospital and medical insurance.' Even so, Struthers concludes 'however much government officials might rail against the arrogance, greed, or growing power of the nursing home lobby, in the final analysis they had nowhere else to place the elderly in need of care.' Struthers reminds us, too, of the often inadequate planning on the part of governments at various levels and how, in the case of nursing homes in Ontario, the public and private sectors became partners, albeit reluctantly, to deliver a social need.

In the final article in this section Dean Oliver, a postdoctoral research fellow at Carleton University in Ottawa, returns to the theme of the emergence of social welfare and veterans' legislation. History offers no guide through the present period, Oliver reminds us, but it does hold some cautionary tales. When Ottawa created a series of social programs in the 1940s, it was very much aware that public opinion favoured government playing a more active role in the area. Oliver presents a case study of veterans' legislation at the end of the

Second World War to explore the connection between public opinion and public policy in Canada. In a paper that examines the multiplicity of factors in the determination of government policy, he concludes that public opinion 'assumed enormous significance' in Canadian public policy on the demobilization and rehabilitation of war veterans. At an earlier time in Canada then, policymakers heeded public opinion in making social welfare policy, and it appears that public opinion remains an important factor—along with others, including bureaucratic imperatives, fiscal requirements, and ideology—in how governments at all levels deal with social policy reform.

Together, the contributors have tried to make a connection between the past and the present. They have shown that the welfare state in Canada has a history and that policymakers and those involved in the debate about the re-invention of the welfare state must attempt to understand change in a historical context. Canada's welfare state has become an important part of what it means to be Canadian and in the debate over the future of Canada's social safety net, it is important for all those engaged in this important process to remember that everything has a history and realize that understanding history is one of the first steps in understanding change.

BEEN THERE, DONE THAT

1890s Precedents to 1990s Social Policies
Affecting the Aged and their Families

EDGAR-ANDRE MONTIGNY

Canadian Studies
Trent University

FAMILY OBLIGATIONS AND THE STATE

From the 1890s to the present day, family obligations have often been the tool used by Western states to help enact various policy changes. This has been particularly true in cases where policies were modified in a manner that forced people to rely upon their families rather than the state when they found themselves in need.

This trend has been evident in Canadian social policy, especially those policies that affect the dependent elderly. Susan Watt argues that the state's interpretation of the family's responsibilities toward the aged have varied over time depending upon the condition of the state's treasury. Watts explains that in the construction of social policy, various models of family have been used. Each model carries with it certain assumptions about the role of the family in the care of its dependent members and the degree to which the state should assist families in their caring functions. When economic times are good, models that accept a large degree of state responsibility for the aged have been employed. In less optimistic economic circumstances, however, models that impose a much greater burden on the family have been initiated.[1]

For this reason, family obligations toward the aged become an especially prominent feature of government policy discussions during periods of fiscal restraint. As the government attempts to reduce its social welfare expenditures, the aged increasingly are spoken of as a 'social problem.' In relation to these discussions it is decided that families must do more if the state is to advert a 'crisis.' Over time these concerns evolve into debates over how the state can force families to assume their proper degree of responsibility for their aged kin.

In combination, the images of social problem, crisis, and family obligations become the justification for the implementation of policies that, to varying degrees, reduce social spending on services for the aged, restrict access to services for those aged people who have kin, or enforce various types of familial responsibility for the aged. It is within this framework that three popular myths emerge, namely the image of old age dependency, the idea that current population aging is unprecedented, and the idea that families somehow have ceased to carry their fair share of responsibility for the aged.

THE AGED AS A SOCIAL PROBLEM

The image of the aged as a social problem usually appears during periods of genuine or at least perceived population aging. Population aging and panic over an impending social crisis often go hand in hand. Yet, the portion of older people in a population does not necessarily have to be increasing for population aging to be perceived as a potential threat. This claim is supported by the findings of Brian Gratton, who studied the aged in the United States, and Jill Quadagno, who examined public policies towards the elderly in England. Both discovered that intense public concern over growth in the size of the aged population arose independently of any significant alterations in the demographic status of the elderly.[2] It is clear that the concept of the aged as a social problem is based more upon people's attitudes, perceptions, and assumptions than upon actual facts.[3] This is because, as Sheila McIntyre points out, a social problem consists of two components, an objective condition and a subjective definition. Once an issue is perceived to be a problem by the public, policymakers, or administrators, the objective condition is often of secondary importance.[4]

This subjective construction of population aging is obvious when one notes that even when populations have been truly aging, the increase in the numbers of old people in and of itself has not often been a cause for concern. The aged are not viewed as a social problem until it is also believed that most old people are destitute and dependent upon other people for their survival. Population aging, therefore, is not the problem. It is the increasing burden on the public purse that they allegedly represent which creates the social problem and the panic over an impending crisis. This trend becomes particularly evident during periods of fiscal restraint when the image of an increasing outlay of funds for a growing population of dependent old people causes policy officials to depict population aging or the aged themselves as a social problem.[5]

THE CRISIS OF A POPULATION AGING

Susan McDaniels argues that it is not by accident that demographic aging has emerged as an important guiding paradigm in recent Canadian public policy discussions and research, or that the aged have become a popular subject in magazines, newspaper articles, and talk shows.[6] Most importantly, the problem of our aging population has taken on greater significance as various government officials and public agencies have responded to the economic crisis that has dominated public policy debates in recent years. Herbert Northcott explains, this 'crisis' definition of population aging arises because it serves the interests of certain groups in society.[7] By creating or at least fuelling the fear that has come to characterize much of the public policy debate surrounding the provision of services for the elderly, governments can help generate public support for policies that involve reducing public spending on the aged.

Despite significant evidence attesting to the high levels of social and economic independence among the aged, much of the current literature on aging emphasizes the dependency of the elderly upon the state, highlighting their needs as recipients of various forms of welfare and social assistance.[8] Northcott argues that this may be because regardless of whether the conclusions have any relevance to those persons who are the object of discussion, the definition of the problem, namely population aging, and the proposed solutions, may serve the vested interests of the problem definers and the policy-makers.[9] Similarly, journalist Thomas Walkom suggests that vote-seeking politicians are guilty of enacting cost-cutting policies that target the elderly in response to 'simmering public resentment,' rather than because the facts reveal that such actions are necessary.[10]

This also explains why government officials and the media regularly equate growing numbers of aged people with growing numbers of dependent people. It is this equation in particular that creates a sense of panic concerning population aging and that permits commentators to depict every increase in the size of the aged population as an automatic cause for alarm because it is assumed that such growth will bring with it enormous penalties in terms of human suffering and financial costs.[11] This is what Northcott describes as population aging rhetoric. The primary goal of this type of information is to persuade and convince people rather than to inform them.[12] Only rarely does this rhetoric present objective information about current circumstances and historical trends.[13] Instead, the simple, but mistaken, translation of demographic projections into social realities is used to encourage the belief that the problem of social dependency exists just because the numbers in a particular age group are increasing.[14]

The truth is that the provision of services to the aged is not the problem. The real social problem is that Western economies are in a state of recession. Nevertheless, even if such arguments are not necessarily correct or based in empirical analysis, it is easy to convince the public that the aged are dependent upon the state and that they represent an unreasonable burden upon the public purse. What becomes more important than scientific validity or determination of causality, Susan McDaniels asserts, is the setting in place of population aging as the unifying explanatory framework for previously inexplicable or unlinked problems.[15] More importantly, this type of argument is used to justify public policies that cut back on services to the aged in the name of fiscal restraint and austerity.

It is widely recognized that the aged are particularly vulnerable in times of fiscal difficulties because they tend to be the largest single group in receipt of government assistance.[16] What is not so often mentioned is the degree to which the families of the aged are vulnerable. Government cut-backs in the realm of support for the aged often target those services that potentially can be provided by family members. Families, therefore, end up bearing the brunt of state initiatives that reduce the amount of money spent on the aged. In this sense, the entire discussion about population aging, old age dependency, and fiscal restraint can be interpreted as a debate over whether the family or the state maintains primary responsibility for the care of the dependent aged.[17] The problem with this debate is that it is guided by the image of the aged as a social problem, which as we have seen is socially constructed and, therefore, may bear little relation to the actual condition of the aged themselves. Hence, policies that are developed in this manner, especially those that redefine the relationship between the family and the state concerning the care of the aged, may not be based on reality. Consequently, they may do little to meet the genuine needs of the aged, their families, or the state.

This was certainly the case in Ontario a century ago. What is more striking, however, is the degree to which the situation in Ontario during the 1890s resembles that which exists today. The government of late–nineteenth-century

Ontario faced an economic crisis. It was felt that this crisis was largely because of the costs of providing overly generous social benefits to the population, and it became evident that spending in this area had to be reduced. Attention was focused in particular upon the aged, since they were the most visible beneficiaries of this system. It was assumed that the aged population was growing rapidly and among this population poverty, dependency, and infirmity were becoming steadily more widespread. In order to avert a crisis, it was decided that the government must abdicate much of its responsibility for caring for aged people. Instead, it was argued, families must bear a larger portion of the burden of providing for the elderly. This course of action was justified by using statistics and reports to demonstrate to the public that the aged had become a burden upon public funds mainly because their heartless families were 'foisting them upon the government.' Since few of these assumptions were based upon social or demographic realities, the cost-cutting measures initiated by the government, while they created much suffering among the aged population and their families, did little to solve the economic difficulties of the province. It is clear that a study of Ontario's nineteenth-century policies in the relationship of the family and the state concerning the care of the dependent aged can reveal much about the potential impact of social reforms upon the aged and their families today.

THE 1890S: THE GOVERNMENT PICTURE

During the last decade of the last century, the provincial government of Ontario faced a financial crisis.[18] As a result, the portion of the provincial budget allocated for social spending was reduced.[19] Even once a recovery was underway, social spending was not increased to keep up with the general growth in the economy. As a result, social spending, which represented 32.4 percent of provincial expenditures in 1893, made up only 14.7 percent of spending by 1911.

In 1893, expenditures on institutions, especially mental hospitals and government-funded charitable institutions such as County Houses of Industry and Houses of Refuge, accounted for over 71 percent of the social welfare budget.[20] This was up from 64 percent in 1878. This was largely because the 1890s was a period of institution building. In 1888 there were sixty-two provincially funded charitable institutions in Ontario. By 1901, there were nearly one hundred. In Houses of Refuge alone the number of beds almost doubled, increasing from 1,260 to 2,268. At the same time, almost two thousand new beds were added to provincial asylums for the insane. In total there was an

80 percent increase in the number of people who could be accommodated in a public institution.[21] Yet the demand for institutional care continued to grow. If social spending was to be limited, it was obvious that this demand had to be curtailed.

In order to reduce the demand for institutional care, the government focused on the fastest-growing institutional population, the elderly. In 1888, elderly people accounted for less than half of the residents of the province's County Houses of Industry,[22] and fewer than 15 percent of the province's asylum population.[23] By the late 1890s the aged constituted approximately 80 percent of the population of Ontario's Houses of Refuge and 70 percent of the province's County Houses of Industry. The aged also formed a larger portion of total admissions to asylums for the insane.[24] It seemed to officials that there was no end to the number of aged people who required institutional care.

Officials argued that this growth in the number of aged people requiring institutional care meant two things. The aged population was growing rapidly, and poverty was becoming an increasingly dominant factor in the lives of these aged people.[25] As well as being poor, the aged who were found inside institutions were usually feeble, infirm, or senile. It was clear to institutional administrators that physical and mental incapacity were necessary attributes of old age. Government reports, therefore, announced that both the financial and physical dependency of the old were expanding rapidly and that they would continue to expand at an ever increasing rate. A major social crisis was predicted.

This crisis was blamed upon families. The main explanation officials advanced for the increase in the number of aged people needing care was that families were using institutions as a means of evading their obligations toward the aged. As institutional administrators noted, the care of the aged was becoming 'an enormous tax upon the state,'[26] largely because families were heartlessly shirking their responsibilities toward the aged and 'foisting them upon the government.'[27] It was also evident to these officials that the: 'very liberality of the government in providing such ample accommodations at cheap rates, or even free, acts as a powerful stimulus in deciding to transfer the burden from the home to the state.'[28] When it came to the care of the aged, therefore, officials argued that the government was being called upon with increasing frequency to assume burdens that 'in all fairness, should be carried by the people.'[29]

It was clear to the government that if spending on institutional care was to be kept in check, the admission of aged persons would have to be curtailed. Irresponsible families would have to be forced to carry out their proper obligations. Officials argued that institutional care had to be limited to help recreate the sense of familial obligation between children and their parents that had been destroyed by the availability of overly generous public relief. As a result, aged people found it increasingly difficult to gain entry into provincial institutions. Old people with relatives were often denied access to institutional care on the grounds that they could be 'easily cared for at home.' Aged people already inside an institution could be ejected if it was discovered that they had relatives whom it was assumed could care for them. By the late 1890s, therefore, only aged people with no family were considered candidates for institutional care.

It does not seem unreasonable that a government faced with a fiscal crisis would restrict people's access to public care when it was apparently obvious that the population was taking advantage of the government's generosity. It was clear to provincial officials that Ontarian families were attempting to turn family obligations toward the aged into state responsibilities. By refusing to allow families to use public facilities to care for their aged, the Ontario government was merely refusing to carry out a function that was supposed to be performed by the family. The government's actions, therefore, were justifiable. Justifiable, that is, if one accepted the government's argument.

THE SOCIAL AND DEMOGRAPHIC REALITIES

The truth is that the actual situation was very different from that presented in various government reports.

POPULATION AGING

To begin with, population aging was not quite the problem government officials declared it was. There is no doubt that the population was aging during the latter half of the nineteenth century. In Canada West in 1851 there were 29,533 persons over the age of sixty and they formed 3 percent of the population. Ten years later, the 55,968 people over sixty constituted 4 percent of the total population. In 1891, some 152,488 aged people formed over 7 percent of the population. By 1901, 8.4 percent of the population of Ontario was over the age of sixty.

These figures reveal, however, that concern over population aging did not necessarily depend upon the actual rate at which the elderly population was increasing. After 1881, for instance, though Ontario's aged population increased in number, it was growing at a steadily slower rate. Even in absolute numbers, fewer additional people were added to the aged population in each of the three final decades of the nineteenth century. The aged population increased at a rate of 46.8 percent between 1851 and 1861, and 36.3 percent between 1871 and 1881. After that date the rate of growth fell to 22.7 percent during the 1880s and 16.6 percent during the 1890s. In absolute numbers the aged population increased by 42,791 people during the 1870s, by 34,697 during the 1880s, and by only 30,247 between 1891 and 1901. It was during this last decade, however, that the growth of the aged population came to be perceived as a social problem by the Ontario government.

It is also evident that despite the general impressions generated by govern-ment reports and newspaper commentaries, the bulk of the aged population was not destitute or dependent. Throughout the nineteenth century, the majority of the elderly population headed their own households or were married to a household head. Most of these people lived independently on their own employment income or savings. In 1901, the census revealed that most elderly men were employed. In St. Catharines, Kingston, and Brockville in 1901, between 64 percent and 76 percent of the aged males worked. Although cost of living estimates for the period are problematic, it appears that the earnings of the majority of these men were sufficient to support themselves and a spouse. Also, despite the common assumption that aged people without employment income were destitute, it is clear that some elderly people had 'considerable capacity for savings accumulation.'[30] The wills of aged people who died in the Brockville region during the 1890s support this hypothesis. Many aged people held wealth in the form of real estate, stocks and bonds, annuities, life insurance, or savings that permitted them to survive without employment income. There were certainly poor elderly people. It is clear, however, that poverty was not nearly as widespread among the aged as govern-ment reports and newspapers often stated.

It is also clear that the elderly were not nearly as physically incapacitated as institutional officials and medical officers reported. Letters, diaries, and obitu-aries indicate that a substantial portion of the aged population led active, productive lives well into old age. Ellen Osler, the mother of Dr. William Osler, remained surprisingly active and alert until shortly before her death at the age of 101. Amelius Irving remained Treasurer of the Law Society of Upper Canada until he was almost 90. Despite his age he seldom failed to put in an appearance at his office at Osgoode Hall every day it was open for business.[31] Meanwhile, upon his retirement at the age of 84, George Cuddy of the Canada Trust Corporation stated that he felt 'rather young to be quitting.'[32] Even less prominent individuals, such as Rev. William Cochrane, a rural minister who lived in constant fear of being unable to provide for his wife, reported visiting 325 families and travelling 11,920 miles in the year he turned 65.[33]

Although the available evidence focuses overwhelmingly upon aged indi-viduals from the middle and upper class, evidence of active, productive, and mentally capable older individuals of any class or income bracket provides proof that the public association of age with dependency and mental decay was inaccurate. The fact that so many of the aged people mentioned were wealthy should also call into question the general equation of age with poverty.

It appears that the government overestimated the poverty and dependency of the aged population as well as the threat posed by population aging. The number of aged people in the population may have been increasing, but the segment of this population that was poor enough or sufficiently incapacitated, either mentally or physically, to require institutional care was small.

Even those people who did require care and support were not necessarily being 'foisted upon the government.' The available evidence reveals that rather than shirking their responsibilities toward the aged, late–nineteenth-century Ontario families were actually working harder to carry out their caring functions and provide shelter and care to their dependent aged members. Brian Gratton discovered that in Boston, even though economic and demographic considerations created a situation in which conflicting responsibilities made it increasingly difficult for adult children to care for their aged parents, the portion of the aged population found living with their children changed little. Rather than witnessing a decline in the degree to which families cared for the aged, the period after 1890 saw adult offspring and other kin working harder to maintain the dependent elderly.[34]

Similarly, in Ontario there is no evidence that families became less willing to provide care as the century progressed despite the fact that it became increasingly difficult for them to do so. The number of aged people in need of care was growing. Families, meanwhile, were getting smaller.[35] During the last half of the nineteenth century, about 15 percent of all couples remained childless. Meanwhile those couples who did reproduce had fewer children. At the same time, child and young adult mortality remained high. The combination of these trends resulted in a large number of people reaching old age with no surviving children.

In addition, people experienced greater geographical mobility. As one newspaper commented, 'keeping up the family attachment' was difficult when business and other pursuits scattered family members to distant homes.[36] The result of these trends was that by the time people reached old age they often found that there were fewer people nearby to provide them with care.[37] As a result, Ann Orloff explains, 'the proportion of adults at risk of supporting an elderly relative increased.'[38] It also meant that communal support networks, which had often been a source of support for caregivers, were weakened.[39] Nevertheless, throughout the latter half of the nineteenth century, the degree to which Ontario's families sheltered and cared for the dependent aged remained unchanged.

Census returns from Brockville, Kingston, and St. Catharines reveal that between 1851 and 1901, family members played a significant role in assisting the aged. Most dependent old people relied upon a married child. In the absence of adult children, however, it is clear that other kin were willing to shelter an aged relative. During the 1890s the number of aged people being cared for by a family member actually increased. In 1891, 67 percent of those aged people who did not head their own household lived with a relative. By 1901 this portion increased to 71 percent.

As well, the records of the Rockwood Asylum for the insane reveal that family members, rather than institutionalizing the aged to get rid of them, played a significant role in keeping them out of institutions. Although asylum administrators reported that aged people were being admitted to Rockwood 'through the importunity of their friends,'[40] case files demonstrate that most elderly patients had received a great deal of care from their relatives before admission and that family members sent them to Rockwood only once they were completely unable to cope and had no alternatives.[41] Rather than being 'easily cared for at home,' most of the elderly people institutionalized by their relatives were senile. As a result they were frequently uncontrollable, suicidal, or violent.[42] Most required amounts and types of care that were completely beyond the physical or financial capacities of their families. Instead of proving that families acted irresponsibly toward the aged, these records reveal that families regularly provided amazing amounts of care for their aged relatives, often under the most adverse circumstances.

INSTITUTIONS

If families were not abandoning their aged kin in institutions in ever increasing numbers, as the government argued, how then can one explain the fact that the aged portion of Ontario's institutional population grew rapidly despite the fact that the government had expanded the capacity of provincial institutions? The fact is that despite government claims that the aged were being institutionalized at an ever increasing rate, the truth was that the aged were no more likely to be institutionalized at the end of the 1890s than they were a decade earlier. Although the government did increase the capacity of provincial institutions they came nowhere near keeping up with the growth of the population, especially the aged population.

In 1889, if every bed in every institution had been occupied by an elderly person, Ontario's institutions could have accommodated only 3 percent of the province's total aged population. In reality, far fewer aged people were found in institutions. For instance, at no time did the aged constitute more than 20 percent of the insane asylum population. In all probability no more than

2 percent of the elderly people in Ontario were housed in institutions before 1890.

A decade later, after families had apparently begun to shirk their responsibilities and abandon the aged in institutions at an ever increasing rate, the portion of the aged population found inside institutions was still less than 3 percent. While the aged certainly formed a larger segment of the population within institutions, the reality was that the overwhelming majority of the aged population lived outside of their walls. For every aged person cared for by the state there were at least thirty-three others being cared for by their families or living on their own.

The explanation for this apparent contradiction is that although the government increased the number of beds in provincial institutions by 80 percent, during the 1890s, it only made room for about 4,000 new people. During the same period the aged population of Ontario increased by over 30,000. While the government did spend money on institutional care, it came nowhere near spending enough to keep up with basic population growth. Officials also ignored the fact that the very economic situation that was causing the government's financial difficulties was also having a major impact upon workers. David and Rosemary Gagan explain that during the 1890s, working-class incomes and standards of living fell, causing considerable individual and familial distress.[43] As the government itself reported in 1895, 'owing to the general depression in business and consequent hard times during the past years, the number of paupers has greatly increased.'[44]

Thus, at the very point when the aged population was growing and their families experiencing an increasing need for assistance, the government, in an attempt to reduce costs, endeavoured to restrict the aged's access to institutions. Since most aged people were not sent to institutions until their families were unable to cope with the care, refusing them access only ensured that they were left with families who were unable to provide them with the care they required, creating hardship and suffering for both the aged and their families.

It is evident that in the late nineteenth century the Ontario government was not as concerned with increasing the familial ties between the aged and their adult children as it may have seemed. Rather, it was employing the concept of family obligations to achieve other goals. It is almost certain that institutional administrators were aware that families were not abandoning the aged in institutions. The government had access to demographic statistics and institutional admission records. It was not difficult to see that the province's institutional facilities were simply inadequate to meet the needs of the population. Instead of expanding these facilities to meet the need, however, the government decided to attack families and accuse them of being irresponsible in an attempt to force them to keep their dependent aged relatives at home.

While the government argued that families were attempting to turn family obligations into state responsibilities, it seems that the opposite was true. It was the state, in an attempt to restrict or cap the amount of money it spent on the needy, which was attempting to force families to carry out functions that had formerly been the responsibility of the state. In other words, in the name of fiscal restraint, the government was trying to redefine the boundary between state responsibilities and family obligations. In this regard, the actions of the Ontario government in the 1890s may shed some light on current social policy reform initiatives and their potential impact upon the aged and their families.

NOTES

1. Susan Watts, 'Models of Family in Health Policy for the Aged,' *Canadian Review of Social Policy* 25 (May 1990), 38.
2. See Brian Gratton, *Urban Elders: Family, Work and Welfare Among Boston's Aged, 1890–1950* (Philadelphia, 1986) and Jill Quadagno, *Aging in Early Industrial Society: Work, Family and Social Policy in Nineteenth-Century England* (New York, 1982).
3. Herbert Northcott, *Aging in Alberta: Rhetoric and Reality* (Calgary, 1992), 87; Sheila McIntyre, 'Old Age as a Social Problem: Historical Notes on the English Experience,' in D. Dingwall, C. Heath, and M. Ried, eds., *Health Care and Health Knowledge* (London, 1977), 42; also see Janet Roebuck and Jane Slaughter, 'Ladies and Pensioners: Stereotypes and Public Policy Affecting Old Women in England, 1880–1940,' *Journal of Social History* 13/1 (Fall 1979), 105–14.
4. McIntyre, 'Old Age as a Social Problem,' 42.; also see Carroll Estes, Robert Newcomer et al., *Fiscal Austerity and Aging* (London, 1983), 14.
5. Northcott, *Aging in Alberta*, 88.
6. Susan McDaniels, 'Demographic Aging as a Guiding Paradigm in Canada's Welfare State,' *Canadian Public Policy* 13/3 (1987), 331.
7. Northcott, *Aging in Alberta*, 5.
8. Sara Arber and Jay Ginn, 'The Invisibility of Age: Gender and Class in Later Life,' *The Sociological Review* 39/2 (May 1991), 263–4.
9. Northcott, *Aging in Alberta*, 4.
10. Thomas Walkom, 'Pensions Will Be Battleground in Attack on Elderly,' *Toronto Star*, 8 Sept. 1994, A25.
11. Christopher Conrad, 'Old Age in the Modern and Postmodern Western World,' in Thomas Cole, David Van Tassel, and Robert Kasterbaum, eds., *The Handbook of the Humanities and Aging* (New York, 1992), 82; and R.F.A. Shegog, *The Impending Crisis of Old Age: A Challenge for Ingenuity* (London, 1981), 4.
12. Northcott, *Aging in Alberta*, 1.
13. See W.R. Bytheway, 'Demographic Statistics and Old Age Ideology,' *Ageing and Society* 1/3 (Nov. 1981), 347–64; Estes et al., *Fiscal Austerity*, 18.
14. See Stephen Katz, 'Alarmist Demography: Power, Knowledge, and the Elderly Population,' *Journal of Aging Studies* 6/3 (Fall 1992), 203–25. and Alan Walker and C. Phillips, eds., *Ageing and Social Policy: A Critical Assessment* (London, 1986), ii.
15. McDaniels, 'Demographic Aging as a Guiding Paradigm,' 331.
16. Fred Pampel and J.B. Williamson, 'Welfare Spending in Advanced Industrial Democracies, 1950–1980,' *American Journal of Sociology* 93/6 (May 1988), 1449.
17. Janet Finch, *Family Obligations and Social Change* (Cambridge, 1989).
18. David Gagen and Rosemary Gagen, 'Working Class Standards of Living in Late-Nineteenth-Century Victorian Urban Ontario: A Review of the Miscellaneous Evidence on the Quality of

Material Life,' *Journal of the Canadian Historical Association* (1990), 171–93.

19. Allan Moscovitch and Glenn Grover, 'Social Expenditures and the Welfare State: The Canadian Experience in Historical Perspective,' in Allan Moscovitch and J. Albert, eds., *The Benevolent State* (Toronto, 1987), 19.
20. Ibid.
21. *Annual Report of the Inspector of Prisons and Public Charities for the Province of Ontario* [hereafter *AR*] (1901).
22. *Ontario Sessional Papers*, no. 61 (1889).
23. *AR* (1897).
24. Edgar-Andre Montigny, '"Foisted Upon the Government": Institutions and the Impact of Public Policy Upon the Aged. The Elderly Patients of Rockwood Asylum, 1866–1906,' *Journal of Social History* 28/4 (1995), 822–3.
25. See Carole Haber, *Beyond Sixty-Five: The Dilemma of Old Age in America's Past* (Cambridge, 1983), 28–35; Carole Haber, 'And the Fear of the Poor House: Perceptions of Old Age Impoverishment in Early Twentieth-Century America,' *Generations* 17/2 (Spring–Summer 1993), 46.
26. *AR* (1896), Appendix (Hamilton), 127; and *AR* (1897), Appendix, (Kingston), 94.
27. *AR* (1898), Appendix (Brockville); *AR* (1897), Appendix (Brockville), 211 and (Toronto).
28. *AR* (1898), Appendix (Hamilton), 151.
29. *AR* (1897), Appendix (Kingston), 93.
30. See James Snell, 'Maintenance Agreements for the Elderly: Canada, 1900–1951,' *Journal of the Canadian Historical Association* (Charlottetown, 1992), 203; Brian Gratton and Francis Rotundo, 'Industrialization, the Family Economy and the Economic Status of the American Elderly,' *Social Science History* 15 (1991), 337–62.
31. Archives of Ontario [hereafter AO], *Biographical Scrapbook*, vol. 1, 524.
32. AO, *Biographical Scrapbook*, vol. 1, 204.
33. AO, MS 409: Diaries of William Cochrane (Sept.–Dec. 1896).
34. Brian Gratton, *Urban Elders*, 52.
35. Cheryl Krasnick Warsh, *Moments of Unreason: The Practice of Canadian Psychiatry and the Homewood Retreat, 1883–1923* (Montreal, 1978), 71–3.
36. 'Keep Up the Family Attachment,' *The Perth Courier* 27 Sept. 1872. This point is important when one considers that it was usually only kin who lived nearby who cared for the aged. See Tamara Hareven, 'Recent Research on the History of the Family,' in M. Drake, ed., *Time, Family and Community: Perspectives on Family and Community History* (Cambridge, 1994).
37. Ann Shola Orloff, *The Politics of Pensions* (Madison, WI, 1993), 3.
38. Ann Shola Orloff, *The Politics of Pensions*, 104; also see M.A. Crowther, 'Family Responsibility and State Responsibility in Britain Before the Welfare State,' *Historical Journal* 25/1 (1982), 134.
39. Cheryl Krasnick Warsh, *Moments of Unreason*, 71–3.
40. *AR* (1896), Appendix (Mimico), 191.
41. See Montigny, 'Foisted Upon the Government,' 831.
42. Montigny, 'Foisted Upon the Government,' 829.
43. Patricia Rook and L. Schnell, 'Childhood and Charity in Nineteenth-Century British North America,' *Histoire Sociale/Social History* 15 (1982), 171; Gagan and Gagan, 'Working Class Standards of Living,' 180.
44. *Ontario Sessional Papers*, no. 11 '27th Annual Report on the Common Gaols, Prisons and Reformatories' (1895), xii.

A NEW TAXPAYER FOR A NEW STATE

Charitable Fundraising and the Origins
of the Welfare State

SHIRLEY TILLOTSON

Department of History
Dalhousie University/University of King's College

For students of Canada's welfare history, the transition from crisis in the 1930s to a new order in the 1950s is a key moment in the development of the welfare state. And it is rightly characterized as a time of expansion in government's (and especially the federal government's) responsibilities for financing welfare programs (in the largest sense, including health and social services) (see Figure 1). But at the same time that public spending on welfare was expanding, charitable donations to the Community Chests were also increasing. In 1959, the collections of these federated fundraising appeals, forerunners of today's United Ways, were somewhat more than eight times their level in 1931[1] (see Figure 2). In the same period, GNP at market prices grew to slightly *less* than eight times the 1931 level (see Figure 3).

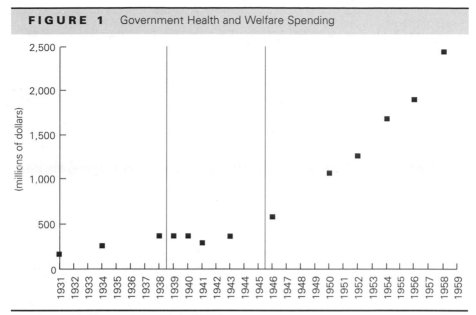

FIGURE 1 Government Health and Welfare Spending

The thinner vertical lines mark the period of WW II.

SOURCE: Dennis Guest, *The Emergence of Social Security in Canada* (Vancouver, 1985).

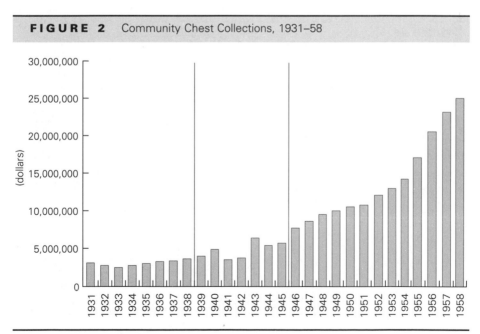

FIGURE 2 Community Chest Collections, 1931–58

The thinner vertical lines mark the period of WW II.

SOURCE: *Canadian Welfare*, various years. Data for 1938 and 1955–6 are estimates only.

FIGURE 3 GNP at Market Prices

The thinner vertical lines mark the period of WW II.

SOURCE: F.H. Leacy, *Historical Statistics of Canada*, 2nd ed., F-13.

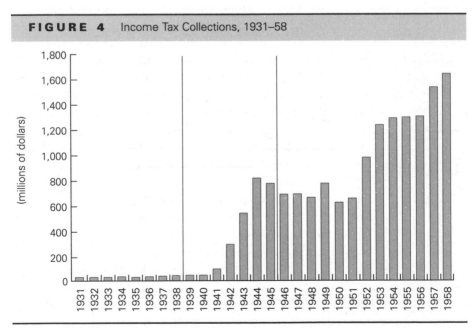

FIGURE 4 Income Tax Collections, 1931–58

The thinner vertical lines mark the period of WW II.

SOURCE: Department of National Revenue, *Taxation Statistics* and W. Irwin Gillespie, *Tax, Borrow and Spend: Financing Federal Spending in Canada 1867–1990* (Ottawa, 1991).

These data on donations in relation to GNP and government spending may seem to contradict those of economist Samuel Martin, who has contributed significantly, in *An Essential Grace*, to the history of the financing of what he calls 'humanistic services.' His data show that personal donations to humanistic services declined between 1937 and 1957, from 1.2 percent of GNP to 1 percent. But his data are, as he admits, derived from a number of broken data series, including, for example, taxation statistics available only after 1946. The Community Chest data, while suffering some minor gaps, are consistent in kind throughout the 1931 to 1958 period to which I attend in this essay. Also, Martin's data count somewhat different things than do mine. He includes, for example, donations to church building funds or to the Queen's University alumni fund, whereas the data on the Community Chest collections show only donations to health and welfare charities. So the increases in donations to the Chests were increases in giving to charities who supported families and cared for the ill and the isolated. Measured by the collections of the Community Chests, this kind of privately funded agency continued to benefit from increasing personal donations from Canadians throughout the 1930s, 1940s, and 1950s.

During these three decades, new government spending on health and welfare was in part financed by increasing income taxation (and, after 1951, the Old Age Security tax, counted with income tax in the federal Taxation Statistics).[2] In 1931, individual income tax collections (shown in Figure 4) were $26.5 million, and Community Chest donations $3 million. By 1959, individuals' tax payments had multiplied to almost $1.5 billion, fifty-six times their 1931 level. At $25 million, Chest donations at the end of the fifties were only 2 percent of income tax collections and, again, only eight times their Depression-era size. But in the period of highest income taxation, after WW II, charitable giving grew faster than tax collections. The 1959 personal tax collection was only 2.2 times that of 1946, whereas charitable donations through the Chest movement grew more than threefold in the same period.

The significance of these data seems quite clear. In the early years of the welfare state, at least, government spending and one of the main types of tax collecting that financed it do not seem to have deterred or impaired Canadians' charitable impulses. Some fiscal conservatives today call for reduced taxation and greater community involvement in caring and giving, and claim government welfare services have fostered selfishness and individualism.[3] In this paper, I want to question the psychological logic underpinning that claim by suggesting that, in the 1930s, 1940s, and 1950s, quite another relationship existed between government welfare provision and private generosity. Rather than being *replaced* by tax paying, charitable giving helped prepare the way in public culture for income tax paying as a feature of citizenship in the welfare state. In effect, the Chests helped shift the political limits on governments' ability to tax.

In particular, the Chests helped prepare the political ground for the great increase in the 1940s in the numbers of payers of *income* tax. Taxation historian W. Irwin Gillespie has argued that the taxpayer is not 'a hapless, helpless victim of a rapacious government that taxes indiscriminately.' Rather, taxpayers' ability to oppose taxation has shaped government's choices about what kinds of taxation to use.[4] If Gillespie is right, then part of taxation history must be an inquiry into the formation of taxpayer opposition—what produces it and, as well, what allays it. It is this latter question—what allayed or reduced opposition to tax paying, and specifically, to income tax paying by lower income groups—that the study of the Community Chest's fundraising practices can help answer. By a nationwide, decades-long campaign of public education, the Community Chest movement helped create a new conception of the taxpayer for a newly expanded state.

THE 'CHEST IDEA'

The Community Chest movement, or the 'federated appeals' as they were more generically known, emerged in the early twentieth century. Montreal's and Toronto's 'Financial Federations' began in the latter years of World War I, another three 'Chests' or 'Federations' began in the 1920s, and another four in the 1930s. By 1939, nine cities (including all Canada's major centres) had federated fundraising appeals. The World War II years and after saw a great flurry of federation of Canadian charities' fundraising appeals, so that by 1949, there were forty-seven Canadian cities with a Community Chest.[5] The 'Chest idea' was that all the charities making public appeals in any given city would unite to make one common appeal each year.[6] Doing so would not only use with maximum efficiency the publicity dollars of each charity; it would also use more efficiently their human resources. Businessmen sitting on management boards and office staffs in the various agencies would be saved the work of planning, managing, and record-keeping for many separate, small campaigns. Door-to-door canvassers, mainly women, would make the circuit once a year, rather than repeatedly. In short, each dollar collected would come at a lower price in collecting costs (usually, costs in volunteer labour).

The federated appeal would be able to avoid labour-intensive fundraising methods that were not only inefficient, but also risky and irritating. The risky ones were those that depended on sales to generate revenue; teas, dances, and fairs did not always succeed in making much money, but they did always consume volunteer energies. The annual appeal was meant to reduce the need for mounting this type of risky event. The annual appeal was also meant to reduce the irritation induced by some aspects of unco-ordinated fundraising. Vancouver retail merchants, for example, complained of two such aspects. One was that 'hours' in their business days were being used up in listening to representatives of individual charities soliciting their firms' support. Another was that retail businesses suffered particularly from the presence in store foyers and downtown streets of 'taggers.' Taggers were women soliciting donations for charity, giving out little lapel labels to each donor. Shoppers had to routinely run a gauntlet of taggers. Merchants wanted this to stop. It was bad for business and not, they believed, especially effective for fundraising. From a business perspective, then, unco-ordinated appeals were not only wasteful of human energies and publicity dollars, they were also a positive nuisance.

The single annual appeal had yet another advantage, in the eyes of its advocates. It was a 'businessman's movement.'[7] Early appeals stressed in their publicity the importance of business expertise in managing fundraising campaigns and ensuring that funded agencies budgeted and accounted properly for the expenditure of the appeal funds. 'Leading businessmen' or a 'Businessmen's Council' or the Board of Trade figured prominently as organizers of the united appeals. They made 'exhaustive inquiry into the finances of each of the institutions,' to provide assurances that charities were not duplicating each others' work or otherwise spending irresponsibly the public's donated dollars.[8] Such scrutiny, they felt, would promote more giving by overcoming perceptions of inefficiency or even of fraud.

Not only were the Chests to be more efficient, they were also intended actually to increase charitable giving. Of course, an image of efficiency was, itself, supposed to invite donations. A second source of greater giving, it was hoped, would be the public's happiness with the reduced number of solicitations. A third anticipated incentive to donating, and perhaps a more probable one, was that the co-ordinated blitz of publicity for the united appeal would heighten public awareness of charitable agencies' welfare work. Each campaign included press releases and advertisements describing the work of member agencies, and provided an occasion for a concentrated flurry of service club speeches and public luncheons, explaining welfare needs and celebrating the work of the member agencies. Whether this method of promotion was more or less effective than earlier, independent fundraising campaigns probably varied for different member agencies. Undeniably, though, the Chest campaign provided publicity resources that the smaller charities had otherwise lacked. Finally, the fourth hope for increased giving, and in my view the most realistic one, was that an appeal organized with the businesslike methods of a 'modern' sales campaign would actually contact more donors and successfully elicit contributions from a larger population. Systematic record-keeping, co-ordinated publicity, team organization, and a military-style chain of command provided fundraisers with data for strategic planning and the means to motivate and support canvassers.

COMPARISON OF THE CHEST IDEA WITH TAXATION PHILOSOPHY AND PRACTICES DURING THE INTERWAR YEARS

The Chest movement's attempt to change the culture of charitable fundraising and giving was inspired by and indeed was part of larger, contemporaneous changes in the culture of public administration. The thinking behind the Chest was cut from the same cultural cloth as contemporaneous thinking about taxation. To understand why that was so, we need to recall that, as Paul Pross has argued, the interwar years saw a symbiotic growth of government bureaucracy and private interest groups.[9] Mediating that symbiosis was a shared language of communication. The development in Canada of one aspect of that shared language (i.e., practices and philosophies) has been described by Doug Owram in *The Government Generation*, in which he shows the increasing use of social science methods by both state and social agencies.[10] Another, further aspect of the shared language or common public culture that linked the growing state to civil society was disseminated and promoted by the expanding Community Chests. One might call this shared language 'tax talk.' Predominantly a language of business expertise, it was also given a collectivist, social democratic inflection in the fundraising practices of the Community Chests, as they sought to induce more Canadians to 'share the burden.' I have identified four areas in which taxation and fundraising languages overlapped: cost-effective collection, accounting controls, use of 'ability to pay' measures, and base-broadening. In the last of these four areas, fundraising innovations preceded their parallels in income taxation.

COST-EFFECTIVE COLLECTION

To begin, let us take the Chest movement's argument that a single appeal was the most cost-effective means of collecting for charity. Reducing costs of collection made for the largest possible net amount of charity dollars available for their intended use. Similarly, governments choosing means of raising revenue weighed the cost of collection against the amounts a tax might raise. For instance, one of the arguments advanced in *favour* of the particular form of the 1920 manufacturer's sales tax, and indeed in favour of sales taxes generally, was the low cost of the administrative methods involved in collecting it. The tax collectors were the manufacturers and wholesalers who handled the taxed goods, and the returns they submitted required only about three dozen additional inspectors and auditors in the Department of National Revenue.[11] By contrast, the chief argument *against* some other tax practices has been that the expense of their administration exceeds the revenue they might generate. For example, tax authority Gwyneth McGregor concluded, on the basis of an analysis of income tax in Canada between WW I and the late 1950s, that government's practice of distinguishing between employees and the self-employed for the purpose of allowing employment expenses could be explained only on the grounds of administrative difficulty and expense.[12] To reduce these, waged and salaried workers' employment expenses, unlike those of the self-employed, were built into the standard personal deduction. This distinction in methods saved 'the Revenue' the cost of checking itemized employment expenses for millions of employee tax returns. Awareness of the cost of collections in determining taxation methods is also apparent in the Taxation Division's publication, in their 1946 *Taxation Statistics*, of data showing Cost of Collections since 1917. When Community Chest promoters argued for a cheaper cost of collections, then, they were thinking in the same way public administrators did in planning tax collection.

ACCOUNTING CONTROLS

Second, the call for particular kinds of managerial expertise was another theme that linked discussion of charity fundraising and taxation in the interwar years. In particular, tax experts and the Community Chest managers agreed that in each of their areas of operation, sound practice required better accounting controls. Indeed, the authorities on taxation and the promoters of businesslike fundraising were sometimes the same people. For example, Horace L. Brittain was director and secretary of the Citizen's Research Institute of Canada, organizer of the annual Canadian Tax Conferences that began in 1923. He also played an active role in the creation of Toronto's Federation for Community Service.[13] In the 1930s, Brittain's Citizen's Research Institute created a Taxation Enquiry Fund to finance the *Special Study of Taxation and Public Expenditure in Canada* by Dr. W.H. Wynne. In 1937, Wynne went from this project to become a member of the economics staff of the Royal Commission on Dominion–Provincial Relations, whose report would help frame fiscal policy in the 1940s and 1950s.[14] We also find some of the leading men of the federated charities active during the 1930s in the Associated Property Owners of Vancouver, an organization devoted to scrutinizing city finances and exposing extravagant spending.[15] These leading businessmen readily moved from promoting proper financial controls in the spending of public money to doing the same for the spending of Community Chest funds.

Wynne's *Special Study of Taxation* furnishes examples of this common language. He criticized public spending in the same technical terms that Chest budget committees brought to their assessments of charitable agencies. One of Wynne's criticisms was that neither provinces nor municipalities used real revenue-expense accounting. Indeed, municipalities facing a revenue shortage had to 'slash rather than prune' public spending because they kept no 'real expense records.'[16] The need for such records, Wynne pointed out, was not only to prevent 'peculation' (although that was one good reason). More important was 'providing the information necessary for administrative and public control.'[17] Public trust required accounting controls. As Michael Piva and Bruce Curtis have shown, colonial Canadian governments had once relied on the good character of public officials more than on routine audit and control mechanisms.[18] Similarly, in Wynne's view, some municipalities (and even provinces) in the interwar years of twentieth-century Canada were still operating as though to require expense records was to impugn the character of officials.

Charities, like nineteenth-century colonial governments, had relied on the prestige of their boards to produce confidence in their spending. When the Community Chest movement promised a businesslike audit of all member agencies' accounts, they were promising as an inducement to charitable giving the same kind of enhancement in administrative control that tax experts were calling for in government as a prerequisite of legitimate taxation. Budget committees on Community Chests queried agency board representatives about particular items in their budgets. Agencies could be removed from the federation if their expense records failed to meet proper standards. That was the fate of several agencies in the early years of the Vancouver Welfare Federation: in 1931, they ousted from their ranks for this reason the Original Great War Veterans Association, as well as the Western Association for the Blind, and the Tuberculous Veterans.[19] What this comparison suggests is that business people viewed both governments and charities as being in need of business expertise. While this view was not new in the interwar years, its expression in the institutional form of the federated appeals was both new and significant. By way of the Chest movement, across the country in major, and later, in minor cities, charitable fundraising became a widespread means of promulgating to a wide audience the gospel of accounting controls as a necessary part of public spending, whether of charity dollars or tax dollars.

'Ability to Pay': The Link Between Income and Obligation

Third, and most important, of the elements in the common public culture I am sketching here, were the means the Chests used in their attempts to increase the numbers of charitable donors. More than efficiency in collections and controls in accounting, the methods adopted to implement this feature of the Chest idea prepared the public to contemplate with a degree of acceptance the expanding incidence of personal income taxation, especially in lower-income cohorts, in the 1940s. The campaign to induce more people to give to the Chests linked income and social obligation in ways that would also appear in discussions of just taxation in the interwar years.

The links of income and obligation in conceptions of tax in the interwar years may be read from the parliamentary debates incited by R.B. Bennett's 1931 federal budget and from changes in the administration of taxation in subsequent years. To put the budget debate in context, we need to realize that, in 1931, paying income tax was still clearly an experience of the middling salary earner, the highly paid, and the rich. Wage earners did not often earn more than the $3,000 that for a married, childless household head was tax exempt in 1930. The 1931 census's income distribution figures for wage earning families showed only 4.48 percent were headed by someone with a *taxable income* of $2,950 or more (i.e., $5,950 or more). Nonetheless, when, in 1931, the exemption level for income tax was dropped to $2,400, more relatively low-income citizens joined the 'elite' ranks of the taxpayers. An economic aristocracy among wage earners, these 52,857 men and 213 women probably all numbered among the 63,276 Canadians who paid tax on *taxable* incomes of less than $2,000. This lowest rank of income taxpayers, many of them solidly middle class in income level, were 38 percent of the country's total 166,972 income taxpayers in 1931.[20] A tax impinging on so few Canadians was hardly a major revenue source. In 1931, personal income tax supplied only 6.61 percent of the federal government's revenue requirements. Over half of those requirements were fulfilled instead by taxes on consumption—sales and excise taxes and customs duties.[21] Quite properly, then, the debate over Bennett's 1931 budget focused primarily on the impact of the customs tariff.[22]

But many speakers commented on the income tax provisions of the budget, too. Even though their remarks showed what can most kindly be called 'confusion' about the incidence of income tax, the MPs also revealed common sense assumptions about the social identities of taxpayers. Among the ranks of the official Opposition, only William Motherwell appears to have grasped the structure of the (admittedly limited) data available from the Department of National Revenue and Bennett's budget speech. He alone seems to have appreciated that Bennett's budget actually *cut* income taxes for 'the small salaried man' whose taxable income was between $3,000 and $8,000. More importantly, Motherwell realized the full import of income tax *increases* to taxable incomes between $9,000 and $137,000. In this range, as he realized, there were conceivably some millionaires whose taxable income had been carved into a smaller shape by means of ingenious tax deductions.[23] There were well over 15,000 taxpayers in this very wealthy group, and under Bennett's budget they were all going to pay more taxes. The rich certainly felt some bite from the 1931 Bennett budget.

But most of Bennett's opponents focused on the tax reductions Bennett proposed to give to a small number of the fabulously wealthy: either the '25 millionaires' or the 523 individuals whose taxable income was greater than $50,000. These were the happy souls whose reduced tax bills under Bennett's new income tax scale gave the 1931 budget its name as 'the rich man's budget.' The image of these few plutocrats was arrayed as the symbol of unjust tax privilege against the sufferings of 'the poor man,' whose cup of tea would now cost more in light of a 3 percent increase in the sales tax. In this rhetoric, the income taxpayer appeared as a figure of privilege, contrasted to the downtrodden ordinary man or woman, the payer of sales tax.

Bennett's critics were right to deplore his government's reliance on increased consumption taxes, regressive forms of taxation that ate away at the pennies and nickels of the poor. But it is equally clear that the moral and symbolic meaning of taxation informed the debate more than did real information about tax incidence.

J.S. Woodsworth's intervention was especially striking in this respect.[24] After noting the fact that most Canadians earned too little to pay income tax, he then pointed out how few taxpayers there were in the 'under $2,000' taxable income class and how little income tax they paid. He went on to offer the figures for the much larger total sums paid by the wealthy and by corporations. 'We are told this country belongs to the people,' he then said, clearly about to puncture a myth, 'and yet, when we come to matters of taxation we find the taxes are loaded upon only a few people.' At this point, it would seem, very oddly, that Woodsworth was deploring the burden of income tax carried by the rich. However, with no apparent regard for consistency, he went on to aver bitterly that 'this government is nothing more or less than a vast debt collecting agency operating to collect from the poor people or the people of moderate means moneys to be turned over to the wealthy people.' In context of comments on the income tax, this view was simply wrong. Although the *sales* tax did indeed collect disproportionately from the poor and the middling sort, the *income* tax did not. Woodsworth's remarks were those of a man completely unused to dissecting the impact of income tax. This should not be surprising, for the income tax in the 1920s had been, in fact, more or less a rich man's tax and a rich man's 'burden.' A tribune of the poor, such as Woodsworth, would have had little reason ever to think of it. When we consider the Chests' effect on public culture, a key focus must be the perception of income tax as a rich man's tax, outside the obligations and taxpaying experience of most working-class and many middle-class Canadians.

The fundraising campaigns of the Community Chests would contribute to changing that perception, both by imitating the methods of the income tax and by enlarging the scope of their application. The model of charitable giving in the Chest idea mimicked in two ways the model of income taxation. One was the use of a progressive scale of giving, tied to income. Figure 5 shows one such scale.[25] Worth noting is that the lowest annual income registered on this (and other, similar scales) is $2,000, also the lowest threshold in the income cohorts into which data on income tax paying were divided. The concept of obligation increasing with greater wealth is also clearly present in the scale. The rate of recommended donation increases with income, albeit slightly less steeply than did rates of income tax owed in Bennett's 1931 budget.[26]

FIGURE 5

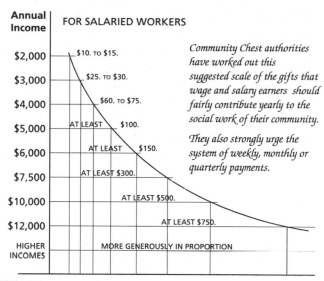

What You Should Give

SOURCE: City of Vancouver Archives, J.S. Matthews files, subject 'Vancouver Welfare Federation,' newsclipping, *Vancouver Sun*, 6 Nov. 1935. The *x*-axis percentages read as follows: 1/2 to 1%, 1%, 1 1/2%, 2%, 2 1/2%, 4%, 5%, 6%.

taxation as citizenship / community obligation

In using this scale, the Chest might be seen to have described charitable giving, like income tax paying, as a rich man's or woman's activity. But to complement the graded scale, the chest also made appeals to industrial workers.[27] And these appeals were tied to income: the suggested donation for those with incomes under $2,000 was a day's pay. In this way, admittedly somewhat loosely, the link between income ('ability to pay' in tax discourse) and obligation to give was maintained. Like the income taxpayer, and unlike the sales taxpayer, the donor to charity in the Chest method consciously paid what he or she 'owed,' knowing that that amount represented something about himself or herself individually.

BASE-BROADENING

The Chest's main purpose was to increase charitable giving, and its main method of doing so was to increase the number of donors. In this aspect of their fundraising, federated appeals anticipated a development that would come in the actual income tax system only during World War II. This 'base-broadening' approach to maximizing revenue was what Mark Leff described as the tax reform approach advocated by some left-of-centre American tax reformers in the 1930s.[28] Within fundraising, the emphasis of base-broadening was on coming to the aid of the 'unselfish few.' (This seems likely to have been the discourse within which J.S. Woodsworth spoke when he lamented the loading of social obligation on the shoulders of a few.) Like fundraisers, the advocates of broadening the income tax base hoped both to relieve some taxpayers of a disproportionate burden and to generate more revenue for social services. Unlike fundraisers, though, these social democratic American reformers were mainly interested in relieving the many, not the few. Specifically, they hoped to relieve lower-income people from the weight of accumulated small consumption taxes.

For these tax reformers, the $2,000 income level was politically important. In the categories identified by economist Henry Simons, for example, the point of base-broadening and the reduction of consumption taxes was to make the tax burden fall 'mainly on people with incomes ranging from $3,000 to $20,000' rather than 'largely on people below the $2,000 level.'[29] The 'common sense' income taxpayer seems to have been the one whose income was greater than $2,000. This income level had a similar meaning for the Chest fundraisers, too. In both taxation and fundraising, then, the middle- and upper-income classes had obligations based on the enjoyment of wealth.

But in pursuit of a larger donor base, the Chest also appealed to those with lower incomes, on different grounds. The 'pitch' to these potential new donors—the elevator operator, the waiter, the sales clerk, the packing clerk—

was that giving to the Community Chest was part payment for the services the Chest provided. For example, in a solicitation to all of Vancouver's 'helping hands,' the fundraisers created a fictive voice of 'tired, unaided domestic hands' that replied 'Yes, indeed, I want to do my tiny share, for did not the Welfare help my little girl last year when we were unable to give her the care she needed so badly?' and 'tough, calloused, work-thickened hands' that expressed appreciation for the summer playgrounds for the kids, and promised 'It won't be much, but I'll do me little bit.'[30] The working-class donors, then, who did in fact give to the Chest were represented as not only fulfiling obligations to the community, but also as helping pay for social services they themselves or their families would use.

From the 1920s to the 1950s, this was the message these co-ordinated fundraising appeals broadcast to working-class Canadians. In a campaign conducted every year in nine major Canadian cites, charitable giving was linked to the concept of insurancelike, income-based contributions to communitywide provision of social services. Chest fundraising educated the mass of Canadians, and not just social elites, in the ways of a modern, rationalized system of funding social services. In this way the Community Chests promoted awareness of welfare services and perceptions of social obligation that applied as well to income tax paying for the welfare state as they did to charitable giving.

Of course, similarities in the philosophies and practices of giving to charity through the Chest and paying income tax should not blind us to the fact that these ways of meeting social obligations have been deemed opposite, with every dollar that is turned over to the state lost to use in private charity.[31] The Community Chests' efforts to create an awareness of welfare need and of the cost of a wide variety of social services was *not* primarily intended to create demand for publicly funded services. Indeed, one of the BC businessmen involved in the Chest's early years argued (with the Chest director's endorsement) that supporting private charity was a crucial defence against communistic appropriation of private wealth (i.e., against high and progressive income taxes).[32] Furthermore, the head of Catholic charities in Quebec warned that 'state charity' might make Canadians 'oblivious to the duty and joy of private charity.'[33] On the left, advocates of a systematically redistributive welfare state correctly saw that some advocates of private philanthropy hoped to forestall tax-funded services.[34]

But intentions do not wholly determine outcomes. It is important, therefore, to understand that there were not only conflicts, but also connections between income taxation and private uses of the welfare dollar. A joke in a 1945 Calgary labour paper played on the overlap between the tax and welfare discourses: 'Officials of the Income Tax Division received the following acknowledgement of a blank [i.e., a tax form] received by a citizen: "Dear Treasury—I received your application blank, but I already belong to several good orders and do not care to join your income tax at this time."[35]

Ruefully, this joke acknowledged that the income tax system occupied the same ground in a worker's life as private welfare spending. And evidently, the humorist had some doubts about being forced to join the impersonal 'order' that was the welfare state. But he understood quite clearly that income taxation was to the welfare state as private insurance systems had been to an earlier, individual-centred welfare regime. The Chest fundraisers' methods had been an attempt to make more collective, to socialize, the process of insuring against hardship. As a result, their campaigns, as one Vancouver social worker claimed, promoted the work of social agencies, not only to charitable givers but also to 'those who contributed through taxation.'[36]

This social worker was right in her conclusion about the Chests' effects, because of the common values and practices embodied both in Community Chest fundraising and in the conception of a broad-based income tax for a welfare state. I have suggested that some aspects of these common values and practices were cost-effective collections, accounting controls, obligation based in ability to pay, and breadth of participation. The latter, furthermore, was grounded in part in a sense of obligation based in anticipated benefit rather than purely a spirit of altruism. These were parts of the emerging public culture from which came both increases in a certain kind of charitable giving and legitimation in the 1950s for increased income taxation.

CONCLUSION

My argument in this paper has not been meant to prove that there has never been at any time *since* the 1950s a diminution in private charitable giving. Martin's data show a drop in charitable giving between 1957 and 1978 from 1 percent of GNP to .6 percent.[37] These years also saw growth in spending on health and welfare from 5 percent of GNP to 18 percent of GNP and, between 1965 and 1970, a striking increase in individual income tax collections. These three phenomena may very well have been connected. But the line of argument I have pursued here does provide historical evidence to suggest that the psychological underpinning to connect these phenomena need not be resentment at increases in income tax paying or apathy about need induced by public provision. When, during the 1930s, 1940s, and 1950s, Canadians paid increasing proportions of their earnings in income tax and state-funded services blossomed, the federated charities also prospered and expanded. This suggests that the willingness to give is not simply the result of a zero-sum calculation about disposable dollars, where more dollars to the taxman means fewer to charity. Nor must the generous charitable giver be cast as the free and morally heroic opposite to the grudging and coerced taxpayer. In the Community Chest's methods of fundraising, charitable giving was described in ways that highlighted the similarities, and not the differences, between the taxpayer for the welfare state and the giver to good causes. In an unintended way, the Chests were fundraising for the welfare state, and not just for private charities. The story of the Community Chest in the period I have discussed here thus recalls to mind a vision of a mutually reinforcing relation, rather than a competitive one, between public and private provision for welfare needs. Something of that vision is worth recapturing.

Notes

1. Community Chest giving was, of course, only one kind of charitable giving. Others may have grown or declined on a different pattern. One advantage of the Community Chest data on giving is that it is a nearly complete and readily available data series for the 1931–59 period, published by the Canadian Welfare Council in their journal, *Canadian Welfare*.
2. W. Irwin Gillespie, *Tax, Borrow, and Spend: Financing Federal Spending in Canada, 1867–1990* (Ottawa, 1991), 215, chart 10-1 and Dept. of National Revenue, Taxation Division, *Taxation Statistics*.
3. See, for example, William Gairdner, *The Attack on the Family*, 84–5. Somewhat less bluntly anti-statist variations on this analysis have been offered by Robert Fulford, 'The Way We Were,' *Saturday Night*, March 1985, 5–6, and the Editors of the *Globe and Mail*, in 'Beyond Public and Private,' 28 Sept. 1995.
4. Gillespie, *Tax, Borrow, and Spend*, 179–80.
5. 'With the Federation Cities,' *Canadian Welfare* 8/5 (1933), 13–20; 'Results of 1948–49 Community Chest Campaigns,' *Canadian Welfare*, 24/8 (1949), 29.
6. This paper's discussion of the 'Chest Idea' draws on the records relating to the initial organizational efforts in the 1920s of the Halifax and Vancouver federated appeals. These are mainly to be found in two collections: Public Archives of Nova Scotia [hereafter PANS], MG20, Records of the United Way of Halifax–Dartmouth and City of Vancouver Archives [hereafter CVA], Vancouver Board of Trade, Add. MSS 300. In the first of these two collections, the key documents are in vol. 1717, a scrapbook. See especially the clippings for May 1925. For the second of these two collections, the key documents are in vol. 5, 319, report by W.C. Woodward, chairman of the Retail Merchants' Bureau of the Vancouver Board of Trade, 4 May 1922; vol. 146, insert at 44, 'Minutes of Meeting of Organizations Called to Receive a Report Prepared by the Special Committee re Community Chest,' 26 June 1923; vol. 8, insert at 487, 'Minutes of a Special meeting of the Council of the Vancouver Board of Trade,' 8 Nov. 1928; and 'Expert Urges Chest System of Charities,' *Vancouver Star*, 13 Aug. 1929, 7. Some of the same themes appear in the origins of Toronto's Federation for Community Service, described in Jacquelyn Gale Wills, 'Efficiency, Feminism, and Co-operative Democracy: Origins of the Toronto Social Planning Council, 1918–1957,' (PhD diss., University of Toronto, School of Social Work, 1989).
7. Additional emphasis on this point may be found in the National Archives of Canada [hereafter NAC], Canadian Council on Social Development [hereafter CCSD] Papers, vol. 158, file 'CWC Divisions—Community Organization, 1935–37,' D.J. Thom, K.C., President of Regina Community Chest, to Marjorie Bradford, secretary for community organization, CWC, 26 Nov. 1936; PANS,

MG 20, vol. 1713, minutes of the Halifax Board of Trade, 'Associated Charities Fund,' 17 Nov. 1921; NAC, CCSD Papers, vol. 158, file 'CWC Divisions—Community Organization, 1935–37,' D.J. Thom, K.C., President of Regina Community Chest, to Marjorie Bradford, secretary for community organization, CWC, 26 Nov. 1936; 'Twenty-Five Years in Toronto,' *Canadian Welfare* 18/4 (1942), 8–9.

8. The quotation is from PANS, MG 20, vol. 1717, 'Community Chest Will Carry On To Finish,' newsclipping, May 1925.

9. Paul Pross, *Group Politics and Public Policy* (Toronto, 1992).

10. Doug Owram, *The Government Generation* (Toronto, 1986).

11. Gillespie, *Tax, Borrow, and Spend*, 120, and H.R. Kemp, 'Dominion Taxation. 1. The Sales Tax,' *Canadian Forum* 3 (July 1923), 298.

12. Gwyneth McGregor, *Employees' Deductions Under the Income Tax: A Comparative Study of Their Treatment in the United Kingdom, the United States and Canada* (Toronto, 1960).

13. Horace L. Brittain,' in *The Canadian Who's Who*, 1936–7.

14. Dr. Wynne's connection to both organizations is documented in the covering letter published with the Citizen Research Institute's *Special Study of Taxation and Public Expenditure in Canada* (1937) and in the list of Commission staff in the final report of the Royal Commission on Dominion–Provincial Relations.

15. CVA, J.S. Matthews clippings file, subject heading 'Associated Property Owners of Vancouver,' 'Property Owners Re-Elect Board,' 9 Feb. 1934; 'Rap Trustees for Increase,' 4 May 1932; 'City Finance Position Shows No Improvement,' 20 July 1936 and annual reports of the Vancouver Welfare Federation. At the time of this research, these reports were held by the United Way of the Lower Mainland. Since that time, they have become part of the collections of the City of Vancouver Archives. My research notes do not, however, contain the City of Vancouver archival citations because these did not exist at the time of my research.

16. Wynne, *Special Study of Taxation*, 50.

17. Ibid.

18. Michael Piva, 'Government Finance and the Development of the Canadian State,' in A. Greer and I. Radforth, eds., *Colonial Leviathan: State Formation in Mid-Nineteenth Century Canada* (Toronto, 1992), 265–7; Bruce Curtis, 'Class Culture and Administration: Educational Inspection in Canada West,' in Greer and Radforth, *Colonial Leviathan*, 116–19.

19. CVA, United Way of the Lower Mainland, Vancouver Welfare Federation minutes binder, 67, minutes of 18 Sept. 1931.

20. J. Harvey Perry, *Taxes, Tariffs, and Subsidies: A History of Canadian Fiscal Development*, vol. 2 (Toronto, 1955), 698; Census of Canada 1931, table 38, 686–7.

21. Gillespie, *Tax, Borrow, and Spend*, 280.

22. Discussion of the income tax appears in Canada, House of Commons, *Debates*, on the following dates in June 1931: 4, 5, 9, 10, 15, 17, 18.

23. Canada, House of Commons, *Debates*, 15 June 1931, 2621–2.

24. Canada, House of Commons, *Debates*, 9 June 1931, 2460.

25. CVA, J.S. Matthews clippings files, subject 'Vancouver Welfare Federation,' 6 Nov. 1935. This scale was used during Howard Falk's tenure as Executive Director, and Falk had been in on the design of federated fundraising appeals in Winnipeg and Montreal. Halifax also used such a scale, as described in PANS, United Way of Halifax–Dartmouth, minutes 1923–1962, 'Constitution,' article 8, section 6, 20 Jan. 1927.

26. Canada, House of Commons, *Debates*, 1 June 1931, 2176–7.

27. Shirley Tillotson, 'Class and Community in Canadian Welfare Work, 1933–1960,' *Journal of Canadian Studies* (forthcoming).

28. Mark Leff, *The Limits of Symbolic Reform* (Cambridge, 1984).

29. Leff, *The Limits of Symbolic Reform*.

30. CVA, J.S. Matthews clippings file, subject 'Vancouver Welfare Federation,' E.S. Roberts, 'Our Whole Town's Working,' *Vancouver Province*, 26 Oct. 1935

31. Seymour Martin, *An Essential Grace: Funding Canada's Health Care, Education, Welfare, Religion and Culture* (Toronto, 1985), 194–5 reports survey results indicating some Canadians hold this view.

32. NAC, CCSD Papers, vol. 13, file 59 'CWC Division—Community Organization "Publicity and Fund

Raising" 1934,' text of broadcast by Robert Cromie on behalf of the Community Chests of Canada, 13 Oct. 1934.

33. NAC, CCSD papers, vol. 13, file 59 'Community Organization, 1933–34, Radio Broadcasts,' 8 Oct. 1933.

34. NAC, CCSD Papers, vol. 13, file 59 'CWC Division—Community Organization "Publicity and Fund Raising" 1934,' Charlotte Whitton to Philip Fisher, 31 Aug. 1934; CVA, United Way of the Lower Mainland, minutes binder labelled 1933–35, Budget committee report, 18 Feb. 1934.

35. *The Call* 1/4 (15 April 1945), 7.

36. CVA, United Way of the Lower Mainland, Mrs. Walter [Alma Gale] Mowatt, 'History of the Community Chest and Council of the Greater Vancouver Area,' Typescript, 1951, 35.

37. Martin, *An Essential Grace.*

Learning from the Past

Marc Lalonde's Pension Reforms of 1982–4

GEOFFREY E. HALE

Department of Political Science
University of Western Ontario

T he federal government is currently considering proposals for the reform of the Canada Pension Plan. These address important concerns with respect to financial sustainability, the fulfilment of existing commitments to older Canadians, the federal–provincial balance of power, and the relationship between public and private pension systems.

However, proposed reforms to the Canada and Quebec Pension Plans (CPP/QPP) will not take place in a political vacuum. The major elements of Canada's mixed public/private pension system are part of what James Buchanan has called the 'economic constitution,' which he defines broadly as 'a set of rules, or social institutions within which people operate and interact with one another...rules [which]...set boundaries on what activities are legitimate.'[1]

As such, it involves both formal, quasi-constitutional rules that require the federal government to obtain provincial consent to changes to CPP laws, along with informal, but potent political and cultural constraints on unilateral federal changes to entrenched property rights and existing entitlements.

Provincial governments—the CPP fund's largest creditors—hold an effective veto on proposed policy changes, thus enforcing the necessity of some measure of political consensus on federal officials. Pensioners are among the best organized, most vocal constituencies in Canada—one capable of mobilizing sizeable political resources to embarrass any government willing to challenge existing entitlements.[2] Any attempt to finance CPP/QPP reform through a pre-emptive raid on private pensions or retirement savings plans would also involve serious political and economic risks.[3] Most proposals for CPP/QPP reform involve an acceleration of premium increases that will either seriously erode federal and provincial income tax revenues in future years—or result in net tax increases that will erode the already anemic growth levels of the 1990s.[4]

Fifteen years ago, there seemed to be much insecurity and little consensus on pension reform as a National Pension Conference convened in Ottawa failed to produce any agreement among competing stakeholders on the optimal conditions of reform.[5] Yet less than three years later, Liberal Finance Minister Marc Lalonde presented proposals for reform of the pension system, which became the basis for a nonpartisan consensus for most of the next decade.[6] Are there lessons to be learned from this process that can usefully be applied to the current debate over pension reform?

A review of the history of Canada's pension reform process between 1981 and 1986 suggests several major principles for the guidance of federal officials in the successful design and implementation of pension reform:

- a measure of bi-partisan consensus is necessary for the successful introduction and implementation of enduring reforms;
- while consensus-building requires the participation of organized interests, there must be centralized political and bureaucratic control of the intergovernmental policy objectives;
- adequate transitional measures, including the phasing-in of large-scale changes, are essential to limit both the political and economic shocks of policy change and to diffuse potential opposition from organized interests;
- the legitimization of large-scale changes, particularly those that require significant sacrifices of money and power by stakeholders in the existing system, largely depends on the federal government's capacity to generate a fiscal surplus sufficient to compensate prospective 'losers' and finance measures to ease the transition to a more sustainable pension system.

This paper will compare the current round of pension reforms with the last major federal pension reform initiative of 1981–4. It will examine the original objectives of pension reform, the process by which they were transformed into legislation between 1983 and 1986, and the basic factors that helped to shape national pension policy consensus which emerged from this process. Finally, it will seek to apply lessons from past attempts at pension reform to the current policy process.

FRAMING THE ISSUES: OBJECTIVES OF PENSION REFORM, 1981–4

The pension reform debate of the early 1980s was rooted in the social and political optimism of public officials who had rapidly expanded the foundations of the national welfare state during the 1960s. Courchene has noted the separation of economic and social policy considerations in Canada and other major industrial nations during the 1960s and early 1970s.[7] Initially, the major elements of the 1960s welfare state were implemented under the assumption that rapid economic and population growth would permit the significant expansion of income transfers and social services without serious tradeoffs against rates of private investment and economic growth.[8] The rising expectations of the 1960s and 1970s evolved into a growing sense of entitlement among program beneficiaries and their patrons in the social policy community. Indeed, Deaton comments that 'liberal social welfare and traditional Marxist analyses...tend to view pensions (state and private) and social security expenditures more generally, as a free good. ...The implicit assumption underlying many current analyses is that pensions are a "free good" because they are a "social right."'[9]

A series of federal initiatives and federal–provincial agreements resulted in the creation of the Canada and Quebec Pension Plans, and the development of a mixed public/private pension system involving four other elements: the income-based Guaranteed Income Supplement (GIS) (and related provincial programs); the universal Old Age Security (OAS) pension, financed from general tax revenues after 1971; registered pension plans, primarily for employees of larger corporations; and Registered Retirement Savings Plans (RRSPs) as a supplemental private arrangement for those who 'fell between the cracks' of the other systems. The social policy community that emerged from these developments was heavily focused on the challenges of eliminating poverty and reducing economic inequality, primarily through the expansion of public programs. Generating the fiscal or economic resources to achieve these objectives was usually seen as someone else's problem.

The pension policy initiatives of the 1970s and early 1980s had three major objectives. First, federal and provincial policy planners sought to achieve universal pension coverage, either through the expansion of universal public programs or a mix of public and private provision. Second, especially at the provincial level, they sought to expand the accessibility, flexibility, and portability of private pension arrangements, particularly in recognition of the growing geographic and career mobility of the postwar 'baby boom' generation. Third, they sought to address the retirement income needs of those underserviced by existing arrangements—particularly women, the self-employed, employees of small businesses, and the single elderly.

For much of the federal social policy community, organized labour and the Canadian left, the preferred means of achieving these objectives was an expansion of the Canada Pension Plan to cover 50 percent of pre-retirement earnings. However, these objectives increasingly brought them into conflict with the growing fiscal constraints of both federal and provincial governments, the jurisdictional constraints on large-scale pension reform, and the capacity of governments and the private sector to generate growing levels of employment, disposable income, economic growth, and taxation simultaneously.

Provincial consent, won with difficulty during the boom times of the 1960s, was even more difficult to obtain as some provinces, most notably Ontario and Alberta, began to question the sustainability of existing social policies. The aging 'baby boom generation' would face tax increases from the current 3.6 percent of payroll to levels then estimated to be in the range of 10 percent by 2010—even without a significant increase in benefit levels. Furthermore, CPP expansion would cut across a wide range of federal and provincial economic policy objectives by reducing overall savings rates, limiting the growth of domestic capital markets and risking increased Canadian dependence on foreign capital—a policy outcome totally at odds both with the economic nationalism of the Trudeau restoration of 1980 and the traditional 'business liberalism' of the federal Tory opposition and several major provincial governments.

The business community, already at odds with federal economic policies, was almost unanimous in its opposition to higher payroll taxes, which are not profit-sensitive, and which fall most heavily on labour-intensive sectors responsible for the bulk of job creation.[10] These factors became even more important as the Canadian economy slid into a major recession in 1981–2. CPP expansion thus became the most politically sensitive issue of the pension reform debate.

The burgeoning federal deficit of the early 1980s made expansion of the OAS a political nonstarter when attempting to address the income needs of current pensioners. However, it was not until the mid-1980s that politicians began to speak about targeting the OAS to lower and middle-income earners through the tax system. While most social policy planners were looking for ways to reduce dependence on the GIS, particularly for single elderly women, a number of factors—the growth in the number of women in the paid work force, the erosion of private pensions by inflation and increasing labour mobility, and increased family instability—meant that a growing percentage of single elderly, especially women, were dependent on the GIS.

At the same time, the federal government attempted to promote uniform standards for private employment pensions in such areas as vesting, portability, and credit splitting and survivors' benefits through a series of federal–provincial meetings. These proposals gradually provided a common ground for incremental pension reform for major business associations, several provinces, and the Department of Finance.

PENSION REFORM: INSTITUTIONS AND PROCESSES

The federal government had initiated a wide-ranging review of social benefits, including pensions, in 1976.[11] This process was complemented by the appointment of an Ontario Royal Commission on Pension Policy in 1977, the study of the Senate Committee on the Retirement Age, released in 1979, and parallel studies in several provinces.[12] While some of these initiatives were stalled by a combination of fiscal constraints, (federal) cabinet preoccupations with constitutional issues and an adverse climate of public opinion towards the large-scale expansion of government during the late 1970s, they received a renewed impetus following the Trudeau government's unexpected return to power in 1980.

The National Pensions Conference was organized jointly by the Departments of National Health and Welfare and Finance in April 1981. Pension, labour, business, women's, and social policy organizations met in Ottawa to exchange points of view.[13] However, a vast gulf emerged at the conference between business and financial sector associations whose preference for pension reform was for a consensual reform and gradual expansion of the private pension system and the network of labour, women's, and social policy organizations pressing for a major expansion of the public pensions system.[14] This was mirrored in the federal cabinet in the split between Health Minister Monique Begin and other 'welfare Liberals' and 'business Liberals' who urged incremental changes to the pension system and a delay of more far reaching measures that might interfere with capital markets and slow the process of economic recovery.

Marc Lalonde's appointment as Minister of Finance in September 1982 facilitated cabinet approval of the latter strategy and its release through a Green Paper by Lalonde and Begin in December 1982.[15] As a former Minister of Health and Welfare, Lalonde was familiar with the file. In contrast to Begin, Lalonde was strongly committed to the principle that the state should encourage individuals to take responsibility to save for their own retirement. Preferring to avoid lengthy negotiations with the provinces, a majority of which had already expressed strong opposition to CPP expansion, Lalonde opted for the development of a consensus package in areas within federal jurisdiction which could be implemented before an election expected in 1984.[16]

The Green Paper addressed five major issues: pension coverage, indexation, portability, flexibility, and women's issues. However, it avoided firm positions on the two major issues: whether and how to achieve increased mandatory coverage and adequate inflation protection. The issue of equal tax treatment of RPPs and RRSPs, while addressed in passing, was left to a subsequent discussion paper to be prepared by Finance Department officials.

In February 1983, the government struck an all-party committee of the House of Commons, led by Begin's former Parliamentary Secretary, Doug Frith, with the objective of developing a consensus on policy reforms capable of immediate implementation. The Committee faced a double challenge: to agree on a package of recommendations that could be implemented prior to the next election within a policy framework that could survive the demographic, fiscal, and political changes of the next generation. The policy process surrounding the hearings took place at three levels: the Committee and its staff, the competition among interest groups to influence the policy agenda, and the federal bureaucracy.

After initial briefings for the Task Force to familiarize MPs with the complex range of issues involved in the Green Paper, Frith attempted to establish a course independent from Task Force staff and Privy Council Office (PCO) officials, most of whom were strongly committed to the Health and Welfare position of expanding the CPP.[17] The Committee identified four major factors that shaped its eventual consensus. Changes in career patterns were pointing towards multi-employer careers for most Canadians, rather than patterns of stable employment with a single company. This suggested the need for greater flexibility in retirement savings plans and a greater emphasis on personal pension ownership. The feminization of the work force and declining family stability meant that women had to have opportunities to accumulate retirement savings in their own right, not just as part of a family savings pattern. Demographic changes pointed to a rapidly aging work force with workers supporting more than twice as many pensioners for longer periods of retirement early in the next century. This in turn made the enormous intergenerational transfers implicit in an expanded CPP unsustainable both on political and economic grounds.[18]

This policy diagnosis was reinforced by Lalonde's strategic decision to pursue policies of co-operation with the private sector, rather than the confrontational approach of the 1980–2 period, to facilitate recovery from the deep recession of the early 1980s.[19] As the Liberals were trailing the opposition Conservatives in the polls through much of this period, the government's political leverage was quite limited in pursuing unilateral policy change.

TABLE 1 Submissions to Pension Task Force, 1983

	Number of Submissions	Percent of Total Submissions
Business/Professional groups	43	26.5
Labour groups	38	23.5
Women's groups	25	15.4
Seniors/Pensioners	25	15.4
Public Sector (prov. & mun. governments, economic councils, and Crown corporations)	10	6.2
Social policy/Anti-poverty groups	8	4.9
Politicians	3	1.9
Pension/Financial groups	3	1.9
Other	7	4.3
Total	162	

SOURCE: *Parliamentary Task Force on Pension Reform*, Third Report (Ottawa, 1983), 113–17.

By early July 1983, the Liberal and PC members of the Task Force had agreed that the broad outline of their report would centre on a package of tax measures, along with targeted improvements of federal programs to meet the needs of specific constituencies. The Committee then hired private sector consultants to reduce its dependence on the data provided by Committee staff and Health and Welfare officials.[20] The Parliamentary Task Force on Pension Reform held extensive hearings in centres across Canada, hearing presentations from 162 organizations (see Table 1).

The battle lines at the Committee hearings parallelled those of the National Pensions Conference two years before. Organized labour, most women's groups, and social policy advocates argued for an expansion of the Canada Pension Plan, mandatory indexing of private pensions, and provisions for 'housewives' pensions.' The major national business groups, while presenting separate briefs on individual sectoral concerns, developed a consensus position through the Business Committee on Pension Policy (BCPP). The BCPP commissioned extensive economic and actuarial research on the costs of various pension reform issues, the extent and nature of pension coverage, and the impact of proposed changes on capital markets.[21] These studies were effective in challenging the economic assumptions of the Green Paper. By emphasizing the probable effects of CPP expansion in displacing private pension savings—much of them recycled into private sector investment—in favour of current consumption on increased social spending, they succeeded in portraying CPP expansion both as a threat to medium-term economic growth and the long-term financial security of Canadians. During the late 1970s and early

1980s, private pension savings accounted for a significantly larger share of net private savings in Canada than in either Britain or the United States.[22] As pension funds had become the fastest growing source of investment capital for business expansion, the corporate and financial sectors had a vital interest in promoting the expansion of the private pension system.[23] Small business and the rapidly growing number of self-employed Canadians had an equally strong interest in the enhancement of the RRSP system.[24] The united business front, and the priority placed on a private-sector-led economic recovery by both Liberals and Conservatives in the aftermath of the 1982 recession helped to shift the terms of debate toward the targeting of specific income disparities as the key goal of pension reform rather than the sweeping, broad brush proposals advanced by much of the social policy lobby.

While this was happening, the bureaucratic policy process resulted in the Department of Finance pre-empting the lead role in pension reform rather than having to negotiate its details through the Privy Council Office or the Ministry of State for Social Development.[25] As changes to the Pension Benefits Standards Act (PBSA) and the Canada Pension Plan would have to be negotiated with the provincial finance ministers, Deputy Finance Minister Mickey Cohen was able to exploit Finance's role as the central agency of fiscal federalism to seize control of the policy agenda. Thus, rather than social policy being designed largely in isolation from economic policy, Finance's success in controlling the internal policy process allowed for a much closer co-ordination of social, fiscal, and economic policies than would have been possible under the cabinet committee structures of the 1970s.

The Parliamentary and bureaucratic policy streams were drawn together at a meeting between Frith and Lalonde in late September 1983. Frith argued that the pension reform package should provide for the equalization of benefits in the tax treatment of RPP and RRSP contributions.[26] The existing RPP ceiling provided for a maximum 'tax assisted' pension of about $62,000— about three times the Average Industrial Wage (AIW). Politically, it made more sense to phase-in an increase in the RRSP ceiling to this level than to reduce the earnings ceiling for defined benefits pensions.[27]

The Task Force Report in November 1983 reflected a consensus of the Liberal and Conservative members, with NDP members preparing a dissenting report. The Committee report recommended a series of technical reforms in the Pension Benefit Standards Acts that supported most of the Green Paper's recommendations—and went well beyond the proposals of the business community. This included proposals for expanding CPP credits for women taking leave from the paid work force for up to seven years. However, the main proposal of the Committee's report was to equalize the tax treatment of RPPs and RRSPs over five years: 'The Task Force recommends that limits on contributions to tax-assisted retirement savings plans be amended so that: (a) the same comprehensive limit applies regardless of the retirement savings vehicle or combination of vehicles used; and (b) for workers with the same total earnings during their working years, the same comprehensive limit applies irrespective of differences in year-by-year earnings.'[28]

The Committee's proposals also included a pension ceiling of one-and-a-half times the average wage and a tax claw-back of individual tax-assisted pension earnings in excess of the ceiling.

PENSION REFORM: THE OUTCOME

While the broad outlines of the Committee's report had been 'sold' to Finance in September–October 1983, the details of its implementation were left entirely in the hands of departmental officials. The Social Policy and Federal–Provincial Relations Branch took responsibility for the proposed PBSA and CPP changes, while the Tax Policy and Legislation Branch managed the tax changes. The two processes took place independently, with co-ordination primarily at a level of mid-ranking and junior officials.[29]

The proposed changes were tabled in two discussion papers in the 1984 budget—one relating to the Canada Pension Plan and entitlements under the Pension Benefits Standards Act,[30] the other to proposed changes in federal tax policies.[31] Inherited by the Mulroney Government after the 1984 election, they became law in modified form in 1986.

The proposals for CPP and private pension reform became part of extensive federal–provincial negotiations between 1984 and 1986. Facing an overloaded federal–provincial agenda, Lalonde's PC successor at Finance, Michael Wilson, agreed with his provincial colleagues on a series of annual CPP premium increases of 0.2 percent between 1986 and 2005 to maintain its medium-term viability. Earlier proposals for 'housewives' pensions' were sharply scaled back as actuarially unsound. Discussions with federal officials suggest that Wilson's flexibility in securing a major fiscal restructuring of the CPP was severely hindered by three major factors: the lack of fiscal flexibility to purchase provincial consent to a major restructuring of the CPP,[32] the Mulroney government's political and constitutional agendas, which placed a premium on the pursuit of co-operation rather than confrontation with the provinces,[33] and the government's declining popularity midway through its first mandate.

Private pension reforms, which were ultimately implemented in January 1987, maintained the voluntary nature of the private system while expanding eligibility to part-time workers and full-time employees with two years' seniority. Improvements were made to vesting regulations and pension portability. Survivor and spousal benefits were enhanced, with the dangers of growing family instability to retirement security recognized through mandatory credit splitting between spouses. Although inflation indexing, a major priority of the early 1980s, was not implemented, this was offset to a degree by the achievement of virtual price stability during the early 1990s.[34]

The tax-based proposals included an increase in the RRSP deduction ceiling to $10,000 in 1985 and a phased increase to $15,500 by 1988, with subsequent indexation.[35] Unused RRSP contribution levels could be carried forward to future tax years for up to seven years. The equalization of RRSP and RPP tax benefits resulted in the reduction of pension entitlements for some upper-income executives.

The Mulroney government accepted the principles of pension reform set out by Lalonde in the 1984 budget, but deferred their implementation for several years due to fiscal constraints. Michael Wilson's 1985 budget renewed the pledge to adjust and index contribution limits by 1989. A White Paper was issued in October 1986, together with detailed rules and procedures extending the phase-in period to 1988–91.[36] Integrated with the 1987 White Paper on Tax Reform,[37] the tax changes were deferred again—to 1989–95.[38] Actual implementation began in the 1991 tax year. Amazingly, through all these changes, while the value of the 1984 tax changes were eroded somewhat by inflation, their basic contents remained unchanged.

The one departure from the consensual approach to pension reform in the 1980s, Wilson's attempt to reduce the indexing of public pensions in his 1985 budget foundered on the outraged response of senior's groups and the Mulroney cabinet's reluctance to challenge the 'sacred trust' of universality.[39] While opinion polls at the time suggested broad public support for the increased targeting of income transfer programs, Wilson was faulted both for acting abruptly to cut entitlements for current pensioners, and for placing short-term deficit reduction considerations ahead of the need to protect the future income security of low-income seniors.

PENSION REFORM IN THE 1990S

Pension reform is one element in the federal government's attempted overhaul of social security policies in the 1990s. The key elements in this process are fiscal sustainability and the targeting of income transfer programs, including pensions, to those in greatest need.

On the surface, the differences between the pension reform exercise of 1982–4 and the social policy reforms of the 1990s are greater than the similarities (see Table 2). Rather than responding to a pattern of growing public expectations, Canadians as a whole are facing the prospect of declining living standards unless significant changes are made in the management of both public and personal finances.[40] Despite the demands of entrenched social policy groups, federal officials—particularly the Minister of Finance, are emphasizing that the purpose of social policy review is the targeting (effectively the rationing) of public benefits—while attempting to maintain the capacity of individual citizens to save for their own retirement. 'The reform of social security cannot be contemplated in isolation from the fiscal realities facing governments in Canada. Until the fiscal situation of governments improves, there will be no

TABLE 2 ˆ Comparing Pension Reform in the 1980s and the 1990s		
	Early 1980s	**Late 1990s**
KEY POLICY PROBLEMS	• universal access to secure retirement incomes	• sustainability of existing public programs - demographic - fiscal
	• inflation protection	
		• growing consensus on targeting of public income transfers
MAIN AREAS OF CONTENTION	• continued emphasis on intergenerational transfers vs. funding of future obligations	• growing consensus on need to limit burden of international ? transfers
	• setting priorities for desirable pension improvements	• maintaining vs. selective reduction of future benefits
	• public vs. private pension systems as dominant element in postreform system	• public vs. private control of pension-related capital accumulation
PROCESS	• gradual shift from isolated focus on social policy within fiscal constraints to integration of social/fiscal/economic policy under finance dept. control	• close integration of fiscal, economic, and social policies - finance dominant actor from the start - fiscal constraints far tighter than in late 1970s, 1980s
	• degree of policy change inversely proportional to need for federal–provincial consensus	• CPP reform much higher priority—major change required in short-term to sustain current benefit levels
	• political and fiscal limits to securing provincial support for CPP reforms	• fiscal constraints limit federal capacity to purchase provincial consensus

RPC privatization plan
A direct challenge to a) growth [?] std. [?]
b) SD equity goals

new money for new programs, including social programs. And existing expenditures must be brought under control and in some instances reduced.'[41]

However, there are also similarities to the 1980s that are worth noting. Just as Lalonde's task in building consensus was eased (and Wilson's hampered) by the nature and political constituencies of their parliamentary opposition, Finance Minister Martin's political position is facilitated by a fragmented opposition whose main English voice, the Reform Party, is committed to an even more thorough restructuring of national social programs.

The slow pace of employment growth following the 1990–2 recession will mean that any debate over CPP reform will be closely watched for its prospective impact both on short- and medium-term job creation and on capital markets. A shift towards steady-state funding of the Canada Pension Plan would produce a CPP reserve fund of almost $130 billion in current dollars—about 30 percent of the total assets of Canadian pension and mutual funds in 1994[42]—raising issues of how such a reserve is to be managed to avoid the manipulation of Canadians' retirement savings to serve short-term partisan political purposes. Although no equivalent to the Business Council on Pension Policy has arisen to challenge the refinancing of the CPP, the campaign mounted by the C.D. Howe Institute and the Reform Party to privatize the CPP through its conversion to a system of mandatory private pension accounts poses an interesting challenge to the prevailing orthodoxy.[43] The biggest challenge facing either the steady-state funding approach or the privatization of the CPP is the challenge to securing existing pension entitlements during the transition period—or selling the Canadian public on a modest reduction in those entitlements.

The proposed reform of public pensions announced in the 1996 federal budget suggests that Finance Minister Paul Martin has learned the lesson of Michael Wilson's periodic attempts to curtail pension entitlements. Benefit changes are being phased-in over an extended period, to ease the potential shocks of change and to make benefit reductions prospective rather than retrospective. (Shades of tax reform!) Benefits will be modestly enhanced for lower-income seniors, but radically reduced for those with annual personal and family incomes over $50,000. The latter have received some compensation by way of increased flexibility in RRSP contributions.[44]

SHAPING CONSENSUS ON PENSION REFORM: 1982–4

The pension reform debate of 1982–6 reflects the increasing difficulty of social policy activists in implementing proposals for policy reform in isolation from fiscal and economic considerations during an era of growing fiscal limits and increasing competition for limited public expenditures. The social policy community's failure to address the consequences of its proposals, particularly for capital formation and medium-term economic growth, played directly into the hands of the business community, which reconciled its often competing interests to head off major structural changes to social policy that it rightly perceived to be detrimental to its fundamental interests. Arguably, integrating social security policies and programs with those promoting medium-term economic growth, business investment, and job creation is the central challenge facing those who would improve our social safety net as we prepare to enter the twenty-first century.

The pension reform debate also illustrates the capacity of the federal Department of Finance to take control of the pensions debate, and indeed, the necessity of such control, in order to balance short- and long-term considerations of fiscal, social, and economic policies and of federal–provincial relations. While the federal government was able to introduce widespread piecemeal improvements to public and private pensions, it did so within a structural framework that respected the existing balance of economic interests and entitlements. This made it possible for Ottawa to co-opt business interests through a major expansion of the tax preferences for private retirement savings and, with them, the expansion of private savings available for investment through capital markets. To balance the short- and medium-term costs and benefits of increased public spending, it is necessary to phase-in changes in ways that avoid untimely increases in business costs, 'grandfather' social entitlements, especially for those in greatest need, and provide adequate transitional arrangements to allow those facing increased costs or reduced benefits to adapt to changing circumstances. Wilson's failure to carry out this balancing act when attempting to limit the indexing of public pensions in his 1985 budget, although subsequently corrected in his later efforts to increase the targeting of social benefits through the integration of tax and transfer systems, squandered much of the political capital necessary for the Mulroney government to sell both deficit reduction and social policy reform to a sceptical public.

Finally, the pension reform debate of 1982–6 illustrates the ability of provincial governments to impose effective limitations on federal tax changes overlapping their jurisdictions. With their veto over possible CPP legislation, their jurisdiction over most private pension plans, and the capacity of the larger provinces to complement or frustrate federal fiscal and social policy initiatives through parallel or countervailing actions, Ottawa can only take direct action within areas under its own direct jurisdiction unless it is prepared to purchase provincial co-operation with fiscal or policy concessions. However, the diversity of provincial interests (and ideological outlooks) and the relative indigence of the federal government in recent years suggest that a strategy of purposeful, incremental change is likely to be more productive than grand strategies for the recasting of large elements of social policy.

NOTES

1. Geoffrey Brennan and James M. Buchanan, *The Power to Tax: Analytical Foundations of a Fiscal Constitution* (Cambridge, 1980), 3.
2. The federal government's abortive efforts to partially de-index its Guaranteed Income Supplement program in its 1985 budget highlighted the political dangers of attempting to reduce pension entitlements for current pensioners. See David Bercuson et al., *Sacred Trust? Brian Mulroney and the Conservative Party in Power* (Toronto, 1986), 93–120.
3. Trial balloons floated by Finance Minister Paul Martin about taxing the build-up of investment income within RRSPs before his 1995 budget prompted a sharp backlash from the rapidly growing financial services industry and many of its middle-class clients.
4. Canada, Department of Finance, *An Information Paper for Consultations on the Canada Pension Plan, (CPP Information Paper) released by the Federal, Provincial and Territorial Governments of Canada* (Ottawa, 1996); Steven James et al., 'The Economics of Canada Pension Plan Reforms,' Working paper 95-09 (Ottawa, 1995).
5. *Proceedings of the National Pensions Conference*, 31 March, 1–2 April 1981 (Ottawa, 1981).
6. Marc Lalonde, *Building Better Pensions for Canadians* (Ottawa, 1984); Marc Lalonde, *Action Plan for Pension Reform* (Ottawa, 1984).
7. Thomas J. Courchene, *Social Policy in the 1990s: Agenda for Reform* (Toronto, 1987); Courchene, 'Toward the Reintegration of Social and Economic Policy,' in G. Bruce Doern and Bryne B. Purchase, eds., *Canada at Risk?* (Toronto, 1990); Courchene, *Social Canada in the Millennium*, (Toronto, 1994).
8. Thomas J. Courchene, 'Path Dependency, Positive Feedback, and Paradigm Warp: A Schumpeterian Approach to the Social Order,' in Elisabeth B. Reynolds, ed., *Income Security in Canada: Changing Needs, Changing Means* (Montreal, 1993), 46–9. This is illustrated by the fact that the actuarial assumptions for the original CPP in 1966 projected that premium rates for a mature CPP would increase to no more than 5.5 percent in 2030; *CPP Information Paper* (1996), 20.
9. Richard Lee Deaton, *The Political Economy of Pensions: Power, Politics and Social Change in Canada, Britain and the United States* (Vancouver, 1989), 9.
10. Ontario, Small Business Advocacy, Ministry of Industry, Trade, and Technology, *State of Small Business 1987* (Toronto, 1988), 120–2.
11. Health and Welfare Canada, 'News Release,' 18 April 1976; 'A Credo of Social Security Values,' 18 April 1976; 'Strategies for a New Social Security System,' 18 April 1976.
12. Canada, Senate, *Retirement without Tears*, Proceedings of the Special Senate Committee on Retirement Age Policies, Issue # 1, 15 April 1980. The *Report of the Ontario Royal Commission on Pension Policy* (Toronto, 1981), along with reports in Quebec and Saskatchewan, had increased pressure for mandatory private pension plans and some form of mandatory indexing.
13. *Proceedings of the National Pensions Conference*.
14. Deaton suggests that this division largely reflects class interests—between those groups for whom financial opportunities are largely dictated by market forces and by those whose power and prosperity is largely dependent upon the regulatory or redistributive activities of governments. Deaton, *Political Economy of Pensions*, 107–8.
15. *Better Pensions for Canadians* (Ottawa, 1982).
16. Interview, Marc Lalonde, Andrea Vincent (Executive Director, Association of Canadian Pension Management), senior Finance Department Official.

17. Interview, Douglas Frith.
18. Interview, Douglas Frith. Intergenerational transfer—the subsidy paid by one generation to support benefits for its predecessors beyond those which can be maintained by the return from pension plan assets.
19. Geoffrey E. Hale, 'The Politics of Canadian Tax Policy: 1978–88,' (PhD diss., The University of Western Ontario, 1996), Chapter 10.
20. Interview, Douglas Frith.
21. Business Committee on Pension Policy, *The Consensus Brief* (Toronto, 1983); William M. Mercer Ltd., *The Costs Study*, 5 volumes (Toronto, 1983); K. Ambachtsheer and D.D. Ezra, *Capital Markets Study* (Toronto, 1983).
22. Deaton, *Political Economy of Pensions*, 170–1.
23. Deaton, *Political Economy of Pensions*, 168–88.
24. The administrative costs of traditional defined benefit plans were and are prohibitive for most small firms. The number of self-employed Canadians, those neither employed nor with employees of their own, rose 61 percent during the 1980s, largely as a result of economic restructuring.
25. A senior Finance Department official comments that 'Mickey [Cohen]'s mastery of the operations of government was vital' to the eventual shape of the 1984 pension reform proposals. Interview, former senior Finance Department official.
26. Interview, Douglas Frith.
27. The latter included not only corporate managers and professionals, but also a large number of unionized workers, whose pensions were usually calculated on the basis of the average of their final three years' earnings. [Author's note: There is a discrepancy here between the text of the Frith Committee's report and the above discussion. The Committee proposed that tax-assisted pensions provide for the replacement of up to 60 percent of pre-retirement earnings to a maximum of $ 55,000—a level that would cover 90 percent of men and 98 percent of women at the time. Accumulated benefits above this level would have been subject to a tax claw-back. This suggests that Frith was able to convince Lalonde of the merits of higher tax preferences for retirement savings, but not his Committee colleagues.]
28. Minutes and Proceedings of the Special Committee on Pension Reform, *The Second and Third Reports to the House*, Issue # 38 (Ottawa, 1983), 101–2.
29. Interview, senior Finance Department official.
30. Marc Lalonde, *Action Plan for Pension Reform* (Ottawa, 1984).
31. Lalonde, *Building Better Pensions for Canadians*.
32. Slow economic growth in 1986 left Wilson well short of his deficit reduction targets; federal–provincial agreements on energy and training policies had contributed significantly to this problem.
33. Interview, former Deputy Minister of Finance.
34. Deaton, *Political Economy of Pensions*, 108–9.
35. These changes were intended to offset the impact of inflation since the last ceiling adjustment in 1977.
36. Department of Finance, *A Better Pension System: Saving for Retirement—Improved Tax Treatment: Detailed Rules and Procedures* (Ottawa, 1986).
37. Michael H. Wilson, *Tax Reform 1987: Income Tax Reform* (Ottawa, 1987), 22–3, 66, 73, 78, 82.
38. The 1996 federal budget froze the RRSP contribution ceiling at $13,500 through 2003, before provisionally allowing it to rise to the planned $15,500 in 2005. The pension limit for RPPs was also frozen until 2004. Paul Martin, *Budget in Brief* (Ottawa, 1996), 20.
39. Bercuson et al., *Sacred Trust?* 102–20.
40. Bruce Little, 'Future Youth to Be Taxed Doubly: Study,' *Globe and Mail*, 26 Feb. 1996, B1.
41. Government of Canada, *Improving Social Security: A Discussion Paper* (Ottawa, 1994), 23.
42. Keith P. Ambachtsheer, *Canada's 20% Foreign Property Rule: Why and How It Should Be Eliminated*, Paper commissioned by the Pension Investment Association of Canada and the Investment Funds Institute of Canada (Toronto, 1995).
43. William B.P. Robson, *Putting Some Gold in the Golden Years: Fixing the Canada Pension Plan*, Commentary # 76 (Toronto, 1996).
44. Canada. Department of Finance, *The Seniors' Benefit: Securing the Future* (Ottawa, 1996).

RELUCTANT PARTNERS

State Regulation of Private Nursing Homes in Ontario, 1941–72

JAMES STRUTHERS

Canadian Studies
Trent University

O ver the past two decades, growing attacks on the welfare state have focused public attention on the merits of private provision of social services through either the voluntary or for-profit sectors. Much of this debate has been 'fundamentally ideological,' Josephine Rekart argues in a recent study, informed by little information about the actual terrain separating public and private which has 'yet to be mapped out.' Through an insightful analysis of what she terms Canada's 'mixed social economy tradition,' Mariana Valverde has also called for a fundamental rethinking of 'the historical relationship of public to private powers in the area of the social.'[1]

Exploration of this 'mixed social economy' is still in its early stages and remains focused, within the work of Rekart and Valverde, upon relationships between the state and the voluntary sector. This article will explore the commercial dimension of welfare provision by analysing the rise of private nursing homes within Ontario in the three decades after World War II, and their gradual incorporation within a regulatory regime by the provincial and local state. Nursing homes provide an important yet relatively unexplored site for research into the relationship between private and public within welfare policy. Within a health care sector otherwise dominated by the much-celebrated expansion of public responsibility for hospital and medical insurance, the provision of long-term care remains a rapidly growing island of private profit. In Ontario, these trends are particularly strong as the province leads every jurisdiction except PEI in its reliance upon the for-profit sector in meeting the health and caregiving needs of the aged.[2]

Why did private nursing homes come to play such a key role within the field of long-term care within Ontario? What role did different branches of the state, at both the local, provincial, and federal level, play in balancing the needs of the elderly against the search for profits within an aging population? Does the history of Ontario's experience with private nursing homes provide support for contemporary arguments favouring the delegation of more state responsibility for caregiving to the profit-making sector? By looking at the rise of private nursing homes in Ontario after World War II, I hope to shed some light on these questions.

THE ORIGINS OF NURSING HOMES

As elsewhere, the origins of private nursing homes in Ontario are obscure. Although boarding of the aged, particularly widows, was not uncommon in the nineteenth century, the earliest references to private accommodation targeted specifically to the elderly date back to the 1930s.[3] Public health officials in that decade describe dwellings, usually run by single women, who 'believed they [were] operating Boarding House[s] for elderly people.' No medical or nursing care was provided within them, however. If taken ill, the 'onus [was] put on the patient to make arrangements.' Over time 'some of their guests became ill and bedfast,' nursing home owners later recalled, 'and before they knew it, boarding house operators in effect had become nursing home owners for there was no real place to send these unfortunate individuals.' Other homes, government officials noted, were launched by registered nurses wishing to go into business for themselves, who drew upon a supply of untrained, 'middle-aged women who [found] it difficult to obtain employment elsewhere,' as poorly paid attendants. Within Toronto, a city faced with an acute shelter shortage in the 1940s, public health officials pointed to growing numbers of the elderly 'lying sometimes in filth and squalor in a rooming house with no one to feed or attend them, sometimes in rooms so cold that they cannot be bathed by a visiting nurse and no hospital will accept them.'[4]

Increased demand for private nursing home care derived from a number of sources. The most obvious was population aging. Between 1900 and 1930 the number of Canadians over age sixty-five jumped by 115 percent, and leaped by another 34 percent during the decade of the 1930s. Within Ontario the percentage of the population aged sixty-five or older ballooned from

5.5 percent to 9.0 percent between 1901 and 1951. Despite this rapid growth in the numbers of elderly, institutional accommodation for their care failed to keep pace. Within Ontario, residents living within charitable or county Houses of Refuge quadrupled between 1900 and 1948 despite no new construction of these facilities. As a consequence, all public and charitable homes for the aged, by the beginning of World War II, were plagued by severe and often dangerous overcrowding. By 1947 Ontario's county Houses of Refuge reported five hundred beds in their attics, basements, and hallways, yet still were plagued by long waiting lists in the hundreds for admission. Toronto city officials pointed out that while their city's population had grown five times between 1900 and 1941, institutional accommodation for the elderly had only doubled, resulting in the 'rise of unsupervised, commercialized accommodation' for those with 'minor and serious illnesses common to aged people.'[5]

Rapid urbanization and a worsening housing crisis during the wartime economy of the 1940s also reduced the ability or willingness of children to take in their bedridden elderly parents. 'With the best of intentions,' government spokespersons commented, 'younger members of families are finding it increasingly difficult to maintain the older members who have not been able...to look after themselves.'[6] One reason was the changing labour market participation of married daughters, traditional caregivers for the elderly, from the 1940s onwards. Reflecting on changes in family life during the 1950s, newspapers pointed out that chronic illness among the elderly 'requires almost constant attention and care *which the busy housewife of today feels she cannot provide* while looking after her own children or working at the same time.' As a result, 'each year an increasing number of elderly people had to look for some other place where they could be looked after.'[7]

The market for paid caregiving also received an enormous boost through the creation of means-tested old age pensions in 1929 and the arrival of universal Old Age Security payments in 1951. Through public pensions, growing numbers of the elderly for the first time could offer cash on a regular monthly basis in return for room, board, and perhaps a modicum of personal care. 'Some...are kept by two people, sometimes a couple, sometimes a widow, sometimes two or three people, getting together and getting a big house in a village or town and taking in these old age pensioners,' CCF Party veteran Agnes Macphail informed the Ontario legislature in 1950. 'Unfortunately, they have to take most of their pensions in order to run the place.'[8] By the mid-1960s, two-thirds of Ontario's four hundred to five hundred nursing homes still had less than twenty beds, most having been created out of such converted private housing.[9] The availability and adequacy of such nursing home care in subsequent years would remain closely tied to the monthly amounts provided through Canada's public and private pensions.

THE ROOTS OF REGULATION

The shortage of acute care hospital beds first drew the local and ultimately the provincial state into subsidizing, licensing, and inspecting nursing homes. By the end of the Great Depression cash-starved local hospitals in Ontario were filling up with nonpaying patients, many of them elderly and in need of chronic bed care. They 'come from rooms where they were caring for themselves but because of their disabilities cannot return to them,' Toronto health officials complained. 'These patients are not wanted by anyone...so they are doomed to remain in General Hospital at $2.35 per day until death intervenes. In the meantime they are occupying beds urgently required for acute cases.'[10]

Beginning in 1941, Toronto began exploring less expensive alternatives by discharging elderly welfare patients into selected nursing homes at a subsidized rate of $40 per month, about half the cost of their hospital care. Although officially justified as an emergency measure and limited to only thirty patients, by 1947 Toronto had placed over six hundred elderly within nursing homes and cut the average length of stay within civic hospitals in half.[11] With the opening of Toronto's first municipal Home for the Aged in 1949, city officials hoped that wartime reliance on private nursing homes could come to an end. Yet the clientele, as in most of Ontario's new public Homes for the Aged built after 1947, quickly reflected a fundamental misdiagnosis by the provincial and local state of the emerging long-term care needs of the elderly. Three-quarters of that institution's seven hundred residents were ambulatory, and only 7 percent required full bed care. Seven out of ten were over the age of seventy and were totally reliant for income upon the inadequate $40 monthly old age pension. Ninety percent were single, widowed, separated, or divorced.[12]

The crisis addressed by the new public Homes for the Aged was poverty, isolation, and exploding shelter costs for the elderly, not the acute shortage of beds within hospitals. Yet Homes for the Aged across Ontario, throughout the 1940s and 1950s resisted building infirmary wards or admitting a larger proportion of bed-care patients, on the grounds that their intended clients were the poor, not the sick elderly.[13] Ontario's postwar aged desperately needed more adequate pensions, low-cost housing, and homecare programs that would allow them to remain living within the community, along with a sufficient supply of long-term care beds within or outside of hospitals. What they got were new institutions, called Homes for the Aged, intended for a mostly ambulatory residential population, to replace the hated county poorhouse.[14] By the early 1950s all of Ontario's public Homes for the Aged were filled to capacity and had long waiting lists. Meanwhile the number of subsidized welfare cases filling up private nursing homes remained as large as ever. What initially began as a temporary solution to a wartime hospital bed crisis, had quickly evolved into a permanent, unintended partnership of convenience between municipal welfare departments and private nursing homes.[15]

Until subsidized elderly welfare clients were placed in nursing homes, the issue of licensing these homes did not arise. '[T]here are *apparently* numerous private homes in Toronto admitting old age pensioners as boarders,' city welfare authorities acknowledged complacently in 1946. '[S]ome of them provide satisfactory care and some doubtful care, but under present circumstances adequate or effective supervision is impossible.'[16] This indifference drew increasing criticism by the end of the decade. In the legislature and within newspapers, complaints about 'boarding houses for pensioners' began to appear with growing frequency. 'You do not know where they are—they are not listed, they are just under private names and a great many old people are crowded into a house with no provision at all for recreation, nor for anybody to see whether they are getting the "breaks" for the money they are paying— just nothing done about it at all,' CCF members of the legislature argued. Church congregations protested against homes in which 'all [the elderly] could do was sit or lie in bed.' Similar sentiments surfaced inside the Ontario cabinet: '[S]hould we not take up with local governments the question of seeing that these homes are habitable and that the people are at least reasonably fed?' Health Minister Russell Kelly asked his colleagues. '[M]any are ill and they need some person in authority to help them.'[17]

The startling frequency of deaths in some Toronto nursing homes as reported by physicians and investigators from the provincial Old Age Pension (OAP) Commission finally galvanized city authorities into action. The bureaucratic scrutiny of the pension commission provided the state, for the first time, with a vehicle for correlating the incidence of death with specific locations. When thirty-six old age pensioners died over a two-year period at one Toronto nursing home—a death rate almost triple that of the much larger Queen Elizabeth Hospital for Incurables—pension commission officials became suspicious. 'Practically every one in the house had severe colds, all the old people were coughing, and one...was very ill in bed with pneumonia,' an OAP investigator noted during a surprise visit. A 'slim frightened looking person' had 'two black eyes and a badly swollen face.' Another elderly lady had a 'bad bruise on the left temple' and 'blood...oozing [from her] stocking...from the knee to the ankle.' Further inquiries revealed a home swarming with cockroaches and packed with thirty-five sick, elderly patients locked in, seven to a room, where doorknobs had been removed so doors could not be opened from the inside. Six men slept in the basement beside the furnace. Five more were housed in the attic. Residents who protested recalled that they were either 'treated worse

[or] put out, and as there are no homes for...old people we have to like it.' City welfare authorities reluctantly agreed. Without regulatory bylaws to force improvements, 'any drastic action might...only add to our troubles....[With] the shortage of institutional accommodation for this type of case, they would probably be left on the street.'[18]

Toronto's city council finally took action in July 1947 by passing Ontario's first bylaw providing for the registration, licensing, and inspection of private nursing homes. The bylaw soon became little more than a symbolic gesture. Unlicensed nursing homes continued to operate within the city and even to receive per diem stipends from the welfare department for the care of indigent elderly patients. They simply were paid less than licensed homes. It was an 'embarrassing situation,' local health officials confessed five years later, but there was little they could do to enforce compliance in the absence of alternative accommodation for the elderly or clear definitions to distinguish boarding house care from nursing home care. Hospitals and homes for the aged already had waiting lists in the hundreds.[19]

Throughout the next two decades, with the encouragement of provincial cost sharing, local governments did embark on a major program of building or renovating seventy modern Homes for the Aged, tripling the population living within state facilities. The 'astounding increase in the number of persons living beyond 65 years of age is the greatest social problem of our day,' government spokespersons acknowledged in announcing funding for the program. But this transformation of the 'old 19th Century "House of Refuge" or "poorhouse"' into what Ontario officials continually termed 'one of the finest systems of up-to-date Homes for the Aged in the world,' failed to meet growing demand for long-term care of the elderly as Ontario's population aged and family structures continued to change.[20] Side by side with public Homes for the Aged emerged an even more rapidly expanding private nursing home industry, which throughout the same two decades mostly escaped government regulation altogether. By 1957 only twelve municipalities licensed nursing homes and the licences granted 'were not in accordance with any real standards,' health officials agreed. Often the task was delegated to the 'municipal clerk, tax collector, or a member of Council who...knew little or nothing of patient care.' Few homes provided much more than room and board 'with practically no nursing care of a skilled type.' Local Medical Officers of Health seemed 'generally [to] show little or no interest in a Nursing Home,' provincial welfare officials conceded by the end of the 1950s.[21]

Public attention to these conditions was awakened by the First Ontario Conference on Aging, a three-day event organized by the Ontario Welfare Council (OWC) in June 1957. At this gathering, social workers, doctors, gerontologists, government officials, and nursing home operators came together for the first time to talk about the problems of an aging population and long-term care. A principal focus of the conference became conditions within private nursing homes. As Simcoe County health officials pointed out, 'we know very little about the exact number or kind of nursing homes which exist,' nor was there even a commonly accepted definition of what they were. Although most homes were unlicensed they could hardly be closed. 'What would we do with patients if it were decided to close them?'[22] Provincial treasury department officials agreed. 'The keepers of the private homes cannot be penalized too heavily,' they argued, 'because the only funds they have available, in many instances, is the $40 per month pension on which the unwanted old person must live.'[23]

Over 150 private nursing home operators also attending the conference came together two years later, with the help of the Ontario Welfare Council, to form the Associated Nursing Homes Incorporated of Ontario (ANHIO), the first provincial lobby group for the industry. Over the next decade the ANHIO, working in tandem with the OWC, would lead the campaign for provincial licensing, regulation, and subsidization of private nursing homes across the province.[24]

THE RELUCTANT STATE: PROVINCIAL LICENSING OF PRIVATE NURSING HOMES

Two federal initiatives after 1958 drew the province ever more deeply into the nursing home business. The first was Ontario's entry into Ottawa's unemployment assistance program in 1958. The second was the launching of publicly funded hospital insurance a year later. The Unemployment Assistance Act provided Ontario with 50 percent federal funding for the cost of unemployable indigents living within so-called 'homes for special care.' With the infusion of this new money, the province for the first time offered to relieve municipalities of 80 percent of the cost of caring for elderly welfare patients housed in private nursing homes. A government study revealed that the arrival of this funding created a major stimulus 'to the opening of many...homes with the proprietors, sometimes with no previous experience and few qualifications, applying for licensing.'[25]

Rapid expansion of the business intensified demands from established operators for provincial licensing and regulated standards within their industry to prevent unfair competition. It also forced Ontario's department of public welfare to begin paying some attention to the quality and conditions of care received by the elderly living within these homes. Provincial welfare authorities in 1958 drafted a model bylaw that municipalities could use for licensing and inspecting nursing homes in order to receive subsidies for the indigent. They rejected any suggestions that the province should undertake this responsibility itself, however, arguing such a task 'would require a large staff and continual policing.'[26]

Hospital insurance had a complex and more far-reaching impact. Within communities where there was a 'shortage of hospital beds for chronically ill patients' the legislation allowed for insurance coverage of private nursing home care 'on a temporary basis.' About forty-eight nursing homes were singled out for insured coverage by the Ontario Hospital Insurance Commission (OHSC), an action it undertook only with the greatest reluctance. Most nursing homes, OHSC officials argued, 'provided only the service any individual would receive from his family in his own home, if he were ill with the "flu" or the type of care given by a mother to an infant, at home.' To incorporate these beds within hospital insurance would open up the floodgates: '[A]ll patients who are receiving this care at home will demand coverage because it would then become "universally-available" under the intent of the Act.'[27]

The arrival of the new scheme also created a marked discrepancy between insured chronic care for the elderly within hospitals and expensive private care for them within nursing homes. Policing this medical borderline was 'indeed a very perplexing question,' Health Minister Matthew Dymond conceded:

> When do they stop being a patient who is chronically ill and in need of...hospital care and when do they become a patient who is essentially a...custodial care patient? It is not a medical diagnosis to say that a patient has nowhere else to go and I know...perfectly well that we have kept many such patients in our hospital beds over the past years for this very reason....I cannot see how these can ever be brought into such a hospital care insurance plan....It would become a mixed up polyglot of many things including health, welfare, and I do not know what else.[28]

The whole issue was surrounded by 'confusion,' he concluded, and would 'have to be threshed out.'[29]

The more provincial health officials learned about private nursing homes after 1959, as they attempted to determine which ones might be suitable for the temporary placement of chronic care patients, the more alarmed they became at the health of the elderly within them. 'Conditions in the majority of them [are] dreadful,' Dymond warned Premier Leslie Frost. 'The patients are overcrowded, inadequately and improperly cared for, by staffs which obviously have little or no training to equip them for the job....[W]e have...to decid[e] what responsibility, if any, we have to these people,' he argued, echoing statements made by his predecessor Russell Kelly a decade earlier. Two years later, Dymond was still urging Frost to act. Nursing homes were 'in such dreadful condition...that I have feared for many months a virtual explosion....[T]hey should be licensed by a central body, preferably the Department of Health...and...licensing should only be granted after certain minimal standards have been met.' Clearly influenced by conflicting advice from Deputy Welfare Minister James Band, who warned that regulating nursing homes 'would be a herculean task,' the Ontario Premier told Dymond he 'did not want to be involved in this at all.'[30]

The health minister's alarm received backing from nursing home operators themselves. In a petition sent directly to incoming premier, John Robarts, the Associated Nursing Homes Incorporated of Ontario argued that only provincial licensing and inspection could improve shoddy standards of care within the industry. Municipal licensing was so haphazard and 'unduly influenced by...political considerations and personal favouritism' that conscientious owners interested in providing quality care faced unfair competition from unscrupulous operators. Because welfare clients comprised 'more than half of the patients in nursing homes,' local governments most often 'overlooked substandard conditions because of the necessity of stretching the public dollar as far as it will go.'[31] Dymond agreed. 'In many cases there is no fire inspection,' he warned Robarts. '[O]nly good fortune has protected us from serious calamity.' For the time being the Ontario premier remained unconvinced. Although not willing to accept provincial responsibility for nursing homes, he did authorize the health minister to conduct a study of them in 1963 in order to gain more information.[32]

While this research—contracted out to the Ontario Welfare Council—was underway, two other government inquiries into aging focused an intense media spotlight upon nursing homes. Between 1964 and 1965 the Senate Committee on Aging, chaired by David Croll, and the Ontario legislature's own Select Committee on Aging heard deeply disturbing public testimony about conditions within nursing homes. Burrell Morris, former president of the ANHIO, shocked Ontario's select committee and garnered widespread media publicity by claiming that some nursing home operators were making 'profits as high as 30 and 40 percent in homes where blind patients were served scrapings off the plates of others.' In other homes record-keeping was so poor the operators 'don't even know how long some patients have been there.' As for medication, he said, 'in most cases there is little or no control.'[33]

After six years' experience in placing chronic care patients within carefully selected nursing homes, the chairman of the OHSC could only say 'we would much sooner be out of this thing, completely, as soon as we can. ...[F]rom what I have seen of nursing homes and I have seen a lot of them, I hope that if I become chronically ill, somebody will not put me in one.'[34] In Ottawa, expert witnesses from the nonprofit long-term care sector told David Croll's Senate Committee on Aging that current subsidies for private nursing homes were 'financing public psychological slums' in which people 'sit...and rot by the thousands.' Conditions in nursing homes were 'downright disgraceful,' the Croll committee concluded.[35]

An Ontario government enquiry into standards of nursing home care provided equally damning evidence. Almost half had no fire alarms, only one in five employed a registered nurse, and 'very few...consulted nutritionists' in preparing meals.[36] By 1965 all three government investigations into aging reached identical conclusions. At the very least, they concluded, nursing homes should be licensed and inspected by provincial departments of health so that conditions within them could be brought up to minimal standards of safety and decency.

The impact of these investigations along with damning newspaper publicity, vigorous prodding from his own health minister, and the prospect of an upcoming election finally moved Roberts to act.[37] In 1966 his government passed the Ontario Nursing Homes Act, establishing for the first time a provincial licensing and regulatory regime through the Department of Health for all nursing homes within the province. For those operators belonging to the ANHIO this was a key policy victory. Provincial regulation promised to bring some semblance of order through regulated competition to their expanding industry. It also cemented an uneasy partnership between private enterprise and the Department of Health to ensure that profitability could be reconciled with Ontario's burgeoning fiscal priorities as well as with the long-term care needs of the elderly.

FROM REGULATION TO INSURANCE

Because of the previous indifference of local governments, medical officers of health, and the OHSC to conditions within nursing homes, provincial health officials had a weak knowledge base from which to assert control over the industry—a problem compounded by an explosive 114 percent growth in nursing home care from 8,500 to 18,200 beds during the first three years following the onset of the provincial licensing and inspection. The industry simply grew 'without rhyme or reason' during these years observed Deputy Health Minister Dr. K.C. Charron, as new operators flooded into the field and began building homes

Ideas as info sources for policy
as policy advocates
policy beneficiaries

'before we know anything about it.' By the decade's end, over half of all nursing home operators in Ontario had been in business less than six years. Within the Ministry of Health, officials conceded that their own quality of knowledge with regard to nursing homes was little more than an educated guess.[38]

Nowhere was the problem more critical than in attempting to determine the per diem costs of nursing home care. 'At best the original rate...struck was a guess,' health officials commented in regard to the $6.50 daily subsidy level established between the OHSC and selected private homes after 1959 for the temporary placement of insured hospital patients. Welfare department payments to nursing homes similarly were based on 'no factual material,' because few nursing home owners either kept or made available standardized accounting records of their real costs.[39]

In the face of a burgeoning demand for long-term care, an increasingly militant nursing home lobby, according to health officials, took maximum advantage of the department's lack of knowledge of their industry to extract ever higher levels of financial support from taxpayers. 'When they were first organized, at a time when there was no order or co-ordination in the operation of nursing homes, they did seem to be doing a good job,' an exasperated Matthew Dymond complained to Robarts only a year after provincial licensing came into effect, 'but since the Province got into the business of regulating nursing homes, they have constituted themselves a pressure group to beat the Government over the head.' Two years later, the Health Minister was even more disparaging in his comments about private nursing homes: 'I have learned to my bitter sorrow,' he warned cabinet, 'that they are concerned about one thing only, making as much money as possible and giving as little as possible in return to the patients. ...[T]he sooner this is gotten into on a public basis, the sooner we will be able to provide good quality health care for this segment of our population.'[40] *public favoured over reg'd + funded private homes*

Public nursing homes were proposed and tentatively developed by the province's department of public welfare through its Rest Homes Act of 1966, which provided 50 percent capital funding and a 70 percent operating subsidy to municipalities willing to construct and administer 'Rest Homes,' separate and distinct from Homes for the Aged, to provide long-term bed and nursing care for the elderly. Unless a majority of nursing care facilities were developed under public or nonprofit auspices, welfare officials argued in defence of the bill, 'there would be a never-ending pressure on the Government from proprietary operators to meet increased rates in order that they might maintain an adequate profit level.' In the United States, they warned, state authorities were 'completely over a barrel due to their over-reliance on proprietary nursing homes.' Increased competition from public homes within Ontario would be 'highly desirable.'[41]

✻ *private not internally competitive: acting*
as a bloc.
∴ creat competition w/ public homes
RELUCTANT PARTNERS
running as a not-for-profit basis.
181

Only two public rest homes, one in Sarnia and the other in Port Colborne, were ever built, despite recognition by government officials that 'a considerable body of opinion...believes that the profit motive should be eliminated from care...and that care services should come only under public or state administration.'[42] Private nursing home owners, through the ANHIO, lobbied furiously against the bill, arguing that state-subsidized competition was both unfair to them and a waste of taxpayers' money, especially when 'private enterprise is eager to fill the need.' Ontario health department officials for the most part agreed, even though they too could not make up their mind whether the unceasing nursing home quest for higher per diem rates was 'impelled by a real economic necessity or merely a desire for higher profits.' With 14,000 private nursing home beds now established within Ontario 'it would be impractical and unjustified to eliminate private enterprise in favour of charitable non-profit or Governmental agency operations,' health officials argued. As long as private operators could meet public need and 'provide a satisfactory level of service...then it would not seem necessary for Government to enter this field.'[43] Any significant competition from the public Rest Homes Act was also undermined by the freeze on new capital spending implemented by the Robarts administration shortly after the legislation came into effect.[44]

Despite private ownership of nursing homes, by the late 1960s almost two-thirds of the clientele were receiving some form of public subsidy from either local welfare departments or the Ontario Hospital Insurance Commission. As a result, the provincial ceiling set for the cost of their care was a critical item for determining the overall profitability of the industry, as well as the total cost of long-term care for government. For state officials accustomed to working alone to determine levels of fiscal support for nonprofit charitable or public agencies, the task of negotiating with the profit-oriented nursing home owners was a new and trying experience. 'When we started this programme three...years ago we set the rate at $6.50 per day,' Dymond complained: 'This was heartily endorsed by nursing home operators. We had hardly got going when they demanded an increase. We raised it the next year to $7.50. The same thing happened all over again last year and we raised it to $8.50. No sooner had that rate been struck than the Associated Nursing Homes retained Woods, Gordon [Consulting Co.]...to come up with a proposal that $12.50 was the amount necessary.' Unless Queen's Park held the line, there would be 'no end to the demands of the nursing home operators.'[45]

The issue came to a boil during the summer of 1968 when homes in Toronto threatened to evict all their welfare patients unless the city agreed to the $12.50 daily rate proposed by the Woods, Gordon report commissioned by the ANHIO. Refusing to be intimidated, the city in turn proposed moving all its clients into nursing homes outside of Toronto that were willing to accept the going rate of $8.50. Outraged patients simply refused to be moved away from their families, friends, and traditional surroundings into other cities—a resistance that received widespread newspaper and public support. 'Metro would be ill-advised to consider...shipping the old folks out of town,' the *Globe and Mail* commented sarcastically. 'This does not seem too far removed from the traditional Eskimo ceremony of placing the old and infirm on a small ice-floe and leaving them to drift away.' Eventually both government and nursing home operators agreed on a new compromise rate of $10.50 but the ugliness of the incident was a harbinger of how difficult it had become to reconcile caring and profit. A similar showdown would occur once again in 1971. By that year some government officials conceded privately that neither the province's health nor welfare department 'possesse[d] any accepted criteria or information to ascertain what the per diem subsidizable rate should be in Nursing Homes.'[46]

The key breakthrough for the industry was over inclusion within public hospital insurance. On this issue nursing home operators had powerful middle-class allies once the coming of medicare in 1968 solidified an emerging public consensus around universal coverage for all catastrophic costs of health care. Nursing home owners had long argued that their patients should be eligible for hospital insurance coverage in order to 'remov[e] the fear, anxiety, and concern especially present in the older person.' Their views received backing from the 1966 final report of Ontario's Select Committee on Aging, which also recommended that hospital insurance should be extended 'to assist aged persons...cared for either in hospitals or in approved nursing and convalescent homes.'[47]

Within Ontario's Hospital Insurance Commission, let alone the provincial Department of Health, there was initially little sympathy for such views. '[T]he future hospital care needs of the Province can best be met through our public hospitals, and it is not our plan to extend the hospital system into the nursing homes,' OHSC officials testified before the Select Committee on Aging.[48] Health Minister Matthew Dymond was equally opposed to the committee's recommendation. More chronic care beds and extension of hospital insurance into nursing homes were 'not the answers' he warned Robarts.

> What [the Select Committee] really recommend is that Government pay (either by grant or insurance) for the maintenance of the aged in facilities of some sort, when the families cannot, or will not, any longer maintain them....Too often, it is concluded, since an old person has to spend much time in bed and have his personal wants and needs attended to by others, he should be kept in hospital. This is wrong.[49]

Here was the crux of the matter. The need for hospital care was a medical matter, to be determined by doctors, hence it should be an insured benefit. Care in nursing homes, however, was mostly custodial, not medical. For those without sufficient means, its cost was properly a needs-tested welfare, not an insured health responsibility. But in practice, were the boundaries really that clear-cut? Not according to nursing home operators. As they argued in a brief before the Senate Committee on Aging, the difference between 'chronically ill care' covered by hospital insurance, and 'ordinary chronic care' within nursing homes was 'so indistinguishable as to be hardly discernible by the experts, let alone the uninformed public.'[50]

Ontario doctors were inclined to agree. Faced with condemning their elderly patients to the ruinous costs of nursing home care, or to dangerous two- and three-storey climbs in older buildings, many refused to discharge them from hospital care to private nursing homes, much to the annoyance of the OHSC. As a result, too many of the elderly were occupying $20 a day hospital beds rather than $7 a day nursing home beds, the OHSC complained, 'simply because it was a convenient place for them to be and simply because somebody was able to pay for it.'[51] As long as the costs of chronic bed care in hospitals were available by right to all Ontarians by virtue of hospital insurance, but nursing home care was either a private or needs-tested welfare responsibility, the system remained deeply biased toward the provision of expensive hospital care. 'Failure to include nursing homes as an insured service may distort the utilization of those facilities which are insured,' OHSC officials warned by 1969. Since almost two-thirds of nursing home residents were already 'being paid for by some government agency' the current situation was also 'full of inequalities,' health officials acknowledged. 'All the other [bed-care patients] are on their own and may be impoverished by illness.'[52] Doctors within the Conservative caucus added their own support to these views. 'If nursing homes were brought into the hospital insurance plan many patients now in active care hospitals could be transferred to less expensive institutions.'[53]

Powerful arguments for such a move also came from outraged taxpayers, appalled in the new age of universal medicare to discover the catastrophic financial consequences of discharge of themselves, their spouses, or their parents from hospital into nursing home care. 'So please explain this injustice to me,' one daughter of a former Conservative cabinet minister wrote to John Robarts. 'I went to the Convalescent Home. The OHIP paid for the Hospital but the Convalescent Home cost me $280.00....What can you do about this? I have always paid my insurance...but I can't understand why, when I was not able and needed help, that my OHIP was not a help....Don't send me a "form" letter, John, please.'[54]

A distressed constituent told Robarts that 'my wife...is now in the hospital and if she [has to enter a nursing home] it will take every dollar we have saved for our old age and there will be nothing for me at all. Our whole income will have to go for her care....You surely must know there are hundreds in my position.' '[We've] paid premiums for this coverage,' another reminded the Premier. 'If you can't put people in General Hospitals, you should pay every cent of the cost of a private nursing home....These are seriously ill people who cannot be pushed aside. If your Government does not act promptly on this, I think you'll find the handwriting on the wall—and it will say, "Out!"'[55]

These letters and many others like them expressed a rising sense of entitlement in the fields of health care and aging, which had been building throughout the social security reforms of the 1960s and which reached a peak with the coming of universal medicare in 1968. They also reflected shifting conceptions of family responsibilities by the end of the 1960s. As the *Toronto Star* argued in making the case for bring nursing homes into medicare:

> Consider the professional man with children and an aging father. The old man becomes a burden on the woman of the house. When she can cope no longer, they look for a nursing home. Maintaining Dad there, they're told, will cost them $77 to $133 a week. The professional man, too, has paid his share; but now he faces a cruel choice. He must balance his father's need for skilled care against his son's need for college....We know that Ontario runs medical and hospital insurance schemes, that their costs come out of our earnings, that they protect us when we're ill. This principle must be extended to the care in our nursing homes.[56]

Within this transformed political context, arguments that singled out long-term nursing home care as an island of family or needs-tested responsibility in an ocean of public health entitlement were no longer acceptable.

By 1969 even Health Minister Matthew Dymond, long an opponent of extending medicare to nursing homes, had become convinced the time had come for a change in policy. He advised Robarts:

> The quality of nursing homes leaves much to be desired. Most...are operated by private enterprise...[and]...the profit motive is a dominant factor in practically all of [them]....[I]n health care of this kind it is rapidly becoming intolerable and will have to be faced up to very soon. This is an area in which it has been impossible to interest any of the insurance groups....Only if an insurance programme were broadly based, as in OHSC, could a reasonable premium rate be established....Most recent figures estimate nursing home care to cost $130 million this year.[57]

Although the cost seemed huge, in practice it worked out to an extra $4 per family in monthly health insurance premiums. Increased spending on nursing home care would also be offset by reduced demand for more expensive hospital beds. Dymond recommended that the government should go ahead. Without assured coverage of private nursing home costs, he argued, efficient utilization of beds within the entire health care system, the modernization and expansion of nursing home facilities, and the attraction of more efficient operators into the industry would not occur.

Two years later, incoming premier, William Davis, Robarts' successor, announced prior to his first upcoming election that nursing home care would be covered by OHIP under a separate Extended Care Plan, beginning on 1 April 1972, with two conditions.[58] First, insured coverage would apply only for medical not residential need, defined as those patients requiring at least one and a half hours of skilled nursing care per day. Second, co-insurance or user fees of $3.50 a day also would be part of the insured $12.50 daily cost of standard ward nursing home care.[59]

With their inclusion under public health insurance, private nursing home owners achieved their most important victory. Under the impetus of health insurance coverage, from 1972 onwards the industry grew by leaps and bounds transforming itself, within five years, from small, single-operator dwellings of less than twenty beds, often owned by women, into highly profitable, modern one-hundred- to two-hundred-bed facilities, owned by corporate chains earning up to 15 percent rates of return for investors and dedicated, as Matthew Dymond argued, 'to one purpose, and one purpose only, to make money for the shareholders.' By the 1980s, these chains would control 86 percent of the more than 30,000 nursing home beds across Ontario.[60]

CONCLUSION

After World War II, the state and private nursing homes entered into a partnership driven primarily by expediency, not ideology. Neither local governments nor the province were committed in principle to creating an enclave of profitability in a field of long-term care otherwise constructed around public and voluntary institutions. Nor was either level of the state anxious to assume responsibility for the licensing and regulation of nursing homes. Instead, from the 1940s until the mid-1960s, municipal authorities, public health officials, and the province continued to insist that reliance on private nursing homes was a temporary measure until an adequate number of chronic care hospital beds and public homes for the aged could be put into place. Not until after the passage of the 1966 Nursing Home Act did provincial politicians and civil servants begin to say it was 'natural that private enterprise should step into the gap' in providing caregiving for the elderly.[61]

Ontario's dependency on private nursing homes was driven by a largely unanticipated growth in demand for long-term care. From the 1930s, onwards provincial officials had warned of the aging of Ontario's population, but their attention remained focused upon the implications of this phenomenon for old age pensions. The extent to which population aging would also dramatically increase the numbers suffering from disabling chronic illness and needing long-term nursing care was largely unforeseen. This misjudgment is evident in the construction of new public homes for the aged as refuges for an ambulatory, residential population, not as the quasi-medical facilities they, along with private nursing homes, would eventually become. It would also be evident in the growing hospital backlog for chronic care beds. As Dr. Keith Stuart, geriatric specialist for Ontario's welfare department, pointed out to the 1965 Select Committee on Aging, the 'suddenness with which modern society has been presented with the necessity of providing Long Term Care' was responsible for 'much of the confusion...in our Province' surrounding nursing home care and defeated attempts at 'leisurely' planning.[62] Failure to construct low-cost accommodation for seniors, to develop minimally adequate public pension entitlements, or to explore seriously the possibilities of home care alternatives until the 1960s also intensified the dependency of elderly citizens and their children upon institutional models of public and private caregiving.

Hospital insurance after 1959 brought these pressures to a head by taking bed care out of the realm of needs-testing and transforming it into a new insured social right. From 1959 onwards the creation of a two-tiered structure of caregiving for the elderly, one insured and one not, provoked both a growing misallocation of Ontario's hospital beds and rising middle-class anger on the part of the elderly and their children, toward the catastrophic costs facing those discharged from hospitals into nursing homes.

For Ontario's private nursing home owners, the confusion and ambivalence of the state toward their industry provided both strategic opportunities and dangers. On the one hand, the absence of an effective regulatory regime prior to 1966 in the face of mounting demands for long-term care, attracted the unscrupulous, the undercapitalized, and the unskilled into the nursing home business. The result, until the late 1960s, was a small-scale, low-profit, and publicly suspect business that had grave difficulty staking a legitimate claim as a health care enterprise. On the other hand, indecisive state planning created both the shortage of public or nonprofit long-term care beds, and the breathing space needed for nursing home operators to organize themselves into an effective private lobby. From 1959 onwards, through the ANHIO nursing home owners were able to demand and get clearer definitions of what constituted nursing home care, who was entitled to provide it, and how much it should cost. In the face of ongoing shortages of hospital bed care, they were also able to gain incorporation into Ontario's health insurance regime itself, despite initial opposition, within the provincial health bureaucracy, to insuring private profits through public funds. The dearth of nonprofit alternatives to nursing homes placed the industry in a strategic position. However much government officials might rail against the arrogance, greed, or growing power of the nursing home lobby, in the final analysis they had nowhere else to place the elderly in need of care.

NOTES

I would like to thank the Social Sciences and Humanities Research Council of Canada for a research grant in support of this work.

1. Josephine Rekart, *Public Funds, Private Provision: The Role of the Voluntary Sector* (Vancouver, 1993), xi, 3–4, 143; Mariana Valverde, 'The Mixed Social Economy as a Canadian Tradition,' *Studies in Political Economy* 47 (Summer 1995), 33–6.

2. Janet Greb, Larry W. Chambers, Amiram Gafni, Ron Goerree, and Roberta Labelle, 'Interprovincial Comparisons of Public and Private Sector Long-Term Care Facilities for the Elderly in Canada,' *Canadian Public Policy* 20/3 (1994), figure 1, 287.

3. According to Bettina Bradbury one in ten widows, most of them over the age of fifty, boarded with families who were not kin in Montreal in 1891; Bettina Bradbury, *Working Families: Age, Gender, and Daily Survival in Industrializing Montreal* (Toronto, 1993), 207.

4. Archives of Ontario [hereafter AO], Ministry of Health Records, RG 10-154, 'Hospitals and Institutions Central Files,' Reel 180, Central Files—Nursing Homes Cannington–Wallaceburg, 1937'62, Stalker, 'Report of Visit of Inspection—Mrs. R's Home,' Toronto, 21 May 1937; RG 18, D-1-70, Ontario Select Committee on Aging, Hearings, testimony of Burrell Morris, 6 Jan. 1965, 470–1; AO, Ministry of Community and Social Service Records, RG 29-01, Box 28, file 1148, 'General Welfare Assistance Act—Nursing Homes—1961,' Doris Moore, Welfare Institutions Inspector, to James Band, 29 March 1962; Metropolitan Toronto Records and Archives [hereafter MTRA], Department of Public Welfare Records, RG 5.1, file 10.2.1, 'Convalescents—Private Nursing and Rest Homes, 1939–1947,' memo from Dr. C.O. Broad, City Hospitals Officer, to C.W. Armstrong, 25 March 1947.

5. Ontario, Department of Public Welfare pamphlet, 'Caring for the Aged,' (1946); Norma Rudy, *For Such a Time as This: L. Earl Ludlow and a History of Homes for the Aged in Ontario, 1837–1961* (Toronto, 1987), 111–12; Ontario, Department of Public Welfare *Annual Reports* (1942–3), 6; (1943–4), 7, 14–15; (1945–6), 25–6; (1947–8),10–11; MTRA, RG 5.1, file 48, memo from A.W. Laver to the Committee on Public Welfare, 31 Dec. 1943.

6. Ontario, Department of Public Welfare, 'Caring for the Aged' (1946); AO, RG 29-01, Box 1, file 26, 'Committee on the Social Problems of the Aging,' minutes of meeting, 9 July 1952.

7. *Port Arthur News Chronicle*, 'Thinking of the Aged,' 6 Nov. 1962.

8. Ontario, *Legislative Debates*, 29 March 1950, speech by Agnes Macphail, BB-9.

9. AO, Ontario Welfare Council Records, Accession #16383, Series 11, Box 62, 'Study of Nursing Home Facilities in Ontario, 1964–65.'

10. On the fiscal crisis of Ontario hospitals in the 1930s and 1940s see David Gagan, *A Necessity Among Us: The Owen Sound General and Marine Hospital, 1891–1985* (Toronto, 1990), chapter 4, 84–108; MTRA, RG 5.1, file 10.2.1, 'Convalescents—Private Nursing and Rest Homes,

1939–1947,' Dr. C.O. Broad, City Hospitals Officer, to A.W. Laver, 25 Sept. 1939.

11. MTRA, RG 5.1, file 10.2.1, Robena Morris to C.W. Armstrong, 'Private Nursing Homes,' 17 July 1947; Dr. C.O. Broad to A.W. Laver, 2 March 1944; A.W. Laver to Robena Morris, 14 May 1942; G.A. Lascelles to Mayor Robert Saunders, 15 July 1947; Robena Morris to H.S. Rupert, 28 March 1950, 'Allocations of Private Nursing Homes Unit'; 'Minutes of Meeting Regarding Procedures,' 23 Oct. 1951.

12. William Main, 'A Study of Lambert Lodge Home for the Aged,' (MSW thesis, University of Toronto School of Social Work, 1951), 67–9, 72.

13. MTRA, RG 5.1, Box 43, file 48, 'Care of Aged and Aged People's Homes, 1943–1948,' A.W. Laver to Robena Morris, 19 March 1946, 'Re: Construction of a Home for the Aged,' noting that a fifteen-hundred-bed facility would relieve the 'long waiting lists reported of homeless, elderly citizens...going from one institution to another seeking admission and care.'

14. A point recognized by some city officials five years after Lambert Lodge opened. 'We must not confuse the need for institutional care with the need for financial assistance in the form of direct relief. We must differentiate between those persons who can look after themselves in the community with additional financial assistance, and those who require CARE in a Home for the Aged,' MTRA, RG 5.1, Box 47, file 50, 'Homes Care Programs, 1952–1980,' 'Minutes of a Meeting held in the deputy commissioner's office, 18 November 1954 Regarding Special Home Care Program for Elderly Persons.'

15. MTRA, 'Minutes of Meeting Regarding Procedures,' 23 Oct. 1951; Box 46, file 48.4, 'Old Age Security, 1951–1965,' memo on 'Maintenance of Indigent Persons in Private Nursing Homes Pending Transfer to Chronically Ill Hospitals or Homes for the Aged,' 24 Feb. 1953; Ontario, *Legislative Debates*, 14 March 1949, speech by W.A. Goodfellow, 835, 840.

16. MTRA, Box 43, file 48, 'Care of the Aged and Aged People's Homes, 1943–1948,' memo from Robena Morris to A.W. Laver, 19 March 1946, 'Re: Constructing a Home for the Aged' [my emphasis].

17. Ontario, *Legislative Debates*, 14 March 1945, speech by Agnes Macphail, 1351; AO, RG 10-154, Hospitals and Institutions Central Files, Reel 179, 'Nursing Homes—Collective—Cannington, 1948–1962,' Russell Kelly, Minister of Health, to W.A. Goodfellow, 25 Nov. 1949.

18. MTRA, RG 5.1, file 48.1A, 'Old Age Assistance, 1944–48,' letter from D.J. Matthews to William Saunders, 14 May 1944; memo to Mr. A.M. Ivey, Chairman, Old Age Pensions Board, 23 April 1944, 'Deaths Recorded of Old Age Pensioners from the _____ Home as taken from the List of Deaths as furnished by the City Clerk'; file 10.2.1.1., B. Moffatt, investigator OAP, 'Report on _____ Home,' 19 Oct. 1944; 'Convalescents—Private Nursing and Rest Homes, 1939–1947,' letter from Dr. Gordon W. Armstrong to A.M. Ivey, 25 Oct. 1944; A.W. Laver to Robert Saunders, 25 May 1944; memo to Robena Morris from M. Douglas and Alfred Skinner, 13 Nov. 1944, 'Re: Visit to _____ Home'; letter from Commissioner of Buildings to proprietor of _____ Home, 13 March 1946; letter from Charles Green, Old Age Pension Commission, to Robena Morris, 6 Jan. 1947, 'Re: _____ Home'; letter from Dr. G.P. Jackson, Medical Officer of Health, to proprietor of _____ Home, 13 Dec. 1946.

19. MTRA, file 10.2.1, copy of bylaw no. 17001, passed 15 July 1947; Report no. 28 of the Board of Control, adopted by city council on 12 Nov. 1951, 'Increase in Rates Paid for Maintenance of Indigent Patients in Private Nursing Homes,' 24 Oct. 1951; 'Report No.7 of the Local Board of Health: Procedure to Ensure Adequate Control of Lodging Houses, Including Nursing Homes,' 30 May 1952.

20. AO, RG 3, John Robarts Papers, Box 324, file 'Programs—Dept, Jan–Dec 1967,' memo on 'Institutional Care for Elderly People,' n.d. but circa 1967; Ontario, *Legislative Debates*, 22 March 1955, speech by William Goodfellow, 1063. For an informative but somewhat hagiographic history of this process of institution building for the aged see Rudy, *For Such a Time as This*.

21. AO, RG 29-01, Box 28, file 1147, James Band to Dr. Charlotte Horner, MOH, Cobourg, 3 Aug. 1961; RG 10-154, reel 179, 'Central Files—Nursing Homes Collective—Cannington 1948–1962,' J.B. Neilson, Chairman, Ontario Hospital Services Commission, 'Report on Visits to Nursing Homes—for Meeting of Commission,' 28 Jan. 1959; RG 29-01, file 1148, Doris Moore, Welfare Institutions Inspector, to James Band, 29 March 1962; file 1150 Doris Moore to James Band, 30 Jan. 1964; file 1151, Doris Moore to Louis Cecile, 13 April 1965; file 1149, Doris Moore to A.T. Bosanquet, 13 Sept. 1963; RG 6, Box 2, Series III-1, file 'Aging and Old Age Assistance,'

Proceedings of the First Ontario Conference on Aging, 31 May–3 June, 1957, Dr. A.D. Foster, Academy of Medicine, Committee on Nursing Homes.

22. AO, 'Aging and Old Age Assistance,' 167, 175.

23. AO, RG 6, Department of Treasury and Economics Records, Series III-1, Box 18, file 'Conference on Aging, 1957,' memo by G.C. Clarkson on 'First Ontario Conference on Aging,' 3 June 1957.

24. AO, Ontario Welfare Council Records, Accession #16383, Box 62, 'Publications: Aging,' 'Study of Nursing Home Facilities in Ontario, 1964–5.'

25. Ontario, Legislative Debates, 11 March 1958, speech by Louis Cecile, 706; AO, Ontario Welfare Council Records, 'Study of Nursing Home Facilities.'

26. AO, RG 3, Frost Papers, Series E-16-A, Box 158, 'Public Welfare Correspondence,' James Band to Louis Cecile, 'Re: Alternatives to Hospital Care within the Jurisdiction of the Department of Public Welfare,' 22 July 1958; RG 29-01, file 1149, Doris Moore to A.T. Bosanquet, 13 Sept. 1963; file 1149, Louis Cecile to B.D. Morris, 25 Oct. 1963.

27. Ontario, Legislative Debates, 24 March 1959, speech by Dr. Matthew Dymond, 1618; ibid., 21 March 1961; AO, RG 10-154, Reel 179, 'Central Files—Nursing Homes Collective—Cannington, 1948–1962,' Dr. W.E. Noonan to Dr. J.B. Neilson, 'Summary of Activity re: Nursing Homes,' 17 Sept. 1959; Dr. R.S. Peat, 'Nursing Homes and the Ontario Hospital Services Commission,' 21 May 1959; 'Report on Nursing Home Inspection,' 26 Jan. 1959.

28. Ontario, Legislative Debates, 24 March 1959, speech by Dr. Matthew Dymond, 1618–9.

29. Ibid., 1617, 1619.

30. AO, RG 3, Frost Papers, Series E-16-A, Box 64, file 122-G, 'Health, Dept. of: Nursing Homes, 1959,' Dr. Matthew Dymond to Leslie Frost, 29 Jan. 1959; ibid., RG 3, Robarts Papers, Box 140, 'Health, Dept. of Nursing Homes, 1961–68,' Dr. Matthew Dymond to R.A. Farrell, (PMO), 30 Oct. 1961; RG 3, Frost Papers, Series E-16-A, Box 158, memo from R.A. Farrell to Leslie Frost, '"Liberty" article on conditions in Homes for the Aged and Nursing Homes,' 28 Jan. 1958, with handwritten enclosure from James Band, January 1958; RG 3, Robarts Papers, Box 140, Matthew Dymond to John Robarts, 3 Jan. 1963.

31. AO, RG 3, Robarts Papers, Box 140, file, 'Nursing Homes—Health, Nov 61–Dec 65,' B.D. Morris, president ANHIO, to John Robarts, 18 Oct. 1961, with enclosure; RG 29-01, file 1148, 'Petition to the Departments of Health and of Welfare (Ontario), by Associated Nursing Homes Incorporated of Ontario,' 7 March 1961; Canada, Senate, 'Special Senate Committee on Aging, Minutes of Proceedings and Evidence,' testimony of B.D. Morris, 16 July 1964.

32. AO, RG 3, Robarts Papers, Box 140, John Robarts to Matthew Dymond, 26 July 1962; Matthew Dymond to John Robarts, 3 Jan. 1963; John Robarts to Matthew Dymond, 14 Jan. 1963.

33. AO, RG 18, Series D-1-70, Box C121, Ontario Legislature Select Committee on Aging, Submission of Associated Nursing Homes Incorporated, 6 Jan. 1965.

34. AO, RG 18, Ontario Select Committee on Aging, 1964–65, Hearings: Part 2, Submission of the Ontario Hospital Services Commission, 7 Jan. 1965; testimony of Dr. J.B. Neilson, 7 Jan. 1965, 567.

35. Canada, Senate, Final Report of the Special Senate Committee on Aging (Ottawa, 1966), 32–5.

36. AO, RG 3, Robarts Papers, Box 140, file, 'Nursing Homes—Health, Nov 61–Dec 65,' 'Study of Nursing Home Facilities, 1964–65.'

37. Throughout 1965, as public enquiries into nursing homes reached a crescendo, headlines appeared such as 'Woman Tied to Chair in Metro Nursing Home,' and 'Misery Lurks in Fetid Homes,' Toronto Star, 3 April 1965; or 'Woman Charges Her Mother Fed Cold Beans and Tea,' Toronto Telegram, 22 Jan. 1965.

38. AO, RG 29-59, Accession 15296/2, Temporary Box 23, minutes of 'Meeting of the Honourable John Yaremko and the Honourable T.L. Wells with Representatives of the Associated Nursing Homes Incorporated of Ontario,' 16 Nov. 1970; RG 29-01, Box 27, file 1125, minutes of the 'Joint Meeting of the Cabinet Committee on Nursing Homes and of the Technical Committee on Nursing Homes,' 14 Oct. 1969; RG 10-1-1, Box 43, file 15, memo from Dr. Barbara Blake to Dr. C.J. Doherty, 'Re Minister's Action Slip Regarding Maximum Size of Nursing Homes,' 20 June 1969; Ibid., Box 43, file 12, Woods, Gordon & Co., 'Associated Nursing Homes Incorporated Ontario, Survey of Operating Costs,' Nov. 1967, 18; RG 10-106, Box 247, file 247.4, Dr. C.J. Doherty to Dr. G.E. Large, 'Re Nursing Home Program,' 10 April 1969.

39. AO, RG 10-106, file 247, Dr. J.C. Allison to Dr. G.E. Large, 'Financial Responsibility for Nursing

Home Care,' 6 March 1967; see also ibid., Dr. Matthew Dymond to Dr. K.C. Charron, 2 March 1967, 'I find my worst fears confirmed—that very little is actually known about the cost of care in this kind of facility.' As the ANHIO commissioned study of nursing home operations by Woods, Gordon, & Co. observed, 'most nursing homes do not maintain their accounting records in such a way as to provide meaningful information concerning day to day operations of their homes'; RG 10-1-1, Box 43, file 12, 'Associated Nursing Homes Incorporated Ontario—Survey of Operating Costs,' Nov. 1967, 19.

40. AO, RG 3, Box 140, file 'Nursing Homes, Jan 67–Dec 67,' Matthew Dymond to E.M. Mode, PMO, 24 Nov. 1967; RG 10, Series 001, Subseries 01, Box 43, file 14, Matthew Dymond to Robert Welch, 12 June 1969.

41. AO, RG 29-01, Box 27, file 1125, minutes of the Technical Committee on Nursing Homes, 30 June 1969, comments of Lawrence Crawford, Chairman; memo from Lawrence Crawford to James Band, 29 April 1969; memo from Clifford Williams to M. Borczak, 29 April 1969. As Crawford argued disparagingly, 'neither the Nursing Homes in this Province nor those anywhere else in North America have done anything creditable by and large—except achieve a temporary bullishness on the N.Y. stock exchange.'

42. AO, RG 10-106, Box 247, file 247.4, memo from Dr. C.J. Doherty to Dr. G.E. Large, 10 April 1969; RG 10-75, Accession 15133/4, Box 4, N-O, Dr. S.A. Holling, 'Comments on Nursing Homes in Ontario—School of Hygiene,' 26 Nov. 1969. As the *Toronto Telegram* noted, 'a population which tends to glorify private enterprise still harbours mistrust of people who make a profit by housing the sick,' 6 Aug. 1971, 'Toronto's Nursing Homes Have Cleaned House.'

43. AO, RG 10-1-1, Box 2, file 14, George A. Newbold, president, ANHIO, to John Robarts, 19 June 1966; RG 10-106, Box 247, C.J. Doherty to G.E. Large, 10 April 1969; RG 10-106, Box 248, file 248.2, Dr. S.A. Holling, 'Nursing Home Program in Ontario,' 1 May 1969.

44. AO, RG 10-106, Box 247, C.J. Doherty to G.E. Large, 'Nursing Home Program,' 10 April 1969.

45. AO, RG 3, Box 141, file, 'Nursing Homes—Health—Jan 69–Dec 69,' Matthew Dymond to A.M. Allen, 10 April 1969; RG 10, Series 001, Box 43, file 14, Matthew Dymond to Allan Grossman, 12 March 1969.

46. Toronto *Globe and Mail*, 14 May 1968, 'Moving Elderly Patients Out of Metro "A Little Too Hot" for Welfare Board'; 'Metro Welfare Tries to Shift Blame,' 16 May 1968; 'Set a Realistic Rate,' 17 Feb. 1969; AO, RG 29-01, file 1157, 'Nursing Home Rates: General Welfare Assistance Act,' 16 Jan. 1970; RG 29-59, Accession 15296/2, Temporary Box 23, file 'Associated Nursing Homes Incorporated,' memo from Cliff Williams to M. Borczak, 21 April 1971.

47. AO, RG 3, Robarts Papers, Box 140, file 'Nursing Homes, Jan 67–Dec 67,' Frances Watson to John Robarts, 1 June 1966; Ontario, *Final Recommendations of the Select Committee on Aging* (Toronto, 1967), 11.

48. AO, RG 18, Series D-1-70, Select Committee on Aging, 1964–65, Hearings: Part 2, testimony of Dr. Peat, OHSC, 7 Jan. 1965, 547.

49. AO, RG 3, Robarts Papers, Box 318, file, 'Aging: Interdepartmental Advisory Committee, Social &Family Services, Jan–Dec 67,' Matthew Dymond to J.K. Reynolds, PMO, 3 April 1967.

50. Senate, Canada, *Final Report*, 'Appendix P-1,' brief submitted by the Associated Nursing Homes Incorporated, Ontario, July 1964, 1116.

51. AO, RG 18, Series D-1-70, Select Committee on Aging, 1964–65, Hearing: Part 2, Submission of Ontario Hospial Services Commission, 7 Jan. 1965, testimony of Dr. J.B. Neilson, Chairman.

52. AO, RG 10-214, Box 26, file 6, memo on 'Nursing Homes, Facilities for the Aged and Related Matters,' June 1969; RG 10-1-1, Box 2, file 15, memo from Dr. G.E. Large to Dr. K.C. Charron, 14 June 1966; RG 10-214, Appendix 19, Box 26, file 6, 'Nursing Homes—Studies 1966–1969,' memo from Dr. Hugh D. Walker, OHSC, to Dr. Twiss, 20 Aug. 1969.

53. AO, RG 3 Robarts Papers, Box 140, file 'Nursing Homes—Jan 67–Dec 67,' Toronto *Globe and Mail*, 2 April 1968, 'Nursing Homes Should be Covered by Hospital Insurance,' covering a resolution introduced in the Ontario legislature by backbench Conservative MPP Dr. Richard Potter.

54. AO, RG 3, Robarts Papers, Box 140, file 'Nursing Homes—Jan 69–Dec 69,' M.D. to John Robarts, n.d. but circa March 1969.

55. AO, RG 3, Robarts Papers, Box 140, file, 'Nursing Homes—Jan 69–Dec 69,' C.T. to Robarts, 4 July 1969; B.K. to Robarts, 28 Feb. 1970; Box 141, file 'Nursing Homes—Health—Jan. 70–Feb 71,' C.T. to Robarts, 1 Dec. 1969.

56. *Toronto Star*, 7 April 1971, 'Nursing Home Care: Say When, Bert.'
57. AO, RG 3, Robarts Papers, Box 321, file 'Homes for the Aged—Social and Family Services, Jan–Feb 69,' Matthew Dymond to John Robarts, 17 June 1969.
58. AO, RG 3, Box 141, file 'Nursing Homes—Health—Jan 70–Feb 71,' William G. Davis to Eileen Simmons, 6 May 1971.
59. AO, RG 10, Series 214, Box 25, file 1, memo from OHSC to 'Administrators of All Licensed Nursing Homes,' 29 March 1972.
60. *The Financial Post*, 26 Dec. 1970, 'The Fifteen Percenters: Villacentres Expanding Soon.' As the article pointed out, 'the current rate structures and welfare subsidies...are set in part with the smaller operator in mind and they enable efficient and larger-scale operators to make a reasonable return on invested capital'; Vera Ingrid Tarman, *Privatization and Health Care: The Case of Ontario Nursing Homes* (Toronto, 1990), 42.
61. AO, RG 10-106, Box 248, file 15-A-19, 248.2, 'Nursing Homes—General, May–December 1967,' memo by Dr. N. Angel, 'Non-Hospital Bed Care,' 3 Oct. 1967.
62. AO, RG 18 Series D-1-70, 'Select Committee on Aging, 1964–65, Hearings: Part 2,' testimony of Dr. Keith Stuart, 14 Dec. 1964, 287.

PUBLIC OPINION AND PUBLIC POLICY IN CANADA

Federal Legislation on War Veterans, 1939–46

DEAN F. OLIVER

Norman Paterson School of International Affairs
Carleton University

T his essay examines the complex relationship among political, economic, bureaucratic, and public interests that helped determine the timing and parameters of federal veterans' policies during the Second World War, policies that, despite their well-publicized failings, are generally considered to have been among the best in the world. In particular, in light of contemporary debate over the degree to which public policy should respond to or be influenced by populist pressures and public opinion (however measured), it explores the nexus between Canadian public opinion and federal public policy on the demobilization and rehabilitation of war veterans.

Public opinion, it will argue, though difficult to place at the centre of the policy process in the first years of the war, assumed enormous significance as the struggle progressed, looming ever larger on Ottawa's agenda as the success of Allied arms brought victory within reach. Its rising significance, to the Canadian public as well as to a large corps of federal bureaucrats, created for the governing Liberals both opportunities and problems. The political payoff from being on the 'right side' of veterans' issues became increasingly apparent, but the dangers—political and otherwise—inherent in raising public expectations, or of diverting the attention of military personnel from war fighting to peacemaking, were at least as serious. The cynical view of Mackenzie King's attempts to navigate these shoals might be to ascribe his delivery of veterans' programs to partisan and, possibly, reactionary motives, as others have painted the delivery of unemployment insurance and family allowance benefits in the same period. This essay illustrates more mundane, though more complex, concerns, principally the subtle and dynamic evolution of public policy in response to diverse stimuli, prominent among them the desire, shared by a broad range of politicians, bureaucrats, military officers, and civilians, to cater generously to the legitimate needs of Canada's former soldiers. Throughout the paper the central role played by enlightened, articulate federal bureaucrats and a forward-looking federal government are stressed. The degree to which policymakers measured, managed, and responded to public concerns is also highlighted, though the public interest was rarely their only concern. Whereas public pressure, then as now, did not guarantee sound policy, however, party interests and politicking did not guarantee bad ones.

THE STIRRINGS OF INTEREST

Canadian demobilization and rehabilitation planning during the Second World War began barely six weeks after the first shots had been fired and well before the force of public opinion had made itself felt on veterans' legislation. There were other things in the news, after all, and the urgency of addressing postwar questions was not readily apparent, to citizens or to their elected representatives. Accurate polling data for this period does not exist, but evidence drawn from more traditional sources like newspapers, correspondence, government records, and public statements, suggests that public opinion, while important in affecting the context of government actions, was not decisive in its specific influence on postwar planning. This would soon change, but for the next several years, federal bureaucrats worked alone and, for the most part, in secret on the details of Canada's demobilization and rehabilitation program. Public views did influence their deliberations to some extent, but credit for Ottawa's early start on postwar issues was not due to pressure from an informed public. As much as anyone, the credit belongs to Ian Mackenzie, the Minister of Pensions and National Health, and the team of senior bureaucrats he assembled.[1] The war 'encourag[ed] the passage of the most significant social security measures yet passed in Canada,' noted Doug Owram, but Mackenzie 'undertook an almost isolated campaign to convert the government to the support of various social security measures.'[2]

If Mackenzie and his staff were alone within the government, however, their views were broadly supported among the public at large. 'Remembering the experiences and the many mistakes made during the last postwar years, covering the period of demobilization and re-establishment of Canada's soldiers,' wrote one private citizen to Mackenzie King, 'I am strongly of the opinion that serious thought should be given this matter as early as possible. I believe it to be [in] the best interest of Canada that a department should be created or a committee set up to study all phases of the coming problem.'[3] The writer went on to offer his services to the government. The City Council of Hamilton, Ontario, sought to ensure job security for those who enlisted in the war effort. Such practices would guarantee 'that shirkers will not entrench themselves in soft jobs while decent men fight their battles.'[4]

Unions and veterans' organizations would not always be on the same side during the war, but at this point they had a great deal in common. The resolution by UAW-CIO Local 195 forwarded to the prime minister by John Taylor, its financial secretary, in September 1940 was typical in stating that 'the Canadian government be requested to enact legislation making it mandatory upon all employers to guarantee to all workers who have left their regular employment to serve in any branch of Canada's armed forces that their jobs, with full seniority, will be available as soon as they are ready to resume work after their discharge from active service.'[5] The Canadian Legion likewise sought to ensure that the physically unfit or those otherwise exempt from military service not profit from their exemption and that volunteers not be penalized on their return to civilian life. Veterans upon their demobilization should 'be assured of that place in civil life which they might reasonably be expected to attain had they not enlisted,' argued Legion president, Brigadier W.W. Foster.[6]

The Conservative Party under R.J. Manion, sensing the public relations value of a pro-veterans' stand, criticized the government for not acting quickly enough on the postwar front, only to be informed that a Cabinet committee with just such a mandate had already been authorized.[7] Newspapers were enthusiastic as well. When the Legion's War Services division announced an ambitious plan to keep Canada's soldiers 'citizen-conscious' by offering them a range of self-improvement courses, the *Globe and Mail* commended the organization for what it called 'Taking the Forward View.' The paper offered full support for the Legion's plan to raise $500,000 for the project. 'Perhaps the most valuable feature of this undertaking,' it noted, 'is its assurance to enlisted men that while they are engaged in war the Canadian people are preparing now for their return. They are not to be forgotten when the trouble is ended.'[8]

By Christmas 1939, in fact, demobilization and rehabilitation planning were ensconced firmly on the government's wartime agenda. For the next several years a precarious military situation would overshadow efforts at postwar preparation, but even at this stage allowances for military dependants and job protection for volunteers provoked major public debates over society's responsibility for veterans and their families.[9] Rumours of harsh or impersonal treatment by Ottawa's overworked bureaucrats spawned myriad stories of starving mothers and bereft veterans unable to collect what was rightfully theirs, or of individuals whose particular circumstances failed to meet the existing legislation's often stringent requirements. Such tales found their way into Mackenzie King's letter box, MPs' constituency offices, and the briefing notes of Opposition Members of Parliament and were indicative of widespread popular concern.[10]

The government's awareness of popular views on the postwar and veterans' concerns can be traced in official press releases with their announcements of the continually expanding network of benefits.[11] It can also be found in the speed with which government representatives, the prime minister included, sought to reassure Canadians that everything possible was being done by way of preparation. By December 1940 this was far from hyperbole. 'It was recognized from the outset,' Ian Mackenzie noted in a speech to the House of Commons, 'that the demobilization period calls for long range planning, and that no single government department could begin to cope with a problem of such magnitude—affecting as it must every phase of the national life.' He then outlined the composition and mission of the multidepartmental Cabinet Committee on Demobilization and Rehabilitation (CCDR) established 8 December 1939, parent body to the General Advisory Committee on Demobilization and Reestablishment (GACDR), and assured his colleagues that a spirit of nonpartisanship would inform the task at hand.[12] Certainly not everyone was as convinced of Ottawa's good intentions, but the government, as the dates indicated, had moved quickly.

If more had not been done it was only because other pressing issues, like staving off military defeat, had intervened. Turf wars between the government and the House of Commons and among the ministers themselves likewise played a role. Postmaster-General C.G. Power, for example, ran into a barrage of criticism from Mackenzie when he proposed a House committee on reconstruction be established to complement the work already being done on postwar problems. Mackenzie's real concern appeared to be who would run the new agency;[13] after first dumping on the proposal, he then suggested himself as its chairman.[14] The scepticism of other ministers was also an impediment at this point, J.L. Ilsley foremost among them. The Minister of Finance and National Revenue informed Power that it 'would be premature' to get into such detailed planning at this stage when 'no extended consideration of the matter is now opportune.' 'It is amazing,' Ilsley suggested, 'how much can be done in the way of getting facts together and framing policies in a few weeks if people set their minds to it.'[15] Such a lackadaisical approach had been responsible in large part for the near fiasco of 1918–19 and few in Ottawa shared such views. Walter Woods' opinion was far more typical. 'If the men now serving, particularly those overseas, feel that definite planning is going on for their future,' he wrote in early 1942, 'I think it will have a tendency to dispel any feeling of disquietude or apprehension that they are going to get poor treatment upon discharge.'[16]

THE RISE OF PUBLIC INTEREST

The lead over public opinion on postwar issues enjoyed by Ottawa's policy mandarins in the opening months of the war eroded gradually. Not until early 1943, with the return of large numbers of Canadian casualties from overseas,[17] the prospects of eventual victory, the Marsh and Beveridge Reports,[18] the Conservatives' Port Hope resolutions,[19] and a growing number of books and articles in the popular press dealing with the postwar, reconstruction, and veterans' affairs, did public demand for information on and policies regarding demobilization and rehabilitation threaten to outstrip government's ability to provide them. Federal officials often appeared remarkably sanguine about this growing information gap. Perhaps because of their initial successes, the realization that special effort was needed to convince Canadians of the complexity of the problems and the nature of their proposed solutions dawned slowly.

In December 1942, it was still understandable for Robert England to inform Mackenzie that there 'does not appear to be any measure requiring legislation at this time' and that 'it would appear as if matters [were] reasonably well in hand.'[20] In October of the following year, however, Mackenzie was still inclined to agree, telling the prime minister that 'Canada has achieved the greatest progress of the English-speaking nations in putting into law its plans for rehabilitation of men discharged from the armed services.' As proof, he sent King copies of three favourable and, presumably, representative reviews of the program from the *Winnipeg Free Press* (October 9), *Fortune* magazine (October issue), and a United Nations report by Lewis L.L. Lorwin for the 20th Century Fund.[21] The views of Mrs. Herbert S. White, one of Mackenzie King's many individual correspondents, on the government's plans were not universally held, but they did support a certain complacency in official circles. 'May I thank you and your Cabinet,' she wrote the prime minister, 'for your comprehensive post-war plans for the boys coming back from overseas....All you do for the boys in service, overseas and here, will command our most earnest cooperation. Thank you from our hearts.'[22]

Mackenzie's level of satisfaction with public support for his department's efforts was unwarranted. It was becoming increasingly apparent, for example, that the Army's overseas commanders were not entirely comfortable with civilian officials lecturing the troops about their postwar prospects. It was a needless distraction, they argued. J.L. Ralston, the Minister of National Defence, supported his senior officers and in 1942 resisted plans by Walter Woods to institute a regular series of lectures and radio programs overseas on postwar topics.[23]

Woods' suggestion derived from reports that the troops overseas were not aware of Ottawa's progress on rehabilitation. Leonard W. Brockington, an advisor to the government on public relations and a former chairman of the Canadian Broadcasting Corporation, wrote in August that they 'seem never to have heard' of the rehabilitation program. 'I am apprehensive,' noted Woods, 'that, for lack of proper information, the boys may get anti-social in their attitude, and develop a frame of mind that is difficult to handle.' Ian Mackenzie, despite his report to the prime minister the following month, had endorsed this view, but Ralston remained unco-operative. Control over the overseas information spigot remained firmly in military hands. 'I do not want Army personnel to become demobilization-minded before the present job is done,' Ralston noted, but 'personnel who are definitely on their way out' should get the appropriate demobilization and rehabilitation information 'in sufficient time before discharge to enable them to lay plans and make arrangements.'[24]

Officials at the Wartime Information Board shared Woods' concern over the government's public relations campaign. The WIB had replaced the Bureau of Public Information in September 1942 as the government's main information directorate. The Bureau's crude and unco-ordinated propaganda had been ineffective in bolstering Canadian morale after the 1942 conscription plebiscite and had not created the positive image for the country's war effort demanded by the prime minister and his senior advisors.[25] Acting on the recommendations of Charles Vining, president of the Newsprint Association of Canada, who reported in July on the weaknesses in the government's information program, the Cabinet War Committee scrapped the Bureau and made Vining the WIB's first director. After a slow start,[26] by early 1943 the new organization had begun regular, systematic surveys of Canadian public opinion using both traditional methods and newer opinion sampling techniques.[27] This had not been possible previously, one official suggested, because until 1943 postwar issues did not 'produce "hot" news stories.'[28]

This was no longer the case. John Grierson, Vining's successor, and organizations like the Canadian Association for Adult Education, were now convinced that support for Canada's war could only be bolstered by the firm promise of a better future, 'that war was futile unless it led to better postwar life for all.'[29] Concrete benefits, including housing, health services, and better working conditions, would have to be stressed. Grierson, in particular, was a committed reformer and idealist who, according to Gary Evans, sought 'to create an active sense of social progress.'[30] The goal was to engender a nonpolitical, nonpartisan consensus on the benefits of Canadian citizenship and the efforts required to defend it. Rather than singing the praises of government initiatives, the WIB would convince Canadians that a better world was just around the corner and that government policy was working to ensure that its enjoyment would be shared by all. This could only be done by the careful coordination of information and public expectations; it also required that public relations policy be backed by actual legislation and by fiscal evidence of Ottawa's commitment to postwar prosperity.[31] Those elements of the government's rehabilitation program that had already been announced helped fulfil this mandate, but the WIB realized that the importance of postwar planning to the general public would soon surpass all other concerns.

Mackenzie King did not immediately share Grierson's views. Nominally, Evans writes, the WIB's aims 'coincided precisely with the prime minister's 1939 war aims of social security and human welfare.'[32] WIB surveys also provided useful information to government, much of it, needless to say, of great partisan utility. The director's thinly veiled hope of making the Board into a 'Ministry of Education' to mould public attitudes in support of official policy and in anticipation of the postwar, however, meant a diminution in coverage of topics dealing purely with the war itself and implied a political agenda that Grierson had promised to avoid. Brooke Claxton, a parliamentary assistant to the prime minister, had appreciated this danger in June. 'The Government cannot and does not want the information service to be an instrument for securing the implementation of government policy,' he wrote, 'except in so far as this is generally accepted by other considerable groups.'[33] Grierson's plan to use *Canadian Affairs*, a magazine for the troops overseas, and a radio series entitled 'Of Things to Come' to articulate a plan for postwar rehabilitation and reconstruction placed him well in advance of official government thinking, which was still focused on the war itself, and smacked of CCF policy. The prime minister ordered Grierson to refrain from postwar planning. That was a matter of government policy, he argued, not propaganda.[34]

The new organization's reliance on polling techniques also was not accepted by Cabinet without reservations. In January 1943, the Cabinet War Committee halted Grierson's plans to use polling as an indication of Canadian public attitudes and in February continued to question 'the statistical reliability of the [polling] method,' much to the annoyance of the Canadian Institute of Public Opinion's (CIPO) A.A. Porter, who was 'inclined to feel we are pretty damned accurate fellows.'[35] The Board finally received permission in March, with the Cabinet's warning to 'exercise careful judgement and discretion in the use of this method of examining opinion, particularly as regards the nature of the questions asked.'[36] Both the WIB and the military services were considerably more enthusiastic about opinion sampling techniques, however, and as early as February 1942 the Army had employed Opinion Surveys, a Montreal firm, to 'bring to light certain elements in morale.'[37] After Cabinet's belated blessing, WIB surveys, and those conducted directly by the CIPO, proliferated.

Whatever means were employed, however, the political implications of providing generous rehabilitation programs and accurately assessing public views of the postwar period were enormous. No one appreciated this more than Brooke Claxton, a rising star in the Liberal caucus. Critical of government information policy since 1941, Claxton encouraged both the civilian departments concerned with postwar planning and the military services to strengthen and formalize their public relations procedures.[38] This would 'create confidence that our government is on the job,' he wrote the GACDR in July 1943, 'and that the men will be looked after better in Canada than anywhere else. As the numbers [of personnel demobilized] increase, there are bound to be complaints and invidious comparisons....Positive publicity is needed to create a proper atmosphere.'[39] 'All the evidence shows,' Claxton wrote in December 1943, 'that the comprehensive program of rehabilitation is known neither to the public nor to the men in the armed forces. Time and again I find people urging that the government do things which it has already done. The anti-government attitude the men in the armed forces have today is partly due to their ignorance of what the government is offering them.'[40] A concerted campaign of moving pictures, radio talks, pamphlets, and orchestrated publicity would be essential. Not to do so would be 'ruinous' from a political standpoint, Claxton added in a follow-up memo on December 29.[41]

These proposals corresponded closely with those of the WIB (an organization whose establishment he had supported), but Claxton and other Liberal MPs also emphasized the political benefits of a revamped information structure, despite what they had earlier told Grierson.[42] Their opinions had been influenced by changes in the political situation during 1943. Mackenzie King, despite his 'undoubted' personal commitment to social security, had responded cautiously to both the Beveridge and Marsh reports and in early 1943 Ian Mackenzie was the Cabinet's only committed proponent of an expanded social welfare platform.[43] 'The demands of war,' wrote J.L. Granatstein, 'were still too pressing for attention to be diverted to post-hostilities planning on a major scale.'[44] Mackenzie's efforts and the Marsh report itself kept social reform on the government's agenda paper, but the defeat of Ontario's Liberals by George Drew's Conservatives in the August provincial election, the CCF's strong showing in the same contest, Liberal defeats in four federal by-elections, labour unrest, and a national poll result putting the CCF ahead of both the Liberals and the Tories finally convinced the prime minister that the government 'had to confront the need for social-welfare legislation.'[45] Warnings that the government's public relations machinery was in need of reform therefore found a more receptive audience as 1943 wore on[46] for they complimented Ottawa's new-found desire to bolster its social reform credentials and the Liberal party's efforts to reorganize for the next federal election. 'It seems to me,' wrote the WIB's J.D. Ketchum in September, 'that you could make a good case for arguing that the Government is losing elections because of their [sic] failure to meet these post-war demands.'[47]

There was much truth in this assessment. Throughout 1943 and 1944 the polls indicated increasing levels of public interest in postwar questions, broad support for generous rehabilitation measures and swift demobilization, universal concern over employment, and considerable dissatisfaction with the information available regarding postwar plans. In April 1943, for example, 78 percent of those polled by the CIPO expected to be able to keep their present jobs,[48] but by December that number had fallen by 10 percent.[49] In October, almost the same number, 71 percent, believed Canada should make 'many changes or reforms' (particular measures were not specified), and by the following January 58 percent expected there would be a jobless period after the war.[50] Another survey in April asked respondents what questions they would have if granted an interview with the prime minister. The three most popular answers all dealt with postwar matters: 15 percent on postwar questions other than demobilization; 13 percent on demobilization and rehabilitation; and 7 percent on social legislation. By comparison, only 4 percent would have selected 'questions concerned with Quebec' or the war effort and a mere 3 percent would have discussed conscription.[51] Canadians' willingness to pay for postwar programs was also growing. In another April poll, 75 percent of respondents expressed themselves willing to pay a 'small part' of their income to 'receive medical and hospital care whenever [they] needed it,'[52] while a month previously 87 percent had approved of demobilization payments to military personnel leaving the service.[53] Fifty-seven percent approved of family allowances (81 percent in Quebec) and 69 percent did not believe that the unemployment insurance plan, by itself, would be enough to provide them 'with enough money to tide you over any period of depression in which you might be unemployed after this war.'[54] By November 1943, the WIB finally considered postwar planning a 'hot subject.'[55]

Meeting the demand for more information and more programs was complicated by the military's, especially the Army's, continuing insistence that the war must be won before attention shifted to postwar concerns. In August 1943, for example, one year after his first clash with Walter Woods, Ralston shot down another public relations proposal, this one to publicize information dealing specifically with military demobilization. Both he and the Adjutant

General believed such facts should 'be kept secret and confidential...to publish anything indicating extent of demobilization, persons who would be retained, priorities as to demobilization, etc., would embarrass, jeopardize and make most difficult, if not impossible, intelligent and effective planning of the Armed Services post-war.'[56] In this case, the reasons for secrecy were more apparent, however, and Ralston's views on rehabilitation publicity appear also to have mellowed. He now conceded the GACDR's right to publicize such material, and in late August CMHQ approved 'in principle' the Department of Pensions and National Health's expanded plans to provide postwar education to the troops, if the Army's Educational Services directorate took the lead. The RCAF, by comparison, 'was very pleased' with civilian efforts, concurred 'heartily' with them, saw no reason why they would interfere in operations, and was prepared 'to give every assistance in the implementation of them' whenever Mackenzie's people were ready to proceed. The Army's unco-operative attitude, despite its improvement from a year earlier, is striking.[57]

So were its effects. By mid-1943 the need for a strong public relations organization to reduce military disillusionment with the civilian government was becoming acute. In May, of nine hundred soldiers surveyed 66 percent believed that better jobs and a more favourable economic climate would not follow the war. Only 21 percent believed they would be 'better off' in the postwar period, versus 30 percent who thought things would get worse. Thirty-nine percent, by contrast, believed civilians would gain from the war, nearly twice the comparable military figure. In September, a survey drawn from morale reports of 270 units based in Canada found that 'the post-war period is generally thought of pessimistically.'[58] In early February 1944, as WIB reports emphasized the public's insistence on 'the most generous possible treatment of discharged men,' another poll of military personnel revealed 'the need for clear and authoritative statements on post-war plans and on provisions for the rehabilitation of service men in particular.' One unit reported that the 'provisions for care and re-employment seem to be neither clear nor adequate,' while another commented on the 'lack of definite policy re disposition of the troops after the war. Men feel that their jobs will be snapped up by [Home Defence and reserve] personnel while they will be kept overseas for an indefinite time.'[59] But Ralston and senior military officials continued to caution against distracting personnel from the task at hand by informing them of their postwar prospects. Civilian bureaucrats and military officers involved in demobilization planning, auxiliary services, and educational and training programs warned of the linkages between information and morale largely in vain. Winning the war was the first priority; winning the peace could wait.

ATTACKING THE PROBLEM: MORE COMMITTEES
AND THE NEED FOR 'DEFINITE INFORMATION'

While the battle continued over strengthening the government's information management process and increasing the amount of information available to the troops, the potential danger to the government's image and to the governing party's re-election prospects grew apace. Attacks on Ottawa's rehabilitation plan by M.J. Coldwell and Tommy Douglas, for example, soon led to calls for veterans' issues to assume the central role in the Liberal Party's next election platform.[60] Confusion amongst the press as to the division of labour between military and civilian authorities and, by implication, the effectiveness and efficiency of the rehabilitation program, served the same purpose.[61] In June 1944, the WIB reported that after nearly five years of preparation, 46 percent of Canadians still wanted more information on the country's plans for its veterans. Even worse, 'those who are not informed of existing measures are inclined to take at face value the stories circulating in many centres about callous or unintelligent handling of discharged men. Criticisms recently heard concern long waiting for discharge, heavy deductions for living expenses while in hospital, and the "calling-up" of men discharged after overseas service.'[62]

'Comments over the past few weeks,' noted a WIB report in mid-October 1944, 'suggest a growing need for information on all matters connected with rehabilitation.'[63] Government publicity had been well received and the plans themselves 'have met with nothing but praise,' but the information was still deemed insufficient, and practical problems in implementing the plans were discussed widely. Rumour and anecdote were, as always, rife, and as the report noted, 'the justice or otherwise of the complaints has, of course, little bearing on their effect on public opinion.' The Toronto Heliconian Club's demand in January 1944 for the establishment of a separate commission for the rehabilitation of actors, musicians, and artists indicated the extant to which postwar issues now dominated the public agenda.[64]

C.B. Macpherson, in a brief for the Wartime Information Board, outlined the impact of this change in public attitudes by specific references to poll results.[65] During 1943, Macpherson stated, the WIB had attempted an active postwar information program but, 'for various reasons,' it had failed. In the latter half of the year, a single individual had handled inquiries, written articles for WIB publications, and kept track of relevant legislation, committee reports, and newspaper coverage of postwar topics. National WIB surveys in April and again in October 1943 indicated that this would no longer suffice. When asked what issues they would like to know more about, 45 percent of respondents in

April and 57 percent in October answered 'plans for after the war.' These were easily the highest figures in each survey. 'Price and wage control,' the next most popular response, was cited by 29 percent and 34 percent respectively, 'labour relations and working conditions' by 22 percent and 29 percent. Also in October, another poll asked what question people would most like answered by their Member of Parliament. The broad category of 'postwar employment, rehabilitation, reconstruction, and social security' was cited by 47 percent; no other topic was mentioned by more than 7 percent of respondents. In light of such figures, what the WIB needed now, Macpherson urged, was a special information service devoted to postwar and reconstruction issues. The main task of this section would be to produce a series of postwar 'reference papers' that would be distributed to Members of Parliament, newspaper editorial writers, government officials, and nongovernment groups working on postwar questions, a distribution list of some two thousand people in all.

Had this been tried earlier in 1943 or in 1942, background information might have been difficult to assemble, but by early 1944 the volume of material from governmental and nongovernmental sources was increasing almost daily. A 'Selected Bibliography on Problems of Demobilization, Adjustment and Rehabilitation' prepared for the WIB and the Canadian Library Council in June by Eleanor Barteaux of the Windsor, Ontario, Public Library ran to 20 pages and listed 43 books (13 of them on Canadian topics) and some 240 government documents, pamphlets, and periodicals (113 of them Canadian).[66]

The effect of the printed word and the machinations of political parties, industry and trade associations, and social welfare groups, however, paled in comparison to the impact on public attitudes caused by the growing number of wounded Canadians returning from overseas. This had three effects on the Canadian public, the WIB reported in March: 'it brings the actual war home to them as never before, it stimulates enthusiasm by providing an opportunity to do small services for the wounded, and it strengthens public determination that these men must be well provided for in the future.'[67]

As Macpherson's memorandum had urged, the WIB's response to these pressures included establishing a special section on postwar issues, a new publication series, and increased efforts to communicate with other government agencies, the press, lobby groups, and the general public. Civil unrest would be the price for failure to address the public's postwar concerns, the WIB argued, and veterans especially must be made part of the national consensus. The Board had believed since 1943 that Canadian soldiers would only continue fighting if they had 'something beyond fighting to fight for.' By 1944, this policy goal had been translated into a campaign to convince the troops that they were 'citizen-soldiers' whose future was connected intimately with that of the nation. In this process, crude, patriotic sloganeering would be avoided in favour of straightforward assessments of the facts, encouragement for public debate, and a broad campaign to keep military personnel attuned to social, economic, and cultural events on the home front.[68] Government programs were explained as simply and as matter-of-factly as possible through booklets, radio programs, and public lectures. The Board also warned soldiers of the likely problems readjustment would bring, while promising the support of government and the general public and the probability that a planned transition would eliminate most of the difficulties encountered after the last war.[69]

The creation of interdepartmental and interservice organizations was another response to the pressure being exerted by an increasingly attentive, informed public.[70] The military established an Inter-service Demobilization Committee (ISDC) in January 1944, while civilian and military agencies formed the Demobilization and Rehabilitation Information Committee (DRIC) in October.[71] More committees were probably the last things Ottawa needed at this point in the war, but regular consultations between the key players guarded against ad hoc solutions, if only by having senior representatives of the groups involved run drafts of proposed publications, press releases, and policy memoranda through a co-operative screening process. It also helped ensure that official publications were equally applicable to all potential clients of government programs: that rehabilitation grants, for example, took into account the particular terms of service of all branches of the armed forces, or that industrial release policies were in accord with the Department of Labour's employment allocation strategy and the military's discharge procedures. Postwar planning was afforded further structural recognition later in the year by a major departmental reorganization. Two new departments, Veterans' Affairs under Ian Mackenzie and Reconstruction under C.D. Howe, would focus exclusively on postwar problems, while National Health and Welfare (formerly Pensions and National Health) under Brooke Claxton would run the widening array of federal social welfare programs.

Organizational reforms alone were not a quick fix. The government's delay until September 1944 in announcing its overall demobilization priorities was part of the problem, lending an annoying vagueness to official pronouncements that bewildered and infuriated military personnel and civilians alike.[72] The sheer time involved in producing appropriate documents and public relations material was another factor, as was, inevitably, the logistical impediment of formal committees, multidepartmental agencies, and multiservice planning. The minutes of the Demobilization and Information Committee, however, reveal clearly the pitfalls avoided by constant contact between the key planning authorities. They also demonstrate clearly the competing forces at work in Canada's postwar planning process.[73]

Everyone involved, for example, feared the consequences of lifting public expectations higher than the various departments and agencies could hope to meet. As one representative from the Department of Veterans' Affairs put it, 'some of the material going out might be holding out the prospect of "pie in the sky," leaving the Department with the responsibility of producing the pie.'[74] Despite the more realistic propaganda focus of the WIB, realism also had its limits. 'Back to Civvy Street,' a key booklet on the demobilization and rehabilitation process, did not include case studies of individuals for fear of creating an unflattering impression.[75] Case studies were deemed essential in visual displays at rehabilitation centres, but they could not depict 'too promising a picture of the rehabilitation story.' The displays would also emphasize that although 'provisions and organizations are made available...ultimate responsibility is the individual's.'[76] After a test screening of the film *Future for Fighters* a number of senior military officers advised 'that the film not be shown to the troops at the present time as it painted too rosy a picture of easy transition from military to civil life.'[77] 'The problem,' the committee concluded after viewing another film entitled *Industrial Re-establishment,* 'was to give the men confidence, without minimizing the very real difficulties they will have to face.'[78]

Concern over civilian and military attitudes towards postwar problems continued into the winter of 1944–5, but by this time as well there was some evidence that public fears might have peaked, even if demands for information and programs had not slackened. In July 1944, 55 percent of respondents to a CIPO poll believed that a period of prosperity would follow the war; 34 percent predicted a depression. The breakdown of optimists versus pessimists by political party was equally encouraging. Liberals split 60–31 in forecasting prosperity, the Progressive Conservatives 57–34, and the Co-operative Commonwealth Federation 52–35. The following month CIPO asked Canadians between the ages of 15 and 24 whether they believed that postwar opportunities for young people would be better or worse than before. Fifty-three percent said 'better,' 16 percent said 'about the same,' and only 17 percent said worse.[79] Even in the military services, the Royal Canadian Navy's representative on the Demobilization and Rehabilitation Information Committee reported in January that naval personnel seemed 'reasonably happy' with Ottawa's plans, despite their great concern over postwar jobs.[80]

The immediate beneficiary of such optimism was the Liberal Party of Canada. Since September 1943, when Mackenzie King had been rattled by a poll placing the CCF as the most popular party among decided voters, the government's approval rating had increased steadily, while that of the Tories, the CCF, and the Bloc Populaire had each declined. From a low of 28 percent, Liberal popularity rose to 31 percent in December 1943, 34 percent in March,

35 percent in June, and 36 percent in November 1944. This was still a far cry from the 55 percent enjoyed in 1940, and other factors besides the postwar question affected the government's image, but it demonstrated clearly that the measures announced to date regarding social security, reconstruction, rehabilitation, and, after September 1944, demobilization were having the desired effect.[81] One of the ironies of federal information policy, William R. Young has argued, was that it sought initially to manufacture a nonpartisan national consensus on Canadian citizenship but wound up bolstering the image and electoral fortunes of the governing party.[82]

But no one was complacent any longer about the public's perception of government efforts. To be caught on the wrong side of a veterans' issue was political suicide, even though, as King and many in the Cabinet acknowledged, the economic needs of a postwar civilian economy might not coincide at all points with an unmitigated espousal of veterans' rights. An August poll showed that 62 percent of youths and 71 percent of adults wanted to see 'many changes or reforms made in Canada' after the war.[83] In Britain, only 57 percent had expressed similar sentiments, in the United States, a mere 32 percent, leading the CIPO's Wilfrid Sanders to refer to the 'evidence of social ferment' in Canada.[84] The WIB also reported in October evidence of growing public 'concern at the hint that [Home Defence personnel] may be demobilized before the men overseas, and fear of a bitter struggle between the two for re-employment.'[85]

If many Canadians remained apprehensive, however, they could no longer complain about a lack of information. The string of rehabilitation programs, grants, courses, and benefits already announced, the establishment of the departments of Veterans' Affairs and Reconstruction, and the espousal by all political parties of the rhetoric of postwar planning and social improvement contributed to a gradual easing of public anxiety and growing faith in government promises. The public relations blitz on general postwar problems, which coincided with official pronouncements in 1943–44 regarding various aspects of the demobilization plan, had in large measure succeeded. In response to the growing tidal wave of information, Canadians placed increasing reliance on Ottawa to manage the postwar period. In mid-October, 49 percent of those surveyed believed the federal government 'should take the lead in setting up and carrying out plans to provide post-war employment'; only 23 percent cited industry and business, and 16 percent said other levels of government.[86] 'It is indeed a great pleasure,' wrote one 1918 veteran to Ian Mackenzie, 'to come into contact with a government as much concerned with the "coming back" as the "going over." It happens so seldom.'[87]

Federal political parties demonstrated their adherence to the 'planning wisdom' in 1945 by incorporating postwar and rehabilitation/reconstruction issues into their election platforms. The Liberals, for example, trumpeted a 'New Social Order for Canada' in the 1945 campaign, and from early 1945 onwards the King government publicized its demobilization and rehabilitation plan across the country and overseas in a bewildering array of forms. Extensive pamphlet and audiovisual material was available months before the war in Europe ended and Ottawa, together with the military authorities, had repatriation booklets in the hands of the troops overseas within days of the German collapse. A typical meeting of the Demobilization and Rehabilitation Information Committee on 16 May 1945 discussed printing a 'Handbook on Rehabilitation' and a guide to the 'Common-sense of Re-establishment,' reports on a series of film and radio projects, a CBC pamphlet on 'The Soldier's Return,' a report by the national speakers' committee, plans for a series of citizens' conventions, and a request to the newspapers to provide copies of relevant articles to service personnel to keep them in touch during the transition period.[88]

By the end of April the polls showed 'an improvement in attitudes...and considerable approval' of the Liberals' plans. Fifty-five percent of respondents felt the government's measures for returned soldiers were 'about right,' while 31 percent said they were 'not enough,' a significant change from the 44–40 split of the previous quarter. Fifty-six percent also said returned men had no cause to complain about their treatment.[89] The public also appeared to support the military's demobilization program. In May, the WIB reported that 'comment on the repatriation program is generally favourable, except for a few remarks from strong conscriptionists about "bribing men to volunteer against Japan." '[90]

But if the public relations battle was being won at home, overseas it was still hindered by the Army's continuing reluctance to expose its troops to postwar information before the Germans had been defeated. Army educational and auxiliary service personnel did inform soldiers of postwar plans whenever possible, and the Army did publish most official statements of government policy in Routine Orders, but especially among the troops of First Canadian Army on the continent, there was a marked reluctance to waste valuable training time on postwar information sessions. This was done on an informal basis wherever occasion permitted, but until May 1945 a comprehensive postwar strategy was nowhere in evidence.[91] As Colonel Hague, the Army Advisor on Discharge Affairs, noted in early April, 'there should be no talk about rehabilitation overseas until after victory.'[92] Hague informed the DRIC a week later that 'the Army Commander overseas [General H.D.G. Crerar, General Officer Commanding-in-Chief (GOC-in-C), First Canadian Army] has expressed the view that no material on the subject of rehabilitation should be distributed to the troops in Europe until he gives the word.'[93] For a service which had planned so carefully for repatriation and for the educational needs of its troops while based in Britain, this was an unfortunate, inconsistent attitude. It stands in marked contrast to the RCAF's official view, announced in July 1944 when it inaugurated a Personnel Counselling Program designed to prepare fliers for postwar employment, build morale and help 'repatriates and convalescents to restore purpose to their lives and ease tensions.' An 'appeal to a person's self-interest is likely to result in a constructive activity of benefit to the individual while he or she is still in the service,' the air force believed.[94] By the end of September, 150 RCAF counsellors had already interviewed 10,762 personnel. In the Royal Canadian Navy, Staff Officers Rehabilitation had talked to 75 percent of all naval personnel by the end of October. But in the Army special personnel counsellors had not yet been trained and existing agencies, mainly the Educational Services, handled most issues.[95]

CONCLUSION

The relationship between public opinion and veterans' policy during the Second World War evolved in response to the military situation, trends in Canadian politics, and the ability of federal planners to manage public demands for government services. Ian Mackenzie began in 1939 by leading an otherwise preoccupied government down the path of long-range planning at a time when the military situation was highly fluid and total defeat a distinct possibility. Calls for demobilization and rehabilitation planning were scattered and unfocused at this time (with a few notable exceptions), more a reaction to the perceived problems of the last war and the Depression than concrete demands for programs this time around.

By 1943, postwar issues had become a subject for public debate across the country, in large part as a result of major British and Canadian reports on the postwar provision of social welfare services and the widespread perception that victory over the Axis was now only a matter of time. The attention did not show federal policy initiatives in an especially flattering light. Much had been accomplished by 1943, but Canadians worried about a repeat of 1919 or, worse, another Depression. Further, they complained that information regarding those programs that did exist was contradictory, incomplete, and often ineffective. They also expressed themselves willing to do much, much more. The shock such findings administered to the demobilization and rehabilitation bureaucracy, now reading public attitudes regularly and, most assumed, scientifically, thanks to WIB and CIPO opinion surveys, drove home the need to dispense, analyse, and, if necessary, manipulate public information more quickly and more accurately. A period of frantic federal planning ensued as Ottawa revamped its information management system and changed the nature, tone, and size of its information effort. Centralized planning appeared to have fallen seriously behind public opinion. The war effort and the political instincts of the governing Liberal Party now dictated that the government make every effort to catch up.

The most visible organizational aspects of this transformation were the formation of the Wartime Information Board, several interservice and interde-partmental committees the following year, and the new departments of Veterans Affairs and Reconstruction. Its most physical manifestation was the series of pamphlets, books, radio programs, and other instructional and infor-mational material that flowed from federal offices in a torrent by the spring of 1945. It was a difficult but successful campaign. By May 1945 opinion polls showed that, despite their concerns, most Canadians believed the commitment of the governing Liberals, if not the complete veracity of all their promises. In August 1945, 61 percent of Canadians polled still believed that a jobless period would follow the end of the war, but just two months previously they had re-elected the King government on the basis of its pledge to 'Build a New Social Order for Canada.'[96] Canadians were still worried; they were no longer terrified.

But increasing public faith in federal promises carried its own cost, which demobilization planners had been quick to point out. Members of the Demobilization and Rehabilitation Information Committee had warned that presenting 'too rosy a picture' of the transition process might raise expecta-tions that no government could hope to meet. Ottawa had placed itself squarely at the forefront of postwar planning. What if something went wrong? The Army's continual rejection of civilian pleas to conduct extensive pre-demobilization briefings was a constant cause of worry. The high command had prepared an extensive repatriation plan, which kicked in the moment peace was declared, but until that point the delivery of postwar information to army personnel was severely curtailed. Formation commanders and morale reports had commented repeatedly and in vain on the troops' desire for basic postwar information; Ralston, CMHQ, and, most vigorously of all, General Crerar opposed such diversions on principle.

Public opinion affected demobilization planning in one other way, as well. It established the validity of two mutually conflicting but equally popular public demands: to bring the troops home as fast as possible to jobs, veterans' programs, and a stable domestic front; and to transform the economy smoothly but rapidly to civilian production to facilitate re-establishment and guarantee employment for civilians as well as soldiers. Over the employment and demobilization of NRMA personnel the conflict between these two points of view was total and almost irreconcilable. J.L. Ralston had been on solid ground in fighting for the rights of overseas volunteers in the Cabinet's 1944 debate on demobilization priorities, as nearly every poll of English Canadian attitudes revealed, but so too were Mackenzie King and C.D. Howe in emphasizing the economic dimension of government policy and the need to free military manpower to begin the reconversion process. The compromise eventually adopted, the use of 'key personnel' and the temporary release of NRMA troops to the industrial labour pool did not please anyone completely, but it at least retained official preferment for those overseas and the cloak of respectability for federal policy.

Such compromises and the efficacy of civilian and military planning would be put to the test in the summer of 1945. Ottawa and the armed services believed strongly that the demobilization program was sound, strong, and flexible enough to handle any contingency that might arise. The Army's point system, for example, was thought to be fair, technically feasible, and popular with the troops. Civilian and military opinion surveys had in large measure informed this process and Canadians were generally convinced that the transition to peace could be managed, not easily perhaps, but at least quietly. All would now depend on the careful implementation of those plans already written; on the continued faith of those in uniform in the system's efficiency; on its adaptability to change in the face of unforeseen circumstances; and, more immediately, on the availability of ships to repatriate the hundreds of thousands of personnel overseas. In the long run, however, the Veterans Charter—the name given to the collection of federal veterans' programs consolidated in a single volume in 1946—would depend on another set of factors entirely: the dedication and professionalism of DVA bureaucrats; the depth of the federal treasury; and the support of the Canadian public.

NOTES

1. Dean F. Oliver, 'When the Battle's Won: Military Demobilization in Canada, 1939–1946' (PhD diss., York University, 1996), chapter 2; and Dean F. Oliver, 'Canadian Military Demobilization in World War II,' in Granatstein and Neary, eds., *The Good Fight* (Toronto, 1995), 367–86.
2. Doug Owram, *The Government Generation: Canadian Intellectuals and the State, 1900–1945* (Toronto: 1986), 276 and 279.
3. National Archives of Canada [hereafter NAC], W.L.M. King Papers, vol. 230, file N-305-22(G), A.E. Nightingale to King, 15 Dec. 1939.
4. *Globe and Mail*, 13 Oct. 1939, 4.
5. King Papers, vol. 230, file N-305-22(G), John Taylor to King, 18 Sept. 1940.
6. *Daily Star*, 20 Sept. 1939, 19 and 34.
7. King Papers, vol. 228, file 2187, 'Analysis of Criticisms by Mr. Manion on Government's War Policy,' n.d., C155161.
8. *Globe and Mail*, 6 Feb. 1940, editorial, 'Taking the Forward View,' 6.
9. See, for example, *Globe and Mail*, 24 Oct. (6), 2 Nov. (7), 12 Dec. (11) and 16 Dec. (1), 1939.

10. Parliament was a key battleground in the formulation of postwar policies, even if the government preferred to reserve as much as possible of the planning machinery for its own control. For several dozen examples of personal representations to the prime minister, see King Papers, vol. 230, file N-305-22(G), 1941.

11. See Mackenzie Papers, vol. 68, file 530-11, 'Press Releases—Pensions and National Health and Veterans Affairs, 1944—11/9/45.' The gradual expansion of benefits for women has been documented by Neary and Brown.

12. Canada, House of Commons, *Debates*, 6 Dec. 1940, 784. Most measures to date were the result of orders-in-council, which Mackenzie defended on the basis of the need for a speedy response. 'Nevertheless,' he said, 'there is no desire on the part of the government or the department [of Pensions and National Health] to assume the role of omniscience in connection with this very human and very complex problem.'

13. Mackenzie Papers, vol. 56, file 527-10(2), unsigned memo to Power, 24 April 1940. Mackenzie is almost certainly the author.

14. Ibid., Mackenzie to King, 10 May 1940. Mackenzie sought to make the Commons committee a very junior partner to his own. It should not create the impression, he argued, 'that the government is undertaking any liability, or making any pledge to carry out the various suggestions that may be advanced.'

15. Ibid., Ilsley to Power, 10 April 1940.

16. NAC, J.L. Ralston Papers, vol. 56, file 'Rehabilitation,' vol. 2, Woods to Mackenzie, 12 March 1942.

17. NAC, Records of the Privy Council Office (PCO), vol. 12, file W-34-10, Wartime Information Board (WIB) memo to Cabinet by A.D. Dunton, 13 March 1944, 1.

18. Leonard C. Marsh, *Report on Social Security for Canada* (Ottawa, 1943) and Sir William Beveridge, *Social Insurance and Allied Services* (London, 1942). See also Beveridge, *Full Employment in a Free Society* (London, 1944). The contemporary literature on postwar planning in Canada from about 1942 to 1946 is vast. See, for example, the series of articles in *Canadian Forum* in 1943 (volume 23) under the general heading 'Planning Postwar Canada'; Alexander Brady and F.R. Scott, eds., *Canada After the War: Studies in Political, Social, and Economic Policies for Post-war Canada* (Toronto, 1943); H.G. Cochrane, 'Plan Today for Reconstruction Tomorrow,' *Canadian Business* 15/4 (April 1942), 40–1, 93–4; George F. Davidson, *Canada Plans Security* (Ottawa, 1944); and Dorise W. Nielsen, *New Worlds for Women* (Toronto, 1944).

19. J.L. Granatstein, *The Politics of Survival: The Conservative Party of Canada, 1939–1945* (Toronto, 1967), 113–50. Excerpts from the Port Hope report of September 1942 are in Appendix 2, 207–10.

20. Mackenzie Papers, vol. 87, file 'Minister's Correspondence,' England to Mackenzie, 4 Dec. 1942.

21. King Papers, vol. 345, Mackenzie to King, 296973-7, 15 Oct. 1943.

22. Ibid., vol. 353, Mrs. Herbert S. White to King, n.d., but probably early December 1943, 306837-9.

23. Unless otherwise noted, all correspondence on this issue is in the Ralston Papers, vol. 56, file 'Rehabilitation,' vol. 2.

24. Interestingly, at around the same time Ralston was fending off Woods' requests for access to the troops before their release because of the benefits to morale and to the government's image, the Army, in response to similar concerns, modernized and expanded its own public relations structure. On 22 May 1943, the Directorate of Information (Army) became the Directorate of Public Relations (Army). NAC, Records of the Department of National Defence (DND), vol. 13329, War Diary, Directorate of Public Relations (Army), May 1943, appendix 21. One month later the DPR announced the appointment of Educational Officers for all Military Districts in Canada. The courses offered by these officers sought to 'increase a man's efficiency as a soldier' and to '*prepare him for return to civilian life*' [emphasis added].

25. William R. Young, 'Building Citizenship: English Canadian Propaganda During the Second World War,' *Journal of Canadian Studies* 16/3-4 (Fall–Winter 1981), 125; Gary Evans, *John Grierson and the National Film Board: The Politics of Wartime Propaganda* (Toronto, 1984), 83–8.

26. Evans, *John Grierson*, 88. Vining resigned due to ill health in January 1943.

27. Private polling companies had been lobbying the WIB for contracts throughout 1942. A.A. Porter, Director, Canadian Institute of Public Opinion, wrote Charles Vining of the WIB on 27 August regarding his company's willingness 'to co-operate to any extent to gather the facts that are necessary in directing Canada's war effort.' An extended correspondence ensued, but by early

October it had fixated on tracking the nature and influence of wartime rumours. This correspondence is in NAC, Records of Boards, Offices and Commissions, Series 31, Wartime Information Board (WIB), 1939–1946, vol. 13, file 8-7-A.

28. Ibid., A.A. Porter to J.D. Ketchum, 1 Dec. 1943. Ketchum had written Porter on November 30 to inquire about the 'poll gap' on postwar questions in the government's opinion surveys.
29. Young, 'Building Citizenship,' 125.
30. Evans, *John Grierson*, 89.
31. Young, 'Building Citizenship,' 126 ff.
32. Evans, *John Grierson*, 90.
33. Cited in ibid., 98.
34. Ibid., 100–1.
35. WIB, vol. 13, file 8-7-A, Ketchum to Porter, 13 Feb. 1943, and Porter to Ketchum, 16 Feb. 1943.
36. Ibid., vol. 1, file 1-2-12, WIB meeting number 12, 8 March 1943, copy of letter, A.D.P. Heeney to John Grierson, 5 March 1943.
37. DND, vol. 13271, War Diary, Deputy Adjutant General (DAG), Feb. 1942, appendix 13, 'Weekly Report,' 2.
38. Evans, *John Grierson*, 83.
39. Mackenzie Papers, vol. 93, file 'Chairman, General Advisory Committee, 2/10/1941 to 31/5/1943,' Claxton to McDonald, 1 July 1943.
40. King Papers, vol. 356, file 3816, Claxton to King, 21 Dec. 1943.
41. David Jay Bercuson's contention that 'no one was actually *doing* anything' about postwar planning when Claxton became a parliamentary assistant in late 1943 is false. Claxton knew that planning was going forward in several areas (probably, as Bercuson points out, too many areas) and quickly became immersed in it himself. Claxton maintained, however, that the government had done a poor job of communicating its plans to the public because the information process was not well co-ordinated. David Bercuson, *True Patriot: The Life of Brooke Claxton, 1898–1960* (Toronto, 1993), 114.
42. Young, 'Building Citizenship,' 125.
43. J.L. Granatstein, *Canada's War: The Politics of the Mackenzie King Government, 1939–1945* (Toronto, 1975), 262–3.
44. Ibid., 262.
45. Ibid., 264–5.
46. In May 1943, 32 percent of those polled by the Canadian Institute of Public Opinion did not know what 'social security' meant, another 19 percent had only a 'vague' awareness and 7 percent were just plain 'wrong.' *Public Opinion Quarterly* 7/2 (Summer 1943), 328. Poll conducted 19 May 1943.
47. WIB, vol. 13, file 8-7-A, Ketchum to A.A. Porter, 23 Sept. 1943.
48. *Public Opinion Quarterly* 7/2 (Summer 1943), 339. Poll conducted 28 April 1943.
49. Ibid., 8/1 (Spring 1944), 159. Poll conducted 15 Dec. 1943.
50. Ibid., 7/4 (Winter 1943), 748 and 8/1 (Spring 1944), 158. Polls conducted 1 Oct. 1943 and 22 Jan. 1944, respectively.
51. Ibid., 8/2 (Summer 1944), 289. Poll conducted 22 April 1944.
52. Ibid., 292. Poll conducted 8 April 1944.
53. Ibid., 299. Poll conducted 11 March 1944.
54. Ibid., 8/3 (Fall 1944), 446. Polls conducted 2 Aug. and 15 July 1944, respectively.
55. WIB, vol. 13, file 8-7-A, Ketchum to A.A. Porter, 23 Nov. 1943.
56. Ralston Papers, vol. 56, 'Rehabilitation,' vol. 3, Ralston memo to file, 17 Aug. 1943.
57. Ibid., CMHQ memo, 26 Aug. 1943, and H. Edwards, RCAF Overseas, to Woods, 14 Sept. 1943.
58. Department of National Defence, Directorate of History (DHist), 113.3R4.003(D1), vol. 1, 'Special Reports,' 'What the Canadian Serviceman Thinks,' 15 Sept. 1943.
59. Ibid., 'Current Rumours Among Units of the Army in Canada,' Special Report Number 107 by the Research and Information Section, Adjutant General's Branch, Army, 7 Feb. 1944.
60. King Papers, vol. 377, T.H. Wood to King, 14 June 1944, 328540.
61. Queen's University Archives, C.G. Power Papers, Box 65, file D-1094, memo by W.S. Woods, 17 May 1944.
62. King Papers, vol. 359, WIB memorandum to Cabinet by J.D. Ketchum, 5 June 1944.
63. Ibid., WIB memo to Cabinet by A.D. Dunton, 16 Oct. 1944, 1–2.

64. Ibid., vol. 365, Toronto Heliconian Club to Mackenzie, 13 Jan. 1944.
65. WIB, vol. 2, file 1-3-1, 'Reconstruction Information,' by C.B. Macpherson, n.d., but either late February or early March 1944.
66. Ibid., vol. 14, file 8-14C, part 1, 'June 1944,' 'Selected Bibliography on Problems of Demobilization, Adjustment and Rehabilitation of Men and Women from the Armed Forces,' compiled by Eleanor Barteaux, Windsor Public Library, June 1944.
67. Ibid., vol. 12, file W-34-10, WIB memo to Cabinet by A.D. Dunton, 13 March 1944.
68. Young, 'Building Citizenship,' 128.
69. Ibid., 129.
70. It is worth reiterating that pressure at this point for attention to postwar problems was both intense and widespread. It also frequently displayed an overtly political tone. In May 1944, for example, the mayor of Prince Albert, Saskatchewan, lobbied Ian Mackenzie to have No. 6 Elementary Flying Training School transformed into a rehabilitation and hospitalization facility. King Papers, vol. 355, George Brock to Mackenzie, 11 May 1944.
71. WIB, vol. 11, file 6-3-1, part 1, Interdepartmental committee meeting, 6 Oct. 1944. It was established officially by Privy Council Order 8096 on 17 October.
72. DHist, 181.009(D5902), Acting Adjutant Tucker, 406 Squadron RCAF to Air Officer Commanding-in-Chief (AOCIC), RCAF Headquarters Overseas, 3 June 1944.
73. In November 1944, its membership included: Colonel H.M. Hague, Army Advisor Discharge Affairs; Lieutenant Commander J.H. McDonald, Director of Demobilization, Navy; Group Captain A.C.P. Clayton, Director of Demobilization, Air; Walter S. Woods, Deputy Minister, Department of Veterans Affairs; Arthur MacNamara, Deputy Minister, Department of Labour; W.A. Mackintosh, Deputy Minister, Department of Reconstruction; Malcolm Ross, National Film Board; Charles Wright, Radio Station CBO; A.D. Dunton, WIB (Chair); and G.C. Andrew, Secretary.
74. WIB, vol. 11, file 6-3-1, part 1, DRIC meeting, 8 Nov. 1944, 3.
75. Ibid., DRIC meeting, 29 Nov. 1944.
76. Ibid., DRIC meeting, 5 Jan. 1945.
77. Ibid., DRIC meeting, 10 Jan. 1945, 3.
78. Ibid., DRIC meeting, 7 Feb. 1945, 2.
79. *Public Opinion Quarterly* 8/3 (Fall 1944), 455–6. Polls conducted 12 July and 26 Aug. 1944, respectively.
80. WIB, vol. 11, file 6-3-1, part 1, DRIC meeting, 17 Jan. 1945, 2.
81. *Public Opinion Quarterly* 8/4 (Winter 1944–5), 580. Poll conducted 22 Nov. 1944.
82. Young, 'Building Citizenship,' 130.
83. *Public Opinion Quarterly* 8/3 (Fall 1944), 455–6. Polls conducted 22 July and 26 Aug. 1944, respectively.
84. Wilfrid Sanders, 'Canada Looks Toward Postwar,' *Public Opinion Quarterly* 8/4 (Winter 1944–5), 528.
85. PCO, vol. 12, file W-34-10, WIB memo to Cabinet by A.D. Dunton, 23 Oct. 1944.
86. *Public Opinion Quarterly* 8/4 (Winter 1944–5), 601. Poll conducted 18 Oct. 1944.
87. King Papers, vol. 365, Basil Warrens to Mackenzie, n.d. but forwarded to the Prime Minister on 31 Oct. 1944.
88. PCO, vol. 99, file R-70-10 (vol. 2), 1945 'Rehabilitation and Demobilization,' DRIC minutes, 16 May 1945.
89. Ibid., vol. 12, file W-34-10, WIB memo to Cabinet, 30 April 1945, 2.
90. Ibid., WIB memo to Cabinet, 28 May 1945, 2.
91. First Canadian Army did prepare a detailed posthostilities educational plan, however. See DND, vol. 13610 (microfilm reel T6671), War Diary, A Plans - Headquarters First Canadian Army, 4 Dec. 1944.
92. WIB, vol. 11, file 6-3-1, part 1, DRIC meeting, 4 April 1945, 4.
93. Ibid., DRIC meeting, 12 April 1945, 2.
94. Ibid., vol. 28, file 'Reference Papers, 1944,' 'RCAF Personnel Counselling Program,' 3 Aug. 1944, 3.
95. Ibid., vol. 11, file 6-3-1, part 1, RCAF, RCN and Army memos, 20 Oct., n.d. and 23 Oct. 1944 respectively.
96. *Public Opinion Quarterly* 9/3 (Fall 1945), 375. Poll conducted 1 Aug. 1945.

PART THREE

Implications for Change

A T SOME POINT IN THE LAST HALF CENTURY, CANADA AS A NATION BECAME associated with the concept of the welfare state. The timing is imprecise, and the degree to which Canada is regarded as the epitome of the welfare state, both domestically and abroad, is probably surpassed by the reputation Scandinavian countries have acquired. Nevertheless, a recent Angus Reid poll indicates that the majority of Canadians regard their government-sponsored social welfare programs as second to none, and that foreign respondents (with the obvious exception of northern Europeans) also had the impression that Canada offered generous and all-encompassing state social benefits.[1] Whether or not the international perception has changed in the last two years, there is increasing domestic concern that our much-vaunted social programs are on the verge of destruction, either because of inherent weaknesses in their design or because of a failure on the part of elected officials to continue the commitment to providing programs and benefits. However, as positive as the response to the Canadian social welfare system is, and as fearful as its collapse may be, a simplistic view of the welfare state has the unfortunate effect of blinding us to both the complexity of its design and the concomitant complexity of its redesign. The authors in this section attempt to put colour back in the black and white picture of the Canadian system as either good or bad, and in so doing offer some solutions to the problems that confront policy-makers today.

In the years before the Second World War, Canadian governments implemented, often reluctantly, a few welfare programs designed to fill in the holes left by overused charitable institutions and family support mechanisms. These were specific programs aimed at providing limited relief for special target groups and included provincial policies of worker's compensation, mother's allowances, and a national, although seriously restricted, system of old age pensions. The provincial programs varied greatly and even the federal foray into the field of social welfare was characterized by a singular disregard for federal social responsibility in general. In the global context, Canada lagged far behind western Europe and even the United States in its appreciation of the state role in providing for the well-being of the population.

Wartime centralization changed the government response to social welfare policy somewhat, but the policies remained haphazard and piecemeal. Less able to use the excuse of the constraints of the federal system despite the fact that the provinces controlled most of the social jurisdiction, the national government was moved to provide central organization in all fields after the outbreak of war. Ottawa still remained reluctant to conceptualize social policy as an integrated component of domestic policy. The programs that the federal government did implement were designed to address very specific problems, and were timed to maximize the government's public appeal. Unemployment insurance was introduced during wartime, at a juncture that saw most Canadians employed and therefore able to contribute to, rather than put pressure on, the insurance fund. Family allowances were offered at the moment when the threat from the political left seemed the greatest, and successfully disarmed opponents of the government. The decade following World War II saw the introduction of grants for medical research, the extension of the old age pension program, and the beginning of joint federal–provincial action in the provision of hospital insurance. While there were clearly more programs introduced and more money spent on social welfare in the years between 1940 and 1956 than had been witnessed before, it was still a piecemeal social welfare system. For the most part, the benefits were still directed at specific target groups—the unemployed, mothers, and the aged poor. Those programs that were theoretically universal, most particularly hospital insurance, which would provide hospital and diagnostic services to any who required them, were still not designed as part of a larger commitment to government responsibility for the well-being of the public.

The 1960s witnessed the change in this ad hoc approach to social welfare. When the final threads of the Canadian social welfare net were woven into place, they were understood to have implications not just for the pre-existing policies but also for the overall levels of employment, productivity, and economic growth in the Canadian state. Universal health insurance, a contributory old age program, and the rationalization of welfare benefits under the Canada Assistance Plan were the first programs to be truly integrated and thus not only completed the social welfare system but also established a real net through which it was assumed few would fall. That, in the final stages, the Canadian social welfare state was designed as an interrelated body of policies with far-flung effects has meant that the process of redesigning the system will be equally complex.

Most of the contributors to this collection recognize that any changes made to our present system will have much wider implications than merely saving a few dollars or providing services to an underprotected group. They accept that the integrated design of the welfare state makes it more vulnerable to fiddling at the edges. The authors in this section, however, not only appreciate the difficulties inherent in restructuring the welfare state, but all are also prepared to offer suggestions for avoiding these difficulties without entirely eliminating the government commitment to social welfare.

R. Brian Howe and Katherine Covell turn their attention to the rights of children in times of fiscal restraint. Despite mid-century national initiatives in the elimination of child poverty, the authors argue that these measures did not meet their objectives of increased economic security for children. Recent Parliamentary and international commitments to the principle of children's rights, including the right to economic security, represent the important shift in Canadian policy away from the traditional concept of child welfare 'justified on the paternalistic grounds of the welfare and needs of vulnerable and deprived children' to one based on the stronger and more demanding principle of a child's inherent right to economic security. Unfortunately, they contend, Canada may have embraced this principle in rhetoric but not in fact. While warning that the ultimate financial and social costs of poverty will continue to be high if the health and psychological well-being of Canada's children are ignored, they offer a prescription for governmental change that would result in the fulfilment of the oft-repeated commitment to child welfare.

In her article, Therese Jennissen examines the implications of the new Canada Health and Social Transfer, particularly in its effects on women, and points to some way in which this one policy could be altered to address the needs of the female portion of the population. She argues that in allocating a greater responsibility to the provinces, the federal CHST threatens to produce a welfare system with various regional differences and one which leaves those most vulnerable to economic fluctuations at the mercy of provincial governments with competing priorities. In attempting to decentralize social policy, and therefore reduce the demands on the federal budget, she argues that policymakers have failed to assess adequately how this transfer will affect individuals. She sees a failure to consider the implications of the CHST, and proposes a greater attention to gender-based analyses of federal policies and a greater role for women in the policy-making process.

Tom Kent, one of the architects of the integrated system of the 1960s, takes a broader view of current social security policies and problems, and offers both a solution to the dilemma as politicians perceive it, and a partial agenda for expansion. He contends that it was the failure of Canadian governments to tax fairly and thoroughly that has led to the enormous deficit with which we now find ourselves, and not the expansion and growing cost of social programs. By taxing every dollar earned, regardless of the source of that income, he argues that we can in fact afford to fix some of the tears in the social welfare net. A system of national childcare and assistance for low-income parents, he says, should be the starting point for a renewed social contract, although he is insistent that these are not the only areas in which action needs to be taken. Ultimately, he finds our legitimacy as a nation resting on the existence of national social policies and national standards and thus fears for the future of Canada if the programs are not retained.

Bruce Campbell turns his lens once again on the social welfare system as a whole, and offers an alternative means of financing that would allow the retention of its key features. He contends that governments need to emphasize job creation, social investment, and a more equitable tax system in order to get the Canadian social welfare state back on track. By rejecting the fallacies that have become the new orthodoxy, most particularly that full employment is a modern impossibility and that globalization limits the role national governments can play, he offers an alternative budget that would protect social welfare while at the same time assisting economic growth.

None of these contributors see the present policies as perfect or inevitable. All suggest changes of varying degrees that would protect the benefits that Canadians now enjoy, and extend those benefits to people who the welfare state has failed. All recognize that changes cannot be made without the effects being felt in all areas of the social welfare system and, moreover, all areas of the Canadian polity. There is a certain degree of cautious optimism here, but it is mitigated by the recognition that, in order for change to occur, policymakers at all levels of government must be prepared to make a firm commitment to the welfare state and take proactive measures to protect it. Whether that will happen remains to be seen.

NOTES

1. Angus E. Reid and Margaret M. Burns, *Canada and the World: An International Perspective on Canada and Canadians* (Winnipeg, 1992).

IMPLICATIONS FOR WOMEN
The Canada Health and Social Transfer

THERESE JENNISSEN

School of Social Work
Carleton University

O n April 1, 1996, the Canada Health and Social Transfer (CHST) formally replaced the Canada Assistance Plan (CAP) and the Established Programs Financing (EPF). This change marks the beginning of a new era for social policy in Canada as the federal government moves away from cost-shared programs. The CHST both reduces the total amount of money that is transferred from the federal government for social programs, and it alters the structure of this funding arrangement. These features of the CHST raise some fundamental social policy questions: what is the future of national standards, what will constitute minimum standards and how will they be determined, will social policies serve the principle of advancing equality in society, including equality for women? With these questions in mind, this paper explores some of the implications of the CHST for women in Canada.

There is little doubt that the CHST will have important negative effects on both men and women, especially those who are living in poverty and who are most dependent on the social programs and services provided by the welfare state. However, there are compelling reasons to explore the impact that this legislation will have specifically on women.[1] Historically, women in Canada have had a particular association with the welfare state both as recipients of services and as workers in the fields of health, social services, and education.[2]

Generally, women in Canada have lower-paying, less-secure jobs than men, are poorer than men, and are more likely than men to end up living in poverty.[3] This is notably the case for single women with children, elderly women, women with disabilities, and aboriginal women. Many women are dependent, at some points in their lives, on the welfare state for financial support and/or on services such as subsidized childcare, counselling and referral services, homemaker services, and legal aid. Women, especially those of child-bearing age and older women, use the health care system more frequently than men.

As workers, women are heavily represented in the sectors governed by the CHST—social services, health, and education. In many provinces these sectors of the economy are facing major funding cuts that threaten jobs.

Although the Canada Health and Social Transfer has only been in operation since 1 April 1996, and its precise impact on women is not yet fully determined, it is possible to make predications based on the Budget Implementation Act, 1995, and the 1996 federal Budget. Before doing this, the paper examines the key features of the CHST focusing on two central aspects of the legislation—reduced federal funding and a restructured transfer mechanism.

THE CANADA HEALTH AND SOCIAL TRANSFER (CHST): WHAT IS IT?

In the 1995 Budget Speech, Finance Minister Paul Martin announced a reduction in the size of the transfer payments to the provinces and the territories. At the same time it was announced that the transfer for health, postsecondary education, welfare and social services would be combined into a single block fund called the Canada Health and Social Transfer. The CHST replaces the Canada Assistance Plan (CAP) and the Established Program Financing (EPF). Developed within the Department of Finance, the CHST followed a year-long social security review by the Department of Human Resources Development and the Standing Committee on Human Resources Development. Martin clearly stated that the driving force behind the CHST was improved federal–provincial relations and deficit reduction; the CHST is 'both better suited to contemporary needs and fiscally sustainable.'[4] Alongside deficit reduction, the transfer 'will end the intrusiveness of cost-sharing under CAP and will reduce the federal–provincial entanglement that has been a source of irritation with current cost-shared arrangements.'[5]

Under the CAP and EPF arrangements, money was transferred with more specific purposes in mind. The EPF was a block transfer consisting of cash and income tax points to the provinces by the federal government. Although this transfer was intended for health and postsecondary education, the provinces had the authority to spend it according to their own priorities as long as the principles of the Canada Health Act were not violated. Provinces not complying with the Canada Health Act were subject to reduced EPF transfers. Since 1989–90, total EPF transfers per capita have not increased.[6]

CAP, on the other hand, was a cost-shared program. Money was transferred from the federal government to the provinces and territories originally at a rate of 50 percent of the full cost for social assistance and social services. The design and delivery of programs was the exclusive responsibility of each province and territory, which had to adhere to the general principles outlined in the CAP in order to be eligible for the transfer. In 1990, the federal transfer payments for CAP were limited to 5 percent of annual growth per year, for two years, for the three richest provinces–British Columbia, Alberta, and Ontario. In 1991 this ceiling was extended until 1994–5. The 1994 budget froze transfers for CAP to all provinces and territories at the 1994–5 levels and stated that the combined CAP–EPF entitlements for 1996–7 would not exceed levels that existed in 1993–4.[7]

Combining CAP and EPF in the CHST gives the provinces and territories more control over how this transfer will be used. Theoretically, in order to receive CHST funding, the provinces and territories must adhere to the principles of the Canada Health Act, and they are prohibited from imposing residency requirements on social assistance applicants. However, there is nothing to ensure that the provincial governments spend money on welfare or postsecondary education.

The Canada Health and Social Transfer resembles the EPF in that it consists of a combination of cash and tax points to the provinces. In the 1995 budget, the funding levels were set for two years. For 1996–7, total funding under the CHST is $26.9 billion—$2.5 billion less than the projected transfers under CAP and EPF. In 1997–8, funding will be further reduced to $25.1 billion or a reduction of $4.5 billion from projections of CAP and EPF.[8]

To ensure that the cash portion of the transfer would not eventually be eroded as the tax component continues to grow (a fear expressed by a number of social policy analysts) the last budget provides 'an iron-clad guarantee' that the cash portion of the CHST will never fall below $11 billion at any period during this five-year time span. The cash portion of the transfer for health and social services will remain a strong part of the CHST.[9]

The Canada Health and Social Transfer: What Will It Mean for Canadian Women?

The CHST is largely about cuts to social spending and a devolving federal role in social policy. These two features have complex and widespread implications for the future of the Canadian welfare state and for those Canadians who most depend on it. This section of the paper explores some important implications that the CHST has for women in Canada.

The CHST Reduces Federal Funds for Social Expenditures

The CHST provides the federal government with a way to abandon the costly, open-ended CAP arrangement—a social expenditure that continued to rise during periods of high unemployment. The new block fund transfer provides less money to the provinces/territories. For the 1996–7 fiscal year, the size of the transfer is $2.5 billion less than the projected amount under the old CAP and EPF regimes. The total transfer for the following fiscal year will be an even further reduction, a cut of $4.5 billion from the projected amounts under CAP and EPF.

Reduced transfer payments to the provinces and territories mean that they have less money to spend on social programs and services, and it most likely means, as we have already seen in Ontario and Alberta, that the provinces will reduce social benefits to compensate for the shortfall.
Reduced social benefits

Social Assistance

Social Assistance Social assistance has been an important financial support for Canadian women. Because of women's more tenuous relationship with the labour market, their roles as child bearers, nurturers and caregivers, and because older, single women are often impoverished, it is no surprise that women are more likely than men to use social programs and services. More than half of the people supported by welfare are women, and more than 69 percent of lone parents, most of whom are women, receive some type of social assistance.

Lone-parent families in Canada are particularly vulnerable to poverty, especially those headed by women. According to the National Council of Welfare, in 1994 nearly 83 percent of single mothers supporting young children were in the poverty range. A Statistics Canada report, *Lone Parent Families in Canada,* states that 61 percent of single-mother families were living below the poverty line in 1991 compared to 10 percent of two-parent families. Single mothers often turn to social assistance for financial support because of poor job opportunities and inadequate, inaccessible childcare. Financial cuts to social assistance therefore will be particularly problematic for lone mothers who depend on this for their livelihood.

Of all women in Canada, aboriginal women and women with disabilities are among the most impoverished. For aboriginal women generally, levels of education are low, unemployment is pervasive, and access to jobs and job training is problematic. Aboriginal women, moreover, are often lone parents, and aboriginal people, in general, have twice the rate of disabilities than nonaboriginal Canadians.[10] For all of these reasons, cuts to social assistance benefits will have a negative impact on aboriginal women who depend on social assistance and social services for their basic needs.

Although social assistance recipients with disabilities are comprised equally of men and women, women with disabilities have an overall higher poverty rate than men with disabilities. According to statistics from 1991, 50 percent of women with disabilities lived on less than $10,000 a year.[11] These women regularly face barriers to employment and sometimes encounter mobility problems. According to a recent study of women and the Canada Assistance Plan, women with disabilities receive less support from social services than they feel they need. Men with disabilities, on the contrary, report that they receive more help and support from community and social services.[12] Cut-backs to funding through the CHST will almost surely mean that social services will become less available to women with disabilities. This is particularly problematic considering the relatively high incidence of violence that women with disabilities experience.

Older women, especially those who live alone, are at risk of living in poverty and many have been dependent on CAP-funded income supplements in order to live. With the reduction of transfer payments to the provinces it is likely that these provincial supplements will cease, in which case older women may witness a direct decline in income. The federal budget of 1996 made some modifications to the Canada Pension Plan and is developing a new seniors package which combines the Old Age Security Pension and the Guaranteed Income Supplement, and although the implications of this for women are not yet clear, it remains an area that requires close scrutiny.

Social Services Funding to social welfare under CAP included money for social assistance and for social services. Reductions in transfer therefore not only threaten social assistance benefits but also the availability of social services. Social services often have critical significance for women. Women regularly depend upon subsidized childcare, counselling and rehabilitation services, homemaker services, child welfare services, noninsured health benefits, and residential care including special care and shelters for women who have been subjected to violence. A withdrawal of funding for these services, and a competition over funding therefore, will have a disproportionate effect on women.

Reduced Spending for Health

Reduced payments under the CHST could mean that health care services would also be cut, and as we have already seen an opportunity for increased privatization of health care facilities and services. When the federal government reduced the size of its transfer payments to the provinces and territories under the CHST, it also reduced its power to enforce the conditions outlined in the Canada Health Act. The last budget, however, established a cash floor, and while theoretically, this gives the federal government more clout than it had the year before, it remains to be seen if this will erode the principles of the Canada Health Act. Since women, especially women in their child-bearing years and elderly women, use health care more than men, cuts to health care will have a disproportionate impact on women and women in child-bearing years and elderly women. Health expenditures for women past the age of fourteen account for a larger portion of total health expenditures than for men. The average per capita health expenditures for women of all ages in 1994 was $2,722 and $2,228 for men. For senior women the per capita expenditures were $8,206 compared to $7,879 for men.[13]

Reduced Spending for Postsecondary Education

The CHST imposes few obvious changes to postsecondary education because under the EPF arrangement no national standards existed and this remains the case with the CHST. There is, however, no assurance in the CHST that postsecondary education must receive funding from this transfer. Whereas under the EPF, approximately 30 percent of the block fund went to education, it is possible that this can be reduced with the CHST.[14] In that event we can expect to see increased tuition fees, and possibly regional disparities in terms of educational opportunities. Higher tuition can be a barrier to education for women, especially if childcare expenses are an issue. In turn, without a postsecondary education, women's job opportunities are limited.

Less Paid Work and More Unpaid Work for Women

Many women are employed in the social service sector in nursing, education, health and childcare work. Almost 40 percent of women in the paid labour force in Canada are employed in teaching and related work, medicine and health and service work. Approximately 80 percent of health care workers are women.[15]

Cutting back funds in health, education and social services means that women working in these sectors might lose their jobs. When social services are cut, it is usually women who end up providing the caring services without pay.

The CHST—A Restructured Block Funding Arrangement

Since the CHST has imposed the most serious changes to the former CAP and since CAP has been so important for women, the following discussion centres on what the elimination of this cost-shared program may mean for Canadian women. Before that, however, a broader view of the implications of the new funding arrangements is provided.

Lumping Programs Together and Eroding National Standards

The Canada Health and Social Transfer is a block funding arrangement that is being deployed by the federal government to cut costs and decentralize social policies. By combining the former CAP and EPF programs into a single block fund with fewer enforceable conditions, the provinces/territories are given significantly more discretion in determining how and where money will be spent without guaranteeing that funds will actually be allocated for designated purposes. Few enforceable conditions means that there is no guarantee that particular programs and services will even exist. Part of the concern is that the block funding arrangement has a built-in disincentive for provinces and territories to spend money on social programs since their expenditures are no longer matched by the federal government. It also means that there will be no national standards across the country.

In order to understand the significance of the restructured transfer payment, however, it is essential not to lose sight of the fact that a central part of this restructuring is about cutting costs. So, while the federal government casts the CHST as providing 'flexibility' and autonomy to the provinces and territories by removing some conditions, in fact, the flexibility is seriously circumscribed by a reduced amount of money moving from the federal to provincial/territorial government. The provision of programs and services is dependent, therefore, not only on the importance that a provincial/territorial government may place on the provision of health, education, and social services, but also on its ability to afford these programs and services. Ultimately this means that social benefits across Canada could be widely varied from region to region, or there could be a lowering of standards in all regions, or, it could mean the elimination of some services altogether.

As it stands now, the CHST imposes stronger conditions on the provinces and territories for health than it does for postsecondary education or social welfare. While the provinces must adhere to the principles outlined in the Canada Health Act, there are no conditions for postsecondary education, and only one condition for welfare. In this competition for scarce resources, welfare services that benefit the most vulnerable segment of society, and those with the least political representation, have the most to lose. Women, particularly lone parents, senior women, and women with disabilities are highly representative in this group.

In the past, cost-shared programs were intended not only to help the provinces and territories maintain a level of service but also to ensure that there was some consistency in service across the country. The elimination of most of the standards for social welfare means that there is no mechanism for ensuring that at least some basic level of similar services will exist across the country. Ultimately, 'the result will be increased regional inequality, a less united country and a less sharing society.'[16] This means that women will have to organize around their issues in at least twelve jurisdictions; and smaller numbers usually mean a smaller political voice, less political power, and subsequently fewer policies that work in the interests of women. This is not to say that provincial/territorial governments committed to advancing the status of women will not be elected in Canada but even in this event, the benefits will only be felt in that province.

Changes to Social Assistance and Social Service Benefits: A Retreat from a Civilized Society

The National Council of Welfare has referred to CAP as the 'true mark of a civilized society' because it provided a social safety net of last resort to men, women, and children who were unable, for whatever reasons, to provide for themselves.[17] Transfers under CAP were contingent on the provinces/territories adhering to a set of principles outlined in legislation. These principles included: (1) the right to an income for persons in need, (2) the right to a level of income that meets a person's budgetary requirements, (3) the right to appeal a welfare decision, (4) the right not to work while receiving assistance, and (5) the right to an income based on need regardless of what province the person is from. All but one of these conditions have been eliminated, and their elimination will have serious detrimental implications for Canadian women.

Elimination of Entitlement

Theoretically, anyone in need of social assistance under the old CAP regime was entitled to it. While the word 'need' was always open to interpretation, and while levels varied widely across the country, the elimination of these conditions heralds the beginning of an entirely different philosophy of welfare. It harkens back to former decades when social assistance was based on 'deservedness.' For women, especially lone parents, this means that they will be under more pressure to accept less than adequate childcare, lower-paying jobs, and workfare arrangements. The elimination of this condition also threatens child welfare and the increase of child poverty because there will be less money available for basic living expenses, childcare services, and child protection services.

Levels of Adequacy

The elimination of levels of adequacy based on a person's budgetary requirements will almost surely mean a reduced standard of living of people dependent on social assistance and social services. While CAP has never set minimum levels of adequacy, at the very least, it ensured that a welfare system be put in place, and that assistance be provided to any person on the basis of need.[18]

Social policy critics and activists have called on the federal and provincial governments to determine a mechanism to incorporate and enforce a number of national standards for social policy. One important standard is to set adequacy levels that must consider the recipients' needs using the market basket approach.[19] In the market basket approach, welfare benefit rates are based on the actual costs of a reasonable basket of goods and services necessary to live with dignity.[20] Without this standard there is no assurance that even the most basic needs of women and children would be met.

Elimination of the Right to Appeal

The CHST does not contain a mechanism for appealing welfare decisions. This is to deny the most vulnerable populations in Canadian society a basic and standard right. This fact places the single condition for social assistance (prohibition of residency requirement) under the CHST at risk. Without an appeal mechanism, it is unclear how violations of this one condition will be dealt with.[21]

Work as a Condition for Social Assistance

The CAP prohibited provincial administrations from requiring those on social assistance to work for their benefits but this principle was removed in the CHST. Making employment a condition for social assistance raises serious issues for all those in need of assistance. This has particularly important implications for women. Since women have fewer opportunities for 'good' jobs, and are often solely responsible for childcare, they may be placed in positions of having to take dangerous, low-paying, dissatisfying work with little choice. The National Anti-Poverty Organization regards workfare as 'a violation of the basic human right to freely choose work,' and worse than that, 'people on welfare will be forced, by law or necessity, to compete for and even take other people's jobs—in most cases for about one-third or half the pay and no benefits.'[22]

CONCLUSION

The Canada Health and Social Transfer will operate against the best interests of many Canadians, particularly those who depend most on the social welfare system. Women are an important group that fall within this category. Canadian women have had a unique relationship with the welfare state and will undoubtedly be negatively affected by the changes that the CHST will bring. The most problematic part of this new legislation for women is that the jobs in which women are concentrated are particularly vulnerable to cuts, and the services and social assistance benefits upon which many women depend are being reduced.

The CHST represents a serious contradiction between the federal government's formal commitment for advancing the status of Canadian women and its substantive policies. On the one hand, the federal government endorses, particularly in international forums, the advancement of the status of Canadian women, but in practice it develops policies that work against the best interests of women. This is particularly disconcerting given the government's commitment to perform gender-based analysis on federal government policies to ensure that they do not differentially affect women. The CHST was not subjected to a gender-based analysis despite the fact that this issue was repeatedly raised by women's organizations at the hearings of the social security review that preceded the 1995 federal budget and despite the fact that the Standing Committee on Human Resources Development identified gender-based analysis as a recommendation in its report.[23]

Women must play a central role in future federal–provincial negotiations over the CHST. Data concerning the impact of the legislation on women must be collected and a gender-based analysis must be applied to the legislation. A gender-based analysis of the CHST will almost surely support the notion of a separate fund for social assistance under the CHST.

To develop gender-sensitive social policies, however, it is not sufficient for governments to simply include the word 'women' in the legislation. Policies that promote the advancement of women require an understanding of the systemic barriers to women's equality and comprehensive strategies for redressing them. Until this is done, the move toward equality for women will remain incremental and vulnerable to reversal during times of economic crises.

NOTES

1. In Canada, the federal government formally supports the notion of advancing the status of women. This was done through a number of forums including the *Canadian Charter of Rights and Freedoms*, its endorsement of international covenants such as the *Nairobi Forward-Looking Strategies for the Advancement of Women*, the *Convention on the Elimination of All Forms of Discrimination Against Women* and the *Beijing Document*. More recently, the federal government adopted a policy that requires gender-based analysis be conducted on future government policies in federal departments and agencies 'where appropriate.'
2. Carol Baines, Patricia Evans, and Sheila Neysmith, 'Caring:Its Impact on the Lives of Women,' in *Women's Caring: Feminist Perspectives on Social Welfare*, (Toronto, 1991), 11–35.
3. Morley Gunderson, Leon Muszynski, Jennifer Keck, *Women and Labour Market Poverty* (Ottawa, 1990), 1–13.
4. *Budget Plan* (Ottawa, 1995), 52.
5. *Budget Plan*, 53.
6. Odette Madore, *The Canada Health and Social Transfer: Operation and Possible Repercussions on the Health Care Sector* (Ottawa, 1995), 3.
7. *Budget Plan*, 52.
8. *Budget Plan*, 55.
9. *Budget Speech* (Ottawa, 1996).
10. Frances Woolley, 'Women and the Canada Assistance Plan' (Ottawa, 1995), 18.
11. Woolley, 'Women and the Canada Assistance Plan,' 23.
12. Ibid.
13. Health Canada, *National Health Expenditures in Canada, 1975–1994, Summary Report* (Ottawa, 1996), 23.
14. Madore, *The Canada Health and Social Transfer*, 3.
15. Karen Messing, *Occupational Health and Safety Concerns of Canadian Women* (Ottawa, 1991), 19.
16. CUPE, 'Our Country Under Attack: A Report of the Canada Health and Social Transfer and What It Will Do to Our Way of Life' (Ottawa, 1995).
17. The National Council of Welfare, *The 1995 Budget and Block Funding: A Report by the National Council of Welfare* (Ottawa, 1994), 4.
18. David Robinson, 'Standing on Guard for Canada's Social Programs' (Ottawa, 1995), 8.
19. Helen Berry, 'The Federal Government and Canada's Social Programs,' *Fact Sheet* (Ottawa, 1995), 4.
20. Social Planning Council of Ottawa–Carleton, 'Could You Live on Welfare? A Market Basket Approach to Adequacy' (Ottawa, 1994).
21. NAPO, 'Poor People Have a Right to Fair Treatment: 30 Million Reasons to Have National Standards for Welfare' (Ottawa, 1995), 4.
22. NAPO, 'Poor People Have a Right,' 4.
23. Therese Jennissen, 'The Federal Social Security Review: A Gender-Sensitive Critique,' in J. Pulkingham and G. Ternowetsky, eds., *Remaking Canadian Social Policy: Social Security in the Late 1990s* (Halifax, 1996), 238–55.

CHILDREN'S RIGHTS IN HARD TIMES

R. BRIAN HOWE

Department of Political Science
University College of Cape Breton

and

KATHERINE COVELL

Department of Psychology
University College of Cape Breton

T he social and economic well-being of children has been a long-standing concern of the Canadian welfare state. Since the Second World War, programs of economic support have been put into place to assist children and families in providing for children's basic material needs. However, during the 1990s, these programs have been caught between contradictory pressures. On the one hand, government efforts to assist children have been bolstered by the reconceptualization of economic security for children as a basic right. With the signing of the United Nations Convention on the Rights of the Child in 1990, Canada officially has become committed to the principle of children's rights—including the right to economic security—and to the implementation of the principle. This commitment has set into motion legal pressures on behalf of the economic well-being of children. But on the other hand, programs of economic and budgetary restraint during the 1990s and cut-backs to the welfare state have set into motion counterpressures working against the legal obligation. Whereas Canadian policy has remained fixed on the goal of increased economic security for children, the lack of policy implementation has resulted in a major gap between promise and reality.

This paper explores the development of these opposing pressures and the implications for children's rights in Canada. It is divided into three parts. The first examines the evolution of Canadian policy on economic support for children and the legal obligations that flow from the UN Convention. The second looks at the current gap between promise and reality in the context of budgetary restraint programs. The third part offers a critique of current policy directions based on long-term considerations of child poverty.

THE EVOLUTION OF CANADIAN POLICY

The economic security of children was a concern of Canadian public policy well before Canada signed the UN Convention on the Rights of the Child in 1990. Since the Second World War (and to a degree before), influenced by the growing belief that the social welfare state has a moral and political obligation to assist children in need, policy was established to provide economic support for children.[1] This policy rested on following three considerations. First, it was believed that the principal means of economic security for children are jobs for their parents or guardians. Thus the principal means of state assistance to children is to ensure economic growth and high levels of employment. Second, it was assumed that there will be times and circumstances when parents are unable to secure employment and provide for their children's needs. Thus there is a need for general programs of income security such as unemployment insurance, social assistance, housing subsidies, and disability benefits to assist parents in providing for their children as well as for themselves.

Third, it was believed that the economic security of children could be advanced through special programs of income supplements and tax benefits to help families meet the costs of raising their children. Thus a child benefits program was put into place—beginning with family allowances in 1945 and continuing with a revised child benefits program in 1992—which provided parents or guardians with direct payments for children. A program of child tax credits also was put into place beginning in 1979 to provide additional after-tax income to families with children. Finally, a childcare expense deduction was established to allow parents to deduct a portion of their childcare costs from their taxable income.

But despite the operation of this network of programs, economic insecurity and child poverty persisted as a problem during the 1970s and 1980s. The problem was finally recognized by Parliament and on 24 November 1989, all the parties in the House of Commons made a resolution to achieve the goal of eliminating child poverty in Canada by the year 2000. Critics cynically said that the chances of the government actually doing this were one in a million. But it was an important public policy statement and one that could be referred to by child advocates in prodding the government into action. The advocacy group Campaign 2000 was formed to monitor progress.

In the 1990s an important shift occurred in Canadian policy regarding children, which served to further strengthen Canada's commitment to children's economic security. This was a shift from a policy based on the traditional concept of child welfare to one based on the stronger and more demanding principle of children's rights.[2] Under the traditional child welfare concept, a policy of economic support for children was justified on the paternalistic grounds of the welfare and needs of vulnerable and deprived children. But under the new principle of children's rights, officially adopted with Canada's signing the UN Convention, the policy was justified on the grounds of economic security as a basic human right. It was no longer a question of working towards the worthy goal of child welfare, but one of providing for a child's inherent human right to economic security.[3]

A number of steps occurred at the international level that led to the adoption of this new rights-based policy. In 1959, with other nations, Canada recognized the principle of children's rights by signing the UN Declaration of the Rights of the Child. This declaration was important, but it was a statement of moral and aspirational principle rather than of legal obligation. To put children's rights on a firmer legal foundation, Canada became involved during the 1980s (the Government of Poland took the lead) in helping to draft the UN Convention on the Rights of the Child. The Convention would bind Canada, as well as other nations who signed it (state parties), to the principles and legal obligations set forth in the Convention. The Convention was adopted by the United Nations General Assembly on 20 November 1989. Canada officially signed it on 28 May 1990, and following consultation among federal, provincial, and territorial governments, ratified it on 13 December 1991. Only Alberta did not support the Convention but has co-operated since the ratification.

The Convention deals with a wide spectrum of children's social, economic, political, civil, and cultural rights.[4] For convenience, these may be summarized into three basic categories: (1) rights of protection, including protection from abuse and neglect, (2) rights of participation, including rights to freedom of expression and education, and (3) rights to social and economic well-being, including rights to health care and economic security. The overriding principle of the document is to provide for the 'best interests of the child.' The key provision dealing with economic security is article 27 of the Convention which requires that state parties recognize the right of every child to a standard of living adequate for the child's physical, mental, spiritual, moral, and social development. It further requires that, in accordance with national conditions and within their means, state parties shall take all appropriate measures to assist parents and others responsible for the child to implement this right. Furthermore, under article 4, state parties are obligated to translate the rights of the Convention into actuality and to make resources available for economic as well as other rights.

In signing the Convention, Canada has assumed the legal obligation to implement children's rights as defined in the Convention through a special reporting system. The system works as follows. Two years after ratification and every five years after, Canada (as well as other state parties) is to report to the UN on its progress in implementing the Convention. Federal, provincial, and territorial governments are to consult with each other and other interested groups (e.g., the Canadian Coalition for the Rights of Children and aboriginal organizations) and prepare a report on developments and issues (Canada's first report was made in 1994). The report is to go for review to the UN Committee on the Rights of the Child, a special body of ten experts nominated by state parties. It also is to be made widely available within Canada for information and comment by concerned citizens and advocacy groups. These concerned citizens and groups may then send their comments and possible criticisms of Canada to the UN Committee for consideration.

The UN Committee in turn makes a report to the UN General Assembly. The purpose of the Committee is not to develop a lengthy critique or make a judgment or assign blame. Rather it is to provide constructive commentary and advice. In its review, the Committee may seek further information and may question the country under consideration, but it is not to act as an investigating police officer or judge. Its main role is to be a consultant and facilitator, providing practical advice and suggestions on improving the situation of children. Whereas it does not have powers of enforcement, its role is assisted by the fact that the Convention is international law, representing the will of the international community. While the international community has only limited powers to enforce the Convention and punish those who do not comply, international peer pressure exists which prods state parties into complying with the Convention. State parties are legally responsible and accountable for implementing the Convention. They have an interest in maintaining their international reputations as law-abiding states and avoiding the negative publicity that would flow from their inaction or inertia in regard to international law.

After signing the Convention, and in conjunction with its agreement to the goals set forth at the 1990 World Summit for Children, Canada has taken five follow-up steps in implementing children's rights.[5] First, it established the Children's Bureau within the Ministry of Health and Welfare in February 1991. The mandate of the Bureau was to closely monitor children's issues, to follow up on Canada's international policy commitments on children, and to ensure consistency and co-ordination for all federal programs and policies for children. Second, a new child tax benefit was announced in February 1992, to come into effect in January 1993. It consolidated family allowances, refundable child tax credits, and nonrefundable child tax credits into a single tax-free monthly payment. It also included an additional amount for low-income working families. The new benefit was to represent an increase of $2.1 billion in federal support for children and families over the next five years (1993–7). Third, a new Action Plan for Children was announced in May 1992, called Brighter Futures. This was in response to the Declaration on the Survival, Protection, and Development of Children, issued at the 1990 World Summit for Children. It was a comprehensive plan, to be co-ordinated by the Children's Bureau, aimed at providing support to children in the broad areas of health care, education, childcare, and economic security, particularly young children at risk. Fourth, as a follow-up to the Action Plan, a new Child Development Initiative was announced in 1992. It involved the establishment of a group of long-term programs designed to deal with conditions of risk during a child's earliest years of life. Funding for the Initiative was to be $500 million. Finally, fifth, Canada made its first Report to the UN Committee in May 1994. It was a lengthy report (262 pages), pointing to the progress—legislative, constitutional, and administrative—that federal, provincial, and territorial governments had made and were making in response to each article of the Convention. We now review this progress.

THE GAP BETWEEN PROMISE AND REALITY

It has now been six years since Canada signed the UN Convention and only four years until the year 2000 when child poverty is to be eliminated. What concrete steps have Canadian governments taken to implement the right of the child to economic security? What effects have government policies had on working towards ending child poverty?

In Canada's First Report to the UN Committee on the Rights of the Child in 1994, the governments of Canada presented what they had done to implement children's rights. They did so in a self-congratulatory manner. In the Report, the federal government refers to its continued support of the Canada Assistance Plan (CAP) to share social assistance costs with the provinces. While it notes that it had to limit increases to CAP (by 5 percent) to the three wealthiest provinces (Ontario, Alberta, British Columbia), it emphasizes the high level of financial support given. The federal government also refers to housing assistance through the Canada Mortgage and Housing Corporation and through Indian and Northern Affairs for low-income families. Finally, it points to more generous family support after 1992 through the expanded Child Tax Benefit, a benefit that targeted low-income families and their children. Provincial and territorial governments refer to income support programs such as social assistance, family benefits, housing subsidies, and daycare support. Saskatchewan and Newfoundland mention school programs to relieve child hunger while the Northwest Territories, PEI, and Ontario point to new child maintenance enforcement programs. Quebec refers to the fact that the economic rights of children are part of the Quebec Charter of Rights. Overall, whereas the report does recognize the continuing problem of child poverty despite all of these measures, its main message is one of substantial progress in dealing with the problem.

In May 1995, following a review of Canada's report, the UN Committee made the following recommendation to Canada in regard to the issue of child poverty.[6] The Committee emphasized the need for Canada to implement article 4 of the Convention calling for the allocation of resources to ensure the economic as well as social and cultural rights of children. The Committee further emphasized the need for Canada to take immediate steps to tackle the problem of child poverty, making feasible efforts to ensure adequate resources and facilities for all families, especially single-parent ones. This was a polite and diplomatic way of suggesting to an affluent nation that it is time to clean up its act.

Were the critical comments of the Committee warranted? Let us review the current situation of child poverty in Canada. But before we do, it may be helpful to define the meaning of child poverty. Children in poverty refers to those who live in a family with a total income below the Statistics Canada low-income cut-offs (poverty line). In general, the poverty line base is one under which families spend 54.7 percent or more of their incomes on the necessities—food, clothing, and shelter. This line varies, however, in accord with the costs of living in different parts of the country. The child poverty rate refers to the percentage of children whose family incomes are at or below the poverty line.

In 1989, when the House of Commons resolution was made to end child poverty in Canada, the child poverty rate stood at 14.5 percent with 934,000 living in poverty. Between 1989 and 1993, the child poverty rate increased steadily. In 1993, Canada had its highest child poverty rate in 14 years, 20.8 percent. A further 481,000 children had been added to the ranks of the poor.

TABLE 1 Child Poverty Rates 1989–93

Year	Number of Children (under 18) Living in Poverty	Poverty Rate (%)
1989	934,000	14.5
1990	1,105,000	16.9
1991	1,210,000	18.2
1992	1,218,000	18.3
1993	1,447,000	21.3

SOURCE: Statistics Canada.

Many of these children are recipients of social assistance. According to the National Council of Welfare, in 1993, 27 percent of welfare recipients were children. The actual numbers show a startling increase of 69 percent. In 1989, 687,000 children were in families receiving social assistance; in 1994 there were 1,162,700 such children. Thus we can assume that many of the children among the ranks of the poor are well below the poverty line. In fact, whereas the current poverty line for a family of three in a mid-size city is $22,000, the average poor family income is $8,300 below that. Increasingly, it would appear, poor children are deeply poor.

The growth of child poverty can be seen as a result of economic developments and social and economic policies that together have created (1) an overall decrease in family income, (2) an increase in unemployment, and (3) an increase in the numbers of single parents. Each of these trends has contributed to the increasing numbers of children living in poverty. This is not to ignore certain progressive government measures. Children are better off than they otherwise would be through the new federal Child Benefits program, the federal Child Development Initiative, and new provincial measures in the areas of maintenance enforcement, and child hunger programs in schools. But when we consider other developments—persisting unemployment and underemployment, cuts in social spending, tightening of unemployment insurance—the net impact has been an increase in child poverty. In the area of unemployment insurance, for example, since 1981, there has been a reduction of benefits and benefit periods and an increase in qualifying periods. When benefits run out and jobs are in short supply, people turn to social assistance more quickly. But in the area of social assistance, during the 1990s, federal transfers to provinces under the CAP have levelled off while provincial welfare benefits have lessened. This increases child poverty. And the future offers little consolation. Beginning in 1996–7, the CAP will end and federal transfers will

TABLE 2	Average Family Incomes (in constant 1993 dollars)
1989	46,250
1990	45,231
1991	44,040
1992	44,152
1993	43,225

SOURCE: Statistics Canada.

occur under the new Canada Health and Social Transfer. As this new arrangement will involve block funding, allowing the provinces to direct monies as they see fit with few federal standards, there is little incentive for provinces to provide minimum standards or ensure adequate benefits to take care of the needs of children.

According to Statistics Canada, real family income fell steadily between 1989 and 1993. As shown in Table 2, between 1989 and 1993 there was a 6.5 percent shrinkage in average family income. The figures here are in 1993 dollars and represent the after-tax income. Average family incomes decreased across income levels; even the poorest quintile with an average income of $10,657 lost 5.4 percent. The poorest families are disproportionately those with young children in which the older parent is thirty years of age or younger.

The overall drop in family income results not only from cuts in social spending, but also from the continual elimination of many well-paying blue-collar jobs. With a shift toward a more high-tech industrial economy, we see increasing job polarization to employment either requiring specialized education, or few skills and paying minimum wage. Minimum wage rates are constantly losing value against increases in the cost of living. Not surprisingly, the 1995 Child Poverty Report notes that in 1993, 244,000 families in which a parent worked were below the poverty line.[7] This number represents a 37 percent increase in the number of children living in working poor, two-parent families.

A further problem is that many parents have had their full-time jobs replaced with part-time jobs: such jobs typically have little security and few benefits. Figure 1 describes the increase in part-time employment. Over the past two decades part-time employment has grown from 12.5 percent to the current 19 percent.

Increases in involuntary part-time employment tend to accompany increases in unemployment as indicated in Figure 2. Unemployment, although somewhat cyclical, has remained relatively high. Global competitiveness is often cited as the reason for continuing high levels of unemployment; however, Canada has among the highest unemployment rates of major industrialized nations.

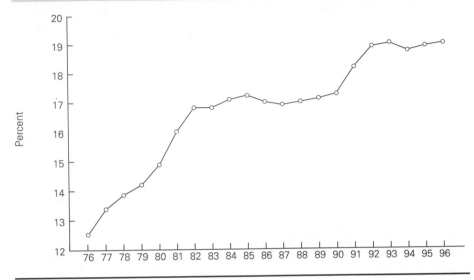

FIGURE 1 Part-time Work as a Percentage of All Employment

SOURCE: Statistics Canada.

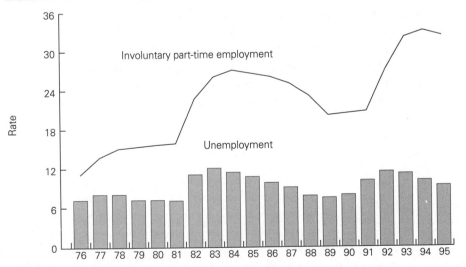

FIGURE 2 Involuntary Part-time Employment and Unemployment Rates

SOURCE: Statistics Canada.

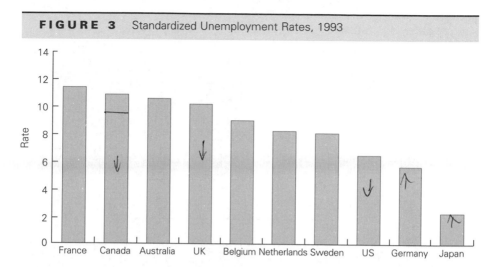

FIGURE 3 Standardized Unemployment Rates, 1993

SOURCE: OECD Employment Outlook, 1993.

The percentage of children experiencing the unemployment of at least one parent for twenty-seven weeks or more has steadily grown from 8.8 percent of children in 1989 (7.5 percent unemployment rate) to 13 percent of children in 1993.

TABLE 3 Children in Families Experiencing Unemployment of at Least One Parent for at Least 27 Weeks

Year	Number of Children	Percent of Children
1989	570,000	8.8
1990	617,000	9.4
1991	806,000	12.1
1992	837,000	12.4
1993	839,000	13.0

SOURCE: Statistics Canada.

With the current unemployment rate at 9.6 percent (February, 1996), the numbers of affected children are likely around 11 percent. Again, young families are most affected. As indicated in Figure 4, unemployment rates for parents under thirty years, already higher than those of older parents, have increased 92 percent compared to a 65 percent increase among older parents. Whereas young parents in two-parent families are more likely to be working poor or unemployed, compared to parents over age thirty, the child most likely

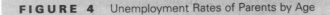

FIGURE 4 Unemployment Rates of Parents by Age

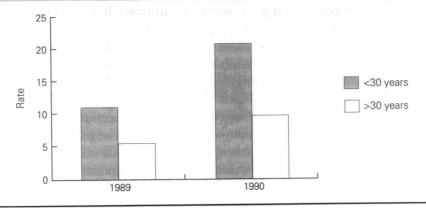

SOURCE: Statistics Canada.

FIGURE 5 Child Poverty Rates by Family Structure

SOURCE: Centre for International Statistics in Economic and Social Welfare, 1994.

to be in poverty is that of the single parent. The rate of child poverty in single-parent families is much higher than in two-parent families.

According to the Centre for International Statistics in Economic and Social Welfare, the single-parent child poverty rate actually declined by about 5 percentage points between 1991 and 1992.[8] However, the absolute number of poor children in single-parent families grew during the same period by 33,000 because of a growth in the overall numbers of single-parent families. By 1993, 595,000 children were living in one-parent families below the poverty line. Figure 5 shows the numbers of poor children in single-parent families.

In summary, the data demonstrate significant increases in child poverty, and identify the single-parent child or the child of parents under age thirty as most at-risk for poverty living. In contrast to promises, it appears that the best interests of children (the overriding principle of the Convention) have been subjugated to the goals of deficit reduction and global competitiveness. It is ironic that justification for such policies and their concomitant toll on families has been concern with future generations. Does the public policy of snip, cut, and chop, indicate increased welfare for the next generation? Policymakers may argue so, but significant bodies of research by developmental psychologists suggest the opposite.

CRITIQUE OF CURRENT POLICY

The effects of growing up in poverty are well documented. Poverty, regardless of family structure or demographics, poses risks to most areas of child development. Statistics described by the Canadian Institute of Child Health show clearly how infant health and physical development are compromised. Poverty is associated with low birthweight, infant mortality, contagious diseases, childhood injury, and childhood death.[9] Intellectual development is affected. Poverty is associated with developmental delays in intellectual development and school achievement.[10] School-related skills are measurably lower among children in poverty from the time they enter preschool; their progress through school is slower and dropout rates are significantly higher.[11] Socioemotional development similarly is jeopardized. There is considerable evidence that poverty is associated with high rates of behavioural problems, with anxiety, social withdrawal, low self-esteem, aggression and delinquency.[12] The ultimate costs to society—financial and social—will be high.

It is noteworthy that the statistics on child poverty described above identify the younger or single parent as most likely to be in poverty. Although poverty affects all children, it is also the case that poverty's effects will be greatest among such parents since these are the family structures also most affected by the daily stresses associated with child rearing. The effects of poverty on child development are mediated by parenting behaviour.[13] Parenting behaviour is affected by income; stress is exacerbated by poverty.

Parents living in poverty not only report more financial stress than their more affluent counterparts, but also more depression and more psychological stress.[14] In turn these stresses affect parenting. Among poor families there are more negative attitudes toward infants, greater use of harsh discipline and punitiveness, and low levels of warmth and support, leaving the children at heightened risk for abuse as well as for poor social competence, aggression, and delinquency.[15]

It is important also to note that stress created by uncertainty, such as in the fear of layoff, as well as income change by job loss affects parenting behaviour. It has been shown, for example, that children's behaviour problems (a reflection of unmet needs) increase when a family's income level is reduced to poverty levels, and decrease if the family moves out of poverty.[16]

The developmental processes and outcomes of poverty suggest, if nothing else, that there is a pragmatic justification for a child-centred design of public policy—policy that takes into account the provisions of the Convention. It is not just trite to say that children are the future. The current cohorts of children are the future parents, workers, and citizens of Canada. The failure to invest in their well-being today is likely to lead to greater economic difficulties. For example, according to the National Council of Welfare in 1993, 58 percent of welfare recipients are high school dropouts. Lack of attention to the present needs of Canada's poor children will lead to increased skill shortages, to high health care costs, to increased crime and the related costs of increased crime, and overall to a nation much unlike our current ideals of caring and equality.

In addition there is a moral justification for giving children centrality in policy design and implementation. The UN Convention asserts that a primary consideration in all activities concerning children is furthering their best interests. Article 3 (1) provides that 'In all actions concerning children, whether undertaken by public or private social welfare institutions, courts of law, administrative authorities, or legislative bodies, *the best interests of the child shall be a primary consideration.*' This provision reflects an underlying belief of those who designed the Convention, and presumably by those who sign it that children are possessors' of rights. Whereas what is in a child's best interests may not always be clear, as described above, the effects of poverty are. Goals to eradicate child poverty must be accompanied by policies and practices that will do so.

Yet, as Huston noted, policy goals continue to be defined in economic terms; in addition, she notes that when children are mentioned in welfare policy, typically they are described as economic burdens interfering with their parents' workforce participation.[17] Although Huston was writing of conditions in the United States, a country whose government has yet to ratify the Convention, the same conditions are apparent here. The health and psychological well-being of Canada's children are far from a government priority.

To the extent that children's needs are not met by their families, policies must explicitly be directed toward fostering their development in accord with the provisions of the Convention. Without adult interventions children's rights are meaningless. Taking children's rights seriously, especially in hard times, requires some changes.

1. *Changes in policy*

   We urge that in order to comply with the Convention, policy should be altered to give greater economic support to children. Accordingly we urge an expanded child benefits program, expanded daycare, and expanded school programs for children in need. Although criticism based on considerations of costs and the deficit is to be expected, we believe the public is concerned enough about child poverty that were the impact of poverty on child development explained to them, they would accept increased taxation to support expanded programs.

   In the long term, at the constitutional level, we suggest that following the approach of Quebec, children's basic economic rights be put into the constitution, possibly as part of the Charter of Rights or a social charter. Such a step would not only signify commitment to the UN Convention, but it would also create additional legal pressures on governments to fulfil their responsibilities. Experience has shown that when push comes to shove, economic considerations tend to come before moral and even legal obligations concerning children's rights. We can expect even more of this under the new system of block funding with few national standards on income security. Against such a tendency, it would be beneficial if children's rights were plugged into the constitution, obligating governments not to sacrifice children's rights on the altar of economic considerations.

2. *Changes in social science research*

   We suggest that more attention be paid to the regular collection of data on children themselves. The child should more frequently be the unit of analysis. It would be helpful if there were less focus on statistics such as the number of children in poor families, and more description of such figures as the percentage of children in poor health by family income; the percentage of infants with congenital or neonatal disorders by family income, the percentage of children in inadequate childcare facilities; the amount of childhood that is spent in poverty, and so forth.

   We suggest further that there be more multidisciplinary approaches to the study of children; that those whose concern is public policy work with those whose concern is developmental psychology, that economists work with child psychologists, and that children's needs be given at least as much focus as economic goals.

3. *Integration of research with public policy*

   The gap between academic research and policymakers must be lessened. Researchers concerned with child physical and mental development and health should both design their research to address public policy needs, and ensure that the results of their research are accessible to policymakers.

Too often, research findings are presented only within academia, and are embedded in jargon.

4. *Widespread education*

We suggest that more attention in public policy be given to increasing public awareness of the UN Convention and Canada's obligations. Indeed such a need was noted by the UN Committee in its review of Canada. In the long term, increased awareness would help to create additional public and political pressure on behalf of children's rights. Moreover, it would be helpful to build knowledge of children's rights (in an age-appropriate fashion) into the school curricula. Rights are of little use to those who are unaware they possess them. The content would include information about one's own and others' rights under the UN Convention and about Canada's obligation to implement those rights. Parents also should be informed about the provisions of the Convention. Those who work with children should be made aware of the Convention and shown how to be advocates for children. Furthermore, public policy courses and textbooks at the university level should include sections on policies on families and children. Likewise, developmental psychology courses should include public policy.

In summary, pressures flowing from the UN Convention and the growing belief that children are bearers of rights have been an effective force in prodding policymakers to make a greater effort to provide for children's economic security. But as we have seen, economic counterpressures have been undercutting this effort. Our suggested changes are intended to assist in the reduction of child poverty and in the fulfilment of the principles of the UN Convention.

NOTES

1. R.B. Howe, 'Evolving Policy on Children's Rights in Canada,' in K. Covell, *Readings in Child Development* (Toronto, 1995), 3–27.
2. Ibid.
3. S.N. Hart, 'From Property to Person Status: Historical Perspectives on Children's Rights,' *American Psychologist* 46/1 (1991), 53–9.
4. N. Cantwell, 'The Origins, Development, and Significance of the United Nations Convention on the Rights of the Child,' in S. Detrick, ed., *The United Nations Convention on the Rights of the Child* (Dordrecht, 1992), 19–30.
5. Canadian Heritage, *Convention on the Rights of the Child: First Report of Canada* (Ottawa, 1994).
6. United Nations Committee on the Rights of the Child, *Concluding Observations on Canada's First Report* (Geneva, 1995).
7. Centre for International Statistics on Economic and Social Welfare, *Child Poverty Indicator Report* (Ottawa, 1994).
8. Centre for International Statistics, *Child Poverty*, 7.
9. L.V. Klerman, *Alive and Well? A Research and Policy Review of Health Programs for Poor Young Children* (New York, 1991).
10. G.J. Duncan, J. Brooks-Gunn, and P.K. Klebanov, 'Economic Deprivation and Early Childhood Development,' *Child Development* 65/2 (1994), 296–318.
11. S. Gilbert, L. Barr, W. Clark, M. Blue, and D. Sunter, *Leaving School: Results of a National Survey Comparing School Leavers with High School Graduates 18–20 Years of Age* (Ottawa, 1993); S.S. McLanahan, N.M. Astone, and N. Marks, 'The Role of Mother-Only Families in Reproducing Poverty,' in A.C. Huston, ed., *Children in Poverty: Child Development and Public Policy* (New York, 1991), 51–78; C.T. Ramey and F.A. Campbell, 'Poverty, Early Childhood Education, and Academic Competence: The Abecedarian Experience,' in Huston, *Children in Poverty*, 190–221.
12. J. Garbarino, 'The Meaning of Poverty in the World of Children,' *American Behavioral Scientist* 35 (1992), 220–37; V.C. McLoyd and L. Wilson, 'The Strain of Living Poor: Parenting, Social Support, and Child Mental Health,' in Huston, *Children in Poverty*, 105–35.
13. R.D. Conger, X. Gi, K. Elder, F.O. Lorenz, and R.L. Simons, 'Economic Stress, Coercive Family Processes and Developmental Problems of Adolescents,' *Child Development* 65/2 (1994), 541–61.
14. A.C. Huston, 'Children in Poverty and Public Policy,' *Developmental Psychology Newsletter* (1995), 1–8.
15. K.A. Dodge, G.S. Pettit, and J.E. Bates, 'Socialization Mediators of the Relation Between Socioeconomic Status and Child Conduct Problems,' *Child Development* 35 (1994), 649–65; P.Y. Hashima and P.R. Amato, 'Poverty, Social Support and Parental Behavior,' *Child Development* 65 (1994), 394–403.
16. P. Garrett, N. Ng'andu, and J. Ferron, 'Poverty Experiences of Young Children and the Quality of Their Home Environments,' *Child Development* 65/2 (1994), 331–45; Huston, 'Children in Poverty,' (1995), 1–8.
17. A.C. Huston, 'Children in Poverty: Designing Research to Affect Policy,' *Society for Research in Child Development Social Policy Report* 8/2 (1994).

How to Strengthen the Welfare State

TOM KENT

This paper begins with a brief discussion of how Canada built a welfare state with approximate national standards despite the constitutional assignment of social responsibility to the provinces. The main instrument—federal sharing of the costs of provincial programs—is now too weak for revival. The most it can still do is to sustain the principles of medicare. New nationwide programs will have to be direct federal programs, utilizing the spending power to make transfers not to the provinces but to individuals.

There is no point in proposing such programs, however, unless they can be reconciled with elimination of the federal deficit; that is, unless federal revenues can be increased. The middle part of the paper makes the case for tax reforms that would raise more revenue more fairly while encouraging economic efficiency.

On that basis, the paper outlines a federal voucher program as the way to finance childcare of consistent quality. This is the top priority. Next, as a step towards a minimum income, would be an enlarged child benefit in the form a refundable tax credit scaled to income and family size. The third priority suggested is to replace the present patchwork of disability benefits by a comprehensive program providing support on consistent principles whatever the nature and the cause of disability. Improvements to medicare are also proposed. The concluding emphasis, however, is that major social progress requires, above all, higher levels of employment.

THE SOCIAL UNION

Canada as a whole has to be a successful welfare state; if not, its survival as any kind of state is doubtful. That is true for the Canada we have, Canada including Quebec. If we have to reorganize without Quebec, the welfare state will be an even more compelling imperative. Otherwise, the cements keeping us together are unlikely to hold for long against the centrifugal forces of regionalism.

This is not, of course, how we began. Confederation was a political contrivance that found a national purpose in building an east–west economy when market forces would have run largely at right angles. The instruments were tariffs, railways, immigration. The economy they produced was never a greatly impressive fulfilment of Canada's potential. We had to wait until the Second World War for a flower of Canadian industrial development. And it was the postwar situation that stimulated our extensive, diversified boom in resource development.

However, the Canadian economy that enjoyed postwar prosperity was not the tariff-protected, east–west economy of the national policy. Globalization has become a catchword only in recent years, but in truth the transformation began in 1947 with the GATT. Progressive lowering of trade barriers gave scope for the quick global reach of new technologies and the associated growth of transnational corporations.

Globalization has an inevitable consequence for our relatively small, trade-dependent economy. Our economic union has become less significant to us. The change has been rapid. As recently as 1981, the total of interprovincial transactions in goods and services was somewhat larger than our external truncations. Now it is the other way round, and by a large margin. In 1994 Canada's transactions with the rest of the world were bigger by 70 percent than the total of interprovincial transactions. PEI was the only province that sold more to the rest of Canada than it sold to other countries.

Obviously, this does not mean that we no longer have a national economy. It does mean that, in the ways we earn and spend, the parts of Canada are less important to each other. The economic union is no longer the strong glue of nationhood that Macdonald's national policy made it.

The postwar generation developed another glue: our social union. The war had strengthened Canadians' sense of identity and confidence. We shared in the worldwide determination not to return to prewar deprivation. Prosperity provided resources for social programs. We were slow by European standards, but over a period of twenty-five years we built a fairly thorough welfare state.

The brake that made us slow was the structure of our federalism. The Canadian state from sea to sea had been built despite geography and in defiance of economics. The Canadian welfare state was built despite the constitution and in defiance of politics. It began with specific constitutional changes, for unemployment insurance and pensions, but the provinces would not go far on that road. Ottawa turned to the financial instrument. By sharing their costs it induced the provinces to expand postsecondary education and to establish health and welfare programs of a reasonably consistent nature. Canada became a social union despite the Constitution's assignment of social responsibility to the provinces.

But to do so, it defied the norms of politics. When they can, politicians are happy to spend the money that gains notice and support—for them. Levying taxes so that other politicians can do the program spending is, to put it mildly, less appealing. The federal cabinets of the fifties and sixties were exceptional in their willingness to do this. Prosperity made them confident about federal revenues. The political pressure for the welfare state was strong. There was still a hangover from wartime centralization, reflected in some spirit of 'noblesse oblige' in Ottawa's attitude to the provinces. Federal politicians were confident that the public expected them to lead and would give them credit for initiating programs even though they were carried out by provincial governments.

This altruism, if we can call it that, did not long outlast the spacious days. Almost as soon as it was conscious of slowing economic growth and tightening finances, Ottawa began to renege on its commitments to 50 percent cost sharing. The process began in 1977 and has continued in increasing steps. This year we have come to the point where the minister of finance claims to be the saviour of the welfare state by undertaking that he will not reduce social transfers to the provinces below $11 billion; that is, below 8 percent of current federal revenues, 1.3 percent of gross domestic product. Thanks to the popularity of medicare, this small fiscal lever may be enough to secure nationwide adherence to its essential principles. But it certainly will not prevent strains on the quality of care.

Much as it might wish, the federal government cannot entirely escape from transfers to the provinces. In addition to the promised floor for social programs, approximately $9 billion is committed for equalization payments to the poor provinces. Altogether, 14 percent of present federal revenues is still required for the provinces.

The cause of Ottawa's fiscal stringency is, of course, its debt. Paying interest to bondholders currently takes 36 percent of federal revenues. When this is combined with the minimum commitments to the provinces, the federal government's financial position is that, for every dollar it obtains in taxes, it has only 50 cents to spend on all its own programs.

The political reality is plain. Finance Minister Martin's line is not drawn in sand—it is in concrete that will hold. To urge the federal government to restore its cuts to money for the provinces is a waste of breath. The road that served us well in the fifties and sixties is now closed. If we are to improve the welfare state today, it has to be through federal programs, providing their benefits directly from Ottawa to individual Canadians.

THE BARRIER

Such programs are entirely possible. I shall discuss them shortly. The prior question is how far, if at all, we can afford them. The necessity of deficit reduction cannot be set aside. There is nothing progressive about piling up obligations to pay yet more interest to bondholders. Our inheritance from the economic mismanagement of the past twenty years is that we can now increase expenditures only if we increase government revenues. Many people think that is impossible; the taxes we already pay are too crippling to the economy.

The truth, I think, is different. The real barrier to advancing the welfare state is a paradoxical shift in ideology. When the economy was performing well, politicians were fairly ready to intervene in the public interest. As the economy began to perform badly, politicians became increasingly cowed by business interests asserting mastery, claiming that their interests must take precedence while increasingly deprived segments of society wait for relief of their pain.

Hardly anyone now disputes that the market is by far the most efficient mechanism for production in a sophisticated economy. To nurture it is one of the major responsibilities of government. But there is a downside. It is the nature of the market economy that nothing succeeds like success, nothing fails like failure. In consequence, it generates extremes of incomes and wealth; very many people are insecure; far too many people experience unemployment, often prolonged.

These defects of the economy have been growing worse. While there are cycles, the trend is that they are continuing to grow still worse. Naturally so. Polarization of incomes reduces the effective demand that creates employment. More unemployment widens income disparities. And so on, in a vicious spiral.

The welfare state is the intervention of citizens to lessen social ill consequences, the inequalities and insecurities, of an unfettered economy. The need for that intervention increases, not decreases, because our economy is in a poor way. We should not be cutting social spending but increasing taxation. My contention is that this is politically practicable. It does not require higher tax rates. It requires only that politicians have the courage to face down some minority interests, for the sake of reforms that a majority of voters would approve. And if they were done right, the reforms would not discourage but encourage the competitive efficiency and enterprise of a growing economy.

RSPs and Flat Taxation

Our formally progressive tax system is shot through the devices that help the rich to get richer. As a first illustration, take the RSP program that is so much boosted as the way ordinary Canadians can make themselves self-reliant in their old age.

If your annual earnings are $75,000 or more, you can reduce what is taxed by $13,500, setting it aside in an RSP. This is commonly represented as merely a tax deferment: you have to take out the money as taxable income when you are old. But that is only a bit of the story. The returns on your savings—the interest, dividends, capital gains—accumulate year after year, also tax-free. That is the great benefit. It makes compounding magic indeed. A person fortunate enough to be able to save $13,500 a year for forty-five years of working life would not need particularly good investment advice to build up, by the age of sixty-nine an RSP of $10 million, thanks to the tax-free accumulation.

And when it is converted to a RIF, the returns on the capital continue to be tax-free. You can live well for a long time, and what is left can be passed on to your spouse, still tax-free.

I have taken, of course, the extreme case, but Mr. Martin has just made it easier to approach by providing that, if you don't save all the $13,500 a year while, say, you have children to look after, you can make it all up later. And he is going to raise the $13,500 to $15,500 and escalate it thereafter.

Of course, we should encourage saving for retirement. But only the already wealthy can save $13,500 a year. A reasonable RSP scheme would provide for tax-free saving not of 18 percent of earnings but of 10 percent, to a maximum of $7,500, with corresponding adjustments in pension-plan provisions. For the majority of people, the benefit would be just as much as they can in practice get from the present system. Only the well-to-do would lose some of the favouritism now given to them. Public revenues would benefit by growing billions of dollars.

The RSP example touches only the fringe of favouritism for the well-do-do. Its core is that government has never accepted the simple wisdom of the Carter Royal Commission on Taxation: a dollar is a dollar is a dollar. Personal tax remains related almost entirely to a narrow definition of income. Tax accountants and lawyers are therefore often able to demonstrate that people with a good deal of money nevertheless have little, if any, income that is taxable.

A fair and efficient tax would be a flat tax, but not in the sense that some conservatives would like. I mean flat in the sense of making no distinction among the sources from which people get money. Earnings, other forms of

compensation, interest dividends, capital gains, benefits of all kinds, inheritances, gifts: all would be included, all liable to tax at the same graduated rates.

The practice could not be quite so simple. There should be considerable, though by no means unlimited, exemptions for inheritances of spouses and dependent children. Since an income including inheritances and the like could fluctuate greatly from year to year, there would need to be full provision for forward averaging of tax liabilities. Still, the fine print would be much less elaborate than is needed for the present income tax. The scope for evasion would be greatly narrowed.

The great merits of a flat tax in my sense are that it would be far fairer; it would lessen the resentments of people whose receipts are almost entirely income as now taxed and who rightly feel that richer people get off more lightly; and present rates of tax would yield, on the broader base, many billions more revenue for public needs.

This massive reform should not be tarnished by an accompanying increase in tax rates. On the contrary, it could better pave the way to a more gradual slope for marginal rates. While the effect of taxes on incentives, and perhaps on the inclination to migrate, is often exaggerated, nevertheless in a global economy it cannot be lightly dismissed. If additional revenue should be necessary later, a better source would be a surtax not on income but on consumption. That is, people with more than (say) $75,000 taxable might pay a surtax on their spending, the difference between their income (as broadly defined) and their net saving. Purchases of major durables, such as houses, would be appropriately amortized. The surtax could begin at a small percentage but be significantly graduated. It would not be a direct disincentive to earnings and would encourage savings. The imposition would be that people who spend heavily on themselves would be required—fairly, I think—to contribute more to public purposes.

A consumption surtax would also be a protection against some forms of tax evasion. Undeclared gifts or undisclosed transfers to the Cayman Islands would show up as taxable spending.

Unlike most developed countries, Canada taxes wealth hardly at all. A flat tax base would change this for future accumulations. But thorough reforms of the kind I am suggesting could not be put in place quickly. As an interim measure, it would be entirely equitable to impose for a year or two a levy on wealth that has hitherto gone untaxed.

CORPORATE TAXATION

Our taxation of corporations is also comparatively light. In one respect, I would make it lighter still. Businesses should not be taxed at all on income they distribute to their shareholders or proprietors. That should simply be taxed like any other personal income, in the hands of the owners if they are individual Canadians. If the owners are other Canadian companies or foreigners, the income distributed to them should be subject to a withholding tax equal, in fairness, to the top rate of personal tax; any required offsets to the withholding would be provided by Revenue Canada, in the case of Canadian companies, or determined according to tax treaties in the case of foreign owners.

Corporation tax would then be confined to profits retained in the business. A rate somewhat higher than the top rate of personal tax would give shareholders more incentive to demand the income that is rightfully theirs. They would thereby combat the worst restrictive practice in our economy: that is, the retention of profits in the control of managers of established companies, which gives them a major advantage over the smaller enterprises that are often more enterprising and innovative but have to attract their capital from the restricted supply of funds available for new investments. The market forces to which big business pays lip-service are in fact stifled at the point where they could do most good, determining the directions of enterprise and innovation. Tax reform would shift some decisions, at least, to the hidden hand of a genuinely competitive market reflecting the judgments of many individual investors.

There are related tax changes that could reinforce this economic reform besides yielding increased revenues for government. One is to stop providing artificially rapid capital cost allowances. They provide many companies with large, interest-free loans from the taxpayer. For companies making regular capital investments, it is a loan account that rolls on and on. The so-called deferred taxes are deferred indefinitely. They thus become a significant subsidy to capital relative to operating costs. That is, they perversely encourage the prevalent downsizing of labour forces.

Another example, introduced into the tax system twenty-five years ago, is that a company is allowed to deduct from its taxable profits the interest on loans borrowed not only for its own business, but also to purchase other companies. Government revenues are thereby reduced in order to further more concentrated control of the economy. Competitive efficiency is reduced rather than enhanced. A similar objection applies to the way in which the previous losses of a purchased company can be set off against the taxes of the purchases, even when the real effect of the purchase is to put the old company out of business.

Corporate managements have also been highly successful in gaining acceptance for their spending of shareholders' money on purposes besides the operation of the business. Political contributions, lobbying, propaganda are the worse examples, as well as many tax-free perquisites. Some of these expenditures should be illegal anyway. But in so far as they are not, there is no reason why government should subsidize them by allowing them as expenses in the reckoning of taxable profits.

Again, corporate managers have become increasingly generous in the valuation of their own work, for better or for worse, in success or in failure. The limit is what shareholders will stand for. It would be a more effective and fairer limit if the taxpayer did not help. Individual compensation over some multiple of the average earnings of Canadians—say, to be generous, ten times—need not be an admissible expense for tax purposes. The extra revenue would pay for a good many childcare places.

These discursive comments on taxation are far from complete, but they establish the essential point: we are not taxed to destruction; substantially more revenue could be raised, more fairly and in ways that would strengthen, not weaken, the efficiency and entrepreneurship of our economy.

I emphasize that this is the essential point. Otherwise, the prospect is further lowering of our social standards. True, some good can be done by redesigning programs within present funding. Mr. Martin's new plan for basic retirement income, in effect absorbing Old Age Security and the elderly credits into an enlarged Guaranteed Income Supplement, is a case in point. On the other hand, some of the redesigns being discussed are steps back.

In any event, program fiddling, however well designed, is too slight a response to the severity of our social problems. Too many people are unemployed too long; too many are poor and insecure; too many children deprived; too many youth alienated from civil society. The cumulating effects are too clear for complacency. The need to halt the trend, to make a major thrust for social betterment, is now.

CHILDCARE VOUCHERS

With so many interrelated problems, it is tempting to propose a wide range of desirable programs. But even if tax reform is pushed to the practicable maximum, in speed and scope, extra resources will be tight. Trying to do something everywhere is likely to mean doing nothing much anywhere. The 'alternative budget,' suggested by the Canadian Centre for Policy Alternatives, seemed to me to fall into this trap. It would be a wiser strategy to choose one or two priority needs, mount major programs to deal effectively with those, and go on to other problems later.

Accordingly, my first proposal to improve the welfare state on a national scale is to mount a comprehensive program for preschool children. This requires two components: income supports for poor parents and childcare. I would give first priority to the care.

With so many lone parents as there now are, and so many conventional families in which both parents work, many children are deprived of the attention and stimulus they need. Childcare has become a major priority for social policy. If we are serious in our boasted concern for equality of opportunity, it must be quality care; and that means not only tending the children, providing healthy meals, socializing them, but also helping them to begin the learning process.

Such care will be a long time coming, on any adequate scale, from the provinces alone. In the present political and fiscal situation, the conventional prescription of federal cost sharing gets some lip-service but no action. Constitutionally, the federal government cannot itself operate daycare. But it can make the need for care effective by purchasing it on behalf of the children.

I am proposing that the federal government issue vouchers for childcare, usable either at provincial and municipal institutions or at privately run but nonprofit centres licensed by the province. These would not be subsidized places. To ensure an adequate response, the vouchers would cover the full cost of care, as negotiated with each province. The program could best apply initially to preschoolers from the age of three, but its extension to younger children should not be ruled out.

The vouchers would be universally available to working parents, subject to two financial conditions. First, there would be income testing in the sense that parents with low-middle to middle family incomes would be liable for partial cost recovery, on a sliding scale, through their tax returns for the current year. Parents with incomes above the ceiling could have vouchers if they wished, but their current year's taxation would require full payment.

Second, there would be provision for income-contingent repayment. Most families that cannot afford good childcare when they need it are better off later. Parents who had received the vouchers entirely or partially free at the time of use would be liable, again on a sliding scale, for repayment through taxes on later incomes. If the parents had in the meantime split up, the liability would have to be divided according to their relative tax positions.

There will be other equity issues. For example, parents who are entitled to a voucher, but for one reason or another are unable to use it, should be able to claim a special tax allowance for, in effect, babysitting costs.

A childcare program seems to me to be the most appealing of social initiatives. There is growing realization that early experience, childhood health, socialization and beginning of education, are crucial to personal development. There should be no pretence that the program is cheap. The initial costs would be substantial and the cost recovery would never be complete. But no program is more clearly an investment in our future. The resentment to being taxed for it would be minimal.

Income Supports and Medicare

Income supplementation is a harder sell. The death of the Canada Assistance Plan will result in further cuts to welfare payments, with even more provincial variations. Ideally, the deteriorations should be more than offset by a direct federal program delivered through the tax system. Enlarged refundable tax credits, appropriately scaled to income from whatever source, could remove the poverty trap of welfare. Unlike present arrangements, they would help the working poor as fairly as the unemployed.

A progressive government would not be afraid to restore the sense of a national social contract by committing itself to the goal of a minimum income. It would be delivered through refundable credits in the tax system; credits sufficient, by their amount and scale-down rate, to make poverty avoidable and almost entirely avoided. But we will have to have full employment before that light becomes visible at the end of the tunnel. A Canada Fair Income Program, as I would like to call it, can be achieved only as resources develop and political will is strengthened.

The best beginning—and my priority next to the childcare program—is an enlarged child benefit. It would be a refundable tax credit scaled to income and family size. It would at least mitigate the poverty that is most damaging for our futures.

My third priority takes us to a more difficult arena of federal–provincial relations. It is to provide consistent income security when disabled. I would remove disability benefits from the Canada Pension Plan, which is not the appropriate place, and join them with the existing tax credits. Further, it would be necessary to negotiate with the provinces to bring in workers' compensation and existing welfare provisions. Many anomalies, and a good deal of dropping-between-the-cracks, could be cured if there were a comprehensive national program. It could best be federally delivered through the tax system. But if that is more than the provinces will swallow, some co-operative way to secure a co-ordinated benefit, at a national standard, should be discoverable.

The removal of disability benefits would considerably ease the financing of the Canada and Quebec Pensions Plans, but it will still be necessary to anticipate the aging of baby boomers by accelerating the rise of contribution rates. Proposals for reducing the benefit rate should, in my view, be rejected. And as long as unemployment is heavy, we certainly should not think of raising the pensionable age.

I have already suggested that medicare is the program on which Ottawa should concentrate its remaining commitment to cost sharing. The attack on its principles can therefore be warded off. But problems about the quality and scope of service will remain. As long as doctors insist on fee for service, there will be some perverse incentive to inflate treatments at the expense of prevention; and fiscal restraint will be largely a matter of rationing resources, with inevitably arbitrary effects on service.

In these circumstances, discussion of what are the medically necessary services concentrates on what can be removed. There are still some frills, such as the generosity to snow birds that the present Ontario government has recently restored. But there are also serious and growing deficiencies. Lengths of stay in hospital have properly been reduced but very little has been done to balance this with the necessary improvements in homecare. Accurately prescribed drugs are medically necessary, but their cost is covered only for arbitrarily defined groups and to a decreasing extent varying among provinces.

I can see no prospect of removing these defects unless we at last adopt a proposal that I have always favoured but which horrifies universalists. It is a device to bring awareness of costs into play, for both the providers and recipients of service. The conventional proposal of user fees is grossly inequitable. Reasonable fairness could be achieved by using the tax system.

The medical expenses attributable to an individual or family would then be totalled for the year and become, like other benefits, an item for the tax return. They would be treated as taxable income, but only up to a ceiling of, say, a 10 percent addition to other personal or family income in any year. The charge would be nil for people with incomes too low for tax liability. For others it would be an extra tax at their marginal rate, but never on more than a 10 percent addition to income.

The revenue yield would not be enormous, since medical costs are heaviest in childhood and old age; that is, at the time when marginal tax rates are at their lowest for most families. But the tax claw-back would be an equitable way to introduce a direct sense of individual costs into the medicare system. With it, wider inclusion of drug and homecare services would become practicable. Without it, we will wait for a long time before medicare becomes more complete.

That is the end of my priority proposals to strengthen the welfare state. I would greatly like to add a new scholarship scheme for postsecondary education. Realistically, however, it has to wait. A more urgent need is to raise the quality of the education that teenagers take from school to work or to college.

I have also ignored the boiling pot of unemployment insurance, training, workfare. I have done so because we should not fall into what I call the Axworthy error, though many others have made it. The error is to think that the problem is with the services supplied to the unemployed. Those indeed have defects. But the real problem is excess demand; that is, there are too many unemployed.

Jobs, Jobs

By this route I come to the concluding, and crucial point. The best social policy is work. Widespread unemployment is too corrosive of civil society to be neutralized by income supports, however well arranged. The indictment of contemporary governments is that they have resigned themselves to failure in a fundamental purpose: that people who can work and want to work should have work almost all of the time.

There is, of course, a circular relationship between work and welfare. The social programs I have suggested are in themselves labour-intensive. They would stimulate consumer spending and hence further employment. They would supplement the necessary shift in macroeconomic policy, a shift to consistently lower interest rates.

In our period of postwar prosperity a quite tight fiscal policy was joined with a fairly easy monetary policy. That was the winning combination. But for twenty years governments made the disastrous reversal to a loose fiscal policy and tight, at times very tight, monetary policy. In consequence, they got themselves strangled by too much debt. Mr. Martin has made the necessary change in fiscal policy. But monetary policy has been only partially relaxed. Interests rates are still too high for the stimulus to consumption, production, and employment that we need.

There is a cost. Because of the magnitude of our external debt, consistently lower interest rates will require acceptance of a lower exchange rate as a structural, not temporary, change. That in turn will require other policy measures, including encouragement to Canadian enterprises not only in the promotion of exports but in the development of production to compete at home with dearer imports.

Employment policy is, of course, more complex than this thumbnail sketch. But the problem is not in the detail. It is in the will of politicians who have lost their way. We need above all a renewed insistence that the economy can operate at reasonably adequate employment. Advancing technology is altering many jobs. Globalization is limiting the number and the wage levels of occupations in which developing countries have comparative advantages. But adaptation to such changes is not impossible. What is necessary for employment must be done. Then the calls on unemployment insurance and welfare will shrink while government revenues will grow. There will be resources for further improvements in social policy.

I am not suggesting an unrestrained optimism. The legacy of twenty years of confusion in public policy, in many countries besides Canada, will continue to slow us down. But the main point is firm. There is nothing to prevent us from beginning to move again along the path of a more equitable and equable society that has common standards for Canadians in whatever province they live. What is missing is political leadership.

BRUCE CAMPBELL

Executive Director
Canadian Centre for Policy Alternatives

A re we as a society doomed to a future of mass unemployment, pervasive insecurity, and growing inequality? Is the Canadian welfare state terminally ill and with it the dream of a just society? Or can it be reclaimed and renewed? I believe it can. I will demonstrate using our Alternative Federal Budget that it is possible to move from the economics of despair to the economics of hope. But first, how did we come to be in the current mess and will the current federal policy agenda improve the situation? The welfare state, whether through incompetence or design, has been under great stress for some time and is now entering a stage of accelerated disassembly. Median family incomes have been falling throughout the 1990s. The universality of social programs and the accompanying notion of social rights of citizenship is crumbling, and in some areas has disappeared altogether. Unemployment has been very high for too long. There has been an explosion of insecurity in the labour market, a surge of part-time and short-term jobs, with low wages and with few benefits. Roughly two of every three jobs created since 1991 lasted for less than one year. The social security system was never designed for such conditions.

· The fiscal weakness of governments—the product of high interest rates, a stagnant economy, high unemployment, and alleged tax fatigue—has resulted in the heavy accumulation of debt. Policymakers have, for the most part, abandoned the notion that government can take active measures to promote stable and balanced growth and job creation, as unrealistic, if not undesirable.

The so-called golden age (1945–75) during which the welfare state was built and the vision of a just society, though far from realization, was beginning to come into focus, has been replaced by the neo-conservative, or neo-liberal, era and the vision has receded.

The current orthodoxy says we have reached the limits of our tax/transfer capacity and with debt continuing to spiral we can no longer afford our social programs. Therefore we have to cut back spending, continue to jettison universality, and target remaining resources to the poorest.

The current orthodoxy says, usually tacitly, though sometimes explicitly, that mass unemployment is here to stay for an indefinite future. Why? Because of technological change which is displacing jobs, and international competitiveness which is transferring jobs from high-wage regions to low-wage regions. Also uncontrollable is high interest monetary policy which has kept the economy in chronic recession for more than fifteen years. Global financial markets, we are told, will not allow us to lower interest rates until we eliminate our deficit and reduce our debt. At the same time we are told that high interest rates, which stifle job creation and drive up debt service costs and the debt itself, are necessary to prevent a resurgence of inflation—a classic catch-22 situation.

These are part of a general orthodoxy which says that the scope for national policies in the era of globalization—a world of mobile capital—is extremely limited, and therefore citizens' expectations about what governments can actually do should be reduced accordingly. This is the TINA syndrome—'there is no alternative.' Citizens must learn to swim with the tide of the New Economy, which has put the welfare state beyond reach.

Finally, the current orthodoxy says that, besides being inevitable, the deregulation, privatization, so-called small government agenda will be better for us in the end. Strangely, it is never made clear who is 'us' and when is the end. Governments for the last twenty years have—for the most part willingly, often enthusiastically—pursued this path.

The origins of the current malaise of the Canadian welfare state are both internal and external. Without downplaying the effect of the breakdown of Bretton Woods international monetary and financial management structures and the failure by the major powers to find a workable replacement, I believe on the basis of divergent national policies and performance since 1973, that Canadian policy choices still bear most of the blame.

The main policy responses to the economic problems of the early 1970s were twofold: a turning back toward pre-Depression monetarist orthodoxy as the way of dealing with inflation with its predictably adverse consequences for unemployment; and secondly, a reduction in taxes benefiting, notably, corporations and the wealthy. The consequence was a fall in the flow of government revenue, the vital oxygen of the welfare state, and the opening up of a series of deficits. By 1980, full-blown monetarism, now firmly at the helm of public policy, thrust the country into recession the depth of which had not been seen since the 1930s. More deficits resulted in rising debt—$200 billion or 42 percent of GDP by 1985 (national accounts basis).[1] Increases in tax revenue during 1975–85 were the second lowest in the OECD.

Under Mulroney the situation reversed to some extent. Taxes rose considerably. However, throughout the 1980s real interest rates remained far above the rate of economic growth. The inevitable consequence was that debt continued to spiral upward as the portion of growing interest bills not paid from operating surpluses (which were the norm in this period) was rolled over as debt. It should be noted that the Mulroney government produced these surpluses by chipping away at the social infrastructure.

Then came John Crow who, with the enthusiastic support of Michael Wilson, and two of the most powerful interest groups in the country, the C.D. Howe Institute and the Business Council on National Issues, launched the great Canadian war to squeeze the last drops of inflation out of the economy. This was surely one of the great pyrrhic victories of our time. The social and economic costs have been immense—deep and prolonged recession, a new wave of still higher unemployment, renewed pressure on the social security system, collapsing government revenue, yawning deficits, interest bills now approaching two-fifths of federal revenue, and a steadily growing debt/GDP ratio.

As the landmark Statistics Canada study by Mimoto and Cross found, social spending remained roughly constant in relation to the economy despite the additional pressures over the last two decades.[2] Even Paul Martin and at least one bond rating agency have acknowledged that social spending bears little blame for the debt. This basic truth has not, however, stopped most of the business establishment and right-wing politicians from continuing to bludgeon Canadians with the myth of rampant overspending requiring that they kick their addiction to the 'nanny state.'

Finally, the predicament of the Canadian welfare state can be seen by contrasting the macroeconomic variables of two periods—the golden age (1950–80), and the neo-liberal period (1981–95), the era of the 'permanent recession.'[3] In the golden age, federal budget surpluses more than offset deficits. The federal debt burden in relation to GDP fell steadily (bottoming out at 22 percent in 1975). Unemployment averaged under 5 percent; annual growth averaged 4.9 percent; real interest rates averaged 3.9 percent; growth exceeded real interest on federal debt by an annual average 1 percent. In the neo-liberal era average growth fell by half to 2.5 percent; unemployment doubled to 10 percent; real interest rates doubled to 7.7 percent; interest on debt exceeded growth by an average 5.2 percent. The government was in deficit in every year and debt climbed steadily throughout the period, reaching 63 percent of GDP in 1995 (national accounts basis).

The gap between the growth rate and real interest on the federal debt is the critical factor because it produces what James Stanford calls the 'fiscal knife-edge' effect.[4] If a deficit opens up under such conditions, that is, when the real interest rate far exceeds the growth rate, then deficit and debts will mushroom because interest payments are growing much faster than tax revenue (unless of course program spending is reduced immediately to close the revenue shortfall). Stanford estimates that this toxic mixture of high real interest rates and slow growth accounted for 83 percent of the accumulation of debt from 1981 to 1995.

Notwithstanding the many flaws in the welfare state and the stresses that have been placed upon it, it has done rather well in mitigating the effects of the massive changes in the labour market over the last two decades.

The final distribution of total income—the main income quintiles—has remained relatively stable despite rapid polarization of market income (i.e., from earnings and investments).[5] This has been due to an increase in government transfers to lower income sectors. The market income of the top 40 percent of families has been rising while earnings of the bottom 60 percent of families has fallen dramatically. The gap between earnings of well-paid and poorly paid workers in Canada grew faster than in any country except the United States and Britain. The decline of wages of the young (under thirty-five years) relative to the rest of the work force was the worst in the OECD. Exacerbating the wage polarization have been the changes in work time, with well-paid workers working longer hours and poorly paid workers working less.

A progressive income tax system up to $60,000 (after which it becomes flat) has helped to offset market inequality. However, when all taxes are considered, we have, as the work of Gillespie et al. has shown, close to a flat tax system with low-, middle-, and high-income groups paying between 30–34 percent of their income in tax.[6] Their work suggests that the tax system is not playing the role it should in offsetting market inequalities and in fact is playing a perverse role by taking a proportionally larger share of tax from middle-income groups than from the wealthiest income earners.

The big winners have been the top 5 percent and probably even more, the top 2 percent who have seen their earnings and interest income grow rapidly at the same time as their tax burden has fallen relative to other groups. Average CEO compensation in Canada is now thirty-six times greater than the wage of the average worker, second only to the United States. In Japan, by comparison, the ratio of CEO compensation to the average industrial wage is only sixteen times.[7]

Contrary to the current orthodoxy, the failure has not been the failure of the social security system but rather the failure of the market to create sufficient jobs, especially good jobs, which is driving social polarization. This dramatic 'market failure' has, until recently, been mitigated, albeit with increasing difficulty, by social transfers. We are now entering a period where the magnitude of cuts at all levels of government is beginning to spark social protest not seen since the 1930s.

I believe that the majority of Canadians, wherever (if at all) they place themselves on the left or right, support the main purpose of the welfare state. They want to earn a decent living and to feel confident that the same opportunities will be available to their children, particularly with the help of a public education system. They also want protection against unexpected or uncontrollable contingencies of life such as unemployment, illness, and old age. They expect government to play a central role in all these areas, although there is much confusion and misinformation around governments' capacity to do this under current circumstances.

Moreover, many middle-class citizens are angry and frustrated with government. They have seen their taxes rise at the same time as the quality of public services has declined, at the same time as their earnings have dropped and their jobs become less secure. They blame political mismanagement and bureaucratic waste for the current malaise. Governments elected on promises to create jobs and halt the damage to social programs, etc., have not delivered. The free trade agreement was supposed to be the ticket to prosperity; then it was wrestling inflation to the ground. Now it is the deficit/debt dragon that must be slain before jobs and growth will return. And all the while the crisis worsens and anxiety grows. So there has been a loss of confidence in government.

This is borne out in a year-long attitudinal survey by Ekos Research.[8] Ekos found unmistakable signs of fragmentation within the middle class along the lines of access to education and economic insecurity. The Ekos survey also found new and growing faultlines of attitudes based on social class—with elites preoccupied with the deficit, competitiveness and minimalist government, and the general public preoccupied with jobs, social issues, and hands-on government. A year-end Angus Reid survey provides further evidence of this polarization—the upper middle and wealthy say governments have not cut enough, the poor say they have cut too much. All classes agree that the rich have grown richer and haven't suffered their share of the pain, according to Reid.[9]

The current climate is also accentuating the dark side of the Canadian psyche. Many in the middle class are fearful about their future and are looking for scapegoats to blame—immigrants, lazy welfare bums, UI cheats, single mothers, youth, natives. Most among the upper-middle and wealthy classes are lulled by a false sense of security that the problems are those of others far away, unconnected to their world. Social solidarity is increasingly replaced by division and mean-spiritedness. As in past times of economic and social breakdown, there is no shortage of politicians to feed on this rancor.

Canadians voted in the Chrétien Liberals in 1993 on a commitment to revitalize the economy, create jobs, maintain the social security system, and restore public finances. Saying that the solution to the country's woes was not 'another five years of cutbacks, job loss and diminished expectations,' the Red Book promised 'a balanced approach...one in which faster economic growth and reduction of unemployment is a prerequisite for sustained deficit reduction' (p. 20). (The soundness of this approach is reinforced in a study by Bellemare and Poulin-Simon which found that a full employment economy in 1993 would have generated an extra $47 billion for federal and provincial treasuries from high revenues and lower payouts.)[10]

The policy reversal has been stunning. The Liberals are undoing the social infrastructure at a rate their predecessors would not have dared. Now they are saying deficit reduction through spending cuts is a prerequisite for job creation and economic growth. Clever public relations and the absence of effective parliamentary opposition have enabled them to maintain their 'good guy' image as the protectors of social programs relatively intact.

The details of these changes have been described elsewhere so I will not repeat them. It bears noting, however, that by 1997–8, they will have cumulatively cut $33 billion out of program spending from where it stood in 1994— ironically the same amount in *extra* interest that will have gone to holders of government debt. Program spending will have fallen to 12.6 percent of GDP, down from 16.8 percent in 1993–4. And the debt/GDP ratio will have climbed from 71.3 percent to 73.7 percent.[11] The Finance Minister boasts about bringing spending down to 1950 levels, but does not mention that this was a time when 77 percent of hospital costs were covered by the patient, and when only 6 percent of young people were enrolled in a university or college compared to 30 percent in 1990.

THE ALTERNATIVE FEDERAL BUDGET

For the last two years the Canadian Centre for Policy Alternatives and CHOICES, a Winnipeg-based social justice coalition, have sponsored an Alternative Federal Budget (AFB) initiative. Bringing together from across the country activists and academics, representatives from labour, women's, church, students', and other social action groups at both the national and community level, the project seeks to replace the economics of despair with the economics of hope. As part of this project, we start from the premise that choices do exist and that budgets are political documents that reflect the priorities and values of those who put them together.

The alternative budget is grounded in the following priorities and values: full employment, a more equitable distribution of income, the eradication of poverty, economic equality between men and women, environmental sustainability, the protection of basic social and economic rights including basic labour rights, and the strengthening of social programs and public services.

The AFB acknowledges that current realities impose constraints on national policy. It acknowledges that the problems of unemployment and the erosion of the social infrastructure cannot be reversed overnight. However, it rejects the position that national governments are impotent—in a world of mobile capital and heavy debt—to do much except cut, deregulate, privatize and hope for the best. On the contrary, the federal government can and must play a central role in the social and economic life of our country.

Our alternative is based on a three-pronged strategy of job creation, social investment, and rebalancing the tax system. It is based on the premise of a government that can take action, starting with the Bank of Canada lowering real interest rates and keeping them low, as well as holding a greater share of government debt. It proposes a number of measures to regulate capital flows: for example, lowering the current ceiling on investment abroad of tax-subsidized pension money; and measures to encourage financial institutions to invest in productive (as opposed to speculative) job-creating activities in *Canadian* communities. It halts the public sector cuts and introduces a number of direct public sector investment measures designed to create jobs in vital areas—childcare; physical, ecological, and communications infrastructure; social and co-op housing. It contains a number of tax and regulatory job creation measures—e.g., a tax cut for low-income groups and proposals for reducing working time and redistributing work.

It holds, contrary to prevailing wisdom, that we cannot afford *not* to make these social investments. As many (including the World Bank) acknowledge, they are *the* most important determinants of the future social and economic well-being of our society. Rejecting the Canada Health and Social Transfer, which slashes funds, removes national standards and enforcement mechanisms, and abdicates federal responsibility, our alternative creates a number of distinct but interdependent national social investment funds—from health care and education to childcare, housing, and income support. Overall program spending in our plan is modest, rising in line with the economy at about 14 percent of GDP, which is substantially below the 1993–4 level.

Finally, our alternative would selectively increase taxes on those groups that are best able to pay, namely, profitable corporations and wealthy Canadians. Our measures include: an inheritance tax on estates over $1 million, two new marginal tax brackets for income earners over $100,000, closing some of the most wasteful of corporate tax subsidies or loopholes such as the lobbying, meals and entertainment, high salaries deduction. It should be noted that over a five-year period 80 percent of the revenue to pay for our budget would come from a revitalized economy with more employed people and healthy businesses paying taxes, fewer depending on social assistance.

Our budget plan would eliminate the deficit and more importantly significantly reduce the debt by the year 2000–1. Although we are a year behind Martin in eliminating the deficit, we make a much bigger dent in the debt, reducing the debt-to-GDP ratio to 59 percent compared to Martin's 65 percent. One reason for this is that our annual interest bill falls throughout the next five years while Martin's interest payments continue to rise. Thus, by the year 2000 annual interest payments under the AFB plan are $42 billion compared to $51 billion under the federal government's plan.[12]

Recognizing the need for co-operation among nations to deal with the problems that global integration and mobile capital pose for national efforts to create jobs and raise living standards, our alternatives include: the Tobin tax to regulate private speculative capital flows, as well as international measures to limit the ability of transnational capital to push down social and environmental standards and taxes. The AFB recognizes that without co-operation among nations to establish international mechanisms to promote stable, equitable, and sustainable development, the success of national efforts is necessarily diminished.

Is our budget alternative realistic? Is it really possible in the current climate for a government to reduce unemployment and begin to rebuild its social infrastructure? We asked one of the country's leading economic forecasters to run our budgetary alternative through its model, to assess its viability. The company, Informetrica, concluded that we would meet or exceed our key macro-targets, including reducing the unemployment rate to 7 percent by the end of the next fiscal year. We also sought and received endorsements from 150 economists and political economists in universities across the country.

Whether one agrees with our approach depends to a large extent on whether one thinks a national government in an age of globalization and NAFTA can, through its central bank, lower real interest rates, take a more active role in monetary and debt management, re-establish some controls on capital, and increase taxes on privileged players without catastrophic consequences—inflation, capital flight, and economic collapse.

I believe that it can be done. While it is important not to downplay the power of mobile capital vis-à-vis national policy-making, it is just as important not to overstate it, for this perversely reinforces the neo-liberal argument. Obviously the national policy space has narrowed, but there is still room. Our targets for real interest rate reduction, debt management, and capital reregulation are quite reasonable. On the monetary policy question we do have the weight of considerable informed opinion on our side, which cannot be dismissed by the 'authoritative voices.' While acknowledging that corporate mobility has everywhere pushed down corporate income tax rates. Canada is in the middle of the pack of OECD countries in terms of the burden of such taxes (and near the bottom in the area of payroll taxes). What we are proposing is not out of line with international norms. Regarding wealth taxation, for example, Canada is one of only three industrialized countries that does not have some form of wealth tax. Our proposal is very much in line with what currently exists in the United States.

Would the money markets veto our budget because it is out of step with neo-liberal orthodoxy. There might well be a period of short-term financial instability, but we are confident our budget meets the test of fiscal soundness and macroeconomic consistency. Our budget plan anticipates a modest decline in the exchange rate (in the 70 cent range) as financial markets adjust their expectations in accordance with cumulative reductions in real interest rates. Overall, any short-term costs are far outweighed by the benefits to the great majority of Canadians.

In my view, the most important obstacle to implementing our kind of budgetary alternative, is the ideological spell of crippling passivity in the face of what are claimed to be uncontrollable global forces. This powerful myth subverts democracy and breeds a politics of resignation and despair. The immense challenge before us is to break this spell, to provide the Canadian citizenry with the educational means to see through the lie that sustains rule by corporate elites, and to demand real democracy in our politics.

NOTES

1. The debt figures are from the *Bank of Canada Review*—various years, and *Bank of Canada Statistical Summary*—various years. I am grateful to Jordan Grant of the Committee on Economic and Monetary Reform who compiled the detailed statistical series, from 1929 to 1994.
2. H Mimoto and P. Cross, 'The Growth of the Federal Debt,' *Canadian Economic Observer* (June 1991), 3.1–3.18
3. These statistics are drawn from James Stanford, 'Growth, Interest and Debt: Canada's Fall from the Fiscal Knife Edge,' *Alternative Federal Budget 1996 Technical Paper #2.*
4. Ibid.
5. There are many studies on this subject. See, for example, Rene Morissette, John Myles, and Garnett Picot, 'Earnings Polarization in Canada 1969–91' in K. Banting and C. Beach, eds., *Labour Market Polarization and Social Policy Reform* (School of Policy Studies, Queen's University, 1995).
6. I Gillespie, F. Vermaeten, and A. Vermaeten, 'Tax Incidence in Canada,' *Canadian Tax Journal* 42/2 (1994).
7. See *CCPA Monitor* (July/August 1996) (Ottawa, Canadian Centre for Policy Alternatives).
8. Ekos Research Associates, *Rethinking Government,1994* (Ottawa).
9. Cited in Ken McQueen, *Ottawa Citizen*, 4 January 1996.
10. D Bellemare and L. Poulin-Simon, *What Is the Real Cost of Unemployment?* (Ottawa, Canadian Centre for Policy Alternatives, 1994).
11. Government of Canada, *Budget Plan, 1996.*
12. Since the government has not made projections beyond 1997–8, the AFB team extended these projections to 2000–1.

Contributors

PAT ARMSTRONG is the Director of the School of Canadian Studies at Carleton University in Ottawa and an accomplished scholar in the study of Canada's social welfare policy.

RAYMOND B. BLAKE is Director of the Centre for Canadian Studies at Mount Allison University. He is the author of *Canadians at Last: Canada Integrated Newfoundland as a Province* and coeditor (with Jeff Keshen) of *Social Welfare Policy in Canada: Historical Readings*. He is currently writing a book on the history of family allowances in Canada.

PENNY BRYDEN is Assistant Professor of History at Mount Allison University. Her forthcoming book, *Planners and Politicians: The Liberal Party and Social Policy. 19571968*, examines the design and implementation of a contributory pension plan and national health insurance.

BRUCE CAMPBELL is a political economist and Executive Director of the Canadian Centre for Policy Alternatives. He has written extensively on economic and social policy issues. He is coauthor (with Maude Barlow) of *Straight Through the Heart: How the Liberals Abandoned the Just Society* (1995). He is coordinator of the CCPACHO!CES Alternative Federal Budget Project.

GUY CHIASSON is a doctoral student at the University of Ottawa in Canadian Politics, where he is working on a thesis on the general theme of local development and its contribution to democracy. He is also involved with the evaluation framework for the local management initiatives in the "New Forms of Governance-Ecosystem Management Project" of the Institute for Research on the Environment and Economy at the University of Ottawa.

THOMAS J COURCHENE is Jarislowsky-Deutsch Professor of Economic and Financial Policy and Director of the John Deutsch Institute for the Study of Economic Policy at Queen's University. He is one of Canada's most influencial public policy analysts.

KATHERINE COVELL is an Associate Professor of Psychology at the University College of Cape Breton as well as CoFounder and Director of the U. C. C. B. Children's Rights Center. Her work reflects her interest in policy related research. She teaches developmental and adolescent psychology, and children's rights. Her research has focused on family and community influences on child development, most notably in the area of children's rights, and the implementation of the United Nations Convention on the Rights of the Child.

GEOFFREY HALE presently works for the Government of Ontario. He is a graduate of Princeton University (B.A., 1976) and the University of Western Ontario (M.B.A. 1978, Ph.D., 1996) where he has taught Canadian politics and business–government relations. He served as Vice President of the Canadian Organization of Small Business between 1983 and 1987.

R. BRIAN HOWE is Associate Professor of Political Science at the University College of Cape Breton. He has published extensively in the areas of children's rights, human rights legislation, and Canadian policy dealing with the implementation of the UN Convention on the Rights of the Child and with the enforcement of human rights law.

THERESE JENNISSEN teaches social policy at the School of Social Work, Carleton University in Ottawa. She has a Ph.D. from McGill University, and has been a researcher for the Library of Parliament and for the Royal Commission on New Reproductive Technologies.

TOM KENT was deeply involved in the establishment of the social and economic programs of the 1960s. In the Pearson government he was coordinator of Programming and Policy Secretary to the Prime Minister. Among other positions, he has been Deputy Minister of two federal departments, president and C. E. O. of two Crown corporations, Chairman of the Royal Commission on Newspapers, editor of a daily newspaper and of magazines, and Dean of Administrative Studies at Dalhousie University. He is the author of several books on public policy and is now a Visiting Fellow in the School of Policy Studies at Queen's University.

EDGAR-ANDRE MONTIGNY is a PostDoctoral Fellow (SSHRCC) researching the economic status of Canada's elderly. He teaches various courses on Nineteenth and TwentiethCentury Canada, especially Ontario and Quebec, including courses on immigrants and race relations and social welfare at the University of Ottawa, University of Toronto (Scarborough Campus), Trent University (Oshawa Campus), and Ryerson Polytechnical University.

ALLAN MOSCOVITCH is Professor of Social Work and Director of the School of Social Work at Carleton University where he has been a member of faculty for 20 years. He is the author/editor of three books and many articles on social welfare policy and has worked with various social service organizations in Ontario. He is currently at work on a study on the use of social assistance funds for community employment programs for Aboriginal people.

DEAN F. OLIVER is a Postdoctoral Fellow at the Norman Paterson School of International Affairs, Carleton University, where he teaches conflict studies and Canadian defence policy. In 199596, he was Assistant Director at the Centre for International and Security Studies, York University. He is currently the contributor for "External Affairs and Defence Policy" to the Canadian Annual Review of Politics and Public Affairs, the official bibliographer for the Canadian Historical Review, and a contributing book reviewer for Canadian Military History.

LESLIE A. PAL is Professor of Public Policy and Administration at the School of Public Administration, Carleton University. He is the author or editor of a dozen books and over 30 articles or chapters on various aspects of public policy. His most recent books are Border Crossings: The Internationalization of Canadian Public Policy (edited with G. Bruce Doern and Brian Tomlin) and Beyond Policy Analysis: Public Issue Management in Turbulent Times.

ANDREW PARKIN is a political sociologist and writer. In 1995, he was a Killam Postdoctoral Fellow in the Department of Sociology and Social Anthropology at Dalhousie University, and from 1989 to 1993 he was a Commonwealth Scholar in the Department of Peace Studies at the University of Bradford.

J. FRANK STRAIN is Associate Professor and Head of the Department of Economics at Mount Allison University. His published research includes work on higher education, federalism, and the welfare state. His current research focuses on complex dynamical systems and institutional change.

JAMES STRUTHERS is a professor in the Canadian Studies Program at Trent University in Peterborough, Ontario. He is the author of No Fault of Their Own: Unemployment and the Canadian Welfare States 19141941 (1983), and The Limits of Affluence: Welfare in Ontario. 19201970 (1994). He is currently researching aging and social policy in Ontario after World War II.

SHIRLEY TILLOTSON is a member of the History Department of Dalhousie University. Her welfare history research focuses on community organization. The essay in this volume is part of her current work on the foundations of the welfare state in the community.

M.